$15⁰⁰ S

THE *ARABIAN NIGHTS* IN ENGLISH LITERATURE

The *Arabian Nights* in English Literature

Studies in the Reception of *The Thousand and One Nights* into British Culture

Edited by

PETER L. CARACCIOLO
Lecturer in English
The Royal Holloway and Bedford New College
University of London

St. Martin's Press   New York

First published in the United States of America in 1988

Printed in Hong Kong

ISBN 0-312-01608-5

Library of Congress Cataloging-in-Publication Data
The *Arabian Nights* in English literature.
  Bibliography: p.
  Includes index.
  1. English literature—Arab influences.
2. Arabian nights.   3. Arabic literature—Appreciation—
Great Britain.   4. Literature, Comparative—English and Arabic.
5. Literature, Comparative—Arabic and English.
6. Arab countries in literature.
I. Caracciolo, Peter L., 1933–
PR129.A65A7   1988   820'.9   87–35622
ISBN 0-312-01608-5

In memoriam

Allan Grant

Contents

List of Illustrations

1 'The Lady of the Glass Case', by R. Smirke for the Forster edition (William Miller, 1802) vol. I

2 (a) 'Sindbad . . . on the Whale's back' from *The History of Sindbad the Sailor* (E. Newbery, 1784)
  (b) Sindbad on 'the Island of Serpents', from *The Oriental Moralist* (E. Newbery, c.1791)

3 'Shacabac, the Barber's Sixth Brother', sharing the imaginary meal with the Barmecide, by R. Smirke for *The Adventures of Hunch-back* (William Daniell, 1814)

4 'Transformations', by William Harvey for 'The Story of the Second Royal Mendicant' in Lane's translation (1839–41) I, 174–5 (the page reproduced here is from the single-volume edition, 1853)

5 (a) 'Zobeide prepares to whip the dogs', from 'The History of Three Calenders, Sons of Kings, and of Five Ladies of Bagdad'
  (b) 'The journey of Prince Firouz Schah and the Princess of Bengal', from 'The Story of the Enchanted Horse'
  Both these are by A. B. Houghton for *Dalziel's Illustrated Nights* (1863–5)

6 'The Transformation of King Beder', Houghton's 1874 water-colour based on his illustration of the tale recounted in the Dalziel edition

7 'Zobeide discovers the young man reciting the Koran', by J. E. Millais, for 'The History of Zobeide' in the Dalziel edition

In text

Preface and
Acknowledgements

Originally placed between the half-title and full-title pages of *The Book of the Thousand Nights and a Night*, Richard Burton's celebrated late-nineteenth-century translation, the black-and-white device reproduced above at first glance seems to offer little to detain the reader. Following as it does the magnificently dramatic front cover (the binding of the 'Library Edition' is particularly impressive, its black cloth elaborately stamped in gold with a rich synthesis of Islamic ornament), the device initially may escape notice altogether.

Yet when that apparently unimportant black-and-white pattern reappears in volume after volume, continuing to be used however much the design of the binding may vary from one edition to the next, then the device begins to claim our attention. It is not a chessboard, of course, and hardly a crossword puzzle; a labyrinth perhaps but if so an impossible one; yet less of a nightmare than a vision of some harmonious and meaningful cluster of shapes like the notation of a dance. Gradually one begins to suspect that a hint is being dropped, a hint as to the spirit of the *Nights* themselves, that protean and vitalising spirit as it was glimpsed by Burton's contemporary W. H. Henley:

> He that has the book of the *Thousand Nights and a Night* has Hashisch-made-words for life. Gallant, subtle, refined, intense, humorous, obscene, here is the Arab intelligence drunk with conception. It is a vast extravaganza of passion in action and picarooning farce and material splendour run mad.[1]

Thus imaginatively stirred, realisation dawns on Burton's reader: the significant markings of this enigmatic device are another version of Arabic script (square Kufic) that spells out the Arabic for *The Book of the Thousand Nights and a Night*.

'The purest angular [type] of Kufic was manipulated to form intricate geometric patterns . . . on minarets and mosques and in maze-like' calligraphy.[2] Ornamental Kufic reached its peak during the later period of the Abbasid Caliphate, the same Abbasid dynasty which supplied the *Nights* with its great caliph, the charismatic Harun al-Rashid, around whose idealised figure was constructed one of the collection's most distinctive features: a lively pseudo-historical cycle of tales. The Abbasids also built away from Baghdad a magnificent, labyrinthine, fortified city-palace which seems to have helped inspire aspects of the City of Brass and the Copper Castle of the *Nights*.[3] For the later Abbasid centuries are much the period too when the collection itself began to take shape. It was between the tenth and twelfth centuries that within a Persian framework some Graeco-Indian elements of folklore coalesced with more realistic Baghdadian stories, and, from the eleventh century on, shrewd Egyptian tales (among them some of the most ancient in the collection) were added. The *Nights*, which by now had become an encyclopaedia of genres (its 'dynamic metabolism' incorporating a multitude of stories within stories),[4] 'this book without an author' settled little by little into its penultimate form in the fifteenth century, and awaited final improvement in its social status at the hands of Antoine Galland in early-eighteenth-century France, the first volumes of *Les Mille et une nuits* appearing in 1704.[5]

Joseph Jacobs, the Victorian folklorist and rival editor of the *Nights*, summed up the growth of these tales as 'Queen Esther telling Persian tales after the manner of Buddha to Haroun Alrashid in Cairo during the fourteenth and fifteenth centuries.'[6] Jacob's witty anachronisms, though, are surpassed by the ingenuity displayed in the black-and-white ornamental Arabic title commissioned by Burton. The aptness of the square Kufic script chosen is further enhanced by a characteristically Arabic series of puns. Embedded in the Arabic lettering is an intricate play on the English words 'square' and 'key'. For 'counterchange' and chequerboard effects of the kind which is approximated here are commonly known as 'key-patterns'.[7] An intriguing example of bilingual paronomasia, this emblem fuses word and image, letters and geometry with the virtuosity of an ideogram. The inscription KITAB ALF LAYLAH WA LAYLAH is repeated four times in so convoluted a manner that the 'square Kufic' title creates a giddy recession of patterns within patterns; the spokes of a wheel (within a square within another square of script) formed from the quadrupled Arabic *'wa'* ('and') assuming at the centre of this maze of letters a kinetic swastika-like unity. This recalls not only the Occidental *tétrascèle* or *gammadion* but also the significant labyrinth of India – *nandyavarta*. In Europe as in Asia this design partook of the nature of a talisman. Besides being a symbol of solar movement and, by analogy, of heavenly bodies more generally, here, in the Burton device, the square swastika shape fittingly invokes the fusion of male and female principles.[8] Furthermore, as it is the property of the goddess herself, it recalls Scheherazade weaving her endless nocturnal tales for dear life and, by her teaching-stories, winning the Sultan Shahriar back to love and humanity – the heroic task which the resourceful Scheherazade eventually accomplishes in the frame tale of *The Thousand and One Nights*.

The foregoing exegesis does not exhaust the messages encoded in this paradoxical ornament. The black-and-white rectangular pattern which Burton commissioned is a reminder that, like such games as chess, the *Nights* have been 'naturalised' far longer than one had realised. Some of the stories landed on English soil at least as early as the fourteenth century and not just in the shape of the Magic Horse that the Squire contributes to Chaucer's own masterpiece; arguably the entire structure of *The Canterbury Tales* reveals a debt to the East.[9] Only during the late seventeenth century was Polichinello anglicised to Mr Punch, while *The Arabian Nights Entertainments* (in the form of the anonymous Grub Street translation of Galland) appeared in 1706, just a generation later – and, indeed, a decade or so before the advent of the English pantomime.[10]

As the black-and-white device further hints, the *Nights* are also a specific instance (and, in England, the major example) of how the Orient served as '*alter ego*' to the West, evoking dread as well as fascination.[11] The Muslim character of the *Nights* both in its religious and in its erotic aspects aroused mixed feelings. While the monotheism appealed to the deist, paradoxically a work that many others among the learned first judged as fit merely for women and children became from the nineteenth century on more and more the victim of censorship.[12] Apart from the Galland, the finest example of such 'a family version' of the *Nights* is Lane's (1839–41) in which the scholarship to some degree compensates for the bowdlerisation.

Once the size, intricacy and, at times, the sexual frankness of the collection were made apparent in the last decades of the century, the labours of Payne and Burton proved counterproductive – at any rate initially. Even a reader so responsive as Henley preferred the more accessible Galland, as many have done since. Confronted by the Burton, Henley was forced to qualify his praise:

> You would say of their poets that they contract immensity to the limits of desire; they exhaust the inexhaustible in their enormous effort; they stoop the universe to the slavery of a talisman, and bind the visible and invisible worlds within the compass of a ring.[13]

It is a paradox none the less that, forming part of what Kipling admiringly characterised as a 'meditation – illumination – inspiration', Henley's critique comes close to discovering one of the great secrets of the *Nights*.[14] Within its inexhaustible plenitude the Burton collection hides this secret, whose key is encoded in the calligraphic pattern. Latent in what may justifiably be seen as a mandala is yet another pun. Through the arrangement whereby the framed swastika interlocks with script of the enclosing set of squares, there

is created an example of one of 'the most fundamental and
pervasive of all Islamic design concepts, that of the infinite
pattern',[15] whose presence here plays upon the idea of 'an indefinite
. . . number' as is suggested by the title *The Thousand and One
Nights*.[16] This link with infinity signals more than merely the many-
layered and open-ended structure of the book which we are about
to read;[17] also by this association we are alerted to the *Nights'*
affinity with another 'infinite sacred book' – the history of the
universe.[18] More than just mirroring the hierarchies of body
and soul, Burton's quasi-counterchange emblem functions as a
microcosm. It reminds us that the narrative recurrence typical of
the tales – the imbrication, interweaving and discontinuities, the
way the tales nest one within another, replicating theme, plot,
character and structure, or doubling back on their tracks – is
yet another example of the 'infinite patterns' that mirror the
observations of the Arab astronomer–philosophers, the cycles of
sun and moon, the conjunction of stars, the retrograde of planets,
and the connection between such celestial phenomena and the
tragi-comic history of humankind.[19]

The influence of the *Nights* has been diffused in many ways:
by travellers, translators, moralists, mythographers; through the
feedback of poets, novelists, critics, the entertainers of children in
theatre and cinema; not least by the efforts of illustrators. For,
indeed, just because it is characteristically Muslim in its apparent
aniconism Burton's learned and witty emblem serves to remind us
that the history of the *Nights'* impact on English culture belongs
predominantly to what has been termed 'the Oriental Renaissance'.[20] As Raymond Schwab notes during his magisterial conspec-
tus of its continental manifestations among the scholarship,
literature and the other arts of the eighteenth and nineteenth
centuries, this second renaissance is closely linked to the Romantic
movement. Yet, perhaps even more than is the case with the
companion school of Orientalist artists, the *Nights'* influence has
continued to be felt in the development of English literature
through Realism to the Modernist avant-garde and beyond.[21]
Although understandable (given the range of European reactions
to the Orient), Schwab's comparative neglect of English literature
reinforces the more general failure of scholars to understand
adequately the important part played by the *Nights* in our culture.
This collection of essays, it is hoped, will in some way redress the
balance. However, the influence of the *Nights* on English literature

covers so vast an area that this collection of essays can only attempt to map certain pathways through to its extraordinary but often hidden treasures. Still perhaps, in their turn, the discoveries that we have made may stimulate further exploration of the process by which the *Nights* came to enrich not just British but also other cultures, in Europe, North America and the Third World. For as W. J. Ong's illuminating *Orality and Literacy* (1982) makes clear, the full story of how the *Nights* were transformed from spoken narratives into elements of printed novel, long poem and drama has yet to be told.

No more than the merchant in the Arabian tale had I any thought of what powers of the djinn I should let loose when first I wondered how Wilkie Collins ever could have expected the Victorian reader of *The Moonstone* to comprehend the implications of that reference to *The Thousand and One Nights* which is jocularly concealed at the epicentre of his most disturbing novel. Fortunately, in the decade that it has taken me to plumb this question, I have found more helpers that just the three wise sheiks who came to the rescue of the Arabian merchant with their life-saving tales. Therefore I should like to thank the many institutions, libraries and individuals who have aided me so generously in the preparation of this book. I gratefully acknowledge grants from the Leverhulme Trust and the Central Research Fund of London University to study the origins of Wilkie Collins's fiction; these funds allowed me to pursue my investigations abroad. Without several grants of study leave from the Royal Holloway College – now Royal Holloway and Bedford New College – I should not have been able to make such use as I have of the collections of manuscripts, periodicals and books at my own college; at Birkbeck College, the School of Oriental and African Studies, Senate House and University College, London; at the British and London Libraries, the Bodleian, and Cambridge University Library; at the Bibliothèque Nationale, Paris; and, in the United States, at the Berg Collection in the New York Public Library (Astor, Lenox and Tilden Foundation), the Pierpont Morgan Library, the libraries of Princeton University, Yale, Harvard, the University of California at Los Angeles, and Stanford, as well as the Huntington Library, San Marino, California: I owe much to the staff of these institutions. In their different ways all these collections are types of Aladdin's Cave, but particularly I am grateful to the Pierpont Morgan Library, Princeton University Library and Stanford University Library, as also to the copyright holder, Mrs Faith Clarke (*née* Dawson), for permission to use, in the essay on Wilkie Collins that I contribute to this book, material from the novelist's manuscripts and letters. I am also grateful to William M. Clarke and Andrew Gasson for further information concerning Collins.

My researches into the *Nights'* influence widening, it soon became clear that any further investigation would have to be a collaborative effort. Even if the inquiry were restricted to the *Night's* influence on English culture, the field was still dauntingly vast. As a previous explorer, tantalised by like ambitions, warned, the *Nights* have had 'an impact on the artistic imagination of novelists, dramatists, poets, musicians and painters that, even in the twentieth century, may be too kaleidoscopic to measure'.[22] Thus alerted, the basis for the present book was laid in a series of intercollegiate lectures which I organised at London University. From my colleagues who participated in this series I learnt much. However, since then death, alas, has taken from us Allan Grant; and other contributors – Antonia Byatt (then of University College) and David Nokes (King's College, London) – have had to drop out from our enterprise. Regrettable as have been these losses, subsequently there have been gains: Cornelia Cook has enlarged my perception of mid-nineteenth-century poetry; Brian Alderson has been generous with his extensive knowledge of children's literature and its illustrators; John Heath-Stubbs provided not just a poet's intuition of how deeply Eliot's *The Waste Land* is rooted in myth as well as more modern literature, but, importantly too, a folklorist's caution against overstating the case for oriental influence on Western culture; while Professor Fatma Moussa-Mahmoud has given me the benefit of her knowledge of both Egyptian and Saudi society.

My own understanding of the *Nights'* genesis has been much increased thanks also to the hospitality that I have received in visits to Egypt and India. Among the helpful staff in the English department at Ain Shams University, Cairo, I am grateful particularly to Professor Mary Massoud, Dr Samira Basta, Dr Fawzia Elsadr, Dr Affaf Roushdy and Moustapha Riad. Likewise I am grateful to Peter A. Connell, OBE, and his staff at the British Council, Bombay; the advice which I received on my two stays there enabled me to make the most of visits to Buddhist and Hindu cave temples at Elephanta, Karle, Ajanta and Ellora as well as to the shrines, mosques, palaces and astronomical observatories of Mughal and Rajput India; for discussions about the more recent culture and history of the sub-continent I am indebted to Dr Atul M. Setalvad, Charles Correa and the distinguished collector of Hindu art Haridas Swali.

At home, through the agency of Michael Darby of the Victoria and Albert Museum, who organised the 1983 exhibition 'The Islamic Perspective' under the auspices of the World of Islam Festival Trust, and (at the invitation of the Trust's director, Alistair Duncan) in a lecture at Leighton House I was able to explore some of the material that now constitutes the Introduction to the present volume. I am indebted to Catriona M. Lawson, then the director's assistant, for much more information than just the fact that Granville Bantock composed a piece entitled 'The Arabian Nights'. It was also through the Trust that I met Wolfgang Köhler, who not only presented me with a copy of his enlightening thesis on Hugo von Hofmannsthal's use of the *Nights*, but also generously let me have on long loan his own precious copy of Nikita Elisséeff's *Thèmes et motifs des Mille et une nuits*.

Similarly I am grateful to the staff of Arthur Probsthain, Oriental Bookseller, 41 Great Russell Street, and of M. Ayres, Museum Street, to Marius Kociejowski of Bertram Rota Limited, 30 Long Acre, and especially to Peter Stockham at Images, 16 Cecil Court, for supplying me with a stream of out-of-the-way books, articles and other items related to the *Nights* and their illustrators. In this respect I should like to acknowledge the help also of Pamela Bickley, Gerlinda Bolton, John Cumming, W. A. Davenport, Doug Hack, Grevel Lindop, Paula Neuss, Roger Palmer, Roger Parisious, Charlotte Stoudt, Elissa Swinglehurst and Jo Udall.

For a number of the pictures illustrating this book, I am indebted to the reprographic departments of the British Library (Plates 2b and 3) and the Victoria and Albert Museum (Plate 6) but the majority are reproduced from photographs taken from items in my own possession, or, in the case of the oldest image in this book, from Stockham's collection. Again I am grateful to him, as indeed I am to David Margolis and David Ross, who took the extra photographs for me.

For permission to reproduce those images that are still in copyright or belonging to others I should like to thank the owners. In addition to the institutions named above, acknowledgements are due to Hodder and Stoughton for Plates 15 and 16, and to the Detmold estate for the cover illustration (every effort has been made to trace any remaining copyright holders). I am grateful also to Grevel Lindop and his publisher, Michael Schmidt of the Carcanet Press, for allowing me to use his poem from *Tourists* (1987) as an epigraph to this book.

Professors John Creaser, D. J. Enright, A. Norman Jeffares, and also Brian Southam have provided welcome encouragement. Professors Angus Easson, Joan Grundy, Barbara Hardy and Kathleen Tillotson, as well as Deirdre Toomey, have directed me down many a Victorian byway to catch a glimpse of Baghdad. Likewise my colleagues Professor Martin Dodsworth and Andrew Gibson aided my survey of difficult terrain in the Beckett trilogy. My wife Marie-Jeanne has given me a helpfully French view of the *Nights'* influence, and I am grateful to her and my daughters for their forbearance.

Ysabel Howard, Paulette Hutchinson, Veronica Jones, Andrée Morcom, Val Murr and Christine See have been of great secretarial assistance. And I am particularly grateful to Frances Arnold, Valery Rose and Graham Eyre for their care and attention to the copy-editing of this book, and to Douglas Matthews for the index.

Although the faults that remain are my own, my debt to all these guides is great and to none more so than Warwick Gould and Robert Hampson. Without their intervention this book would never have been completed. Just when the peoples of the *Arabian Nights* seemed transformed to shoals of iridescent but elusive fish that could not be cooked and brought to the table, I too was saved from petrification, and the threatening genie who had escaped from the bottle was brought under control.

P. L. C.

NOTES

Books published in London unless otherwise stated.

1. W. E. Henley, 'Arabian Nights Entertainments', *Views and Reviews: Essays in Appreciation*, I: *Literature* (D. Nutt, 1890) p. 208. Fitzhugh Ludlow, *The Hasheesh Eater* (New York: Harpers, 1857), facsimile in *The Hasty Papers: A One Shot Review* (New York: 1960) sees in the hallucinations experienced by the drug-taker the origins of the energy and imaginative scope of the oriental tale and especially the *Nights*, their elastic use of time and space, endless self-replication and metamorphoses, the oneiric way in which the supernatural intrudes into the everyday world, the *Nights'* basically tragic-comic mood (pp. ix, 21–9, 32–9, 64, 106–8, 123, 216); cf. De Quincey's African magician

who detects 'an alphabet of new and infinite symbols . . . secret hieroglyphics uttered by the flying footsteps' of the young Aladdin in 'Infant Literature', *Autobiographic Sketches*, vol. I of *Collected Writings*, ed. D. Masson (Edinburgh: A. and C. Black, 1898–90) pp. 128–9. See also *infra*, ch. 1, pp. 27–8, 56–7, 69 n. 65, 79 n. 133.

2. Y. H. Safadi, *Islamic Calligraphy* (Thames and Hudson, 1978) p. 12. I an grateful to Kathy Vande Vate, Mr Safadi's assistant in the Arabic section of the Department of Oriental Manuscripts and Printed Books of the British Library for confirming my translation of the Arabic title and helping me to unravel the calligraphic knot; to Peter Stocks for further information about Islamic books, and generally to Barry Bloomfield. In concluding the Foreword to his translation, Burton acknowledges 'that the Arabic ornamentations of these volumes were designed by [his] excellent friend Yacoub Artin Pasha, of the Ministry of Instruction, Cairo, with the well-known writing-artist Shaykh Mohammed Muunis the Cairene – *The Book of the Thousand Nights and a Night*, Illustrated Library Edition, I (H. S. Nichols, 1897) xxxii. Through orientalist scholarship of the calibre evident in Emile Prisse D'Avennes's magnificently illustrated *L'Art arabe d'après les monuments du Kaire* (Paris: A. Morel, 1877) – see esp. ch. 11 – the cultivated Victorian reader came to know something of the value that the Muslim bibliophile attaches to the puzzling and talismanic colophon.

3. See Oleg Grabar, *The Formation of Islamic Art* (New Haven, Conn.: Yale University Press, 1973) ch. 6, esp. pp. 166–73. Where Grabar draws parallels with Versailles, R. A. Nicholson sees Harun as 'the Charlemagne of the East': *A Literary History of the Arabs* (Cambridge: Cambridge University Press, 1907) p. 261.

4. Mahmoud Ali Manzalaoui, 'Arabian Nights', *Cassell's Encyclopaedia of Literature*, ed. S. H. Steinberg (Cassell, 1953) I, 26–9. On the Afro-Asiatic roots of Ancient Greece see Martin Bernal's *Black Athena* (Free Association Books, 1987).

5. Franz Rosenthal, 'Literature', *The Legacy of Islam*, ed. Joseph Schacht and C. E. Bosworth, 2nd edn (Oxford University Press, 1979) esp. pp. 345–6 and n.

6. Joseph Jacobs, 'An Introduction to the *Arabian Nights* . . .', prefixed to the edition of Lane's translation planned for issue by Gibbings and Co. . . . (1896) pp. xv. 'In Persian tradition [the frame tale of the *Nights*] appears to have been partially assimilated to the traditions surrounding the [Old Testament] *Book of Esther*. The names Shahrazād and Dīnāzād . . . given in the *Nights* to the heroine and her sister, occur in Arabic references to Persian history [that are associated] with the Jewish consort of a much married king, a woman considered as a liberator of her people' – 'al Tabari' [*Tarikh al-Rasul wa-al-Muluk*, ed. J. de Goeje *et al*. (Leiden, 1879–1901) I, 688] cited by Manzalaoui in *Cassell's Encyclopaedia*, I, 26–9; II, 1532–3. In his selection *Indian Fairy Tales* (D. Nutt, 1892), Jacobs traces the idea of 'connecting a number of disconnected stories' with the central figure of a saviour back to the appropriation of Indian folk-literature by the Buddhist compilers of the *Jakatas* 'possibly as early as . . . 241 BC' (p. 227). Building on

suggestions of Leo Frobenius that the basic idea of the *Nights* and its Sudanese analogues has its source in the area embracing the littoral of the Indian Ocean, Joseph Campbell speculates as to whether the 'Shehrzad frametale' has not even more ancient roots in the practice of ritual regicide, for which Sir James Frazer found such extensive evidence – *The Masks of God: Primitive Mythology* (Harmondsworth: Penguin, 1976) ch. 4. See also *infra*, Heath-Stubbs, ch. 11.

7. E. H. Gombrich, *The Sense of Order: A Study in the Psychology of Decorative Art* (Oxford: Phaidon, 1979) pp. 89, 140–1, 292–3.

8. On the *nandyavarta* and associated symbolism, see the Count Goblet d'Alviella, *The Migration of Symbols* (1892; facsimile of first English edn [1894], Wellingborough, Northants: Aquarian Press, 1979) ch. 2; also William Simpson, *The Buddhist Praying Wheel* (1896; repr. New York: University Books, 1970) ch. 6. Brahma's daughter and consort Sarasvati, the Hindu goddess of eloquence and learning, is 'the archetype of Scheherazade': R. and S. Michaud, *India of the 1001 Nights* (Thames and Hudson, 1986) p. 1.

9. H. S. V. Jones 'The Squire's Tale', *Sources and Analogues of Chaucer's Canterbury Tales*, ed. W. F. Bryan and G. Dempster (Chicago: University of Chicago Press, 1941) pp. 357–76, esp. p. 364; and Katherine Slater Gittes, 'The Canterbury Tales and the Arabic Frame Tradition', *PMLA*, xcviii (Mar 1983) 237–51. See also *infra*, ch. 1, p. 5 and n. 19.

10. See *Oxford English Dictionary* on how 'Polichinello' mutates into 'Punch'. In 1682 a toy puppet show included Punch, according to Robert Leach, *The Punch and Judy Show* (Batsford, 1985) p. 21. The first real pantomime was Rich's *The Magician; or, Harlequin a Director* in 1721; see Gerald Frow, *Oh Yes It Is! A History of Pantomime* (BBC, 1985) p. 39. On the circumstances in which the first English version of the Arabian collection was published so near the start of the eighteenth century, see *infra*, ch. 1, p. 2 and n. 2.

11. Raymond Schwab, *The Oriental Renaissance*, G. Patterson-Black and V. Reinking, foreword by Edward Said (New York: Columbia University Press, 1984) pp. 4, 483. In a more critical vein, Aziz Al-Azmeh, in his *Islamic Studies and the European Imagination* (Exeter: University of Exeter, 1986) p. 16 and n. 27), cites Paul Valéry on the 'intoxicating *Orient of the Mind*', a 'state between dreaming and waking where there is no logic . . . to keep the elements of our memory from attracting each other into their natural combinations' – 'Orientem Versus' (1938), in *History and Politics*, tr. D. Folliot and J. Mathews (Princeton, N.J.: Princeton University Press, 1963) p. 381. However, the intelligence evident in the creation of the oriental device which Burton commissioned witnesses that the labyrinth is a complex symbol capable of evoking not just 'drunken space' but also the library; see Allen S. Weiss, 'Impossible Sovereignty' in the Georges Bataille issue of *October*, xxxvi (Spring 1986) 133, 135. And Valéry in fact also praises 'the logic and lucidity of . . . the Arabs. . . . Their deductive imagination, subtle above all others' (p. 384).

12. See *infra*, ch. 1, pp. 1–4, 38–42, and Alderson, ch. 2.

13. Henley, *Views and Reviews*, i, 210.

14. Rudyard Kipling, *Something of Myself* (Macmillan, 1937) p. 82. Henley's
    Arabesque influence on *Kim* is also detectable; see ibid., p. 139.
15. Ernst J. Grube, *The World of Islam* (Paul Hamlyn, 1966) pp. 67–8.
16. Rosenthal, in *The Legacy of Islam*, ed. Schacht and Bosworth, p. 337;
    Gittes, in *PMLA*, xcviii, 240–3; and Jorge Luis Borges, 'The Thousand
    and One Nights', *Seven Nights* (Faber, 1986) pp. 45–6, 50, 56.
17. In his illustrations for Edward Lane's translation (1839–41) William
    Harvey is much influenced by the way Middle Eastern and Mughal
    artists decorated books, so in framing the opening of chapters, sections
    and notes with one or more illustrative vignettes enclosed by a
    characteristically Islamic mixture of ornament – geometric, arabesque,
    architectural or calligraphic – Harvey gives the reader clues as to what
    level of narrative 'nesting' has been reached in a particular tale or
    anecdote. Since the Dalziel *Illustrated . . . Nights* (Ward etc., 1863–5)
    also attempts to emulate this Islamic model, the Victorian public
    became familiar with the use of significant patterns as a method of
    signposting the perusal of the *Nights*. On related areas of influence,
    see Michael Darby, *The Islamic Perspective: An Aspect of British Architec-
    ture and Design in the Nineteenth Century* (World of Islam Festival Trust,
    1983); also Donald King and David Sylvester, *The Eastern Carpet in the
    Western World* (Arts Council, 1983) pp. 9–23, for, as Borges observes
    in a magical poem, 'Métaphores des Mille et une nuits', the second
    metaphor is the oriental carpet in which what seems a chaos of lines
    and colours is in truth governed by a secret order: 'comme cet autre
    rêve, l'Univers' – *La Rose profonde; la monnaie de fer; Histoire de la nuit,*
    tr. and ed. Nestor Ibarra (Paris: Gallimard, 1983) pp. 132–4.
18. Jorge Luis Borges, 'Partial Magic in the *Quixote*', *Labyrinths* (Har-
    mondsworth: Penguin, 1970) p. 231. See also Ernst R. Curtius, *Euro-
    pean Literature and the Latin Middle Ages* (Routledge and Kegan Paul,
    1953) ch. 16.
19. See Seyyed Hossein Nasr, *Islamic Cosmological Doctrines*, rev. edn
    (Thames and Hudson, 1979) chs 3 and 14; also K. Critchlow, *Islamic
    Patterns* (New York: Schocken; and London: Thames and Hudson,
    1976) ch. 4 and pp. 152–5; K. Alban *et al.*, *The Language of Pattern*,
    (Thames and Hudson, 1976) chs 2 and 4, and p. 62; and Joachim
    Schultz, *Movement and Rhythms of the Stars* (Edinburgh: Floris, 1986).
    'There is a suspicion [among scientists] that simple laws recursively
    applied could explain the protean complexity of the universe' –
    Benjamin Woolley, *Observer*, 1 February 1987, p. 31.
20. Schwab, *The Oriental Renaissance*, p. 11, notes that the phrase was first
    used by Edgar Quinet in his *Du Génie des religions* (Paris, 1842).
21. For some of the artist–travellers 'the strangeness of the terrain and
    the unfamiliar light provoked both a rethinking of European artistic
    conventions and a discovery of brilliant colour' – Hugh Casson in the
    Foreword to *The Orientalists: Delacroix to Matisse*, Royal Academy of
    Arts exhibition catalogue, ed. Mary Anne Stevens (Weidenfeld and
    Nicolson, 1984). Stevens' illuminating survey 'Western Art and its
    Encounter with the Islamic World' extends into the twentieth century
    as far as Kandinsky (p. 22), from which is but a small step to Wyndham

Lewis and *The Caliph's Design*, especially when assisted by Roger
Bezombes's *L'Exotisme dans l'art et la pensée* (Paris: Elsevier, 1953).
Among late-twentieth-century British artists, at least one visionary
has expressively identified his painting with the magic carpet: see
C. Lampert, *Frank Auerbach* (Arts Council, 1978) p. 17.

22. Sheila Shaw, 'Early English Editions of the *Arabian Nights*; their Value
to Eighteenth Century Literary Scholarship', *Muslim World*, XLIX (1959)
238. Thus only recently have I glimpsed the influence of the *Nights*
on areas as diverse as the following: Richard Jefferies, *Bevis: The Story
of a Boy* (Sampson Low, 1882), *passim*; the late nineteenth-century
occult revival, for, according to R. A. Gilbert *The Arabian Tales* were
an inspiration (see his *A. E. Waite* (Wellingborough, Northants:
Crucible, 1987) p. 88); Georges Perec, *La Vie mode d'emploi* (Paris:
Hachette, 1978), tr. by David Bellos as *Life, A User's Manual* (London:
Collins Harvill, 1987) throughout which Scheherazade's Sultan makes
his presence felt (as he does in the work of Italo Calvino and Umberto
Eco, likewise often holistic in structure); more disturbingly, though,
the *Nights* also figure among the poignant and revealing neurological
case studies of 'organised chaos' in Oliver Sack's *The Man who Mistook
his Wife for a Hat* (London: Picador, 1986) pp. vi, xi, 5, 104: 'We have,
each of us, a life story . . . whose continuity, whose sense *is* our lives.
It might be said that each of us constructs and lives a 'narrative', and
that this narrative *is* us, our identities' (p. 105).

Notes on the Contributors

Brian Alderson is a freelance writer and lecturer. He has been Visiting Professor at the University of California at Los Angeles and at the University of Southern Mississippi. In 1986–7 he staged at the British Library an exhibition on the English picture-book tradition and Randolph Caldecott, for which he wrote the catalogue *Sing a Song for Sixpence*.

Peter L. Caracciolo is Lecturer in English Language and Literature at the Royal Holloway and Bedford New College, University of London. His publications include essays on Le Fanu and Michael Moorcock in, respectively, *Twentieth-Century Crime and Mystery Writers* (1980, repr. 1986), and *Twentieth-Century Science Fiction Writers* (1981, rev. 1986), as well as articles on Wilkie Collins, Joseph Conrad, Wyndham Lewis, Doris Lessing and Brian Aldiss in various learned journals.

Cornelia Cook is Lecturer in English Language and Literature at Queen Mary College, University of London. She is the author of a book on Joyce Cary (1981) and has published articles on George Meredith, Thomas Hardy and Ford Madox Ford.

Warwick Gould is Senior Lecturer in English Language and Literature at the Royal Holloway and Bedford New College, University of London. With Phillip L. Marcus and Michael J. Sidnell he is editor of *The Secret Rose: Stories by W. B. Yeats: A Variorum Edition* (1981), and with Marjorie Reeves is author of *Joachim of Fiore and the Myth of the Eternal Evangel in the Nineteenth Century* (1987). He is editor of *Yeats Annual*.

Allan Grant was Senior Lecturer in English in the Department of Humanities, Chelsea College of Science, University of London. His publications include a commentary on Ford Madox Ford's *The Good Soldier*, *A Preface to Coleridge* (1973) and *A Preface to Dickens* (1984).

Robert G. Hampson is Lecturer in English Language and Literature at the Royal Holloway and Bedford New College, University of London. He has edited Conrad's *Lord Jim* and *Victory*, and Kipling's

Something of Myself. He is Secretary of the (British) Joseph Conrad Society.

John Heath-Stubbs, FRSL, was formerly Lecturer at the College of St Mark and St John, Chelsea, and Professor of English at Alexandria University. His publications include *The Immolation of Aleph* (1985), and translations (with Peter Avery) of *Hafiz of Shiraz* and *The Rubaiyat of Omar Khayyam.* His *Collected Poems* appeared in 1988. He is a member of the Council of the Folklore Society.

Grevel Lindop is a Senior Lecturer in the Department of English Language and Literature, University of Manchester. His publications include *The Opium-Eater: A Life of Thomas De Quincey* (1981), an edition of De Quincey's *Confessions of an English Opium-Eater and Other Writings,* and *Tourists* (1987) a collection of his own poems.

Fatma Moussa-Mahmoud, Professor of English, Cairo University, is currently teaching at the Centre of University Women Students, King Saud University, Saudi Arabia. An authority on William Beckford, her recent publications include work on George Eliot, the translation into English of a major Egyptian novel, *Miramar* by Naguib Mahfouz (1978), and, into Arabic, Shakespeare's *King Lear* and *Henry IV, Part I.*

Leonee Ormond is Senior Lecturer in English at King's College, London. She is the author of a biography of George Du Maurier (1969) and, with her husband, of the standard monograph on Frederic Lord Leighton (1975). A critical study of J. M. Barrie appeared in 1987.

Michael Slater is Reader in English at Birkbeck College, University of London. He was honorary editor of *The Dickensian,* 1968–77, and has edited Dickens' *Christmas Books* and *Nicholas Nickleby.* He has also published *Dickens in America and the Americans* (1978) and *Dickens and Women* (1983).

Deirdre Toomey is editor (with David Bindman) of *The Complete Graphic Works of William Blake* (1978). She is research editor of the *Yeats Annual.*

A Note on Orthography

Over the centuries, the half-dozen or so renderings of the *Nights* into English have had to confront the complex question of the orthography of Arabic words and the transcription of proper names. And each translator has coped with the problem in his own, sometimes idiosyncratic way. Not even in the case of the great heroine of the frame tale is there any exception. No generally agreed spelling of her name exists. As to other memorable beings in the *Nights*, such as the spirits, demonic or benign, there one meets a gamut of spellings such as *genius, genie, genii, jinee, jinni, jinn, djinn, ginn, jann* – not to mention *afrit, afrite, efreet, ifrit*; additionally various speech marks may be added. If a lack of unanimity has prevailed among a succession of scholars, the same is hardly less true of the writers who have felt the impact of their translations. After all, most English writers, largely ignorant of the nuances in foreign lexia that results from differences of gender or number, tend also to be careless about the phonetic indicators. Naturally such diversity of spelling has further increased over the decades as the translations and reworkings have multiplied, the *Nights'* influence taking ever more varied forms. Thus in the late nineteenth and twentieth centuries one may readily find in a given piece (let alone in its author's entire *oeuvre*) that, for reasons chiefly stylistic, the writer rings the changes on the possible spellings of certain names – or indeed the variant titles of certain stories from the *Nights*. Yet in spite of all this diversity, the danger of real confusion is negligible; the reader experiences little difficulty in following the shifts of nomenclature. Therefore, though (like so many before me) I must confess to preference for Galland's elegant simplicity, in my own and other's contributions to this gathering of essays I have sought to impose no more orthographic consistency than that warranted by the history of the *Nights'* transmission and reception, modalities which even today are more oral than literary.

To Scheherazade

GREVEL LINDOP

Your unperturbed voice
with a serenely repeated movement
like the scimitar-stroke
of a great bird's wing, lays open
a rift of clear air
through our silence, a coloured swathe
engrossed with human action:
debate, betrayal, ruse, justice.

Through the page as through a pane
we look out on a spacious real world
where people say 'But Allah alone is wise . . .
finding a baboon an artist in calligraphy
or the lost ring in the belly of a fish.

In that saying, the imperturbable
perspective: they are real
to themselves in the same way
as to us. In that, and the knowledge
(on which especially your love is founded)
that there is a story opening
inside every other story,
and that of these it is given us to know
an infinite number, but still less than all.

1

Introduction: 'Such a store house of ingenious fiction and of splendid imagery'

PETER L. CARACCIOLO

I

There are few who do not recollect with pleasure the emotions they felt when the Thousand and One Nights were first put into their hands. . . . It may be safely asserted, that such fictions as the magic lamp of Aladdin, and the cavern of the Forty Thieves, have contributed more to the amusement and delight of every succeeding generation since the fortunate appearance of these tales in this quarter of the world, than all the works which the industry and the imagination of Europeans have provided for the instruction and entertainment of youth. Such a store house of ingenious fiction and of splendid imagery, of supernatural agency skilfully introduced, conveying morality, not in the austere form of imperative precept and dictatorial aphorism, but in the more pleasing shape of example, is not to be found in any other existing work of the imagination.

(Henry Weber, *Tales of the East* [Edinburgh: John Ballantyne, 1812; London: Longman, 1812, 3 vols] I, i)

Only to a limited extent does Weber's statement hold true today. Pantomime, if nothing else, will have brought Aladdin and, if not Ali Baba, at least Sindbad the Sailor to the attention of late-twentieth-century children.[1] However, they probably will know little of Scheherazade's desperate circumstances which force the telling of these tales. Modern selections from the *Arabian Nights* frequently omit one of the collection's most distinctive features, the frame tale of how the beautiful and intelligent Scheherazade must spin out a succession of nocturnal tales to save not only her life but also the lives of the young women of her country who are

1

in danger of the vengeance of her husband, the Sultan Shahriar.

Antoine Galland's *Mille et une nuits* (1704–17) was the first, though partial, translation of the *Nights*. This, in turn, was translated into English in the first decade of the eighteenth century, and, as early as 1715, this Grub Street version of Galland's translation had reached its 'Third Edition'.[2] It was to be many times reprinted during the rest of the century. Among its first English readers were Swift, Addison and Pope. Charles Gildon dedicates his *Golden Spy: or a Political Journal of British Nights' Entertainments* (1709) to Swift: 'The Arabian and Turkish Tales were owing to your Tale of a Tub.' Pope first mentioned the *Nights* in 1711, when recommending these tales for Trumbull's son, and at least thought 'of writing a Persian Fable in which I should have given a full loose to description and imagination. It would have been a very wild thing . . . but might not have been unentertaining.'[3] Addison's encounter with the *Nights* led to a number of pseudo-oriental tales in the *Spectator*, the most celebrated being 'The Vision of Mirza'.[4]

Among the next generation, the *Nights* found readers in Reynolds, Sterne, Blair, Warton, Hawkesworth and Beattie.[5] Gibbon recorded, 'Before I left Kingston school I was well acquainted with Pope's Homer and the Arabian Nights entertainments, two books which will always please by the moving picture of human manners and specious miracles.'[6] In later life, Gibbon more than once compared these tales with epic: with Homer when conversing with Charles James Fox; with Vergil when in his *Critical Observations on the Sixth Book of the Aeneid* (1770) Gibbon declared that both Vergil's poem and the *Nights* were politically instructive.[7] Others indeed sought to enlist the help of these Arabian stories in the study of the classics. Sir John Pringle told Boswell in 1776 that 'he would teach Latin very easily by having the Arabian tales translated into it, so as to engage children; for what entertainment could they have in the Books which are read at School?'[8]

The tales were not confined to the leisure hours of pupils studying Greek and Latin. Following the publication of *Robinson Crusoe* in regular instalments, the *Churchman's Last Shift* began the weekly serialisation of 'Sindbad the Sailor' in 1720 – and, later, of another series of extracts from the *Nights*. The *Nights* obviously lends itself to serial publication, and in 1723 the *London News*, a thrice-weekly news-sheet, began serialising *The Arabian Nights' Entertainments* – its 445 instalments ran over three years. In 1785, the *Novelist Magazine* serialised the complete Galland embellished with engravings, and in the 1790s the *General Magazine* and the *Lady's Magazine* published extracts serially. Such serialisation, R. D. Mayo observes, 'presumably would have been welcomed by a new audience', many of whom were still unfamiliar with what we now regard as the classics of prose fiction, let alone the Greek and Latin epics.[9]

As early as 1711, Shaftesbury, in his *Advice to an Author*, had deplored the 'Moorish fancy' which 'prevails strongly at this present time': 'Monsters and monsterland were never more in request; and we may often see a philosopher, or wit, run a tale-gathering in these idle deserts as familiarly as the silliest woman or merest boy.'[10] In 1720 a similarly hostile response was elicited from Bishop Atterbury by the gift of two volumes of Arabian tales from Pope. Suspecting the tales were 'the product of some Womans Imagination', the Bishop concedes that 'they may furnish the mind with some new images: but I think the Purchase is made at too great an Expense'.[11] While *Joseph Andrews* (1742) suggests (bk III, ch. 1) a coolness towards these tales was still common, *The Expedition of Humphry Clinker* (1771) provides perhaps the earliest instance of what was to become a trope common in the nineteenth-century:

> below the three bridges such a prodigious forest of masts, for miles together, that you would think all the ships in the universe were here assembled. All that you read of wealth and grandeur, in the Arabian Nights Entertainments and the Persian Tales concerning Bagdad . . . Damascus, Ispahan and Samarkand is here realized. Ranelagh looks like the inchanted palace of a genie . . . enlightened with a thousand golden lamps . . . . (Penguin edn, p. 123)

But we should notice that this letter of 31 May is offered here as from a woman's pen – and that Lydia is writing to a woman correspondent. It is often as important in real life to recall which sex is being addressed, to remember (for example) that Walpole is writing to Mary Berry when, in 1789, he turns to defend the *Nights* against Atterbury's strictures: 'Read Sinbad the Sailor's voyages and you will be sick of Aeneas's.'[12] As Knipp points out, 'it was not uncommon, even with forthright admirers, to consign the oriental tales to the taste of women and children'.[13] In his perceptive *Remarks on the Arabian Nights Entertainments* (Cadell and Davies,

1797), the first book to be devoted to a study of the tales, Richard Hole notes a variety of attitudes to the collection, almost all dismissive:

> The sedate and philosophical turn from them with contempt; the gay and volatile laugh at their seeming absurdities; those of an elegant and correct taste are disgusted with their grotesque figures and fantastic imagery; and however we may be occasionally amused by their wild and diversified incidents, they are seldom thoroughly relished but by children, or by men whose imagination is complimented at the expense of their judgement.   (p. 8)

This passage registers precisely the challenge the *Nights* posed to neoclassical criticism.[14] By 1812, Henry Weber's *Tales of the East* could view such features of the *Nights* as Hole describes not as defects but as qualities.

During the eighteenth century 'nothing is so striking as the degree to which . . . English writers are able to tame and domesticate what comes to them originally in the form of a genuinely exotic item'.[15] Apart from *Rasselas* (1759), a work esteemed by Weber, nothing of any great literary profundity was achieved in the pseudo-oriental genre until the publication of *Vathek*. Beckford used the *Nights* and his knowledge of other oriental materials to create a fantasy that at times is more potent, bizarre and cruelly sensual than anything which had yet appeared among the English imitations of the Eastern tale.[16] But the *Nights* referred to a real world – as travel writings such as Lady Mary Wortley Montagu's correspondence (especially the letter of 10 March 1718) and Patrick Russell's *Natural History of Aleppo* (1794) demonstrated.[17] Weber draws on the testimony of a number of erudite travellers to counter the charge that the *Nights* is 'a spurious production' (I, ii–v), and he displays a knowledge of their origins, growth, quality and influence which compares very creditably with what is known today:[18] that they belong less to the 'literature' of the East than to what has been called its 'orature' ('The recitation of eastern fables and tales partakes somewhat of a dramatic performance' – I, iii); that, unlike the neoclassical work of art, with its unity of action, beginning, middle and end, the *Nights* consists of 'endless' tales which hold the audience in suspense by intriguing discontinuities ('not unfrequently, in the midst of some interesting adventure, when the expectation of his audience is raised to the highest pitch [the professional story-teller] breaks off abruptly' – I, iv). Such narrative ellipses serve not only to draw back the frustrated listeners on the following day, but also, Weber implies, to compensate for the largely stereotypical characterisation and replicated episodes. The similarities between these Arabian tales and those told in the East Indies and Bengal (noted by an earlier editor, Dr Jonathan Scott – I, vi) lead Weber to consider the successive stages by which these stories came to be put together:

> The Arabian Nights . . . is probably a tissue of tales invented at different times, some of them entirely fictitious, others founded on anecdotes of real history, upon which marvellous additions have been engrafted, and which have been altered and varied by different reciters. (I, vii).

Weber is frank as to how the *Nights* vary not only in mood but in quality too: some showing 'the most happy ingenuity, others . . . the extreme of silliness and insipidity' (I, viii). There are no strict limits to the collection; they are the creation of more than one author or culture, as the variety in different manuscripts suggests (I, xxiv). The *Nights* are encyclopaedic in nature, growing both by accretion – thus preserving tales that otherwise might have been forgotten – and by self-replication. Through variations upon its repertoire of motifs, characters and plots, the *Nights* has generated yet more tales. Indeed, not a little of its influence has been through the example it has provided of self-multiplication. Weber of course could not have known of the evidence that suggests that Chaucer himself had been in a sense an oriental traveller too, visiting areas of Spain where vestiges of Moorish culture still lingered.[19] What Weber does have (thanks to the researches of scholars like Warton and Hole) is a good idea of how oriental narratives reached fourteenth-century England – 'The Enchanted Horse [is] evidently the original of the Horse of Chaucer' (I, xxxiii). Through medieval translations (often by Jewish middlemen such as Petrus Alphonsus) aspects of the *Nights* were passed on to the West (I, xviii). Via Persian and, then, Arabic recensions, stories belonging to the *Nights* entered Europe around the twelfth century, the collection incorporating somewhere along the line discrete groups of tales such as *The Seven Wise Masters* (I, xii). Passing through Arabised Sicily and Moorish Spain in the wake of commerce or crusade, many of the tales came to be part of the cultural heritage of the West and were assimilated into its folklore 'till the present day when [they circulate] among the common people in the form of a chap-book sold at fairs' (I, xv).

Galland's achievement in first introducing modern Europe to a collection of the *Nights* receives its proper due. Weber accepts the necessity which led Galland to omit the verses that intersperse the Arabic text, for the European reader would have found them 'an intolerable interruption' (I, xxix). Nor does he find Galland's version excessively elegant or moralistic: 'but very seldom do any moral reflections occur. . . . The whole of the tales are delivered in the plain unornamented language of familiar conversation . . . such as was used by the story-tellers' (I, xxix–xxx).[20]

II

'When Europe was immersed in barbarism'

By 1793 the English Galland had reached its eighteenth 'edition'. During the next forty years, the rate of publication (whether reprint or new translation) was to double. The excitement of having the art and matter of the *Nights* in some degree verified by travellers, the appearance of learned commentaries on the tales, and the increasing use of illustrations were perhaps responsible for this popularity. But of at least equal importance was the discovery of further tales that could be, more or less, legitimately regarded as belonging to the collection. On their translation from the French of Chavis and Cazotte, the authenticity of these Arabian tales was at first questioned. However, the conflicting views that Jonathan Scott, Russell and the more sceptical among their audience expressed in contributions to the *Gentleman's Magazine* (Dec 1797, p. 1020; Apr 1798, p. 305; Feb 1799, pp. 52, 91–2) and Ouseley's scholarly *Oriental Collections* (1797, I.iii, 245–7) served only to whet the public's appetite for this continuation of the *Nights*. In 1792 Robert Heron's *The Arabian Tales*, as his translation of the *Continuation of the Nights* was entitled, appeared in every major city of the kingdom, at London, Dublin and Edinburgh (in the last, Heron remodelled his translation the selfsame year); a further version ascribed to Mr Beloe was published in London two years later; the

Continuation was also included in an edition of the *Nights* issued at Liverpool in 1814. In 1812, Weber also had published these stories alongside the *Nights* in his *Tales of the East*. At least a decade earlier a copy of what seems more likely to have been the Beloe was added to the collection that Wordsworth was making of versions of the *Nights* and their analogues.[21]

In the Preface to *Arthur; or, The Northern Enchantment* (1789), Richard Hole expressed the view that the *Nights* ought to be regarded as a book for adults and retranslated (pp. iv–v). Hole's *Arthur* also was in Wordsworth's library,[22] which from 1810 to 1830 housed much of Coleridge's collection; and John Beer suggests that Hole supplied a source for 'The Ancient Mariner' in his discussion of Sindbad's voyages in his *Remarks on the Arabian Nights* (1797).[23] In fact, what is arguably an even more illuminating commentary on the socio-historical context of the *Nights* had been written in 1795 by J. Dacre Carlyle, Professor of Arabic at Cambridge. In her annotation of Allan Grant's study of 'The Ancient Mariner' (*infra*, ch. 4), Deirdre Toomey traces Coleridge's indebtedness to Carlyle's *Specimens of Arabian Poetry* (Cambridge, Lunn *et al.*; London, Payne *et al.*; Oxford, Fletcher *et al.*, 1796). Not only did Carlyle's academic career at Cambridge overlap with the undergraduate days of Coleridge and William and John Wordsworth, but he also held ecclesiastical office in Cumberland as the Chancellor of Carlisle. Besides 'revealing another and uncharted road to Xanadu' (*infra*, ch. 4, n. 16), Carlyle's account of Arabic poetics plainly interested more than one of the Coleridge–Wordsworth set. In *Thalaba* (1801), Southey refers to Carlyle's translations, which may have influenced his own free unrhymed verse in that work.[24] Although the copy of Southey's poem in Wordsworth's library is a second edition (1809), a gift of the author, nevertheless *Thalaba* was certainly known to Wordsworth long before 1809; from its original publication, its author's name was coupled with his own, and Wordsworth writes knowledgeably of Southey's erudition in a letter to Walter Scott (16 Oct 1803).[25] In all likelihood, before the end of the century Wordsworth could have heard from both Coleridge and Southey of Carlyle's studies. When Carlyle considers the more sophisticated achievements of the Abbasid Caliphate 'the most splendid period of the Mohammedan Empire' (pp. i–ii), he records that, although Arabic has since ceased to be spoken in court or business life, it continues to be the language of science and, above all, religion (pp. iii–v). Therefore, whereas 'the European writer of pastorals' was driven to either 'uncouth dialect' or an 'unnatural refinement', the Arab poet

> described only the scenes which were before his eyes, and the language of his herds-men . . . was the genuine language used by them, by himself and by his readers. . . . [Thus] the critics of Bagdad universally acknowledged the dialect of the Vallies of Yemen to be the standard of Arabian purity.   (pp. vii–viii)

Such an account, a sample of which is cited in Edward Forster's handsome version of the *Nights* (1802) resembles the 'essentially democratic' views expressed in the Preface to the *Lyrical Ballads* (1800–5).

More and more the *Nights* and their continuation appear to have been in Wordsworth's mind as he composed the *Prelude*. After the completion of the 1799 version, brother and sister walked from Sockburn across the Pennines and, as Dorothy records in a letter (24 and 27 Dec 1799), she was unable 'to express the enchanted effect produced by this Arabian scene of colour as the wind blew aside the great waterfall behind which we stood' (*Letters of W. and D. Wordsworth*, I, 280). Five years later, the 1805 *Prelude* completed, Dorothy Wordsworth was working on her *Recollections of a Tour made in Scotland A. D. 1803*.[26] On their tour the Wordsworths were often reminded of the Orient. It is almost as if they found in the Highlands some approximation to the speech of Carlyle's 'Vallies of Yemen' in the 'stately speech/Such as grave livers do in Scotland use' (p. 311). Certainly, the hills and lakes of Morven bring to the tourists' mind a memory of Addison's pseudo-oriental tale ('the islands of the Blessed in the *Vision of Mirza'* – p. 321), and, a little later, there is the more evocative spectacle that was to inspire eventually the composition of 'The Solitary Reaper' (1805) with its image of 'travellers . . . Among Arabian sands' (p. 380). On 16 September from Arthur's Seat, the Wordsworths' impression of Edinburgh below in the mist was 'visionary, like the conceptions of our childhood of Bagdad or Balsora when we have been reading the Arabian Nights Entertainments' (pp. 385–6).

London too had once seemed to the young William Wordsworth more wonderful than 'airy palaces and gardens built/By genii of romance' (*Prelude*, VII.82–3), and in the rough draft of MS Y occur clear references to Aladdin and other characters of the *Nights*, such as the Third Royal Calender shipwrecked on the magnetic mountain, a misadventure that could well have helped suggest a central passage in the *Prelude*: book v's apocalyptic vision of 'the fleet waters of the drowning world/In chace' (136–7) of the Arabian Knight.[27] The Third Calender's story belongs to the frame tale of 'The Porter and the Ladies of Baghdad': with that typically Arabesque recursive structure, it places dream within tale within tale – very like the levels within which the dreamer nests in *Prelude* v (45–165). The Calender recalls how, after being shipwrecked, he had taken shelter on the island and fallen asleep. He dreamed that an old man appeared instructing him how to save mankind from present evil: if he toppled the bronze horseman placed at the summit of the Magnetic Mountain, the sea would rise and over-whelm the dangerous island.

Southey acknowledges he drew the germ of *Thalaba* from the *Continuation*,[28] the 'History of Maugraby' contributing to the nomenclature, characterisation, plot and atmosphere of Southey's poem. *Thalaba* voices the belief (which Southey shares with Words-worth) in the beneficent influence of nature and solitude, and, in *The Arabian Tales*, the reader's attention is drawn to a similar belief by the French editor's comments on the story that immediately precedes Maugraby's narrative. This earlier story is called 'Habib and Dorathil-goase, or the Arabian Knight'. In describing how Habib is hardened by rough living, taught 'to behold with enthusi-asm the wonders of nature', use is made of the trope of the book of creation which is also employed in *Prelude* v. When Habib falls asleep on the seashore having escaped from a cataclysm that he himself triggered, a water-filled sea-shell is used clairvoyantly by naiads to identify the sleeper as 'the Arabian Knight' who, it is prophesied, will liberate the country (Heron, *The Arabian Tales* [Edinburgh: Bell *et al.*, 1792] III, 225, 291–3; IV, 55–60).

The stone and shell (borne by Wordsworth's Arabian Knight), which are also, respectively, '*Euclid's Elements*' and 'a loud prophetic blast of harmony,/An ode' (*Prelude*, v.88, 96–7), have been shown to derive in part from the third of Descartes's pregnant visions.[29] There in a library, a stranger mysteriously attending, the dreaming Descartes consulted two books: respectively the essence of science and of poetry. However, as enlightening about the origins of Wordsworth's 'desert Quixote' is Descartes's first dream. In this vision, unbalanced by a whirlwind of supernatural fears, Descartes makes his way to the college chapel and there is presented with a melon.[30] A similar fruit functions as an image of spiritual rebirth in the story of another sleeper in *The Arabian Tales*: the enchanting story of 'The Dream of Valid Hassen'. The circumstances by which the dream occurs as well as its content parallel the experience of both Descartes and Wordsworth's 'friend'. All three dreamers fall asleep after study (Heron, *The Arabian Tales*, ɪɪ, 319; Kemp Smith, *New Studies*, pp. 33–4; *Prelude*, v.60–70), whereupon both Valid Hassen and Descartes are mysteriously confronted with a melon; similarly, as Wordsworth's dreamer is distressed at finding himself 'in an Arabian waste,/A desert . . . [a] wild wilderness/Alone upon the sands' (*Prelude* v.71–2), so too Valid Hassen is distressed at being transported into a similar imaginary landscape: 'the middle of an arid plain . . . Amid those burning sands' (*Arabian Tales*, ɪɪ, 319). Yet in each case as the mysterious objects of the dreams are analysed it becomes clear that, sustained by the power of the imagination through their ordeal, each dreamer has chanced upon hidden truths by which he may discover his vocation. Thus these Arabian allusions help impart a subtle coherence and density of meaning to an area of *The Prelude* sometimes found wanting in these respects.[31] By a compound of motifs drawn from 'The tales that charm away the wakeful night/In Araby . . . and something in the shape/Of these will live till man shall be no more' (*Prelude*, v.520, 528–9), Wordsworth's Knight, Don Quixote and Descartes are all associated with the preservation of a number of threatened values. 'A race of real children' (436) liable to be swamped by a flood of dehumanising educational reforms are not the sole object of Wordsworth's concern: Burke's reference to the deluge of the French Revolution also reminds us of the political implications of *Prelude* v.[32] Either way, the role of this 'Arab of the desert . . . this semi-Quixote' of *The Prelude* (v.124, 142) seems to be that of preserving culture amid a deluge of ignorance. It is therefore more than just suggestive that exactly such a metaphor is used by Hole of Islam's achievement when Europe was plunged into the Dark Ages. In his *Remarks on the Arabian Nights Entertainments* (1797), Hole acknowledges Mediaeval Christendom's debt to Islamic culture:

> To [the Arabians] we are chiefly indebted for the preservation of those valuable remains of antiquity; and, so fully established was their literary reputation in former days, that, *when Europe was immersed in barbarism* [emphasis added] all polite learning passed under the designation of *studia Arabum*. (pp. 2–3)[33]

III

'The elements of British mythology'

Walter Scott visited Grasmere in 1805 but there is no evidence that he was shown *The Prelude* as De Quincey was.[34] The 'Author of *Waverley*' had to discover for himself how the *Nights* could help him to chronicle imaginatively the process by which the Scots (as Andrew Lang was to comment when editing the Waverley novels) 'a people patriarchal and military as the Arabs of the desert were suddenly dragged into modern commercial and industrial society'.[35] Scott's familiarity with the Arabian tales dates from childhood, when he used to read them aloud to the family circle, and they remained favourites of his throughout his life. Scott's letters and journal are full of references to the *Nights*: in middle years, for instance, grieving over a sick child, Scott has poignant recourse to memories of the paralysed young 'Prince of the Black marble Islands'.[36] There is evidence also that the potential of such references was from the start recognised by his audience.

Thus one reviewer of *The Minstrelsy of the Scottish Borders* (1802–3) remarked of its contents,

> Many of them will serve for the story of future ballads, and the decoration of yet unwritten metrical romances. They constitute the elements of British mythology; *and in the hands of a Modern Ovid*, may be shapen into a wild catalogue of metamorphoses, into amusing anecdotes of sorcery, fableries of romance, or tales of wonder, *into a Thousand and One Nights' Entertainment*, or golden legends of shuddering astonishment. (*Critical Review*, Nov 1803)[37]

Arabesque touches are not difficult to detect in the subsequent verse narratives, though they are on an altogether slighter scale than those employed by another friend of Scott's, George Crabbe, who skilfully drew on the harim intrigues of the Harun cycle in the *Nights* to structure and characterise 'The Confidant' (*Tales*, 1812).[38]

The author's own account of the protracted growth of *Waverley* (in his General Preface, 1829) indicates, more or less explicitly, several crypto-Arabian influences: the inspiring welcome given to *The Minstrelsy*; the favourable impression made by *The Lady of the*

Lake (Edinburgh: John Ballantyne, 1810), which introduced into the Highlands (as Scott himself points out) 'the beautiful Arabian tale of *Il Bondocani*', Harun's alias from the *Continuation of the Nights* (*Lady of the Lake*, vi.xxvi, p. 427n). However, at least as much impact, if not more, must have been made on Scott by the achievement of Weber. In bringing the Galland and its continuation together with other oriental tale groups, Weber clearly reactivated Scott's recollections of childhood reading (just as the appearance of the new Arabian tales in 1792 had stirred so creatively the Lake poets' memories of their first encounter with the *Nights*). From 1804 to 1813, Weber had been Scott's amanuensis and an intimate of the family, who were 'pleased by his stores of knowledge' (*Dictionary of National Biography*). For comprehensiveness as a collection, Weber's *Tales of the East; Comprising the Most Popular Romances of Oriental Origin and Best Imitations by European Authors* (1812) remains without rival, and the erudition and critical sweep of its introduction still command respect.[39] One of the many valuable features of this commentary that surely caught Scott's eye is highlighted by the subtitle: the evidence that Weber provides that, while Homer may have contributed to Sindbad's voyages, in turn the *Nights* had influenced many earlier European writers – the very poets, playwrights and romancers whom Scott so admires that their names recur in his novels. Not only do there appear, over and over again, the names of Chaucer, Spenser, Shakespeare, the seventeenth-century dramatists, Samuel Johnson, but those also of Cervantes, the French *trouveurs*, Boccaccio and the subsequent 'Italian novelists' (i, xiii), this last phrase an ambiguous terminology that might have seemed suggestive to the creator of the Waverley novels.

In the Scottish novels there are regularly allusions to Shakespeare (the history plays and especially *Henry IV* for obvious reasons are prominent). These Shakespearean allusions always outnumber the references to the classical or Italian poets, though in certain of Scott's novels Shakespeare in turn may be outstripped: by the ballads in *The Bride of Lammermoor*; by the Bible in *Old Mortality*, *Heart of Midlothian* and *Redgauntlet*. Admittedly the incidence of allusions to the *Nights* per novel is far less; however, through strategic placing, these Arabian references provide vital clues as to the structure, atmosphere, characterisation, themes and genre to which most conveniently the whole sequence seems to belong. Of all the various strands of allusion woven into *The Antiquary* (1816), for instance, those to 'Abu Hassan or The Sleeper Awakened' (see for example I, ch. 13, p. 164 – Border Edition) are arguably the most significant, since they underline so crucially plot, psychology and other concerns.[40]

Advised by Scott that *Waverley* (1814) rejects the fashionable conventions of the Gothic and the Sentimental, that it is 'neither a romance of chivalry nor tale of modern manners' (I, ch. 1, p. 3 – Border Edition), the reader could miss the hint that the novel escapes being contained by any *one* of these particular categories. This is because Scott here attempts to comprehend a range of such genres. The later dismissal of 'Prince Hussein's tapestry' (ch. 5, p. 42), as its tone should warn us, is a tease; for the story of Prince Ahmed and the Peri Banou (in which the magic carpet is found) to some degree offers a suggestive likeness to the adventures of Scott's hero. Led by romantic feelings into an unfamiliar wilderness, each discovers the underground abode of 'the daughter of one of the most powerful and distinguished genies' (Weber, *Tales of the East*, I, 441) whose charms tend to eclipse the young man's recollections of a previous love, whose male relatives threaten the civilised, if corrupt, world. When first glimpsed the Highlander's beacon resembles 'the fiery vehicle in which the Evil Genius of an Oriental tale traverses land and sea' (*Waverley*, I, ch. 17, p. 151). A thread of such Eastern allusion connects the first references to the *Nights* and its 'instrumental marvellous' (Todorov, *The Fantastic* (1973) p. 56) with one of the finest touches towards the close of the novel. Here a celebrated Arabian formula is pronounced at a moment when clan loyalties could not be more passionately felt. On being condemned to death, Fergus thinks of his leaderless people, but he quickly realises that, to the clan, Waverley cannot be 'Vich Ian Vohr', 'and these three magic words . . . are the only "Open Sesame" to their feelings and sympathies' (II, ch. 40, p. 336). The 'Forty Thieves' allusion recalls tragically the hidden yet genuine riches of Highland sentiment and culture which were now doomed, without letting the reader forget that from their cavernous hide-outs these backward feudal marauders had threatened the progressive settled world. Although the *Nights* is but one thread in Scott's tapestry of allusions, the anonymous reviewer in the *British Critic* (Aug 1814) singled out for praise the Arabesque elements in the pattern, recognising them as particularly apt for Scott's design of serving Scotland by interpreting her to England:

This tale should be ranked in the same class with the Arabian Nights entertainments, in which the story, however it may for a moment engage the attention, is but of little consequence in proportion to the faithful picture which they present of the manners and customs of the east.[41]

There is a relative obviousness about the way in which in *Guy Mannering* (1815) Scott fuses extracts from a young lady's correspondence with oriental story-telling 'half poetry, half prose' (I, ch. 17, p. 153 – Border Edition). In *The Heart of Midlothian* (1818), though, Scott elaborates his art of allusion by capitalising on the repetitiveness of the *Nights*. Jeannie's admirable enterprise in tackling difficulties, which are partly of her own creation, is associated with the adventures of *both* the Second *and* Third Calenders (II, ch. 2, p. 16 – Border Edition). The conflation looks deliberate, for, taken together, these tales exhibit marked affinities with a happier Arabian tale, not of the loss but of the recovery of children, to which Scott refers near the end of his novel. This is the story of Bedreddin Hassan, whose cream tarts Scott uses to point up the comic possibility that a fashionable lady might betray her dairy-maid origins (II, ch. 26, p. 365). This allusion helps to reduce the awkwardness with which the Highland conclusion relates to the earlier parts of the novel.

In *Redgauntlet* (1824) Scott similarly exploits the repetitiveness of the *Nights*, the key reference to the *Nights* occurring in letter 12 of the correspondence between Darsie Latimer and Alan Fairford:

We fools of fancy, who suffer ourselves, like Malvolio to be cheated with our visions, have, nevertheless, this advantage over the wise ones of the earth, that we have our whole stock of enjoyments under our own command, and can dish for ourselves an intellectual banquet with most moderate assistance from external objects. It is, to be sure, something like the feast which the Barmecide served up to Alnaschar; and we cannot be expected to get fat upon such a diet. But then, neither is there repletion nor nausea, which often succeed the grosser and more material revel.   (I, letter 12, p. 174 – Border Edition)

Again Scott conflates two tales: the tale of the Barber's Fifth Brother and the tale of the Barber's Sixth Brother. Like Malvolio, the Barber's Fifth Brother, Alnaschar, falls victim to delusions of grandeur; unlike Malvolio, Alnaschar is wholly self-deluded. Things are quite different in the case of the Barber's Sixth Brother – the resourceful Shacabac only pretends to be deceived. By joining in the make-believe meal to which he is invited by the Barmecide, Shacabac calls his host's bluff. By this three-way connection in which Malvolio is linked with the coalescence of the two contrary adventures of the Barber's brothers, Scott requires his reader to discriminate between varieties of delusion, real and apparent, self-inflicted and otherwise. The point is stressed throughout the novel by the manner in which these distinctions are repeatedly imagined in terms of either feasting or dearth. Wandering Willie's tale, which in a brilliant *mise en abîme* nests within the recursive structures of the Latimer–Fairford correspondence, is also part of this pattern. When Wandering Willie's 'gudesire' 'like a man in a dream' ventures across a different border into the Other World seeking the receipt for the rent he had paid, it is by taking 'neither meat, drink, or siller, except [his] ain' (I, letter 11, pp. 165–7) that he ensures his return. He thus can be seen as an antitype to Shacabac in this escape from the damnable clutches of Sir Robert Redgauntlet. In Scott's late masterpiece the many tales within tales converge far more than many critics have realised.

IV

'A Turkish kiosk rising on the ruins of an ancient temple'

Scott's over-ambitious attempt at combining an all-inclusive corniche with a lengthy chain of witnesses makes *Tales of my Landlord* (but not *Old Mortality*, that noble epic which it frames) an awkward *Caledonian Nights*; however, against this comparative failure can be set the enthrallingly imbricated recursions of *Redgauntlet*. The Waverley novels, of course, have something of those defects of the *Nights* which became progressively more apparent with the gradual editing of the vulgate of *Alf laylah wa laylah* during the early nineteenth century; the translations of this Arabic text beginning with Hammer-Purgstall's French–German one of 1823–4 (an English version by George Lamb followed in 1826) temporarily shifted attention away from the more elegant Galland. Often Scott's prose is sloppy, the plots confused, the history inaccurate, the same stock characters recurring from one novel to the next. Yet the *Nights* help us to make sense of many features of Scott's work, such as (1) the instances of apparently loose construction which prove to be subtle webs of allusion, balance and contrast; (2) the variety of the material handled; (3) the eclectic fusion of genres which makes possible the expansion of the novel-form itself; (4) the *frisson* of the supernatural amid the everyday; (5) the innovative mixture of fact and fiction encompassing successive cultures; (6) the vast distances covered by Scott's travellers; (7) the way he extends the sociological range of the characters beyond the middle class (the usual concern of the conventional novel of his time) so as to comprehend royalty, the aristocrat, peasant and outlaw, the professionals, merchants and proletariat; (8) the resourcefulness of his woman characters. What the *Nights* uniquely provides is a largely secular model of capacious, protean fictions employing an expressive amalgam of prose and verse, realism and fantasy, comedy and tragedy; tales within tales that are responsive to the needs of society, and lend themselves to semi-dramatic reading.[42]

Robert Louis Stevenson, a later enthusiast of the *Nights*, sensed the significance of this Arabesque precedent when he compared Fielding's neo-classical achievement with Scott's prototype of a new kind of fiction:

> The fact is that the Engish novel was looking one way and seeking one set of effects in the hands of Fielding; and in the hands of Scott it was looking eagerly in all ways and searching for all effects that by any possibility it could utilize. The difference between the two men marks a great enfranchisement. With Scott the Romantic movement, the movement of an extended curiosity and an enfranchised imagination has begun.[43]

The Prefatory Letter to *Peveril of the Peak* (1822) suggests, however, that Scott was a more conscious innovator than Stevenson allows. Defending his work against the strictures of the professional historian, whose case is here presented by Dr Dryasdust, Scott gives a thumbnail sketch of the oriental sources for his art of the novel:

> *Author.* . . . . You mean to say these learned persons will have but little toleration for a romance, or a fictitious narrative, founded upon history?
> *Dryasdust.* . . . just as every classical traveller pours forth

expressions of sorrow and indignation, when, in travelling
through Greece, he chances to see a Turkish kiosk rising on the
ruins of an ancient temple.

Author. But since we cannot rebuild the temple, a kiosk may
be a pretty thing, may it not? Not quite correct in architecture,
strictly and classically criticised; but presenting something
uncommon to the eye, and something fantastic to the imagination, on which the spectator gazes wth pleasure of the same
description which arises from the perusal of an Eastern tale.

(i, lxxiii–lxxiv – Border Edition)

In this use of a comparison between the differing architectures of
the two civilisations so as to distinguish their respective literatures,
there is plainly an echo of Hole's brilliant image which Scott had
probably encountered in Weber (*Tales of the East*, i, xxxii). In his
Remarks, Hole observed that 'the Voyages of Sindbad' might not
unjustly be 'denominated *The Arabian Odyssey*':

It seems indeed . . . to bear the same resemblance to that
performance, as an oriental mosch does to a Grecian temple.
The constituent parts of the first may be separately considered
as to their effect and beauty: each forms a little whole by itself
. . . [these features] irregularly placed . . . gilt and ornamented
. . . in gay confusion alternately engage and distract the attention.
But in the Grecian temple all parts harmonize together, and
compose one simple and magnificent WHOLE. The same kind of
Saracenic masonry, more fashionable in Spenser's days than in
ours, is discoverable in his *Fairy Queen*. It constitutes a different
order of poetic architecture from that of the classical Epic; and
its inferiority must be allowed, though it possesses some peculiar
and appropriate beauties. (pp. 17–18)

However, Scott has significantly extended the implications of the
architectural simile by the subtle changes he has made in the terms
of the comparison. These extensions of meaning relate principally
to two matters: first, the applicability of oriental methods of
construction to English culture; and, second, the psychological
conditions that seem to most favour the Western author's recognition of this potential.

By changing Hole's 'Grecian temple' to 'the ruins of an ancient
temple', and by replacing Hole's 'oriental mosch' with a 'Turkish

kiosk' that rises upon (rather than 'alongside') the Greek building, Scott points to historical realities, to specific gains as well as losses that have resulted from the Islamic conquests. For exclusively sacred edifices pagan, Christian and Muslim there is substituted what in the Regency period amounts to the international architectural style for the great magnate. The orientalism which had shaped the pavilions of the eighteenth-century garden was becoming fashionable for the mansion itself, as is witnessed by the design of Sezincote and the Royal Pavilion at Brighton, the latter between 1803 and 1822 mutating from mosque through Chinese pavilion to Mughal palace in a fashion that is reminiscent of the way Hole's simile is transformed into Scott's. The style, like the simile, is at once exotic and familiar: exotic because, apart from the mosque, the oriental originals that inspired such English mansions were literally the 'stately pleasure dome' of Coleridge's 'Vision in a Dream' ('Kubla Khan'); familiar because, like the villas outside imperial Rome, or of the Italian Renaissance and the English eighteenth century, these 'Turkish kiosks' were used by the hardly devout magnates of an epigonic culture.[44] It is in their ability to respond quickly to social needs with a 'flexible and additive system of construction' that the creators of 'the Turkish kiosk' betray their Arabian or Central Asian ancestry in nomadic communities with their tent cities: the Bedouin, Turk, Mughal and Manchu conquerors of the settled civilisations of the East. It was also in their methods of adaptation that these nomadic builders revealed design techniques which nineteenth-century Europe realised it was advantageous to copy.[45] Since the activities pursued in these pleasure domes frequently included music and poetry, the European who was acquainted with the Arabian studies of Carlyle or Hole could easily grasp the link between Moslem architecture and other arts.

Scott's reworking of the architectural–literary parallel so as to explain his own practice as a writer also illuminates other areas of the *Nights'* influence. The fact that Scott would have found Hole's simile most conveniently in Weber reinforces the suspicion that it was *Tales of the East* with its reactivation of memories of childhood's favourite reading which triggered off in the middle-aged novelist such a creative upsurge of allusions to the *Nights* in the Waverley sequence. This hypothesis gains support from consideration of the circumstances in which works such as 'The Ancient Mariner' and the 1805 *Prelude* were composed.[46] It would seem that the psychological conditions most likely to favour the European author's exploitation of the potential in the *Nights* are as follows.

In adulthood the author recaptures memories of childhood by discovering a new perspective on these Arabian tales, which is gained by some combination of factors such as (1) new commentaries, either literary or anthropological; (2) actual travel in Islamic cultures, or the re-creation of that experience by architectural and other designs, or even by the dreams bred of narcotic experiment; (3) the discovery of additional tales belonging to the Arab or analogous collections; (4) new renderings into English; (5) their ornament and illustration; (6) that process of reticulated influence characteristic of the *Nights* – the example set by various great predecessors' use of these stories.[47]

For the Lake poets and for Scott the English precedents had been established by Chaucer, Spenser and Shakespeare. For the generations immediately subsequent to the first Romantics, the situation was rather different. During the first half of the nineteenth century, the only major British addition to the medieval and Renaissance prototypes to appear was the Waverly sequence. Throughout the period from Jane Austen's time until at least Victoria's death, the formative influence of Walter Scott seems to be inextricably linked with the *Nights*.[48]

'We have seen three literary kings in our Time – Scott – Byron – and then the scotch novels', wrote Keats near the start of his own *annus mirabilis*, 1819.[49] It is around this time that, amid the flow of echoes from Antiquity, the Renaissance and the Romantics (among the latter Scott figuring significantly as poet and novelist), there also runs through Keats's poetry, as in his letters, a steady current of allusions to Eastern tales, to masterpieces of imitation such as *Vathek*, as well as to the genuinely oriental, and not least to the *Nights*. Some of the earliest signs of this Arabesque influence are detectable in *Endymion* (1817); in 1819 there is a spate of such Arabian allusions – just six months or so after Keats's praise of 'the scotch novels'; stanza 30 of 'The Eve of St Agnes' seems to draw not only on elements of the 'Story of the Enchanted Horse' but also on the exotic provisions which are gathered by the Porter for what proves to be an increasingly amorous entertainment at the opening of the 'History of the Three Calenders, Sons of Kings, and the Five Ladies of Baghdad'. In his letters, Keats lauds the delicacy of claret, which 'walks like Aladin about his own enchanted palace so gently that you do not feel his step – Other wines . . . transform a Man to a Silenus; this makes him a Hermes' (14 Feb–3

May 1819), and this allusion is followed by Keats's wooing of
Fanny Brawne with references to the melancholy story of the Magic
Basket which gave the tantalised lover but a glimpse of paradise
(15? July 1819) (Letters, ed. Gittings, pp. 215, 269; cf. Lamia, 1.257–
67). Such clues as these confirm Miriam Allott's observation that
Keats is rediscovering the Nights in Weber's Tales of the East.[50]
Its narrative principles and its tolerance of the episodic and
heterogeneous are hardly likely to have escaped Keats.

By contrast, Byron in Don Juan (1818–23) makes the most econ-
omical use of the Nights, placing allusions to these tales mise en
abîme in canto III, stanza xxxiv:

> Afar a dwarf buffoon stood telling tales
> To a sedate grey circle of old smokers,
> Of secret treasures found in hidden vales,
> Of wonderful replies from Arab jokers,
> Of charms to make good gold and cure bad ails,
> Of rocks bewitched that open to the knockers,
> Of magic ladies who by one sole act
> Transformed their lords to beasts (but that's a fact) . . . .
> (Penguin edn, p. 165)

Apart from helping to convey the atmosphere of the festivities
celebrating the union of Haidee and Juan, this vignette deftly
evokes some of the most popular of the Arabian tales: those of
Little Hunchback, Sindbad, Ali Baba, Aladdin, Sidi Numan. This
epitome helps to structure both cantos III and IV, fusing a mock-
heroic version of a modern Ulysses' return home with such tense
episodes from 'The Forty Thieves' as the seizure of Cassim in the
treasure-cavern and the later imposture of the Robber Chief. The
long-delayed revenge of Lambro acts also as an ironic frame for
the song 'The Isles of Greece'. These recursive structures create a
microcosm of the whole poem, reminding the reader of one of the
more expandable genres to which Don Juan belongs.

V

*If the gods would give me the desire of my heart, I should be able to
write a story which boys would relish for the next few dozen of centuries.
The boy critic loves the story: grown-up, he loves the author who wrote*

the story. Hence the kindly tie is established between writer and reader, and lasts pretty nearly for life. I meet people now who don't care for Walter Scott, or the Arabian Nights; *I am sorry for them, unless they in their time have found* their *romancer – their charming Scheherazade.*

(Thackeray)[51]

When Thackeray's contemporaries began to rediscover their 'charming Scheherazade' in Edward Lane's translation of the *Nights* (Charles Knight, 1839–41) they too were reminded of Scott. The *Dublin Review* of February 1840, noticing Lane, turned to an analogue of 'the enlargement and recapture of the Ginn in the fisherman's story [that] is familiar to most readers from its quotation by . . . Scott in the notes to *The Lay of the Last Minstrel'*,[52] The *Dublin Review* at the same time considered Jonathan Scott's edition (London, 1811); the French version of Hammer – the first translation from the vulgate (Paris, 1823–4); Habicht's German taken from various sources (Breslau, 1825); *Alif Laila wa Laila* ('Calcutta II'), edited by William Macnaghten (Calcutta, 1838–9), the most complete text; and, also from Calcutta in the same years, Henry Torrens's incomplete version, still the best English translation as far as it goes. Rival publishers produced two other English versions of Galland in 1839: a revision of Edward Forster's, which continued to be handsomely illustrated if in a somewhat neo-classical style by Smirke; and a cheaper version published in Halifax. These reactions of publishers to Lane recall the earlier responses to the *Continuation* (1792) and to Weber's *Tales of the East* (1812), and set a pattern for later republications in the 1840s and 1850s.

This sort of competition might help to explain why in 'a new edition' of Lane (1853) John Murray made textual changes without consulting the translator. Not only were Lane's copious and informative notes dispensed with, but

The more modern (and undoubtedly the more correct) spelling of Mr LANE, was found to be too formidable an innovation for the adoption of English readers, and threatened to stop the circulation of his admirable translation. . . . therefore . . . it was thought that readers would more easily recognise their old friends Aladdin and Sindbad the Sailor, than 'Alá ed-Deen and Es-Sindbad of the Sea. ('Advertisement')

However, from the mid-1850s until 1864–5 Lane not merely dominated but swept the board of other versions of the *Nights*. So in
their new edition of 1859 Edward Lane and his nephew E. Stanley-
Poole felt confident enough to return to the 1839–41 orthography
and rich annotation:

> The public appreciation of these notes, and of the advantage of
> correctly-written foreign words is . . . proved by the call for the
> present edition. . . . The present generation does not regard
> antiquated blunders as 'the familiar names of childhood' but
> rather strives to attain accuracy in all things.   (Editor's Preface,
> p. viii)

Despised though they were by Lane's editor, 'the familiar names
of childhood' had been celebrated a decade earlier with affectionate
humour in Dickens' 'A Christmas Tree' (*Household Words*, 21 Dec
1850). The way in which the disturbing implications of the two
Eastern kings' encounter with the Lady of the Glass Case (Plate 1)
are so completely lost on the child of Dickens' recollection leads
one to speculate whether Dickens first saw a depiction of this
sexual adventure before he could read.[53] That the early-nineteenth-
century child became acquainted with some of these Arabian
tales at a very early age is not in doubt. Among the stories in
contemporary chapbooks, those of Aladdin, the Forty Thieves and
Sindbad were at least as popular as the tales taken from Perrault,
d'Aulnoy and Grimm, and, moreover, supplied material for other
forms of family entertainment, occupying a vital part of the
repertoire of pantomime, the toy stage and 'dark, dirty, real
theatres'.[54]

Until 1839 none of Dickens' writings, public or private, made
much mention of the *Nights*. Then, on the turn of that year,
when the translations of Torrens and Lane appeared, there were
indications that Dickens was rapidly rediscovering the *Nights*
at the very time when, under the influence of Scott, he was
experimenting with new ways of reaching the public. On 4 January
1839, in answer to a query from John Forster, Dickens wrote, 'If I
had a copy of the *Arabian Nights* [i.e. at hand] I could shew you
where it is in a second. But . . . for the life of me I can't at a pinch
remember the fellow's name, though I think it was Shacabac.'[55]
Towards the end of March, by way of warning an American
correspondent about the dangers of literary ambition, Dickens

viewed the quest for fame in terms of 'the talking bird, the singing tree, and the golden water' sought at such risk of petrification by Parizade and her brothers in 'The Story of the Sisters who Envied their Younger Sister' (*Letters*, ed. House *et al.*, p. 534 and n. 4). Then, on 14 July, Dickens sent Forster his 'rough notes of proposals for the New Work' (i.e. *Master Humphrey's Clock*), which was to combine some imitation of the procedures of eighteenth-century periodicals such as the *Spectator* with a series of papers about London's past, present and future, 'to which I would give some such title as The Relaxations of Gog and Magog, dividing them into portions like the *Arabian Nights*, and supposing [them] to entertain each other with such narrations . . . all night long, and break off every morning at daylight' (*Letters*, pp. 563–4).

Besides the overt references here to the *Nights*, all the eighteenth-century precedents which Dickens cites make some use of the collection and its analogues (note too that Washington Irving's *The Tales of Alhambra* [1832], which Dickens also mentions, answered a request from Scott's illustrator David Wilkie for 'something in the Haroun Al raschid style'). Five weeks after outlining his ideas for *Master Humphrey's Clock*, on 21 August 1839, Dickens warmly recommended to one of his illustrators, George Cattermole, 'A Legend of Montrose, and Kenilworth which I have just been reading with greater delight than ever' (*Letters*, p. 576). Significantly, Dickens opens this 1839 letter by suggesting the very work, *Peveril*, which as noted above, is prefaced by Scott's oriental theory of the novel with its memorable image of 'a Turkish kiosk rising on the ruins of an ancient temple'.

The frontispiece to volume I of the first edition in book form of *Master Humphrey's Clock* (Chapman and Hall, 1840) has a design by Cattermole that teasingly unites the arts of medieval Christendom with those of Islam.[56] At first glance the decorative margins, which provide a sentimental–comic setting for the vignettes of early-nineteenth-century domestic scenes, are mock-Gothic fantasies. On closer inspection the absurdly elongated halberds prove to outline ambiguous 'counterchange patterns' that can be read as the horseshoe arches of Moorish architecture. Although the point of the central arch in Dickens' frontispiece is masked by a shield, and its contours are flattened, there are also nuances of the lambrequin sub-patterns often found in the Islamic arch. These Muslim elements contrast with the classical and Gothic shapes of the doors and alcoves of the genre scenes. The alert reader discovers that the tales within tales stored within the clock case do contain halberd-wielding jinn ('*Giant Chronicles*').[57] But the corniche that Dickens laboriously constructs as a Cockney Nights Entertainments proves to be no less cumbersome than Scott's own experiment. In *The Old Curiosity Shop* itself, on the other hand, the lessons of Scott are better assimilated. There Shakespearean allusions serve to characterise and structure the personages and events of the main action, while the *Nights* performs a similar role for the sub-plot: Quilp is modelled on Richard III; there is 'an extensive parallel with Nell and her grandfather to Cordelia and Lear'[58]; and Dick Swiveller likens himself to those young men in the Arabian tales whose courting is forwarded by the help of a genie or two – Bedreddin Hassan, one such, being shuttled between Grand Cairo and Damascus, exactly the locations specified by Dickens (ch. 64). Swiveller's feverish awakening into what seems 'an Arabian Night' picks up reverberations from far beyond just 'The Story of Camaralzaman, Prince of the Isles of the Children of Khaledan'. There is a distinct touch of Aladdin's manner of wooing about the way in which the idea of marriage to 'the Princess of China' is so soon followed by the expectation of 'black slaves with jars of jewels on their heads' (Penguin edn, pp. 579–82, 714).

This suggests the way in which memories of the *Nights*, apparently reactivated by Lane and Scott, enabled Dickens to move away from the methods of literary construction evident in *Pickwick* and *Oliver Twist* towards the rich integration of autobiography, fiction, social concern, psychological insight, literary and popular lore that is achieved in his mature art.[59] The story book *par excellence* that served Dickens as a template for such a synthesis was *The Arabian Nights Entertainments*. In *Hard Times*, for example Dickens illuminates the connections between the worlds of education, industry, marriage and entertainment by the iteration of adroitly varied references to the *Nights*. Of the five explicit allusions to the tales, the most egregious comes near the opening of the novel with an unexpected parallel between M'Choakumchild's teaching and Morgiana's destruction of all but one of the Forty Thieves (bk. 1, ch. 2). When this cryptic warning of the continuing threat to Ali Baba is reinforced in the following chapter by English nursery rhymes about both the mixed fortunes of those who frequented 'the house that Jack built', and the propensity of pipers to steal, there is foreshadowed Tom's embezzlement. On his sister's visit to their dying mother, there appears an almost imperceptible yet highly potent reference to 'the golden water' (bk II, ch. 9; Penguin edn, p. 223), the successful quest for which enables Parizade to revivify her petrified brothers and so reunite themselves with their father.[60] By this hint Dickens probes the imaginative and moral deficiencies of the training that Mr Gradgrind inflicted on his children, which makes it nigh-well impossible for Louisa to redeem any of her relatives.

The *Nights* also gives mythic depth to Dickens' poignant treatment of man's inhumanity to woman. The antiquity of theological and legal disabilities still endured by nineteenth-century women of whatever class, implied in Rachael's reliance on the precedent established by Christ's defence of the Woman taken in Adultery (bk I, ch. 13; p. 120), and the ironic disclaimer that Mr Gradgrind MP takes after Bluebeard (bk I, ch. 15), are amplified in the reader's memory by the triple links between Sissy's plight and the situation in the frame tale of the *Nights*. Interrogated by the disapproving Gradgrind, Sissy confesses that she had been in the habit of soothing her distressed father by reading to him about 'the Hunchback, and the Genies' (bk I, ch. 7; p. 89). Later, with Louisa for her ill-fated Dinarzade, Sissy continues her account of how the *Nights* create a life-enhancing suspense as to 'whether the Sultan would let the lady go on with the story, or would have her head cut off before it was finished'. The parallel between the Persian sultaness and this Victorian Scheherazade is completed when their nocturnal story-telling is repeatedly interrupted by men bent on cruelly exploitative marriage-making (bk I, ch. 9; pp. 99–101).

VI

'What Genii-elixir or Magi-distillation?'

Emily Brontë used the *Nights* to draw attention not to the 'Fairy Palaces' of Coketown, but to the financial bases of the Industrial Revlution first in the slave trade, then, during the nineteenth century, in the captive markets of British colonial possessions in India and China.[61] The *Nights* figures among the Brontës' books 'so early acquired, assimilated, conned as to be almost coeval with . . . memory', and the key to *Wuthering Heights* is to be found in two references to the *Nights*.[62] One morning the young Catherine informed Nelly that 'she was that day an Arabian merchant going to cross the Desert with his caravan and [needing] plenty of provision for herself and beasts: a horse, and three camels . . .' (II, ch. 4, p. 235 – 1976 Oxford edn). In 'The Merchant and the Jinni' the fatal carelessness of the traveller arouses the wrath of the jinni; in *Wuthering Heights*, young Catherine's breaking of bounds draws upon her the baleful interest of Heathcliff. This 'dark skinned gypsy' (I, ch. 1, p. 6), a foundling picked up in the great slave port of Liverpool, is supplied with a legend of alternative origin by Nelly Dean:

> You're fit for a prince in disguise. Who knows, but your father was Emperor of China, and your mother an Indian queen, each of them able to buy up, with one week's income, Wuthering Heights and Thrushcross Grange together? And you were kidnapped by wicked sailors, and brought to England . . . .
>
> (I, ch. 7, p. 72)

Thus Heathcliff is associated with both the East India Company's expanding colonial hegemony, and also the regal miscegenation fostered by the genie in the *Nights*; for, despite the reversal of the sexes here, the Victorian reader could but be reminded of the story of Camaralzaman and Badoura, Princess of China, nor forget that in its continuation as the story of the princes Amgiad and Assad there are protracted over several generations conflicts between parents and children whose relationships verge perilously on the unnatural.

Charlotte Brontë's aversion to Heathcliff which led her to describe him as 'a Ghoul – an Afreet' (p. 444 and n.) finds more than a little justification in Nelly's testimony. Teased by Catherine about how her sister-in-law dotes on him, Heathcliff denies any response to Isabella 'except in a very ghoulish fashion' (I, ch. 10, p. 131). Later Lockwood is driven to question whether his brutal landlord is 'a ghoul or vampire' (II, ch. 20, p. 403). These overtly 'ghoulish' associations are sustained by numerous references to *diablerie* and the carnivorous. Frequently viewed as 'a fiend' and 'goblin', Heathcliff is twice observed expressing the wish to eat *human* flesh (I, ch. 14, p. 181; II, ch. 3, p. 222), and Isabella points to his cannibal teeth. When to the sense that there is something ghoulish in Heathcliff's feelings for Catherine, a view Nelly and Lockwood share, is added their observation that both lovers eventually refuse normal food, the nineteenth-century reader steeped in the Arabian

tales would be bound to suspect the influence of one of the most
bizarre emotional triangles in the *Nights*, that found in the story of
Sidi Numan. Puzzled by his wife's reluctance to do more than pick
at a solitary grain of rice, he discovers her adultery with a ghoul;
she takes her revenge by transforming him into a dog. The story
of Sidi Numan echoes one of the inset tales told in Lane's version
of 'The Merchant and the Jinni': 'The Story of the Third Sheyk and
the Mule' (I, ch. 1, pp. 56–7). Both tales present a love triangle
and its metamorphic consequence, but one involves a ghoul, the
other a black slave.[63] Originating in a characteristically Islamic
pattern of theme, repeat and variation, the multiplying reflections
between the Arabian tales produce a narrative version of a hall of
mirrors. Emily Brontë not only places Nelly Dean in the role of
Scheherazade to Lockwood's Shahriar, but also deploys the narrative methods of the *Nights* with a subtlety that is rare amongst
novelists of the period. Only a few, such as Scott, Wilkie Collins,
Le Fanu and Stevenson, approach the virtuosity with which
Emily Brontë 'naturalises' the *Nights*' multi-vocal, discontinuous,
imbricated, recursive art of narration.[64]

While there is no exact precedent in the Arabian tales for
Lockwood's nightmare within a nightmare, after Emily's stroke of
genius such a dream sequence appears the inevitable extension of
those awakenings from dream into a day-time world which the
Nights presents as mingling naturalism and fantasy in a fashion
that is itself phantasmagoric and which would seem likely to be
drug-induced. Although when questioned by Mrs Gaskell, who
had been impressed by the authentic account of the effects of
opium in Lucy Snowe's Eastern vision of Brussels *en fête*, Charlotte
Brontë 'replied that she had never in her knowledge taken a grain
of it in any shape' (*The Life of Charlotte Brontë* [1857] ch. 27),
nevertheless there are grounds for believing Emily's sister was not
so entirely reliant upon her unaided imagination as she avowed:
the drug, after all, was widely used in nineteenth-century medi-
cation; the comparable effects of laudanum and hashish, as well
as the intimate connections of such phenomena with distinctive
features of the Eastern tales, were progressively explored by writers
of the period such as De Quincey (the 'Opium Eater's' works,
themselves suffused with references to the *Nights*, were known to
the Brontës) and Fitzhugh Ludlow, whose *Hasheesh Eater* (1857)
has recently been linked to Dickens' hallucinatory experiments with
Edwin Drood; in any case the Brontë sisters had ample opportunity

to witness something of the effects of opium, since their brother Branwell became an addict in the last years of his life.[65] Although the pattern in the carpet of *Villette*'s Eastern references is too intricate for anything approaching a full analysis here, there is an allusion whose wider significance calls for some comment. Charlotte Brontë weaves together Lucy Snowe's feverish chain of recollection and bewilderment with memories of a familiar story: 'Bedridden Hassan, transported in his sleep . . . . Had a Genius . . . as the eastern tale said, . . . borne me over land and ocean, and laid me quietly down beside a hearth of Old England? But no; I knew the fire of that hearth burned before its Lares no more' (II, ch. 16; Penguin edn, p. 240). In Lucy's speculations concerning 'the dark-tinged draught' offered her – 'What Genii-elixir or Magi-distillation?' – Charlotte hints at a phenomenon much discussed in the period, the opiate-like power of the *Nights* to call up one's memories of childhood and its secrets.

In *Jane Eyre* Charlotte Brontë gives Rochester's black gelding the name of one among Haroun's constant companions on his nocturnal wanderings. 'Mesrour' is the Nubian 'chief of the eunuchs of his palace' (Galland), and this reference to the caliph's harim is more than just one of a number of clues derived from the *Nights* as to the hidden and irregular love-life of Jane's master; the punning allusion suggests also the extent to which the *Nights* provided the adult Victorians with a secret language in which they could encode their anxieties about sexual politics. Thus Thackeray's passion for Mrs Brookfield was 'like the genie in the [*Nights*] who would have puffed himself up as big as the world had not the seal of God been on the bottle that contained him'.[66]

With one or two exceptions such as 'Carmilla' (ch. 11), where an ominous reference to Aladdin's lamp introduces the General's interrupted and recursive account of his daughter's fatal relationship with Millarca (the anagram itself is akin to the twinning names of the *Nights*), J. Sheridan Le Fanu's Arabesque allusions are largely confined to his non-supernatural fiction. He seems to have felt that, while a reference to the *Nights* could enhance terror or mystery of a non-supernatural kind, it tended to militate against the authentic supernatural. Thus *In a Glass Darkly* (Richard Bentley, 1872) contains only one other Arabesque reference. This is in 'The Room at the Dragon Volant', a non-supernatural tale. 'Beauty is like that precious stone in the "Arabian Nights" which emits, no matter how concealed, a light that betrays it' (ch. 14): the tantalised

Victorian reader may well have wondered whether the reference was to the light-emitting diamond in the tale of the fortunate Cogia Hassan Alhabbal or to the ill-omened gem that illuminates the palace of the Petrified City discovered by Zobeide. In Le Fanu's tale, as it turns out, the allusion goes further than just enhancing the exoticism of a masked ball into which a note of orientalism has already been introduced in the shape of a Chinese fortune-teller; another function of the Arabesque reference is subtly to prepare the reader for the living death that eventually threatens to overtake the foolhardy protagonist lost like Zobeide in a conquered city (Lane, *Nights*, ɪ, ch. 3).

In *Uncle Silas: A Tale of Bartram-Haugh* (1864) occurs Le Fanu's finest use of the *Nights*. Maud the heroine, concealed in a dark room at night, watches her evil, grotesque governess Madame de la Rougierre rifle her father's desk. The next morning, when the governess sat 'smiling by me, full of anxious and affectionate inquiry, and smoothed the coverlet with her great felonious hand, I could quite comprehend the dreadful feeling with which the deceived husband in the "Araban Nights" met his ghoul wife, after his nocturnal discovery' (ch. 18; World's Classics edn, p. 94). *Uncle Silas* is full of such dreadful nocturnal revelations, which climax in murder. Uncle Silas himself, the epicentre of this dark, unconscious side of human nature, is also seen as a kind of ghoul, 'one of those goblins of the desert, whom Asiatic superstition tells of . . . colder and more awful than the grave' (ch. 52; World's Classics edn, p. 337).

In the minor novels, reference to the *Nights* is for the most part decorative. *Wylder's Hand: A Novel* (Richard Bentley, 1864, 3 vols) contains, in addition to references to the Flying Carpet and to 'our old friend Sindbad' a more serious use of the tale of Aladdin. Mark Wylder, an ill-fated Aladdin, tells the story of the ring (by which his dead hand will be recognised) and elaborately alludes to the *Nights*. He has received the ring from a 'Persian merchant, with a grand beard. We called him the magician, he was so like the pictures of Aladdin's uncle . . . exactly like the pictures in the story-books' (ɪ, ch. 9, p. 93). Wylder's motto is 'resurgam'; it appears (in Persian) on the ring, and his dead body does 'rise again'. The narrator comments, 'better than Aladdin's, for you need not rub it and bring up that confoundedly ugly genii; the slave of your ring works unseen' (p. 95). The 'slave' of Wylder's ring is his murderer, who forges his 'hand'. The allusion to the

Nights thus provides a bizarre, determinist frame for the novel as a whole.

In Le Fanu's masterpiece about the 'caste-system' of eighteenth-century Ireland, *The House by the Churchyard* (1863), the English agent Dangerfield is the 'grand vizir' (Antony Blond, Doughty Library edn, ch. 26, p. 136). In a brilliant trope at the end of chapter 56, 'a Vampire sits in the Church', Dangerfield is described as knowing Charles Archer (i.e. himself) to be 'slave of his lamp' (p. 259). Yet it is possible that the Sturk–Dangerfield plot in the novel is a kind of morbid fantasia on the theme of 'The Sleeper Awakened'. Dr Sturk had, many years ago and while under the influence of *opium*, witnessed the murder by Archer of Mr Beauclerc. When he awoke from his trance he remembered nothing. When Archer/Dangerfield comes to Chapelizod, Sturk does not recognise him, but suffers a 'thrill' when this 'grand vizir' touches him, and begins to suffer nightmares which partly turn upon a subconscious recognition of Archer. One night Sturk sleeps, dreams, and wakes with memory intact (ch. 44, pp. 206–7), but his recall costs him dear and he 'sleeps' again in a coma, having barely survived Archer–Dangerfield's murder attempt: 'the enchanter who met him in the Butcher's Wood . . . whose wand had traced those parallel indentures in his skull' (ch. 57, p. 264). His bandages are like 'a fantastic turban' (ch. 81, p. 374). His 'sleep' is then broken by the ghastly trepanning; he 'wakes' to tell his story and then sleeps for ever (ch. 88, pp. 412–19; chs 92–5).[67]

VII

> *Is it an echo of something*
> *Read with a boy's delight,*
> *Viziers nodding together*
> *In some Arabian night?*
> (Tennyson, *Maud*, vii.iii)

Although as adults they would concede 'the days are gone . . . when the voyages of Sindbad appeared as authentic as those of Ross and Parry' (*Foreign Quarterly Review*, xiv [1834] 350), Victorians used the *Nights* when voicing in tones of mingled wonder and recognition their first impressions of alien experiences: Darwin 'beetle-hunting' in the Brazilian jungle, or Max Müller, relating the

Popul Vuh to the folklore of other peoples.[68] William Morris, indeed, saw the *Nights* as a kind of 'Bible', and men who took such differing attitudes towards Christianity as Newman, R. S. Hawker, J. S. Mill, Matthew Arnold and T. H. Huxley each found the *Nights* apt to his own purposes; so Macaulay excoriated the East India Company's misrule of Bengal for resembling 'the government of evil Genie'.[69] In *Sartor Resartus* (1833, ch. 10) Thomas Carlyle is apprehensive lest as the result of an excessively logical and scientific training, the mind becomes as dangerous as the Doctor's head which in the tale of the Greek King and the Physician Douban was 'screwed off . . . and set in a basin to keep it alive . . . without a shadow of a heart'. In *Modern Painters* (1843–60) Ruskin pictures the imagination successively as the genie in the bottle, and the 'Open Sesame' to the treasure-cave; and literature as the shape-changing princess who redeems the Second Calender from his animality. Ruskin's explicit awareness that their growing popularity had transformed the *Nights* into a kind of shorthand for the age allows him to characterise quickly topics as diverse as Carpaccio's paintings and the means by which one might ideally realise the flexibility of structure desirable in a museum. Significantly Trollope once joked that he was 'the Author of the *Nights*', for the archrealist himself also makes reference to them in his novels.[70]

What is perhaps surprising is that the Victorian poets neglected these Arabian tales.[71] In a handful of poems, criticism of mid-nineteenth-century society drew analogies from the doomed cities of the *Nights*: Christina Rossetti's 'The Dead City' (1847), Meredith's 'The Sleeping City' (1851), James 'B. V.' Thomson's 'The Doom of a City' (1857–67). All are among the poets' lesser achievements: their later verse makes little or no use of the *Nights*. The only exception, Thomson's *The City of Dreadful Night* (1874–80) employs Zobeide's tale of the Petrified City to link the nation's malaise and its colonial empire. The same diagnosis, by employing associated elements in the same Arabian tale-group and its analogies, is more subtly expressed in *The Moonstone* (1868) and *The Master of Ballantrae* (1889), discussed below in chapters 6 and 7. It is reversed by Kipling in 'The City of Brass' (1909; repr. in *The Years Between*, 1917).

The two Victorian poets most indebted to the *Nights* are those whose work shows concern for social problems of the kind which exercised the novel in this period. Although the overall shape of Morris's *The Earthly Paradise* (1868–70) depends more on *The*

Decameron, he derived the plot of 'The Man who Never Laughed Again' from 'The Fifth Wezeer's-Tale' as given by Lane in his abstract (III, 169–73). In 'Hasan of El-Basrah', a neighbouring story (III, 384–518, esp. p. 391), which had earlier fascinated Tennyson, Morris found the name 'Bahram' for a man who allowed his curiosity to destroy his chances of an idyllic relationship with a woman. Another of Morris's verse narratives in *The Earthly Paradise* also draws upon Hasan of El-Basrah. 'The Land East of the Sun and West of the Moon' has diverse origins, but the manner in which the material is worked by Morris as a nocturnal tale within a tale, oneiric and fragmented, suggests that its Scandinavian origins are complemented by the analogue in the *Nights*. It would also seem that the same tale is to be reckoned with in any consideration of the genesis of *The Princess*. It has been argued that Tennyson encountered the Persian sources for his verse medley in the Introduction to Henry Weber's *Tales of the East* (1812).[72] However, since Tennyson conceived the idea of this framed verse narrative in 1839, it seems at least as likely that *The Princess* (1847) is yet another work which to some degree was prompted by the publication (and frequent reprinting) of Lane. Not only does this collection include a succession of learned and resourceful ladies, worthy sisters of Scheherazade. It contains also the tale of how, by a daring act of female impersonation (as in *The Princess*), a betrothed succeeded in entering an Amazonian community and thus saved his marriage. A similar concern with the unhappy consequences to both sexes of 'the ill-usage suffered by women in their relationships with men' finds memorable expression elsewhere in Tennyson's work in the early 'Recollections of the Arabian Nights' (1830) and in *Maud* (1855), where Tennyson calls upon, respectively, 'Noureddin and the Fair Persian' and 'Noureddin Ali and Bedreddin Hassan', for these stories (almost namesakes) handle a common theme of separated lovers.

Scott's panegyric of James Watt in the introductory epistle to *The Monastery* (1820) heralded that roster of ghouls, afrits and peris among the workforce of the Industrial Revolution glimpsed in turn by William Howitt in his *Visits to Remarkable Places* (1842), Disraeli's *Coningsby* (1844) and Charlotte Brontë at the Crystal Palace.[73] Leigh Hunt had rejoiced when reviewing Lane in 1840 that the progress of science, far from putting 'an end to all poetry and romance', had revealed a world as filled with hitherto undetected powers as the jinn-haunted world of the *Nights*.[74] But, by May 1850, F. G.

Stephens in the Pre-Raphaelite journal *Art and Poetry* (continuation of *The Germ*) feared that many of his contemporaries missed 'the poetry of the things about us, our railways, factories, mines, roaring cities, steam vessels . . . which if they were found only in The Thousand and One Nights . . . would be gloried over without end' (IV, 170–1). It is therefore perhaps to be expected that, as E. P. Thompson remarks, 'the very last impression that is given by the majority of Pre-Raphaelite paintings [apart, that is, from a small number of memorable pictures such as Ford Madox Brown's *Work* (1852–65), Holman Hunt's *The Awakening Conscience* (1853–6) or William Bell Scott's *Iron and Coal* (1861)] is that they are engaged in any serious way with the exploration of contemporary experience'.[75] Rather more surprisingly, few of the Orientalists school pay any attention to the *Nights*. Painters as talented as John Frederick Lewis were all too often drawn to the East for reasons that were fundamentally escapist, neglecting, as they did, the poverty, disease and dirt there that Houghton and Doré did not shrink from depicting back home, whether they were recording life in the slums or illustrating the *Nights*.

Since neither *The Golden Prime of Haroun Alraschid* (1866), the water-colour version of Hunt's illustration to Tennyson's 'Recollections of the Arabian Nights', nor Dante Gabriel Rossetti's *Golden Water* (1858) is equal to the *Nights*, one particularly regrets that, of the series of paintings which Houghton based on his contributions to *Dalziel's Illustrated Nights*, the whereabouts of only one, the exquisite *Transformation of King Beder* (Plate 6) is known. The striking embellishments that the Dalziel brothers lavished on their version of the Galland translation were obviously intended to eclipse the similarly planned but more sombrely elegant Lane with its 'many hundred engravings' by William Harvey (Plate 4), a new edition of which had appeared in 1859. Serially published in parts (1863–5), the Dalziel was later bound in red or blue cloth gold-stamped with rather crude Arabesque designs, and with vignettes at the start of each section as a way of signposting the labyrinthine contents, and with other illustrations dropped appositely into the text. The Dalziel lacks the copious annotation of Lane; for knowledge of Islamic architecture, too, the Lane–Harvey is unsurpassed. Among the Dalziels' gifted team of illustrators, Tenniel is noteworthy for aptly importing the terrible frown and gesture of Wonderland's Queen into his serio-comic illustration of Sidi Numan's transformation (Plate 8).[76] Millais's rendering of Zobeide's discovery of the devout prince is less successsful than Harvey's in capturing the utter loneliness of the sole survivor in the Petrified City (Plate 7). Where the Dalziel edition really scores over Lane is in the ninety-two illustrations by Houghton, 'which should have made him as famous as Doré'.[77] Through a combination of circumstantial detail and wide scholarship (Plate 5a), Houghton invariably imparts an air of conviction, no matter how extraordinary the adventure. A splendid instance of this is to be seen when the Enchanted Horse soars over the fastness of the Western Ghats, an appropriately Hindu–Buddhist setting for this tale of Indian inventiveness (Plate 5b). Houghton stresses the matter-of-factness with which the Arabian tales record the irruption of the supernatural into the everyday. Doré emphasises a different aspect of the *Nights*. Largely responsible for the design of the Cassell volume (1874–5, subsequently the Dalziels' chief competitor among illustrated versions of the Galland text), Doré characteristically substantiates the fantastic elements in the *Nights* by locating marvels in topographies reminiscent of his illustrations of Dante's Hell or Coleridge's Antarctic or Xanadu (Plate 9).

In the second half of the nineteenth century there were more than a score of illustrated editions (or reissues) of the Arabian compendium, and for young readers a like number of selections from the tales. However, some adults were unwilling to acknowledge openly the continuing appeal of the *Nights*: 'To read of these things was a sort of intellectual hashish, an intoxicating stimulant to that early imagination', wrote Bagehot, recalling the entertainments of his childhood when he reviewed the new edition of Lane in 1859. Yet, while he welcomed that edition, Bagehot felt 'the thing itself has lost the charm which one held us enchained'.[78] Other adults in the second half of the century, however, did not relegate the *Nights* to an outgrown phase. Like Dickens and Collins before them, they tended to prefer Galland above later translations – it was after all a nineteenth-century English revision of Galland's text that Sir John Lubbock placed no. 57 in his list of the Hundred Best Books (1893). At any rate, memories of that childhood favourite proved to be strong. Henry James possessed the three-volume set of Lane, but it would seem that the text to which he habitually referred was the earlier translation: the 'Grub Street' Galland's spelling of the Arabic names is employed in the many allusions to the *Nights* which run through James's *oeuvre* from the earliest work to his most mature achievement.[79] James in 'The Impressions of a

Cousin' (*Century Magazine*, Nov–Dec 1883) exploits the Arabesque hints in Wilkie Collins's imagery and fuses Count Fosco's machinations with the match-making schemes of the wilful caliph in 'The Porter and the Ladies of Baghdad'.[80]

VIII

'An atmosphere that Western lungs can breathe'

James seems to have sensed that the very deficiencies in the characterisation of the stereotypical personages of the *Nights* make them malleable for those who wish to explore psychological implications ignored by the Arabian story-tellers. One particular Arabian tale which James uses with increasing complexity at each stage of his career is the story of the loves of Prince Camaralzaman and the Princess Badoura, together with (what is less well known) its darker continuation in the tale of their sons the princes Amgiad and Assad. These stories play a usually overt and ever more important role in, successively, *Watch and Word* (1871), *The Europeans* (1878) and *The Golden Bowl* (1904) – though in the last the key to the Arabesque references is concealed in Maggie's puzzled apprehension of that 'wonderful, beautiful but outlandish pagoda' that has reared itself up 'in the very centre of the garden of her life' (ch. 25), even as she attempts to understand the situation between her husband and his ex-lover, who is now the Princess's stepmother.[81] James exploits the shift in this pair of tales from the happy outcome of adolescent love to a troublesome sexuality aroused by distortions in the natural ties of family and friendship.

In *The Wings of the Dove* (1902) again there is almost the effect of an oriental riddle. Milly, in feeling ominously oppressed by the hospitality offered her in London, is 'conscious of the enveloping flap of a protective mantle, a shelter with the weight of an Eastern carpet. An Eastern carpet, for wishing-purposes of one's own, was a thing to be on rather than under' (bk v, ch. 1; World's Classics edn, p. 154). This is a wittily sinister allusion to the Princess Nouronnihar, in the story of Prince Ahmed and the Peri Banou, who lies at death's door and to whose aid fly her three suitors on the magic carpet. The Arabesque references in *What Maisie Knew*, the oblique as well as the direct, have yet more extensive functions.

How then is one to explain the coolness towards the *Nights* which is voiced in the Preface to *The Aspern Papers* (1908)? Clearly it cannot be attributed to that Christian–Hellenist tradition which is perhaps the basic reason why Browning and even Arnold (who, accustomed to 'the splendours of the Arabian Nights', found he could respond to the Persian Passion Play) make few if any Arabesque allusions in their own creative work.[82] Moreover, it would be less than just to suggest that James is here attempting to hide the origins of his use of the frame tale and witness system in *The Turn of the Screw* (1898). The terms that James uses to discuss the *Nights* provide the best clue as to how one is to interpret the Preface to *The Aspern Papers*. There James distinguishes between stories such as those of Cinderella, Bluebeard and Little Red Riding Hood, which are characterised as 'the short and sharp and single, charged more or less with the compactness of anecdote', and

> the long and loose, the copious, the various, the endless, where, dramatically speaking, roundness is quite sacrificed . . . to fullness, sacrificed to exuberance if one will: witness at hazard almost any one of the *Arabian Nights*. The charm of all these things for the distracted modern mind is in the clear field of experience . . . an annexed but independent world . . . we flounder, we lose breath, on the other hand – that is we fail, not of continuity, but of an agreeable unity, of the 'roundness' in which beauty and lucidity largely reside – when we go in, as they say, for great lengths and breadths.
>
> (Penguin edn, pp. 37–8)

Since James is at pains to separate these *Nights* from the 'old familiars of our childhood', one is drawn to the conclusion that what he has in mind here is some version other than the manageable Galland or even the reasonably compact Lane translation. Certainly James's words here will serve to describe the reactions of many a reader who attempts to *read* rather than *consult* the third great translation of the nineteenth century – what in view of the one's indebtedness to the other's labours is best treated as a composite work by Payne and Richard Burton, which is how the urbane W. E. Henley dealt with them in an essay, in *Views and Reviews* (Nutt, 1890), which Kipling so much admired:[83]

> The prose of Mr Payne's translation is always readable and often elegant; Sir Richard Burton's notes and 'terminal essays' are a

mine of curious and diverting information; but for me the real author of *The Arabian Nights* is called not Burton nor Payne but Antoine Galland. He it was, in truth, who gave the world as much exactly as it needed of his preposterous original, who eliminated its tediousness, purged it of its barbarous and sickening immorality, wiped it clean of cruelty and unnaturalness, selected its essentials of comedy and romance, and set them clear and sharp against a light that Western eyes can bear and in an atmosphere that western lungs can breathe.   (p. 213)

Provoked beyond endurance by the thought of Burton's ten volumes (which nightmarishly he foresaw one day multiplying to forty), Henley seized on the diametrically opposed principle licensed by the Islamic aesthetic which admits of contraction as well as dilation: so in 1893 Henley distilled the essence of the Galland collection into a single poem which is one of the most evocative of meditations on 'That centre of miracles/The Sole unparalleled Arabian Nights!' (*London Voluntaries* [Nutt, 1893] p. 42), their place in childhood and later life:

> Then, as the Book was glassed
> In Life as in some olden mirror's quaint
> Bewildering angles, so would Life
> Flash light on light back on the Book: and both
> Were changed.
> ('Arabian Nights Entertainments', p. 51)

Overwhelmed by their first impressions of the bewilderingly immense and various collection that Payne and Burton had assembled, others escaped by taking routes more or less different from Henley's miniaturisation. Some for example focused on drawing out the implication of a single but momentous story, 'The Sultan Al-Yaman and his Three Sons', an analogue of which is better known for having inspired first Voltaire and Walpole, then scientists such as T. H. Huxley, who wrote nearly as celebrated an essay 'On the Method of Zadig: Restrospective Prophecy as a Function of Science' (*Science and Culture and Other Essays*, 1881). Jonathan Scott's 1811 translation from the Arabic had already given this oriental detective story added currency, but its incorporation into the Burton canon brought Zadig's method further publicity, influencing not only the creation of Sherlock Holmes (1887) but, it has been suggested, even contributing to the theories of Freud, who, from another but not unconnected direction, through the agency of Schopenhauer and especially Nietzsche, was absorbing the Buddhist teachings as also the lessons of the *Nights*.[84]

The fusion of the Arabian compendium with another, more inward and coherent collection of Eastern stories offered a further solution as to how greater meaning and order might be given to the embarrassingly heterogeneous riches uncovered by Burton. Introducing an edition of Lane, planned for reissue in 1896, in order to compete with the Burton, the folklorist Joseph Jacobs also finds himself at a loss to comprehend fully the origins of 'a work which in its entirety, and with all its "branches", is one of the biggest books in existence'. Jacobs suggests it all started with

> an application of the Buddhist idea of reincarnation to the universal human interest for tale-telling. Buddha it was who was continually reincarnating himself, and part of his enlightenment consisted in his perfect memory of what had happened to him in all his previous incarnations.   (pp. xvi–xvii)

Such reminiscences of Gautama Buddha, Jacobs explains here – as he had done earlier to the young reader of *Indian Fairy Tales* (Nutt, 1892) – were ultimately gathered together as the *Jatakas* with their characteristic structure whereby a tale of the present frames a tale of the past. In the past (once it has been identified) lies the solution to the current problem – a pattern which is also significantly evident in the varying manner by which the best work of Kipling, Wells, Conrad, Eliot, Joyce, and to a lesser extent the Woolfs, makes use of the *Nights*.

IX

Length . . . is one of the essential qualities, one of the essential virtues of the book. A short Arabian Nights *is as unthinkable as a neat wilderness, or a snug cathedral.*
        (G. K. Chesterton, 'The Everlasting Nights', 1901)

Whereas in the eighteenth century and the first half of the nineteenth, the *Nights* were normally published in a full adult version (a market in which the Galland seems to have held its own against the challenge of Lane and later Payne and Burton), towards the end of Victoria's reign there was a rising flood of selections and abridgements adapted for young readers. The number of these 'short *Arabian Nights*' peaked in 1907 and 1908 with half a dozen or more juvenile versions a year. By the twentieth century most were decorated with attractive pictures and yet were reasonably cheap. What Brian Alderson has called the 'cocoa-table book' formula was applied to the *Nights* as early as 1814, when William Daniell's *The Adventure of Hunch-back* appeared, a handsome selection from Forster's adult version (Wiliam Miller, 1802, repr. 1810) intended as a juvenile complement to the adult book. The latter was produced in a small as well as large format, but, with their magnificent engravings by, among others, William Daniell from Robert Smirke's paintings (Plate 3), all three publications must have been beyond the pocket of most readers. The prices in Mrs E. Newbery's *Catalogue of Publications for Young Minds* (1800) help us to understand the failure of Wordsworth's childhood resolve to save up and buy the 'four large volumes' of the *Arabian Nights* (*Prelude* [1805] v.460–76): the Galland complete, like its *Continuation* (also in four volumes) cost no less than 14s. a set. More within the reach of the young middle-class reader was *The Oriental Moralist, or the Beauties of the Arabian Nights Entertainments* (c. 1791) at 3s. (Plate 2b); for sixpence, though, a child or poorer parent could buy at least one tale (usually, it seems, *Aladdin* or *Sindbad*), often charmingly illustrated; in some instances, such as *The Valley of Diamonds, or, Harlequin Sindbad* (E. Thomas, 1815), '*with a neat frontispiece*' that folded out, these are pioneering examples of the panorama book. By the mid-Victorian period Dean and Munday had elaborated such 'movables' into appealing versions of the peep-show. The success with chromolithography displayed in Owen Jones's evocative decoration of J. G. Lockhart's *Ancient Spanish Ballads* (John Murray, 1841),[85] then in the Dalziels' distinctively Islamic-looking production of Thomas Moore's 'Oriental romance', *Lalla Rookh* (originally published 1817; repr. with engraving of T. Sulman's designs and John Tenniel's illustrations, Longmans, 1860–1), led Gall and Inglis of Edinburgh to use something of the same techniques when illustrating their own abridgement of the *Nights* (1867). Further improvements in colour printing inspired brilliant decoration of the kind found in Walter Crane's *Aladdin's Picture Book* (G. Routledge, 1876). For all the jewel-like appearance of such a publication, some readers may well have been struck more by the almost Japanese use of blacks and whites in Beardsley's graphic depiction of Ali Baba surprised in the wood by the Forty Thieves (Plate 14) published in *The Later Work* (Bodley Head, 1900). Since the beginning of the twentieth century, however, popular taste has favoured coloured illustration. The most opulent expression of developments in colour photography was found in the *de luxe* signed editions of picture-books produced during the first quarter of the century for the Christmas gift trade and, as John Betjeman recalled, kept in the drawing room for when it 'was time for the children to come down to tea'.[86] Although Arthur Rackham's mastery of this sort of book was unequalled, he apparently executed only one *Arabian Nights* illustration – a gripping Old Man of the Sea.[87] This area neglected by Rackham was interesting to rivals such as Heath Robinson, E. J. Detmold and Edmond Dulac (see Plates 15 and 16, and jacket illustration).

The physical awkwardness of the *de luxe* edition as well as its social exclusivity could be rectified in the trade editions and cheap reprints. But catering for the juvenile reader was often the cause of other, less easily remedied defects in these illustrated abridgements. As Brian Alderson shows (*infra*, ch. 2), as early as the end of the eighteenth century the Galland text was being cut to protect a young audience. A century later the scandal of Burton's ethnographical revelations, and subsequently the 'oversexed' nature of Mardrus's version further provoked prudish tendencies towards bowdlerisation as expurgated versions of the tales were graded for different ages. The dropping of the frame story was the greatest casualty sustained. This excision was to be expected of single tales, the most likely to fall into the hands of the very young, but even selections such as *Miss Braddon's Revised Edition of Aladdin . . . and Sindbad . . . Illustrated by Gustave Doré . . .* (J. and R. Maxwell, 1880) lack any indication of the plight of Scheherazade. Rare is the illustrator with the sensitivity displayed by William Strang, who in the frontis- and tail-pieces for *Sindbad . . . and Ali Baba* (Lawrence and Bullen, 1896), wittily shapes a pair of framing icons to suggest the Chinese-box structure of the *Nights*. Nor is it merely that a significant element in the meaning of the collection is lost when the episode of the Lady in the Glass Case is omitted. Such efforts to keep young minds unsullied may create far more damaging misapprehensions. In what is surely the most profusely illustrated of all selections, George Newnes's *Arabian Nights Enter-*

tainments, with 'several hundred' pictures by W. Heath Robinson, Helen Stratton and others (1899), the editor's efforts to avoid disclosing the sexual infidelities of Shahriar's first queen leave the reader with the impression that she was engaged in betraying her country to its foreign enemies. Worse was the effect created by Helen Marion Burnside's selection (R. Tuck, 1893), which contrives to imply that it was not the Sultan's first wife but Scheherazade herself who was the guilty one. Although the barbarity of Shahriar is deplored by the censors, their prudishness can bring them close to an apparent extenuation of his revenge.

Such anti-feminist emphases (perhaps at times barely conscious) were not the only type of propagandist use to which the *Nights* are put during this period. There is more than a touch of *Stalky and Co.* abut the Nister–Dutton edition (1907).[88] In his introduction, the editor, W. H. D. Rouse, stresses that

for Englishmen, whose empire contains so many millions of Moslems, this study of the *Nights* is of high importance; it is not possible to govern well without understanding of the governed and sympathy with their feelings and thoughts, and only through knowledge can come that wise tolerance which wins trust and enables the ruler to control, to improve, to reform. (p. 7)

Sometimes though, in this marketing of the 'short *Arabian Nights*' during the Edwardian period, the opportunity was seized to express liberal views, almost wholly opposed to these patriarchal and imperialist attitudes. This was true of at least one team of story-teller and illustrator to come the way of the rebellious adolescent daughters of the British establishment. Drawn by the elaborately playful imitation of Islamic book design decorating *Stories from the Arabian Nights* (Hodder and Stoughton, 1907; 1st edn Oct, 2nd edn Nov), the first fruit of Laurence Housman's prolific partnership with Edmund Dulac, the proto-suffragettes would find themselves caught by arresting ideas.[89] For, while Housman's introduction begins by celebrating Scheherazade's acievement as 'splendid and memorable' (p. iii), he concludes by shocking his reader into the terrifying realisation that, even as she succeeds in gaining yet another stay of execution, so nightly must Scheherazade 'share . . . the pillow of a homicidal maniac' (p. viii).[90] This challenging introduction was dropped from the cheap reprints of the 1907 book, and there is nothing like it in the next collection of tales which Housman selected for Dulac to illustrate: the sumptuously mock-Persian *Sindbad . . .* (1914). But Housman collaborated again with Dulac on a tale which Housman rightly sees as reflecting 'Scheherazade's own great adventurous self', a story that has 'the distinction of being' in some versions of the *Nights* 'the last of all since it witnesses the accomplishment' of Scheherazade's task of saving her fellow women (p. 3). Indicative of the change in emphasis that he himself effects in this lively retelling of the old story, Housman gives pride of place in its new title not, as is customary, to Camaralzaman but to the heroine, Princess Badoura, 'the woman of beauty and brain, who, personating her husband, ruled a Kingdom'.[91] Housman continues by reminding his reader how 'Scheherazade, her great act of statesmanship concluded, adumbrates what woman set free to use her own resources can do' (*Princess Badoura* [Hodder and Stoughton, 1913] p. 4).

Dulac's own ability to stir the imagination Yeats readily acknowledges in 'Certain Noble Plays of Japan' (1916),[92] and the fame of 'the distinguished illustrator of the *Arabian Nights*' spread further still during the interwar years. For instance, over Christmastide 1931 Boots the Chemists joined Hodder and Stoughton in reprinting a collection of the stories on which the painter had worked with Housman, with the result that by the New Year some 20,000 copies had been distributed.

Although Chesterton underestimated those qualities in the *Nights* that allowed them to survive the ill effects of prudery and economics, he shows great perspicacity about other aspects of the Arab collection, as when he characterises the *Nights* as 'one vast conspiracy to entrap the reader in a condition of everlasting attention' ('The Everlasting Nights', *Daily News*, 7 Nov 1901).[93] Chesterton's insight goes a long way to explaining what exactly it is in these labyrinthine Muslim recensions of Egypto-Hindu, Graeco-Buddhist folklore that so fascinated Eliot, Joyce, Yeats and Wyndham Lewis.

X

'Without the Nights no Arabian Nights!'

John Heath-Stubbs has recently reminded us that what most baffled the first readers of *The Waste Land* was 'the absence of any narrative links . . . accentuated by Ezra Pound's excision of many passages from the original version'. Among Eliot's models for such discontinuities, Heath-Stubbs notes *The City of Dreadful Night* and *Maud*, both of course indebted to the *Nights*.[94] In both the Foreword and the Terminal Essay to his translation (1885; there were over a dozen different editions by 1920) Burton insists 'without the Nights no Arabian Nights!' Such a criterion anticipates one of the basic rediscoveries of Modernism. As Walter Benjamin was to remark of Brecht, 'interruption is one of the fundamental methods of all form-giving. . . . It is, to mention just one of its aspects, the origin of quotation.'[95]

Admittedly the quotation from *Heart of Darkness* was excised from the final version of *The Waste Land*, but the manner in which the Marlow cycle experiments so subtly with bottling up the manifold yet discontinuous *Nights* in the more coherently recursive and thoughtful Buddhist *Jatakas* apparently caught the eye also of Eliot, who as a boy had reworked Sindbad's adventure with the whale, and, as a student of oriental languages at Harvard, had attempted to master the Buddhist fables in their original Pali.[96]

Stimulating too were the models proffered by the various means through which these Eastern tales came to manipulate time and space. One suggestive instance of this nonchalant handling of time arises from the fact that Scheherazade, a Sassanid monarch of pre-Islamic Persia, recounts stories concerning the adventures of the post-conquest Abbasid caliph Harun. That H. G. Wells glimpsed something of what might be developed along these lines is evident from the echoes of both Buddhist and Arab tales that are conjoined in *The Time Machine* and *The Sleeper Awakes*. But not until *Finnegans Wake* (1923–39) and its parody in *The Childermass* (1928) does one begin to see anything like a realisation of what a synthesis of the dislocations typical of the *Nights* and the time-shifts which are as distinctive a feature of the *Jatakas* might accomplish in the way of mirroring the universe of quantum physics and depth psychology.

XI

'Infinitely more instructive and enjoyable than our romances'

In the world of theatre and other public media there was a comparable span of work during this period ranging from the popular to the highbrow that exhibits more or less directly an Arabesque cast. On the stage towards the turn of the century the *Nights* had begun to eclipse the *Commedia dell'Arte* as a source for pantomime. The lavishness of Augustus Harris's production of *The Forty Thieves* (1886) was but one celebrated example of Arabesque influence on developments in late-Victorian spectacular theatre.[97] On an altogether more thoughtful level, in the Preface to his *Three Plays for Puritans* (1901), Shaw had welcomed the unexpurgated *Nights* of Burton as 'infinitely more instructive and enjoyable than our romances, because love is treated there as naturally as any other passion' (Penguin edn, p. 18).[98] And, through Redbrook, Shaw teasingly acknowledges that *Captain Brassbound's Conversion* is indebted for more than local colour to that 'copy of [the Burton] in the library of the National Liberal Club' (Act II). In the first two decades of the twentieth century, though, the most memorable instances of theatre inspired by the *Nights* were imported by foreign companies. Early in 1911 Max Reinhardt brought his Arabian fantasia *Sumurûn* to London for six weeks. Later in the same year, the outstanding success of the Ballets Russes' first visit to London was *Schéhérazade*. In this production Diaghilev ('moved . . . by the legendary brilliance of the sultans of the eighth century') fused Rimsky-Korsakov's music, Bakst's designs, Fokine's innovative choreography and the genius of Nijinsky as a dancer. The dazzling ballet which resulted cast its brilliance far beyond the salons of the *grand couturiers* into the minds of artist and intellectual, affecting, to a degree rare in the history of English culture, such things as poster design and interior decoration, and accounting for the Persian look increasingly evident in the work of book-illustrators such as Dulac, René Bull, E. J. Detmold and Kay Nielsen.[99] Oscar Asche and G. F. Norton's successful musical (based on pantomime's use of the *Nights*) *Chu Chin Chow* ran for almost five years from 1916. In September 1923 James Elroy Flecker's *Hassan* began its London run of 281 performances. The poet's instruction that 'the scenery and costumes . . . should be inspired by . . . Persian miniatures' like those reproduced in 'the illustrations to Mardrus's big edition of the *Arabian Nights*' was complied with; and, with music by Delius, choreography by Fokine himself, and as director Basil Dean, a disciple of Reinhardt, this exercise in 'total theatre' is said to have been 'the most significant musical production the London stage had seen for many a day, opera not excluded'.[100]

Post-war Germany's fascination with the *Nights* made itself felt on English writers through the brilliant cinematic achievements of the 1920s. Lubitsch's atmospheric screen version of *Sumurûn* (1920) is echoed in the burlesque that forms one episode in Paul Leni's *Waxworks* (1924). Arthur Robison's ingeniously recursive *Warning Shadows: A Nocturnal Hallucination* (1922) was deservedly popular with the English picture-goer, and it was reminiscences of the *Nights* suffusing the Chinese tale included in Lang's enthralling story-sequence *Destiny* (1921) which helped lift Douglas Fairbanks's *Thief of Baghdad* (1923–4) above the level of Edison's and Fox's earlier attempts at putting Ali Baba onto film.[101]

More popular literary genres for adults as well as for children were likewise influenced. The dress that Innocent Smith designs 'rich with green and purple . . . like a secret garden in the "Arabian Nights" ' signals that what Chesterton correctly understands as the spirit of carefree generosity pervading 'Noureddin and the Fair Persian' is an important key to the significance of *Manalive* (Nelson, 1912, ch. 3, pp. 67–8). Similarly, the undercover detective operations in which the Caliph as frequently encounters supernatural phenomena as he does less extraordinary mysteries encouraged the use that is made of Arabesque allusions in the Father Brown stories and in many of John Buchan's thrillers, *The Thirty-Nine Steps* (1915) being notable for the complexity of its references to both 'The Little Hunchback' and 'The Continuation of the Sleeper Awakened'. *The Arabian Nights Murder* (1936) by John Dickson Carr – an American long resident in London – tantalises the reader by the blatant manner in which it flirts with allusions to the *Nights*. For all the many explicit references to the intrigues, disguises and detective episodes in the stories told of the caliph and his jealous queen Zobeide, Carr's own narrative in the last analysis eschews the supernatural agencies that so often supply the explanation in the Harun cycle. Carr adopts exactly the reverse procedure in his next book. While the more explicit allusions there are to the vampire tradition of Keats and Stoker, the plot of *The Burning Court* (1937) – the locked-room mystery to end all such – is based on a conflation of the dangerous marriages contracted by the likes of the Young Prince of the Black Islands, or Sidi Numan. Indeed, as late as the 1950s, Carr's Stevensonian propensities were being pointed out as constituting his 'finger-prints' by a fellow detective-story writer, C. Day Lewis.[102]

Perhaps as a result of the limitations inherent in the numerous abridgements, Arabesque allusion in juvenile literature at the turn of the century is not generally very *recherché*: in *The Brass Bottle* (1900) Anstey does not range much beyond the tales of Aladdin, the fisherman and the genie in the bottle; plainly *Kim* (1901) derives a good deal from the Harun cycle, but the degree to which the *Nights* guided Kipling's exploration of the Island's history is barely suggested by the reference to afrits and their kind in *Puck of Pook's Hill* (1906); Edith Nesbit, on the other hand, casts her net more widely through the Arabian 'ocean of story', as she refines the dangerously ambivalent spirits of the *Nights* into meta-parental surrogates, wondrously potent, superficially irritable, essentially benign.[103]

XII

'The educated reader needs to know . . .'

Whereas the nineteenth century produced around half-a-dozen translations from the Arabic (whether directly or otherwise) into English, the modern period so far has managed barely three. Of these, there is only one version that can compete in length with the efforts of Lane and Payne–Burton: Edward Powys Mathers' translation from the French of Mardrus,[104] Initially published privately by the Casanova Society (1923, repr. 1929), eventually it found a wider audience in a trade edition that Routledge brought out in 1937. Rival publishers responded somewhat in the way that their predecessors had done to each reworking of the *Nights* in the nineteenth century – battening onto the success envisaged for, and in fact enjoyed, by the private-press editions of the Mardrus and Mathers. Thus in 1922 Cecil Palmer published Lane's version filled out by extra tales from Galland, illustrated by Frank Brangwyn; in 1930 Chatto and Windus reissued the Lane text embellished with copies of original engravings by Harvey; in the same year Gollancz published in a limited edition *The Magic Horse*, with Lane's text yet again, but illustrated Cubist-fashion by Ceri Richards; the advent of Routledge's trade edition elicited from Hodder and Stoughton in 1938 yet another, though less sumptuous, variant on that longstanding success, Housman and Dulac's collaboration.

During the inter-war period many writers found that the Mardrus and Mathers (or the re-issue of earlier versions published by competitors) acted on their own memories like Proust's 'madeleine'.[105] In 1922 Pound had endeavoured to bring together Mathers and Wyndham Lewis (the latter having published his Vorticist pamphlet *The Caliph's Design* a couple of years earlier).[106] By 1927 Lewis was announcing in *Time and Western Man* (repr. Boston, Mass.: Beacon Press, 1957) that the unconscious is the 'extraordinary Aladdin's Cave' in which (led there by 'that old magician Sigmund Freud') Joyce 'manufactured his *Ulysses*', and 'the duration-flux' of Bergson has 'its source, too, in that magical cavern' (pp. 91, 103, 264, 380). Rebecca West's semi-autobiographical *Harriet Hume* (1929), an amusing fantasy on women's liberation, teasingly uses elements from (once more) the tale of Camaralzaman to tell how a woman's superior insight affects a modern couple's relationship.[107] And onward from *The Apes of God* (1930) through the next decade or so, Lewis's own experiments with a more humane kind of fiction display an increasingly adroit use of the *Nights*.

Believing that among the classics of world literature which 'the educated reader needs to know' are 'the stories told by Scheherazade', in his magisterial survey *The March of Literature* (Allen and Unwin, 1938–9, 2nd imp. 1947) Ford Madox Ford is at pains to make his point about oriental influences on Western society:

> It will be well if the reader gets into his head an image of a vast panorama of the Eastern world across which shimmered two streams of literary influence. The one descended the Nile, the other came from China yet both discharged themselves into the Mediterranean to form that . . . civilisation which is today our own. (pp. 16, 18)

Just as 'the art of the conte-fablist' fed into European medieval literature (pp. 303, 305), Sindbad the Sailor and Ali Baba persisting from the legendary days of Ancient Egypt (p. 450), so Balzac's *oeuvre* is 'a Parisian Nights Entertainments on a vast scale' (p. 740).

Balzac's *Seraphita* hovers over the genesis of *Orlando* (1928) – as Arnold Bennett spotted – yet Balzac himself would not have us forget when reading his fantasy (ch. 3) that such transvestism and androgyny derive partly from the Arabian stories.[108] Certainly from the middle of the 1920s there were signs of an increased interest in the *Nights* among the Bloomsbury circle.[109] Telling allusions to 'Sindbad in the Valley of Gems', Parizade's quest and suchlike in

Vita Sackville-West's *Passenger to Teheran* (Hogarth, 1926), and in her letters from the Middle East, met with a sympathetic response from Virginia Woolf.[110] Retrospectively too there is an intriguingly Arabesque look about aspects of Woolf's most important theorising on the art of the novel in the twentieth century. In 'Modern Fiction' (*TLS*, 10 Apr 1919), when pondering the defects of the Edwardian novel, she comes close to identifying herself with Scheherazade:

> The writer seems constrained not by his own free will but by some powerful and unscrupulous tyrant who has him in thrall to provide a plot, to provide comedy, tragedy, love interest, and an air of probability embalming the whole. (*The Common Reader: First Series* [Hogarth, 1925; new edn 1984] p. 149)

This essay, taken together with her insights concerning the fragmentation typical of Modernism in 'Mr Bennett and Mrs Brown' (1924), raises the question of whether the open-ended form of the *Nights* and its kind might not provide an enlightening angle from which to explore further Virginia Woolf's achievement. Likewise more consideration might be profitably given to this side of E. M. Forster's work. Not only did he possess a copy of Mardrus's translation of the Arabic text into French, but in *Aspects of the Novel* (1927), after reluctantly conceding that 'story is the fundamental aspect without which [the novel] could not exist', Forster introduces into his argument Scheherazade herself:

> Great novelist though she was – exquisite in her descriptions, tolerant in her judgements, ingenious in her incidents, advanced in her morality, vivid in her delineations of character, expert in her knowledge of three Oriental capitals – it was yet on none of those gifts that she relied when trying to save her life from her intolerable husband. They were but incidental. She only survived because she managed to keep the king wondering what would happen next . . . Tuesday after Monday. (Ch. 2; Penguin edn, pp. 34–5)

Here, with that unmistakable echo of the title of Virginia Woolf's 1921 collection of experimental pieces (*Monday or Tuesday*), Forster teasingly invites the reader to view the heroine of the *Nights* as the frustrated prototype of the Modernist.

The impact of Mardrus and Mathers is felt in other genres too.

In addition to Yeats's reworking of *A Vision* (1937) there is the case of De La Mare, another of the small band of English-speaking poets of the twentieth century who are openly drawn to the *Nights*.[111] *Peacock Pie* (1913) had contained one spellbinding but solitary response, 'Alas Alack' being inspired by a magical episode in the tale of the Young Prince of the Black Islands:

> Ann, Ann!
> Come! quick as you can.
> There's a fish that *talks*
> In the frying pan.

The Mardrus and Mathers, or the other more adult translations that competed with the new version, elicited from De La Mare a much greater reaction; it was also a much darker one. *Desert Islands* (1930, rev. 1932) ponders the paradoxical nature of the Arab collection: 'Perhaps the chief charm of the *Thousand and One Nights* . . . is first, the peculiar density of its romance, and next the extraordinary penalties bestowed on the characters who indulge in it' (p. 10). Among De La Mare's most spellbinding poems of the 1930s, there are a number that allude to the *Nights*: 'Dreams', for instance (*The Fleeting and Other Poems*, 1933), which links 'jinn and Sidhe'; or later 'Books' (*This Year, Next Year*, 1937), where once again Sindbad finds himself sailing with Crusoe. By the time that the latter poem was published, it was possible for Aladdin to figure prominently in the brief litany of the heroes, heroines and villains of 'The Pantomime', the incantation of which is all that is necessary to evoke the spirit of that seasonable entertainment. His magic lamp had supplied the brand name of a modern lighting-appliance that writers as various as Virginia Woolf and Graham Geeene had difficulty in getting to work.[112] Only De La Mare contrived to make a poem out of these inadequacies:

> The oil in wild Aladdin's lamp
> A witching radiance shed;
> But when its Genie absent was
> It languished, dull and dead . . .
> ('A Rose in Candlelight',
> *Memory and Other Poems*, 1938)

Herbert Read's interest is most explicit in his *Engish Prose Style* (G. Bell, 1928). In a study that was in continuous demand during the next four decades, *The Thousand and One Nights* is called as witness when Read turns to defend fancy against 'a certain denigration from its association of contrast to imagination' which it has suffered since Coleridge's time: 'with its magnificent apparatus of genii and afrits [the collection] is the greatest work of fantasy that has ever been evolved by tradition and given literary form' (p. 134).[113] As in *English Prose Style* and *Wordsworth* (1930) the Arabian stories are brought into close proximity to North Country traditions, so in 'Surrealism and the Romantic Principle' (1936; repr. in *The Philosophy of Modern Art*, Faber, 1951) the *Nights* is coupled with Kafka.[114] In such a context, it seems less strange to find Arabian reminiscences also in Read's own platonic fantasy *The Green Child* (Heinemann, 1935), specifically of Abdullah of the Land's visit to the submarine utopia of his merman namesake.

There is an amusing aptness about the ingenuity with which Read submerges such an Arabian parallel in the pool at the very entrance to the underworld of *The Green Child*, so that it can only be identified by the reader who has acquainted himself with the preceding work of the author and his associates.[115] While such a covert use of the *Nights* differs from the practice of most of his predecessors, nevertheless Read is not the only writer thus to suppress almost entirely his Arabesque debts. Some Victorian precedents for a like strategy of concealed reference are to be found in the novels of Wilkie Collins, in Emily Brontë's *Wuthering Heights* and of course in James's *Golden Bowl*. The notable examples of T. S. Eliot and Virginia Woolf, however, suggest that the incidence of this literary game of hide-and-seek, as a marked feature of the modern period, bespeaks a new kind of intimacy with the *Nights* among some English-speaking writers and readers.

XIII

The eyes of the departing migrants are fixed on the sea,
To conjure their special fates from the impersonal water:
'I see an important decision made on a lake,
An illness, a beard, Arabia found in a bed,
*   Nanny defeated, Money'.*
                    (W. H. Auden, 'Dover 1937')

In the 1930s and 1940s there was a tendency to regard any departure from realism as escapist, but the inevitable psychological reaction encouraged other traditions which (as with Auden's witty application of desert geomancy to the English seaside) continued to pay attention to the *Nights*.[116] At first sight, however, during these years this alternative evaluation of the fantastical strain apparently found literary expression only in such ghettos as science fiction and children's books.

In the first two volumes of C. S. Lewis's science-fiction trilogy, the *Nights* gradually make their presence felt. In *Out of the Silent Planet* (1938) the desert uplands of Mars may help to explain not just elements of the planet's nomenclature but also the significantly recursive ornamentation of the sacred megaliths of Malcandra: 'these empty and crowded areas turned out to be themselves arranged in larger designs . . . quite often large arabesques included as a subordinate detail intricate pictures' (ch. 17; Pan edn, pp. 122–3). Roger Lancelyn Green has persuasively linked the name of *Perelandra* (1943) with the Persian for 'fairy' (*peri*).[117] Similarly the space vehicle by which Ransom travels to Perelandra (ch. 2) recalls both the legends about the levitation of Mohammed's coffin and the different kinds of 'instrumental marvellous' employed in the Arabian tales to reach the other world. It is in chapter 9 of *That Hideous Strength* (Bodley Head, 1945) that Lewis emphasises his debts to the *Nights*, and in particular associates himself with the use which, in *Sartor Resartus*, Carlyle had made of one central Arabian story.[118] In 'The Saracen's Head' (the chapter-title itself is a give-away) oriental details such as the 'turban'-like head-dressing (p. 221) vividly relate the nightmarish laboratory to the medieval Levantine court of the ungrateful Grecian king who so fatally consults the severed head of the physician Douban. By such an adaptation of the teaching-stories of the medieval East and Victorian England, C. S. Lewis satirises what in certain fields of modern science he considered a heartless pursuit of knowledge.

In his essay 'On Juvenile Tastes', C. S. Lewis confesses to an aversion to the Arab collection: 'I, who disliked *The Arabian Nights* as a child, dislike them still.'[119] Despite Lewis's persistently hostile attitude – and however much he may have preferred the tales and legends of other cultures – any aversion that he may have felt is not to be equated with ignorance of the content and manner of the *Nights*. It is not just that there is a greater incidence of Arabesque allusion in *The Chronicles of Narnia*; Lewis also makes progressively more recondite and inventive use of the characteristic structures as well as the particular details of the *Nights*. *The Lion, the Witch and the Wardrobe* (1950) is based partly on the fate of those 'Sons of Adam and . . . Daughters of Eve' who, discovering the petrified cities of the *Nights*, encounter jinn and ghouls lurking about such ruins (chs 7–9; Puffin edn, pp. 64, 76); in *Prince Caspian* (1951), Lewis tries to make his reader understand something of what it must feel like to be summoned 'when a magician in the *Arabian Nights* calls up a Jinn' (ch. 8; Puffin edn, p. 90); in *The Voyage of the Dawn Treader* (1952), with playful ingenuity he deploys picture-frames and books-within-books to alert the reader to the adroit handling of recursion and narrative interweaving, as well as specific, often complex reference to individual stories such as that of Prince Ahmed and the Peri Banou (e.g. chs 1 and 10); successively in *The Silver Chair* (1953), *The Horse and his Boy* (1954), *The Magician's Nephew* (1955) and *The Last Battle* (1956) there are implied reminiscences not just of the familiar tales, such as that of Aladdin, but also of the two lives of the Sultan Mahmud, and of the Pseudo-Caliph, which help to make an entry into, landscape and populate the other worlds; moreover throughout *The Chronicles* Lewis converts to Christian proselytising ends the Moslem counter-Crusade romances which are also numbered among the *Nights*.

In the meantime an altogether greater religious masterpiece was in the making. Letters from David Jones to Harman Grisewood and the Edes in 1938 and 1939 reveal something of the genesis of 'Balaam's Ass', in which one thing, among others, that Roman legionary and British Tommy prove to have in common is the knack of cornering their listener 'for a thousand and one nights' with 'twice-told tales from East of Suez'.[120] At much the same time William Empson had linked the Spanish Civil War with the Japanese invasion of China, when in 'Aubade' (1937) he made stealthy use of the match-making genies to take 'a bedshift flight to a Far Eastern sky'.[121]

XIV

The story is essentially an encyclopedia in miniature. . . . Its most striking quality, and one seldom attained by didactic works, is however the charming form it has been given.

(Gerhardt, *The Art of Story-Telling*, pp. 343–4)

Scheherazade, or the Future of the English Novel (1927) is an illuminating oddity in the history of the Anglophone reception of the *Nights*.[122] When, in *The Structure of the Novel: Hogarth Lecture No. 6* (1928), Edwin Muir noted it as being a 'packed little essay' (pp. 8–9), he spoke truer than he knew. Although a literary specialist, its author, John Carruthers, was excited more by the modern scientific revolution: 'a veritable second Renaissance in thought is in progress . . . and novelists, backward and complacent though they are, cannot remain unaware of it much longer' (p. 75).

In the name of a heroine who with her life-saving tales is the type of all the learned women in the *Nights*, Carruthers attempts to bridge the gap between the humanities and the culture of science (three decades before C. P. Snow's bid).[123] In thus doing, he shows himself so attuned to the implications of the most advanced theories of his day that the unorthodox remedy which he proposes for the spiritual malaise of our epoch has had to wait half a century before the like was to be heard from studies such as David Bohm's *Wholeness and the Implicate Order* (1980). Again in the sphere of psychology, with his exposition of Whitehead's theories on *prehension*, 'by which term is meant "uncognitive apprehension" or . . . "unconscious patterning" ' (p. 80), Carruthers looks forward to Anton Ehrenzweig's observations in *The Hidden Order of Art* (1967). Moreover in both fields of research – physics, and the nature of intelligence – Carruthers anticipates that recourse to comparison with the *Nights* (e.g. their open-ended nesting structures, manipulation of time and space) which is currently being made by such notable exponents of their specialisms as Douglas R. Hofstader in his study of human thought-processes, *Gödel, Escher, Bach: An Eternal Golden Braid* (Penguin, 1980; see chs 4, 5 and especially 'Little Harmonic Labyrinth'), and Ilya Prigogine's team with their account of 'dissipative structures' in *Order out of Chaos* (Fontana, 1985, p. 277). Unfortunately Carruthers fails to grasp sufficiently the *literary* consequences of his own philosophical discoveries: 'Gestalt . . . imaginatively apprehended . . . changes our whole attitude towards the world . . . it re-affirms values that nineteenth century science did its best to annihilate: most important of all for literature, it reinstates the soul' (*Scheherazade*, pp. 75–6). Ironically, the holistic vision which he sees imbuing the novel of the future eventually began to be realised in the fiction (and poems) of certain Post-Modernists who have built upon the experiments of the self-same twentieth-century *avant-garde* which Carruthers regards so coolly.[124] In the short term his sceptical attitude towards the innovations of the most adventurous of his contemporaries is symptomatic of that anti-Modernism that was to be a marked feature of thirties writing.

XV

'Re-incarnations of Scheherazade, the Teller of STORIES'
(Carruthers)

Deploring 'a general refusal to grasp the importance of fantasy in [his] work', Graham Greene too reminds us, 'I'm a story-teller, unlike writers of the previous generation such as Virginia Woolf and E. M. Forster.'[125] Indeed, his narratives, filled with action and suspense, commonly wearing an uncomplicated look, do seem to derive from the linear aspects of the *Nights* rather than from their more involved patterns, which attracted the Modernists to them. Nevertheless, from his early works to the more recent, beneath the appearance of apparently straightforward realism, Greene's structures are often surprisingly Arabesque. Variations on the frame tale of the *Nights* in particular tend to reappear throughout his *oeuvre*. Some of the most obvious instances are found in *A Gun for Sale* (1936) and *Travels with my Aunt* (1969): in the former, discreetly overarching references to the pantomimes of Aladdin and Sindbad (Penguin edn, pp. 21, 53, 159, 160; see also ch. 5), and, in the latter, one memorably witty allusion to a 'deep crimson' dahlia named 'Arabian Night' (p. 136) help to point up the presence of nocturnal weavers of therapeutic tales at an important crisis in each novel. In *A Burnt-out Case* (1960) and 'Under the Garden' (*A Sense of Reality*, 1963), Greene plays even more ingeniously with this Perso-Arabian motif, turning his story-tellers into men threatened by women. Nor does the teasing of his reader stop there. As with Eliot and Read, who were, Greene has confessed, 'the two great figures of my young manhood',[126] the Arabesque allusions in Greene's work became progressively more submerged. In *Monsignor Quixote* (1982, pt II, ch. 4) the censorship of the innocent priest by his reactionary bishop leads to a sublime use of the imaginary meal that the Barber's Sixth Brother pretends to share with his Barmecide host. Greene's reference here to one of the most famous stories in the *Nights* is all the more potent just because there is no obvious allusion to the tale. Out of a story cherished by the Victorians and their successors Greene creates that deeply poignant scene in which, way past midnight, without the prescribed bread and wine, Monsignor Quixote falteringly celebrates his last mass, and moved by love for his old philosophical sparring-partner, the communist mayor Sancho, receives Holy Communion.

XVI

'Mother of Records . . . Prototype of Tales'

The increasing role that fantasy has come to play in Greene's work since the late 1950s invites an explanation along lines rather similar to those which help to account for Doris Lessing's switch from the mainstream novel into genre fiction, especially science fiction (for the recent return to her earlier mode is more apparent than real). Significantly, Lessing's change of direction occurred at almost the same time as Greene's. True, it was not until the apocalyptic conclusion of *The Four-Gated City* (MacGibbon and Kee, 1969), where the realistic narrative is replaced by a vision of the nuclear holocaust, that an unmistakably Arabesque note was struck. There, although one of the 'survivors' is disgusted by such a mixture, the cultivation of 'irony and St John of the Cross and the Arabian Nights' (Granada edn, p. 667) offers him, as it had once done his family and friends, a mystical hint of salvation. Nevertheless, as her 1971 preface for the paperback reprint is at pains to emphasise, as early as *The Golden Notebook* (1961) there are elements of that experiment in which hindsight recognises traces of exotic and older traditions: above all there is the 'envelope' shape of *The Golden Notebook*, its 'frame', which holds together the fragmented stories of characters as stereotypical as those in 'the old morality plays'.[127]

The changes in direction made by Greene and Lessing might be related partly to the appearance of two new translations of the *Nights*. In 1953 Allen and Unwin published A. J. Arberry's selection *Scheherazade*, and in the following year Allen Lane brought out N. J. Dawood's *The Hunchback, Sindbad and Other Tales* as their Penguin no. 1001. By the mid-sixties there were no fewer than six different paperback versions of the *Nights*. This *embarras de richesses* coincided with a return to the Arabian stories by an older generation of writers. Thus in *The Cocktail Party* (1949), with its envelope of nocturnal tales of the East, tales interrupted but life-enhancing,

Eliot links the Alcestis myth with 'The Story of the Fisherman and the Genie' by a pun on the 'gin and water' requested by Harcourt-Reilly (i.i). Likewise, in 'The Lady of the Pool' (*The Anathemata* [Faber, 1952] p. 167), David Jones gives an Arabesque twist to Bede's story of how Pope Gregory was prompted to send missionaries to England, and, thanks to Gurdjieff, Scheherazade helps introduce Hugh Macdiarmid's vision of world language, *In Memoriam James Joyce* (Glasgow: William Maclellan, 1955, p. 21).[128] In Wyndham Lewis's satire on left-wing clerics, *The Red Priest* (Methuen, 1956, pp. 105, 115), Father Augustine Card is led deeper into temptation by a suspiciously punctual London bus no. 1001,[129] while Rebecca West's late masterpiece *The Fountain Overflows* (Macmillan, 1957) brilliantly reworks Shakespeare's *King Lear* by the use of analogous stories from the *Nights* (e.g. pp. 51, 62, 143, 242, 274 in the Virago edn).

Nor among the contemporaries of Greene and Lessing were British writers unique in exhibiting signs of having fallen again under the *Nights'* spell. While Greene places some of David Jones's work 'among the great poems of this century', it is also evident from the reference to Jorge Luis Borges in *The Honorary Consul* (1973, pt ii, ch. 3; Penguin edn, p. 74) that Greene's interest in the *Nights* was further stimulated by the Arabesque stream which has fed Latin American Magic Realism.[130] Whereas, though, it is a Manichean strain in him that makes Greene so unorthodox a Catholic, for the past quarter-century Doris Lessing has been caught up in Sufism.[131] In a 1972 essay on her teacher, Lessing discusses Idries Shah's influential book *The Sufis* (W. H. Allen, 1964). There, in his introduction, Robert Graves argues that there is a link between the White Goddess and the Arabic title of the *Nights*, which Shah decodes as meaning 'mother matrix, . . . principle of . . . story' (pp. xii, 174–5).[132] Both Greene and Lessing rely on dreams as an integral part of their creative process. Understandably, though, where Lessing sees 'the unconscious artist [residing] in our depths' as a prophetess figure ('the Mistress of the Ceremony' – interview, Oct 1963), Greene, with his memories of the cinema, especially films such as the Arabesque *Warning Shadows*, relates dreams to features of Oriental story-telling: nocturnal, cheap, serial entertainment, recursive and at times otherworldly.[133] In both cases travel and drugs have contributed to these oriental fantasies. For, while the time, place and degree to which these pressures have been felt obviously varied, all the other factors in the expected set of stimuli have been operative in the creative process of these two writers, reactivating their richly intertwined memories of childhood and the *Nights*.

It was not until the 1960s that Lessing became conscious of her debt to Persia, where she was born; then 'under mescaline' she found that it had influenced her unconsciously (interview, Oct 1963). These Persian memories had been reinforced by her early reading of the European classics, among which not a few show Arabesque nuances: Scott, Balzac, Meredith, Proust, Conrad and Karen Blixen (Isaac Dinesen) – the Danish story-teller most nearly approaching Sir Walter Scott in her exuberant employment of the *Nights*. And, like Lessing herself, Blixen is clearly aware that 'the real history of Africa is still in the custody of black story-tellers and wise men'.[134]

As in *The Four-Gated City* reminiscences of the Arabian stories occur during the dark night of the Earth, so, in that account of disintegration of individual personality *Briefing for a Descent into Hell* (1971), Ali Baba – along with Jason, Prometheus, Adam and other morally ambiguous culture-bearers – is linked with the psychopomp Mercury (Granada edn, p. 112). Soul-conducting is again an element in the meaning of the deep structure of *The Memoirs of a Survivor* (1974), where the multi-coloured fish symbolism of the opening clearly points to Lessing's amplification of the tale of the Young Prince of the Black Islands, his drowned kingdom, its transformed citizens who are eventually saved from fisherman and cooking-pot by the lady who comes through the wall. By contrast, the Arabesque borrowings constellated throughout *Canopus in Argos: Archives* (Jonathan Cape, 1979–83) avowedly come by less direct routes, partly originating in Lessing's encounter with an Hispano-Moorish embodiment of that architecture–literary analogy which, as noted above, was a common theme of Hole, Weber and Scott in their theorisings about the nature of the *Nights*.

Interviewed in the *Guardian* (15 May 1981), Lessing explained that during the 1960s, in order to cope with the emotional problems of middle age, she had evolved therapeutic fantasies based on the topography of Granada (which for Lessing has always evoked memories of her Persian place of birth – 'Impertinent Daughters', *Granta*, 14 [1984] 60), only to find some twenty years later these psychic associations of Andalusia revived in the process of composing *The Marriages between Zones Three, Four and Five* (1980). The trigger that reactivated these memories of Moorish Spain apparently was Oleg Grabar's *The Alhambra* (Allen Lane, 1978). In this remarkably illuminating analysis of one of the peaks of Islamic art, Grabar sums up the Arabesque impressions that the Alhambra has left on a succession of English-speaking visitors ever since the days of Washington Irving, Owen Jones and Richard Ford. Besides making half-a-dozen explicit comparisons with the *Nights*, the City of Brass, Harun's Baghdad (pp. 109, 114, 206–10), Grabar demonstrates that, as the tales seem to multiply themselves, so an identical principle of self-generation operates throughout the Alhambra. Certainly this monument seems conducive to the writing of a subtly oriental space epic, with its additive and eclectic architecture, inscribed yet geometrically decorated to the extent that the spectator is irresistibly drawn into a mathematical contemplation of heaven and earth.

Significantly, details of the Alhambra's structure and decoration can be seen paralleled in a number of the often striking illustrations lavished on Idries Shah's *World Tales* (Allen Lane, 1979), which Lessing reviewed under the title 'Some Parables of Human Destiny'. Besides revealing the diffusion of the *Jatakas*, *Panchatantra* and *Hitopadesa* (which had been explored by the Victorian folklorists), in this sampling of 'the extraordinary coincidence of stories told in all times, in all places' Shah suggests that nearly a quarter of the tales he has here collected have some degree of affinity with the *Nights*. That *World Tales* helped to revive yet more of Doris Lessing's memories of the Arabian stories is hinted in the series-title for her space chronicles: *Canopus in Argos: Archives*. As I have explained elsewhere, the opening phrase is an allusion to *The Lights of Canopus*, the Persian variant of the Muslim mirror for princes – *Kalila and Dimna*; indeed Lessing wrote the introduction for a new version (Knopf, 1980) by Ramsay Wood.[135] The final element in the Canopus series-title is a different matter. 'Archives' seems to echo Shah's numerological decipherment of the Arabic title of the *Nights* as meaning something like 'Source of Records . . ., Mother of Records, Prototype of Tales' (*The Sufis*, pp. 174–5).

There is considerable variation in the extent to which the *Nights* have visibly influenced individual volumes in the *Canopus* series: ghouls batten onto the disturbed emotional life of the stricken planet in *Re . . . Shikasta* (Jonathan Cape, 1979, p. 206); when Lessing uses the Preface to *The Sirian Experiments* (1981) to voice the wish that 'reviewers and readers could see this series . . . as a framework that enables me to tell . . . a beguiling tale or two; to put questions, both to myself and to others; to explore ideas and sociological possibilities' (p. iii), one catches glimpses of the open-ended structures of the *Nights* and the teaching-stories that they frame. These sightings are confirmed when in *The Making of the Representative for Planet 8* (Jonathan Cape, 1982) the narrator recalls how 'Canopus had told . . . a thousand tales that would prepare the minds of our people for understanding our role as a planet among planets' (p. 34). Further confirmation comes in this novel's Afterword, when Lessing herself yearns for a modern Harun to go around 'incognito' redressing wrongs (p. 129). Yet, as often is the case with the twentieth-century writer's use of the *Nights*, those places in the *Canopus* series where the Arabesque influence has been most profound are paradoxically just the areas where the traces are most submerged. Among Shah's selection in *World Tales* is an explicit variant on 'The Sleeper Awakened', here entitled 'The Desolate Island' (pp. 114–15): a parable about the need to use this world to prepare for the next that plainly did not go unmissed by the author of *The Making of the Representative for Planet 8*. Again, in *The Marriages between Zones Three, Four and Five* (Jonathan Cape, 1980), there are reminiscences of the Arabian story of Hasan of Basra, who goes in search of his peri wife, she having returned to her motherland and its Amazonian society ('The Bird Maiden', *World Tales*, pp. 238–51) – a tale which Lessing uses in her affecting exploration of the inner space of marital relationships.

From *The Marriages* it is also clear that Lessing responds deeply to oriental painting. In fact published towards the end of the 1970s, Idries Shah's sumptuous *World Tales* was riding a tide of public taste that has brought back into fashion those very illustrators of the *Nights* who had flourished earlier in the century during the 'Golden Age' of children's books. This revival of interest began early in the decade with picture-books; then followed more scholarly studies, one of the most important of these being David Larkin's edition of *The Unknown Paintings of Kay Nielsen . . . with an elegy by Hildegarde Flanner* (Pan, 1977). This publication reproduces a portfolio of 'nineteen remarkable gouache illustrations of . . . miniature size . . . for *A Thousand and One Nights* on which [Nielsen] had worked from 1918 to 1922'; these were intended to accompany a translation from the Arabic into Danish, but it never materialised (p. 14).[136]

It is exactly this protean nature of the *Nights* that helps explain those apparently wild fluctuations in size, quality, mode and genre between one work and the next (indeed, as far as modal and generic variations are concerned, sometimes within the single work itself) which – even more than is the case with Lessing – are so highly characteristic of Michael Moorcock's Post-Modernist *oeuvre*: that recent alternation between, on the one hand, multi-media *bricolage* as found elegantly miniaturised in *The Entropy Tango* (New English Library, 1981) and, on the other, the tumultuous panoramas of the Pyat memoirs *Byzantium Endures* and *The Laughter of Carthage* (Secker and Warburg, 1981 and 1984), at one point in the latter a glimpse is caught of the archetypal cockney Mrs Cornelius 'at the *Shaharazad* cabaret around midnight' (p. 79).

Autobiographical reminiscences in *Letters from Hollywood* (Harrap, 1986) indicate that, as the heterogeneous *Nights* aided the young Moorcock in his exploration of the street life of London's Soho, so now in the middle age, encountering the West Coast styles of California, Moorcock is able to come to terms with Los Angeles by recollecting Housman and Dulac's collaborations (pp. 12, 75, 59–60, 156–7). Among such memories, does the suffragette version of *Princess Badoura* figure? It is tempting to speculate whether Moorcock's feminist allegiances took him in that direction. After all, one of the earliest references to the *Nights* that Moorcock makes occurs in *The Adventures of Una Persson and Catherine Cornelius in the Twentieth Century* (Quartet, 1976), where the tale of Prince Ahmed and the Peri Banou is given an anti-patriarchal twist – while incidentally pretending to claim an operatic connection for the ever-ramifying genealogy of Moorcock's most celebrated hero:

> 'Cornelius,' Ahmed's father spoke suddenly. 'Any relation to the Barber of Baghdad Cornelius? . . . The comic opera, you know. German. Last century. A great favourite of mine when I was a student.'
> 'I'm afraid my family's very ordinary,' she said.   (p. 104)

Again, in that apotheosis of heroic burlesque *Gloriana* (Allison and Busby, 1978) the travesties do not engage only with swords and sorcery, *The Faerie Queene*, *Orlando* and *The Arabian Nights Murder*; Moorcock also presents a parodic reflection of the West's discomfiture at the rise of the oil-rich East in the shape of an alternative history of the Renaissance. Here an apparently secure Albion protects a weak but scheming Arabia, whose London ambassador is none other than Shahryar; he is plotting against the overlord of Baghdad, who is not, as in the *Nights*, Harun al-Rashid but 'the

Grand Caliph Hassan al-Giafar' (pp. 80, 91). In later picaresque chronicles of that collapse of the old European empires which was brought about by the Great War, his anti-hero's struggles to invent a pocket helicopter induce in Pyat reveries about 'a flying prince and princess, those staples of Oriental legend' (*The Laughter of Carthage*, p. 173; these dreams are further parodied in ch. 8). Through such Arabesque allusions, Moorcock drops hints that the *Nights* have provided him with a model of how an encyclopaedia of genres can help anatomise a society.[137]

Whatever degree of truth there may be in the suggestion implicitly made by Hofstadter that the structure of the Arab collection is in some way isomorphic with the processes of the mind, there can be no doubt that the *Nights* continues to exercise an influence over writers working in Britain today, writers as different as J. G. Ballard, A. S. Byatt, Angela Carter, Nuruddin Farah, Robert Irwin, Salman Rushdie, Alan Sillitoe and Ahdaf Souief. And not just writers, for there are Arabesque traces evident in the current revival of oral story-telling by groups such as the multi-cultural Common Lore. Like the *Nights* themselves, the history of their influence is an 'endless' tale. Bordering on the world of the archetypes, in Borges's words, the book of *The Thousand and One Nights* is 'so vast that it is not necessary to have read it, for it is part of our memory.'[138]

NOTES

Books published in London unless otherwise stated. In the case of early editions, the name of the publisher is given for only those books to which specific reference is made and for which there are no modern editions.

1. Gerald Frow, in *'Oh Yes It Is': A History of Pantomine* (BBC, 1985), notes that, while *Ali Baba* is very seldom seen these days, the Forty Thieves being the principal deterrent, and *Sindbad* remains in fairly regular but limited production (p. 116), '*Aladdin* ranks second only to *Cinderella*' (p. 114); however, the *Guardian*, 21 Dec 1985, p. 8, suggested that *Aladdin* is fast becoming the most popular source for pantomime.
2. See Duncan B. Macdonald, 'A Bibliographical and Literary Study of the First Appearance of the *Arabian Nights* in Europe', *Library Quarterly*, II, no. 4 (Oct 1932) 387–420, esp. p. 406. Donald F. Bond (ed.), in *The Spectator* (Oxford: Clarendon Press, 1965) IV, 410n., notes that 'volumes five and six were published in English translation for A. Bell in 1706 (advertised in *Post Boy* 10 December)'. Brian Alderson informs me that copies of the opening volumes of the first Grub Street edition are in

both the Opie and Princeton collections. See also J. H. Hanford, 'Open Sesame', *Princeton University Library Chronicle*, xxvi, no. 1 (Autumn 1964) 48–56; for this last information I am grateful to Charles E. Greene, Princeton University Library. James Beattie (see *infra*, n. 5) suggests that *Gullivers' Travels* owes something to Sindbad's voyages.

3. Joseph Spence, *Observations, Anecdotes and Characters of Books and Men*, ed. James M. Osborn (Oxford: Clarendon Press, 1966) i, 151–2.

4. Addison also borrows from the *Nights* to point some morals in his periodical essays: e.g. *Spectator*, no. 195 (13 Oct 1711), using 'The Tale of the Grecian King and the Physician Douban'; *Spectator*, no. 535 (13 Nov 1714), using 'The Barber's Fifth Brother'; *Guardian*, no. 162 (16 Sep 1713), using 'Shacabac and the Barmecide Feast'. See A. J. Weitzman, 'The Influence of the Middle East on English Prose Fiction 1600–1725' (PhD thesis, New York University, 1964) pp. 169–71.

5. On Reynolds, see Charles Christopher Knipp, 'Types of Orientalism in Eighteenth-Century England' (PhD thesis, University of California, Berkeley, 1974) pp. 23–4. Henri Fluchère, in *Laurence Sterne, de l'homme à l'oeuvre, biographie critique* (Paris: Gallimard, 1961) p. 368, cites a facsimile catalogue of Sterne's library. In his *Hobby-Horses* (M. Allen, 1797), Jenkin Jones, asserting that criticism of Sterne has been too harsh, suggests an approach to *Tristram Shandy* by way of the *Nights* (p. 16; also pp. 10, 12); see too Alan B. Howes, *Yorick and the Critics* (New Haven, Conn.: Yale University Press, 1958) p. 94. The relevant extracts from, respectively, John Hawkesworth (*Adventurer*, no. 4, 18 Nov 1752), Hugh Blair (*Lectures on Rhetoric and Poetry*, 1762) and James Beattie (*On Fable and Romance*, 1783) are collected in *Novel and Romance*, ed. Ioan Williams (Routledge and Kegan Paul, 1970); see esp. pp. 193, 248, 312–13.

6. Edward Gibbon, *Memoirs of my Life*, ed. Georges A. Bonnard (Thomas Nelson, 1966) p. 36.

7. *The Letters of Edward Gibbon*, ed. J. E. Norton (Cassell, 1956) iii, 132 (4 Oct 1788); *The English Essays of Edward Gibbon*, ed. Patricia B. Craddock (Oxford: Clarendon Press, 1972) p. 141.

8. [The Journal of James] Boswell, *the Ominous Years: 1774–6*, ed. Charles Ryskamp and Frederick A. Pottle (Heinemann, 1963) p. 322 (10 Apr 1776).

9. Robert D. Mayo, *The English Novel in the Magazines 1740–1815* (Evanston, Ill.: Northwestern University Press; and London: Oxford University Press, 1962) pp. 41, 58–9, 61, 109, 229, 233, 248, 253, 276, 303, 366, 448, 455–6.

10. Third Earl of Shaftesbury, 'Advice to an Author,' section iii, *Characteristics of Men, Manners, Opinions, Times*, ed. John M. Robertson (New York: Bobbs-Merrill, 1964) i, 221–5.

11. *The Correspondence of Alexander Pope*, ed. George Sherburn (Oxford: Clarendon Press, 1956) ii, 53–6 (23, 28 Sep 1720).

12. *Horace Walpole's Correspondence with Mary and Agnes Berry*, ed. W. S. Lewis *et al.* (London: Oxford University Press; and New Haven, Conn.: Yale University Press, 1944) xi, 20 (30 June 1789).

13. Knipp, 'Types of Orientalism', p. 23.

14. Although in scholarly works such as Thomas Warton's *Observations on the Fairie Queene* (1754, rev. 1762), and Bishop Hurd's *Letters on Chivalry and Romance* (1762), there is a growing awareness of the affinities between medieval European poetry and Eastern literature, no less influential was the witty defence of the *Nights* mounted by Clara Reeve in her elegant discussion *The Progress of Romance* (1785) pp. 22–7 (Evening II).
15. Knipp, 'Types of Orientalism', p. 48.
16. The first important modern study of the Eastern element in the literary achievement of the period is Martha Pike Conant's *The Oriental Tale in England in the Eighteenth Century* (New York: Columbia University Press, 1908). Deficiencies in her work are corrected by Fatma Moussa-Mahmoud, 'Beckford, *Vathek* and the Oriental Tale', and Mahmoud A. Manzalaoui, 'Pseudo-Orientalism in Translation: The Age of *Vathek*', both in *William Beckford of Fonthill . . . Bicentenary Essays*, ed. Fatma Moussa-Mahmoud (Cairo: Cairo Studies in English, 1960) esp. pp. 110, 123–6. Benjamin Boyce, in 'English Short Fiction in the Eighteenth Century: A Preliminary Review', *Studies in Short Fiction*, V (1967–8) 95–112, notes the role played by the *Nights* in the development of this genre. That the heroine of the Arabian frame tale inspires the female romance writers of the age is implied by Patrizia Nerozzi Bellman *et al.* in *Scheherazade in Inghilterra* (Milan: Cisalpino-Goliardica, 1983). On the uniqueness of *Vathek*, see also Roger Lonsdale's introduction to the World's Classics edition (1970, 1983) p. xxv.
17. Robert Halsband (ed.), in *The Complete Letters of Lady Wortley Montagu* (Oxford University Press, 1965) I, 385 n. 1, notes that in 1739 Lady Mary owned *Les Mille et une nuits* in ten volumes. The first publication of her Turkish Embassy Letters was 1763. See also Patrick Russell, *The Natural History of Aleppo . . .* I, 385–6 (G. G. & J. Robinson, 1794) n. 38.
18. See G. E. von Grunebaum, 'Creative Borrowing', *Medieval Islam* (Chicago: University of Chicago Press, 1945) ch. 9; Mahmoud A. Manzalaoui, 'The Arabian Nights', *Cassell's Encyclopedia of Literature*, ed. S. H. Steinberg (Cassell, 1953) I, 26–9; E. Littmann, 'Alf Layla wa Layla', *Encyclopaedia of Islam*, new edn (Leiden: Brill, 1960) I, 358–64; Mia Gerhardt, *The Art of Story-Telling: A Literary Study of the Thousand and One Nights* (Leiden: Brill, 1963); E. J. Ranelagh, *The Past we Share: The Near-Eastern Ancestry of Western Folk Literature* (Quartet, 1979); Joseph Schacht with C. E. Bosworth (ed.), *The Legacy of Islam* (Oxford: Clarendon Press, 1979).
19. Albert C. Baugh, 'The Background of Chaucer's Mission to Spain', in *Chaucer und seine Zeit: Symposium für Walter F. Schirmer*, ed. Arno Esch (Tübingen: Max Niemeyer, 1968) pp. 55–69. On the diplomatic and cultural context see P. E. Russell, *The English Intervention in Spain and Portugal in the Time of Edward III and Richard II* (Oxford: Clarendon Press, 1955); W. M. Watt and Pierre Cachia, *A History of Islamic Spain* (Edinburgh: Edinburgh University Press, 1965); Michael Brett, *The Moors: Islam in the West* (Orbis, 1980). The degree to which Chaucer's masterpiece was influenced by Eastern story collection is a matter that

has been extensively examined: see for example W. F. Bryan and G. Dempster (eds), *Sources and Analogues of Chaucer's Canterbury Tales* (Chicago: University of Chicago Press, 1941), which builds on earlier scholarship. More recent studies include Dorothee Metlitzki, *The Matter of Araby in Medieval England* (New Haven, Conn.: Yale University Press, 1977); Katherine Slater Gittes, 'The Canterbury Tales and the Arabic Frame Tradition', *PMLA*, XCVIII (Mar 1983) 237–51; Helen Cooper, *The Structure of the Canterbury Tales* (Duckworth, 1983).

20. Among others, C. C. Knipp, in 'The Arabian Nights in England – Galland's Translation and its Successors', *Journal of Arabic Literature*, V (1974) 44–54, concurs with this preference.

21. Besides the Galland text in the *Novelist Magazine* (XVIII, 1785) and Jonathan Scott's 1811 translation of the *Nights*, Wordsworth possessed a copy of *The Arabian Tales* (1794), which Chester L. and Alice C. Shaver suggest is the *Continuation*; see *Wordsworth's Library: A Catalogue* (New York: Garland, 1979) pp. 10–11. Additionally Wordsworth owned François Petis de la Croix's *Les Mille et un jours* (Paris, 1712–26) and the Ambrose Philips translation of *Persian Tales* in the *Novelist Magazine* (XIII, 1783); see Shaver, *Wordsworth's Library*, p. 200. A. A. Mendilow, in 'Robert Heron and Wordsworth's Critical Essays', *MLR*, LII (1957) 329–38, establishes other connections between the two writers.

22. Shaver, *Wordsworth's Library*, p. 125.

23. John Beer, *Coleridge the Visionary* (Chatto and Windus, 1959) pp. 145–6, 148, 325 n. 42.

24. *Thalaba*, III.xxiv, *The Poetical Works of Robert Southey* (Longman, 1838) IV, 94–5, 118.

25. *The Letters of William and Dorothy Wordsworth 1787–1805*, ed. E. de Selincourt, rev. C. L. Shaver (Oxford: Clarendon Press, 1967) I, 412–13, 432; see also *The Letters of Sir Walter Scott*, ed. Herbert Grierson (Constable, 1932) I, 288 (10 Apr 1806). In a letter to Daniel Stuart (19 Sep 1801), Coleridge expresses interest in *Thalaba*, the poem having been planned in 1797 – Coleridge, *Collected Letters*, ed. E. L. Griggs (Oxford: Clarendon Press, 1956) II, 413, Coleridge and Southey became friends in 1795, and Thomas MacFarland is not alone in arguing persuasively that during their most creative period Coleridge and Wordsworth were in a state of intellectual symbiosis; see his *Romanticism and the Forms of Ruin* (Princeton, NJ: Princeton University Press, 1981) ch. 1. In 1831 Wordsworth was on friendly terms with a Miss Carlyle who (A. G. Hill suggests) was probably a relation of Joseph Dacre; see *Letters of W. and D. Wordsworth*, V, 416. See also *The Letters of Mary Wordsworth*, ed. M. E. Burton (Oxford: Clarendon Press, 1958) p. 123 (item 58, 5 Oct 1825).

26. *Journals of Dorothy Wordsworth* ed. E. de Selincourt (Macmillan, 1959) I, viii, 195–409.

27. My text here and after is *The Prelude 1799, 1805, 1850*, ed. Jonathan Wordsworth, M. H. Abrams and Stephen Gill (New York: Norton, 1979).

28. Southey, *Poetical Works*, IV, xv.

29. Jane Worthington Smyser, 'Wordsworth's Dream of Poetry and Science: *The Prelude* v', *PMLA*, LXXI (1956) 269–75. Norman Kemp Smith, in *New Studies in the Philosophy of Descartes* (Macmillan, 1952) pp. v, 15–17, 33–9, translates Descartes's dream as it appears in Baillet's *Vie de Descartes*, Christopher Salvesen, in *The Landscape of Memory: A Study of Wordsworth's Poetry* (1965; repr. Arnold, 1970) pp. 9–12, notes that 'A History of my Mind', the projected title of Descartes's *Discourse sur la méthods* makes one think of Wordsworth. Mary Jacobus points to further evidence that Coleridge was reading Descartes through the years 1797 to 1803: 'Wordsworth and the Language of the Dream', *ELH*, XLVI (1979) 638, 644n.

30. The melon shares in the symbolism of the gourd – the paradoxical fruitfulness of the desert; see Harold Bayley, *The Lost Language of Symbolism* (1912; 7th imp., Ernest Benn, 1974) II, 246. Since Yahweh made one grow to cover Jonah's head while he awaited the destruction of Nineveh (Jonah 4), the gourd has come to symbolise the Resurrection; see George Ferguson, *Signs and Symbols of Christian Art* (Oxford: Galaxy, 1966) p. 31. Cf. Stephen's dream in 'Scylla and Charybdis' (Joyce, *Ulysses*).

31. See for example, on the structure and themes of book v, W. G. Stobie, 'A Reading of *The Prelude*, Book v', *Modern Language Quarterly*, XXIV (1963) 365–73; Joel Morkan, 'Structure and Meaning in *The Prelude*: Book v', *PMLA*, LXXXVII (1972) 246–54; Frank D. McConnell, *The Confessional Imagination: A Reading of Wordsworth's Prelude* (Baltimore: Johns Hopkins University Press, 1974) pp. 130–1 – on the implication of the Chinese-box narrative of the dream; David Wiener, 'Wordsworth, Books and the Growth of a Poet's Mind', *Journal of English and Germanic Philology*, LXXIV (1975) 209–20; Michael Jaye, 'The Artifice of Disjunction, Book 5, *The Prelude*', *Papers on Language and Literature*, XIV (1978) 32–50; John Beer, *Wordsworth in Time* (Faber, 1979) pp. 180–5; Ernest Bernhardt-Kabisch, 'The Stone and the Shell: Wordsworth, Cataclysm and the Myth of Glaucus', *Studies in Romanticism*, XXIV (Spring 1985) 455–90. Kenneth R. Johnston, in *Wordsworth and the Recluse* (New Haven, Conn.: Yale University Press, 1984) p. 140, notes that 'the dream is pre-eminently *a vocation*, a story about the proper choice of one's life work'; yet R. D. Havens, whose critique in *The Mind of a Poet* (Baltimore: John Hopkins University Press, 1941) pp. 375–6, occasioned all this defence of book v is also one of the first critics to have glimpsed the connections between the dream, the finding of the drowned man's body and the reading of the *Nights* (p. 397). Though he seems unaware of the *Continuation*, nevertheless the 'Arabian Knight' pun, which has often been noted by readers, demonstrates how peculiarly resonant can be the half or more deeply hidden use of the *Nights*, a subtle effect which in the succeeding centuries would be increasingly explored by writers such as Dickens, James, T. S. Eliot and Herbert Read. On the 'Arabian Knight' pun, see *inter alia*, Elizabeth Sewell, *The Orphic Voice* (Routledge and Kegan Paul, 1961) p. 357; Jacobus, in *ELH*, XLVI, 640.

32. Of lines 158–61, W. J. B. Owen (ed.), in *The Fourteen Book 'Prelude'* (Ithaca, NY: Cornell University Press, 1985) p. 97, comments that they

seem 'to mean that Wordsworth foresaw the imminent collapse of
Western civilization under French aggression'. Ernest Bernhardt-
Kabisch pointing out that cataclysm, especially of the diluvial sort,
appears repeatedly as a metaphor for the French Revolution in the
literature of the period, cites Edmund Burke: 'the most astonishing
Deluge that has hitherto happened in the world' (*Reflections on the
Revolution in France*). Bernhardt-Kabisch also recognises that 'as an
Arab he is one of a nation of preservers and transmitters who rescued
Greek science and metaphysics from oblivion . . . and the age of
Wordsworth also regarded Arabia as a fountainhead of romance and
eloquence, especially of figurative expression, if not the originators of
modern romantic poets as such' (*SIR*, xxiv, 472–3). But Bernhardt-
Kabisch fails to spot the close parallels between *Prelude* v, the
Continuation and the studies of both Hole (see next note) and Carlyle.

33. In the Preface to *Arthur* (1789) pp. iv–v, Hole had anticipated these
views and in similar language.

34. 'Literary Reminiscences: The Lake Poets, William Wordsworth', *The
Collected Writings of Thomas De Quincey*, ed. David Masson (Edinburgh:
A. and C. Black, 1889) ii, 268–70.

35. Editor's Introduction to *Rob Roy*, Border Edition (J. C. Nimmo, 1893)
i, xvi. All text references to the Waverley novels are to this edition.

36. See Arthur Melville Clarke, *Sir Walter Scott: The Formative Years* (William
Blackwood, 1969) pp. 55, 57; Edgar Johnson, *Sir Walter Scott: The Great
Unknown* (Hamish Hamilton, 1970) i, 41; James C. Corson, *Notes and
Index to Sir Herbert Grierson's Edition of the Letters of Sir Walter Scott*
(Oxford: Clarendon Press, 1979) p. 354; Scott, *Letters*, i, 21, and ii, 43;
The Journal of Sir Walter Scott, ed. W. E. K. Anderson (Oxford:
Clarendon Press, 1972) p. 117.

37. 'There is something here as much the spirit of prophecy as of criticism'
comments J. G. Lockhart (ed.) in *The Minstrelsy* (Edinburgh: A. and
C. Black, 1833, repr. 1873) ii, 311n.

38. See René Huchon, *George Crabbe and his Times*, tr. F. Clarke (John
Murray, 1907) pp. 29, 356–7; and, for Scott's praise of Crabbe's work,
Scott, *Letters* iii, 211 (c. Jan 1813).

39. The entry for Weber in *The Dictionary of National Biography* errs in
saying that the introduction for *Tales of the East* 'was borrowed from
the "Tartarian Tales" of Thomas Flloyd of Dublin'. The *Athenaeum*, 14
Apr 1894, p. 474 (which is cited as the authority for this accusation),
in fact says Flloyd's work lacks a preface. It is with the plagiarism of
Flloyd's translation that the *Athenaeum* charges Weber.

40. See also *infra*, ch. 6.

41. *British Critic*, n.s. ii, 189–211, repr. in *Scott: The Critical Heritage*, ed.
John O. Hayden (Routledge and Kegan Paul, 1970) pp. 67–74; see esp.
p. 69.

42. How Scott passed on these lessons of the *Nights* not just to his fellow
Britons but also writers in Europe and America may be gauged from
Hayden, *Scott: The Critical Heritage, passim*; note especially the intense
if varied response of Heine, Goethe, Stendhal, Belinsky and Twain.

See also J. H. Raleigh, 'What Scott Meant to the Victorians', *Victorian Studies*, VII, (1963–4) 7–34.

43. Excerpted by Hayden (*Scott: The Critical Heritage*, pp. 475–6) from an unsigned article, 'Victor Hugo's Romances', *Cornhill Magazine* (Aug 1874) xxx, 179–94.

44. To explain secular artistic developments, Oleg Grabar refers to the *Nights* in *The Formation of Islamic Art* (New Haven, Conn.: Yale University Press, 1970) ch. 6, esp. p. 173, as he does also in *The Alhambra* (Allen Lane, 1978) pp. 109, 114, 206, 208, 210; in this respect Grabar echoes Richard Ford on Cordova and Granada in his influential *Handbook for Travellers in Spain* (John Murray, 1845; 3rd edn, 1855) I, 231, 310, 312. See also Patrick Conner, *Oriental Architecture in the West* (Thames and Hudson, 1979) chs 9 and 10.

45. Nineteenth-century architecture in particular often shows an oriental influence: see plates 67–72 in Francis D. Klingender, *Art and the Industrial Revolution* (1947), rev. A. Elton (1968; Paladin, 1972); and Michael Darby, *The Islamic Perspective: An Aspect of British Architecture and Design in the Nineteenth Century* (World of Islam Festival Trust, 1983).

46. On 'The Ancient Mariner', see not only Allan Grant and Deirdre Toomey, *infra*, ch. 4, but also Hazlitt: 'Coleridge used to laugh at me for my want of the faculty of dreaming; and once, on my saying that I did not like the preternatural stories in the Arabian Nights (for the comic parts I love dearly), he said "That must be because you never dream. There is a class of poetry built on this foundation, which is surely no inconsiderable part of our nature, since we are asleep and building up imaginations of this sort half our time"' – 'On Dreams', *The Plain Speaker* (1826). This echoes Hazlitt's comparison of the grotesque elements in the *Nights* with 'The Ancient Mariner' in 'On Wit and Humour', *Lectures on the English Comic Writers* (1819). See *The Collected Works of William Hazlitt*, ed. A. R. Waller and Arnold Glover (Dent, 1903) VII, 23–4, and VIII, 12–4.

47. This nexus of conditions apparently favouring a writer's use of the *Nights* (which I had noted independently) proves to be almost identical with that 'paradigm' of 'the themes of the self' to which belong 'the worlds of childhood, drugs, schizophrenia and mysticism' explored by, for example, Balzac (so influenced by the *Nights*). See Tzvetan Todorov, *The Fantastic: A Structural Approach to a Literary Genre*, tr. R. Howard (Cleveland, Ohio: Case Western Reserve University Press; and Ithaca, NY: Cornell University Press, 1973, 1975) pp. 146–7.

48. While there was the precedent of Maria Edgeworth's *Belinda* (J. Johnson, 1801), which makes telling use of the Persian Queen's unhappy marriage and the tantalisingly interrupted stories she tells the young Dinarzade just before dawn (I, ch. 3 and 4), it is Scott's example which seems to have influenced the manner whereby the ironic books-within-a-book enclosures framing *Persuasion* (1818) are signalled by Anne's satirical concession that the young 'Mr Elliot's character, like the Sultaness Scheherazade's head, must live another

day' (ch. 23). See Austen's letter of 28 Sep 1814 (on *Waverley*) and 1 Apr 1816, in *Letters*, ed. R. W. Chapman (Oxford University Press, 1952) pp. 404, 452–3. Note too that the origins of Mary Shelley's masterpiece, implied by the Chinese-box construction of *Frankenstein* (1818), are hinted in the reference to Sindbad's burial alive on the Fourth Voyage (cf. ch. 4).

49. *The Letters of John Keats: A Selection*, ed. R. Gittings (Oxford University Press, 1970; repr. 1985) p. 185 (to George and Georgina Keats, 16 Dec 1818–4 Jan 1819).

50. *The Poems of John Keats*, ed. Miriam Allott (Longmans, 1970) pp. 614, 631, 633, 635, 639, 642, 660, 711; other references to the *Nights* are noted at pp. 117, 137, 172–3, 260, 373, 463.

51. 'De Juventute', repr. from the *Cornhill Magazine*, 1863, in *Roundabout Papers* (Smith, Elder, 1863) p. 123.

52. *Dublin Review*, VIII, 118. *Redgauntlet* acts like 'some Arabian charm' at least as late as Mark Rutherford's *The Revolution in Tanner's Lane* (Trübner, 1887) ch. 19.

53. See Michael Slater, *infra*, ch. 5.

54. 'A Christmas Tree', the Christmas 1850 number of *Household Words* (21 Dec); my text here is from Charles Dickens, *Selected Short Fiction*, ed. Deborah Thomas (Harmondsworth: Penguin, 1976) pp. 134, 415.

55. *The Pilgrim Edition of Letters of Charles Dickens*, ed. M. House, G. Storey, *et al.*, I (Oxford: Clarendon Press, 1965) pp. 490–1.

56. This frontispiece is perhaps a parody of Harvey's illustrations that signpost the reader through the labyrinth of Lane's translation and notes. The spine of each of the three volumes of Lane is decorated with a design based on Islamic armour; the title and half-title pages and section openings are likewise decorated with frames or panels that can incorporate both Arabesque ornament and vignette genre scenes. On the expressive use that Dickens makes of the illustrations to his novels, see Joan Stevens, '"Woodcuts Dropped into the Text": The Illustrations in *The Old Curiosity Shop* and *Barnaby Rudge*', *Studies in Bibliography*, xx (1967) 113–33; 'among the narrative purposes for which Dickens increasingly came to organise his inserts, first perhaps is that of helping the reader to keep his hold on the story as it jerked along in its weekly sections' (pp. 116–17).

57. *Master Humphrey's Clock*, New Oxford Illustrated Dickens (Oxford University Press, 1958; repr. 1963) p. 19.

58. Angus Easson (ed.), *The Old Curiosity Shop* (Harmondsworth: Penguin, last repr. 1978) p. 684, n. 6.

59. On the way in which the Arabesque allusions in Dickens' novels interact with the other references, literary as well as popular, see Harry Stone, *Dickens and The Invisible World* (Macmillan, 1979–80).

60. The first critic to glimpse this deeply ironic allusion to 'the tale of the three sisters who envied their sister' seems to have been Margaret C. Annan in her outstanding PhD thesis 'The Arabian Nights in Victorian Literature' (Northwestern University, Evanston, Ill., 1945) p. 203. In his *Hard Times: Critical Commentary and Notes* (University of London Press, 1973) pp. 68–9, while more conscious of the New Testament

echoes, Angus Easson senses that in the world of *Hard Times* the power of 'the golden water' is limited.

61. See *Durham University Journal*, LXX, no. 2 (June 1978) 250–1, where I touched on this aspect in my review of Hilda Marsden and Ian Jack's edition of *Wuthering Heights* (Oxford University Press, 1976) – my text here. See also E. J. Hobsbawn, *Industry and Empire* (Harmondsworth: Penguin, 1970) esp. ch. 7 ('Britain in the World Economy'); Martin Green, *Dreams of Adventure, Deeds of Empire* (Routledge and Kegan Paul, 1980) pp. 8–14, 112–21; E. Williams, *From Columbus to Castro* (André Deutsch, 1970) ch. 10.

62. Winifred Gérin, *Branwell Brontë* (Hutchinson, 1962) pp. 7, 31.

63. There is a similar relationship between 'The Fisherman and the Jinni' and its continuation with the inset tale of the Young King of the Black Islands, the latter containing a lover who is a resentful racial outcast, and a cuckold who is petrified from the waist down (Lane, *Nights*, I, ch. 2).

64. Nevertheless, with tendencies towards centripetal form, and what might be seen as a proto-psychology of characterisation ('The Porter and the Ladies of Baghdad', for instance, displays a memorably coherent and thoughtful mixture of realism and fantasy), the *Nights* fluctuates between the folktale and the novel genres and therefore invites the sort of conflation of its analogous tales and their Western cognates that was particularly common in the practice of nineteenth-century novelists.

65. See Randolph Stow, letter on *Edwin Drood*, TLS, 25 Nov 1983, p. 1321. *The Hasty Papers* (1960) includes a facsimile of *The Hasheesh Eater*. Alethea Hayter is alert to a number of the connections between the *Nights* and narcotics; see *Opium and the Romantic Imagination* (Faber, 1971) pp. 128, 207, 247. See also *supra*, Preface, p. xiv, xxi–ii, also ch. 6.

66. Ann Monsarrat, *The Uneasy Victorian: Thackeray the Man* (Cassell, 1980) p. 215.

67. For the discovery of just how 'The Sleeper Awakened' haunts the deeper recesses of Le Fanu's masterpiece I am indebted to Deirdre Toomey.

68. *The Life and Letters of Charles Darwin*, ed. Francis Darwin (John Murray, 1887) I, 241 (letter to F. Watkins, 18 Aug 1832). See also Gillian Beer, *Darwin's Plots* (Routledge and Kegan Paul, 1983) pp. 10, 263 n. 17. Max Miller, *Chips from a German Workshop* (Longmans, 1868) I, 336.

69. For his review of *The Life of Lord Clive* (Jan 1840), see *The Works of Lord Macaulay* (Longmans, 1873) VI, esp. p. 431. For other examples of Arabesque influence, see *The Letters of William Morris*, ed. Philip Henderson (Longmans, 1950) pp. 244–7 (letter to the Editor of the *Pall Mall Gazette*, 2 Feb 1886); John Henry Newman, *Apologia Pro Vita Sua* (1864) ch. 1; Piers Brendon, *Hawker of Morwenstow* (Jonathan Cape, 1975) pp. 38–9; Matthew Arnold, *God and the Bible* (1875), in the *Complete Prose Works*, ed. R. H. Super (Ann Arbor: University of Michigan, 1970) VII, 288–9; John Stuart Mill, *Autobiography* (1873), ed. Jack Stillinger (Oxford: Clarendon Press, 1977) pp. 6–8; T. H. Huxley, *Evolution and Ethics, Collected Essays*, IX (Macmillan, 1894) p. 293.

70. *The Library Edition of the Works of John Ruskin*, ed. E. T. Cook and Alexander Wedderburn (George Allen, 1903–8) IV, 224, 251; XXVII, 736; XXXIV, 260. Trollope's waggish imposture is noted by Donald D. Stone in *The Romantic Impulse in Victorian Fiction* (Cambridge, Mass.: Harvard University Press, 1980) p. 285. See also *infra*, ch. 6.

71. Elizabeth Barrett, however, alludes to the Arabian stories in her correspondence with Robert Browning, *The Letters of Robert Browning and Elizabeth Barrett Barrett, 1845–1846* (Smith, Elder, 1899) I, 306; II, 103, 215, 244. Uniquely, there is a reference to Aladdin in Browning's *Red Cotton Nightcap Country* (Smith, Elder, 1873) II.811.

72. John Killham, *Tennyson and the Princess: Reflection of an Age* (Athlone Press, 1958) ch. 10, esp. pp. 209, 210, 222. See also ch. 9 for his comments on 'Recollections of the Arabian Nights' and feminism.

73. Walter Scott, *The Monastery*, I, lxxvi; William Howitt, *Visits to Remarkable Places*, pp. 86–7. On the historical context of the above two works, see Klingender, *Art and the Industrial Revolution*, ch. 6, esp. pp. 110–13. Disraeli, *Coningsby*, bk IV, ch. 2. Charlotte Brontë's letter of 2 June 1851 is cited in Mrs Gaskell's *Life* (1857).

74. 'What do you know of the thousand and one causes of the unknown and invisible world which is as close as the air you breathe?' – Leigh Hunt, *London and Westminster Review*, XXXIII (1839–40) 108.

75. E. P. Thompson, *William Morris* (Lawrence and Wishart, 1955) p. 81.

76. De La Mare saw Dodgson as a character out of the *Nights*: 'Lewis Carroll', *The Eighteen Eighties* (Cambridge: Cambridge University Press, 1930) p. 236. William A. Madden also has noted how the Chinese-box structure of the *Alice* books resembles the Arabian cycle: 'Framing the *Alices*', *PMLA*, CI (May 1986) 362–73, esp. p. 372. Borges sees the *Nights'* influence too in the multi-levelled, branching dream structure of *Sylvie and Bruno: Seven Nights* (Faber, 1986) p. 53. As *Punch*'s chief political cartoonist during the period, Tenniel satirised Disraeli's unpopular bill by which Victoria was named Empress of India, caricaturing the Prime Minister as a pantomime version of the wicked magician bartering 'New Crowns for Old Ones' (*Punch*, Apr 1876); see Plate 10. According to Harvey Granville Barker the *Nights* lend themselves to burlesque: see *The Eighteen Sixties*, ed. John Drinkwater (Cambridge: Cambridge University Press, 1932) p. 135.

77. Paul Hogarth, *Arthur Boyd Houghton* (Victoria and Albert Museum, 1975) p. 10. See also Terry Reece Hackford on the illustration of the *Nights*: 'Fantastic Visions', in *The Aesthetics of Fantasy*, ed. R. C. Schlobin (Brighton: Harvester, 1982) pp. 143–75.

78. 'The People of the Arabian Nights', *National Review*, IX (July 1859) 44–71; it was reprinted in Littell's *Living Age*, LXII (1859) – as Muhsin Jassim Ali notes in his valuable study of nineteenth-century English criticism of the *Nights*, *Scheherazade in England* (Washington, DC: Three Continents Press, 1981) p. 101.

79. The Arabesque elements in James's early work are scrutinised by Peter Buitenhuis in *The Grasping Imagination: The American Writings of Henry James* (Toronto: University of Toronto, 1970); and R. E. Long *The Great Succession* (Pittsburgh: University of Pittsburgh Press, 1979). James's

use of Galland is noted by Adeline R. Tintner in her inter-disciplinary study 'Henry James, Orientalist', *Modern Language Studies*, XIII, no. 4 (Fall 1983) 121–52; however, she takes too charitable a view of Harun al-Rashid, and somewhat neglects *What Maisie knew*.

80. James had written about *The Woman in White* in a review of Mrs Braddon's *Aurora Floyd* in *The Nation*, 9 Nov 1865; repr. in *Notes and Reviews*, ed. Pierre de Chaignon La Rose (Cambridge, Mass.: Dunster House, 1921).

81. Gabriel Pearson recognises the sources of James's image: it 'smacks of childhood fantasy, and seems blended out of *The Arabian Nights* and *Alice in Wonderland* – 'The Novel to End All Novels', *The Air of Reality: New Essays on Henry James*, ed. John Goode (Methuen, 1972) pp. 342–3. See also Ruth Bernard Yeazell, *Language and Knowledge in the Late Novels of Henry James* (Chicago: University of Chicago Press, 1976) pp. 13, 46–8, 62–3, 119. One of George Eliot's heroes too is seen as Camaralzaman: *Daniel Deronda* (1876) ch. 16 (Penguin edn, p. 224). Her *oeuvre*, so admired by James, is another area of Arabesque influence that requires further investigation.

82. Arnold, 'A Persian Passion Play' (1871), in *The Complete Prose Works*, VII, 22.

83. Rudyard Kipling, *Something of Myself* (Macmillan, 1937) p. 82.

84. See Michael Shepherd, *Sherlock Holmes and the Case of Dr Freud* (Tavistock, 1985); also Sigmund Freud, 'Original Record of the Case', *Notes upon a Case of Obsessional Neurosis* ['The Rat Man'] (1909), 8 Nov 1907: 'A dream had to do with joking terms of abuse used by his friend V. – "son of a whore", "son of a one-eyed monkey" (*Arabian Nights*)' – *Standard Edition of the Complete Psychological Works*, general ed. James Strachey (Hogarth Press, 1955) x, 151–318, esp. p. 277. Freud here alludes to the nocturnal stories told in 'The Porter and the Ladies of Baghdad', particularly the Second Calender's tale of how he was transformed into an ape; but all three calenders have lost an eye through sexual transgression. The 'Rat Man' case was discussed by the Vienna Psychoanalytic Society in 1907, and the First International Psychoanalytical Congress, Salzburg, 1908; a brief summary was published by Otto Rank, 1910. By 1914 Freud had grown interested in Arab and other oriental interpretations of dreams (*Standard Edition*, x, 4n., 88n.). Besides several nineteenth-century German versions from the Arabic, there were translations from the English versions: first the Dalziel (Dresden, 1881), then the Burton (Leipzig, 1907–8). Interest in the *Nights* was certainly strong in Freud's Vienna. Following Goethe and Rückert's path into the Arabian labyrinth (see K. Mommsen, *Goethe und 1001 Nächte* [Berlin, Deutsche Akademie der Wissenschaften zu Berlin Veröffentlichungen des Instituts für deutsche Sprache und Literatur, 1960]), between 1892 and 1925 more than a score of Hugo von Hofmannsthal's works (a dozen by 1907) are influenced by the *Nights* (see Wolfgang Köhler, *Hugo von Hofmannsthal und 1001 Nächte* [Frankfurt-am-Main: Peter Lang, 1972] pp. 54–7). Both Freud and Hofmannsthal were avid readers of English as well as, in varying degrees, being aware of each other's work: see Michael

Hamburger, *Hofmannsthal* (Princeton, NJ: Princeton University Press, 1972) pp. 28, 86, and especially 'Hofmannsthal's Debt to the English-Speaking World' (pp. 133–55); also Freud, 'Contribution to a Questionnaire on Reading' (1907), in *Standard Editions*, ix, 245–7 (the collection incorporating Freud's 'Contribution' was introduced by Hofmannsthal). Freud, of course, helped Bruno Bettelheim shed further light on the psychological implications of the *Nights* in *The Uses of Enchantment* (Thames and Hudson, 1976); however there 'The Fisherman and the Jinni' is imperfectly recalled (p. 80n.). An indication of Freud's impact on Bloomsbury is given in Leonard Woolf's *Autobiography*, ii (Oxford University Press, 1980) esp. p. 307.

85. Among the other illustrators of *Ancient Spanish Ballads* are Harvey and David Roberts.

86. John Betjeman's memories as cited in Gordon N. Ray, *The Illustrator and the Book in England from 1790 to 1914* (Oxford University Press and Pierpont Morgan Library, 1976) p. 207.

87. Sotheby's, *Children's Book, Juvenilia and Related Drawings* (sale catalogue, 19 June 1986) item 719, p. 146, and colour plate xii.

88. While mirroring the actualities of colonial entertainments, the overarching 'Slaves of the Lamp' symbolism generated by the school pantomime in *Stalky and Co.* alerts the reader to the fact that the skills gained through breaking bounds can be turned later to the defence of the North-West Frontier.

89. See Laurence Housman, *The Unexpected Years* (Jonathan Cape, 1937) pp. 272–3.

90. Housman's brilliant polemic seems to be exaggerated by Dena Justin in 'From Mother Goddess to Dishwasher', *Natural History*, lxxxii (1973) 44, as cited in Diana Cooper-Clark, *Interviews with Contemporary Novelists* (Macmillan, 1986) pp. 20, 26 n. 16: 'so subtly have our nerve ends been twisted against our own reason that we accept the resolution of the *Arabian Nights* as a routine happy ending'. However, this is to mistake the genre. The *Nights* amounts to a mirror for husbands; anticipating Bettelheim's interpretation of the frame tale (*The Uses of Enchantment*, pp. 86–90), Marie Lahy-Hollebecque demonstrates in her profound reading that the *Nights* records the cure of a sick mind through the therapy of teaching-stories: see her *Le Féminisme de Shéhérazade* (Paris: Editions Radot, 1927), esp. chs 4 ('Les procédés éducatifs . . .'), 6 ('. . . un manuel d'instruction royale'), 7 (. . . une apologétique de la femme'), 8 ('un art d'aimer') and 11 ('Les résultats de l'initiation de l'homme par la femme' - 'Shahriar [must become] le premier féministe en Islam' [p. 247]). Housman himself became a politically committed activist whose pamphleteering extended beyond a sustained advocacy of Women's suffrage. His *Articles of Faith in the Freedom of Women* (A. C. Fifield, 1910) notes that a woman, the Ranee of Jhanzee, was the only leader of real military talent produced by the Indian mutineers.

91. This Hodder and Stoughton publication was again as witty a pastiche as it was handsome, the dissemination of subversive ideas under the

cover of a *de luxe* gift-book being worthy of Scheherazade's own teaching-stories.

92. W. B. Yeats, *Essays and Introductions* (Macmillan, 1961) p. 221.
93. Repr. in *The Spice of Life and other essays* ed. Dorothy Collins (Beaconsfield, Bucks: Darwen Finlayson, 1964) pp. 58–60, 174.
94. John Heath-Stubbs, 'Structure and Source in Eliot's Major Poetry', *Agenda*, xxiii, nos 1–2 (Spring–Summer 1985, T. S. Eliot special issue) 24, 26–7.
95. Walter Benjamin, 'What is Epic Theatre?' (1939), in *Understanding Brecht*, tr. Anna Bostock (New Left Books, 1973) p. 19. 'He do the Police in different voices', the cancelled subtitle for Eliot's draft, taken from *Our Mutual Friend*, is an explicit instance of Eliot's use of a Victorian novel influenced by the narrative methods of the *Nights*. Less obvious but perhaps more significant is the reference in Eliot's lines 'bats with baby faces' that 'crawled head downward down a blackened wall' (379–81; see also *The Waste Land: A Facsimile and Transcript of The Original Drafts*, ed. Valerie Eliot [Faber, 1971, repr. 1972] pp. 75, 113, 145), since in *Dracula* (1897), when Jonathan Harker observes that 'this diary seems horribly like the beginning of the "Arabian Nights" for everything has to break off at cockcrow' (ch. 3), Bram Stoker points to a feature of the *Nights* which Burton, unlike the Grub Street translator and Lane, did not neglect. In his 'Mistah Kurtz: He Dead', in *T. S. Eliot: The Man and his Work*, ed. Allen Tate (Chatto and Windus, 1967) p. 356, H. S. Davies sensed the presence of *Dracula* about *The Waste Land*.
96. Evidently the dropping of the *Heart of Darkness* quotation from *The Waste Land* was at Pound's wish, for the epigraph to *The Hollow Men* (again taken from *Heart of Darkness*) seems to point to Eliot's interest in the seminal use that there Conrad makes of both the Arabian and Buddhist fables: see *The Waste Land: A Facsimile*, p. 125, and my 'Buddhist Teaching Stories and their influence on Conrad, Wells and Kipling: The Reception of the Jataka and Allied Genres in Victorian Culture', *Conradian*, xi, no. 1 (May 1986) 24–34 and also my 'Buddhist Typologies in the Marlow Cycle and in *Victory* and Conrad's Contribution to the Modernism of Jacob Epstein, Wyndham Lewis and T. S. Eliot', in *Conradian*, xiii (1988). As noted by Neville Braybrooke in 'T. S. Eliot in the South Seas', in *Eliot: The Man and his Work*, ed. Tate, pp. 3, 82–8, 'A Tale of a Whale' (written when Eliot was sixteen) echoes Sindbad's First Voyage. This Arabesque reminiscence has been remarked also by P. S. Sri in *T. S. Eliot, Vedanta, and Buddhism* (Vancouver: University of Vancouver Press, 1985) p. 8. On Eliot's reading the *Jatakas*, see Peter Ackroyd, *T. S. Eliot* (Sphere, 1985) p. 47; the poet himself confessed to being as deeply moved by 'some of the early Buddhist scriptures' as by 'parts of the Old Testament' – 'The Use of Poetry and the Use of Criticism' (1933), in *Selected Prose*, ed. F. Kermode (Faber, 1975) p. 82. See also Stephen Spender, *Eliot* (Fontana, 1975) pp. 26–7. The fusion of the *Jatakas* and the *Nights* discernible in the 'Fire Sermon' section of *The Waste Land* is most

obvious in Leonard Woolf's *Stories of the East* (Hogarth Press, 1921) esp. p. 12.

97. Michael R. Booth, *Victorian Spectacular Theatre 1850–1910* (Routledge and Kegan Paul, 1981) pp. 86–9, 90, 161–71, esp. p. 87.

98. See also Constantine's acknowledgement of Europe's debt to these educative tales in Rebecca West, *Black Lamb and Grey Falcon* (Macmillan, 1941) I, 394, and on the *Nights'* place in Arab society, Abdelwahab Bouhdiba's illuminating *Sexuality in Islam*, P. A. Sheridan (Routledge and Kegan Paul, 1985) esp. pp. 35, 131, 146, 194, 224–5. See also the 'Anna Victrix' chapter of D. H. Lawrence's *The Rainbow* (1915), and *The Letters of E. M. Forster*, ed. Mary Lago and P. N. Furbank (Collins, 1983) I, 180. George Moore claims (1911) that he encountered his 'primal scene' in the spectacle of the incestuous lovers who are overtaken by divine retribution in the tale of the First Calender. *Freeman's Journal* attacked Moore's proposed translation of the *Nights* into Gaelic: 'he wishes an indecent book to be put in the hands of every Irish peasant' – *Hail and Farwell*, ed. R. Cave (Gerrards Cross, Bucks: Colin Smythe, 1985) pp. 337, 417–18.

99. See J. L. Styan, *Max Reinhardt* (Cambridge: Cambridge University Press, 1982) ch. 3 and p. 135; A. L. Haskell, *Ballet Russe* (Weidenfeld and Nicolson, 1968) pp. 51, 63–4. The most celebrated fashion show of Paul Poiret (1911) was on the theme of the '1002nd Night', and in 1923 he created a perfume named 'Aladin'; see *Le Petit journal de la Musée de la Mode et du Costume* (Paris), no. 3 (5 July 1986) 2, 4. On the degree to which 'The Russian Ballet became for a time the curious centre for intellectual as well as fashionable London', see Leonard Woolf, *An Autobiography*, II, 22, 30, 85; and on the interest of Vita Sackville-West and her family in Perso-Arabesque fashion, see Victoria Glendinning, *Vita* (Weidenfeld and Nicolson, 1983) pp. 72, 110, 117, 295. See also *The Letters of Virginia Woolf*, ed. N. Nicolson et al. (Hogarth Press, 1977) III, 4 and n. 3; and C. Spencer, *Leon Bakst* (Academy, 1978) pp. 183–4.

100. See Dawn Redwood, *Flecker and Delius: The Making of 'Hassan'* (Thames Publishing, 1978) pp. 27–8, 62–6, 87, 90, 94. Flecker's widow had failed to secure the co-operation of Ravel.

101. In turn Fairbanks's film was remade by Berger and Powell (1940). On Robison's achievement, see Graham Greene's film review, *Spectator*, 1 May 1936) repr. in *The Pleasure Dome* (Secker and Warburg, 1972) p. 72. On Fairbanks's debt to Lang, see Paul M. Jensen, *The Cinema of Fritz Lang* (New York: Barthes; London: Zwemmer, 1969) ch. 2, esp. p. 24). On the German cinema of the 1920s, see Siegfried Kracauer, *From Caligari to Hitler* (Denis Dobson, 1947) esp. p. 91, and Lotte H. Eisner, *The Haunted Screen* (Secker and Warburg, repr. 1973) esp. p. 90n.

102. The comparison with 'the Arabian Nights', which C. Day Lewis made on the Third Programme, is quoted among the reactions to *The Dead Man's Knock* on the back of the dustjacket of Dickson Carr's *Scandal at High Chimneys* (Hamish Hamilton, 1959).

103. There is a particular need for further investigation of Kipling's

synthesis of the *Nights* with other oriental genres; a preliminary survey forms part of my 'Buddhist Teaching Stories', *Conradian*, XI, no. 1.

104. Mardrus's original (1899–1904) is a very free translation from the Arabic; it eschews the anthropological emphases of Burton, seeking to gain a hearing for the *Nights* as literature, see Gerhardt, 'The Boulevard Literature of the Paris 1900s', *The Art of Story-Telling*, p. 103. Borges thinks better of it in 'The Translators of the *1001 Nights*', *A Reader*, ed. E. R. Monegal and A. Reid (New York: Dutton, 1981) p. 84.

105. Some indication of Proust's debt to the *Nights* is given in P. A. Spalding, *A Reader's Handbook to Proust* (Chatto and Windus, 1952) p. 138; Terence Kilmartin, *A Guide to Proust* (Harmondsworth: Penguin, 1985) p. 152; and David Ellison, *The Reading of Proust* (Oxford: Basil Blackwell, 1984) pp. 50, 161, 195 n. 26. More generally, see G. Piroue, 'La France et les 1001 Nuits', *La Table ronde*, July–Aug 1958, pp. 104–12; M.-L. Dufresnoi, *L'Orient romantique en France, 1704–1889* (Montreal, 1949); H. Aboul-Hussein and C. Pellat, *Cheherazade* (Alger: SNED, 1976); Jennifer Waelti-Walters, *Michel Butor* (Victoria, BC: Sono Nis Press, 1977), and Pierre Schneider, *Plaisir extrême* (Paris: Editions du Seuil, 1987).

106. In 'The Parable of the Caliph's Design', repr. in *Wyndham Lewis on Art: Collected Writings, 1913–1956*, ed. Walter Michel and C. J. Fox (Thames and Hudson, 1969) pp. 129–83, Lewis conflates such phenomena as the 'mushrooming palace of Aladdin and the building of the City of Many Columned Iram' – Burton, *Nights*, Illustrated Library Edition, ed. Leonard C. Smithers (H. S. Nichols, 1897) III, 236–42; and Lane, *Nights*, II, note to chap. 11, pp. 343–6. See also *The Letters of Ezra Pound and Wyndham Lewis*, ed. Timothy Materer (Faber, 1985) p. 136.

107. Rebecca West's first book, *Henry James* (1915), considers at least two of the very novels where he alludes to Camaralzaman; she also compares Ford Madox Ford to James in her review of *The Good Soldier*: *Daily News*, 2 Apr 1915, p. 6, repr. in *Ford Madox Ford: The Critical Heritage*, ed. Frank MacShane (Routledge and Kegan Paul, 1972) p. 45. Similarly, Ford's novel (Bodley Head, 1915), among other Arabesque allusions, conflates the Camaralzaman and Aladdin tropes (Penguin edn, p. 201).

108. Arnold Bennett, *Evening Standard*, 8 Nov 1928, p. 7, repr. in *Virginia Woolf: The Critical Heritage*, ed. Robin Majumdar and Allen McLaurin (Routledge and Kegan Paul, 1975) p. 233. The sex-change in *Orlando*, ch. 3, takes place in Constantinople at the end of the seventeenth century, much the same time and place as those of Antoine Galland's discovery of *Les Mille et une nuits*. For an analogous case of sexual transformation in the *Nights*, see the tale of the enchanted spring (Lane, *Nights*, III, 162; Burton, Illustrated Library Edition, V, 58), also W. A. Clouston, *Popular Tales and Fictions* (Blackwood, 1887) I, 446–7.

109. Virginia Woolf noted Logan Pearsall Smith's 'delightful adventures – life is like the Arabian Nights' – *Diary*, ed. A. O. Bell, I (Har-

mondsworth: Penguin, 1983) 274 (18 May 1919). As indicated *supra*, n. 96, Leonard Woolf alludes to the *Nights* in 'Tale Told by Moonlight' (*Stories of the East*). The only Mardrus and Mathers in the Woolfs' Victoria Square library was the Casanova Society publication of *The Queen of Sheba* (1923), but its dustjacket repeatedly links this work with the *Nights*.

110. While modern Baghdad (28 Feb 1926) is not as she and Virginia 'saw it in Hassan', the Shah's treasury, for instance, is another matter: 'I have been in Aladdin's Cave. . . . I can't write about it now. It was simply the Arabian Nights, with decor by the Sitwells. Pure fantasy. Oh *why* weren't you there?' *The Letters of Vita Sackville-West to Virginia Woolf*, ed. Louise DeSalvo and Mitchell A. Leaska (Papermac, 1985) pp. 119, 132–3 (Teheran, 8 Apr 1926). See also Vita's account of Kum in *Passenger to Teheran*, p. 134, and Virginia Woolf's almost contemporaneous association of her friend with much the same costume that she herself had assumed in the Dreadnought hoax: *Letters*, III, 238 (3 Feb 1926).

111. The edition I cite is Walter De La Mare, *Complete Poems* (Faber, 1969) pp. 138, 347–8, 368, 820–1, 840.

112. See the entry for 25 Sep 1927 in Virginia Woolf, *Diary*, ed. A. O. Bell *et al.* vol. III (Harmondsworth: Penguin, 1982) 159 and n. 15; and Graham Greene, *A Sort of Life* (Harmondsworth: Penguin, 1972) p. 146. Cf Joyce's 'alladim lamps' in *Finnegans Wake*. For Kathleen Raine, however, the Aladdin lamp seems to have set the scene for a mystical illumination – not so far removed from her earlier association of the *Nights* with a civilised manner of living (see *Farewell Happy Fields* [Hamish Hamilton, 1973] p. 87, and *The Land Unknown* [Hamish Hamilton, 1975] pp. 118–19; cf. *The Lion's Mouth* [1977] p. i).

113. My text here is from the revised edition, 1952.

114. In *English Prose Style*, ch. 9, only six pages separate the two references, similarly, in Read's half-acknowledged source for the English folktale, Thomas Keightley's *The Fairy Mythology* (rev. Bohn's Antiquarian Library, 1850), 'The Green Children' and a comparable Perso-Arabian romance, 'The Peri Wife', are given prominence. See also 'Hasan of El Basrah' (Lane, *Nights*, III, 384; Burton, Illustrated Library Edition, VI, 166; Mardrus-Mathers, *Nights*, III, 213). In *Wordsworth* (Faber and Faber, repr. 1978) pp. 129–31, Read explores MS Y of *The Prelude* (lines 84–100, also 155–8), with its 'stories of magic and traveller's tales' that in fact are drawn from the *Nights* (*The Prelude*, Norton edn, pp. 502–3). For the coupling with Kafka, see *The Philosophy of Modern Art* (Faber paperback, last repr. 1985) p. 124. See also Robert Barker, 'Sources for Herbert Read's *The Green Child* I and II', *Notes and Queries*, CCXXII (Oct 1977) 455–7; CCXXV (Dec 1980) 531–3.

115. Note, for example, references to 'coral', 'sea weed', etc.: Read, *The Green Child* (Harmondsworth: Penguin, 1969, repr. 1979) pp. 125, 127–8, 130, 143, 154.

116. My text here is from Auden's *Collected Shorter Poems 1930–44* (Faber, 5th imp. 1952) p. 121. Robert Medley recollects how he and Auden, as Platonic schoolfriends, were taken to a matinee of *Aladdin* and an

unsurprising revelation of adult hypocrisy: *Drawn from the Life* (Faber, 1983) p. 45.

117. Roger Lancelyn Green and Walter Hooper, *C. S. Lewis: A Biography* (Collins, 1974) p. 172.

118. The Pan edition (1955) is an abridgement. The murderous device of the poisoned page is used in Umberto Eco's arabesque *Name of the Rose* (1983).

119. C. S. Lewis, *Of Other Worlds* (Geoffrey Bles, 1966) p. 39, first published in the *Church Times*, 'Children's Book Supplement', 28 Nov 1958. This essay perhaps expresses some exasperation with the plethora of new translations and reissues of the *Nights* in the 1950s and 1960s; see *infra*, p. 55.

120. In Jones's words, 'seeming to afford a link of sorts between the two widely separated books' (*In Parenthesis*, 1937, and *The Anathemata*, 1952), 'The Book of Balaam's Ass' was apparently begun in 1939: see the letters to Harman Grisewood, and the Edes, 17 Jan and 11 Apr 1939, in *Dai Greatcoat: A Self-Portrait of David Jones in his Letters*, ed. René Hague (Faber, 1980) pp. 89–92. A fragment of the 'Book' was published in *The Sleeping Lord* (Faber, 1974) pp. 97–111; a fuller text appeared as section IV of *The Roman Quarry* ed. H. Grisewood and R. Hague (Agenda Editions, 1981) pp. 186–211 (the *Nights* allusions are at pp. 98–9 and 191–2, respectively).

121. William Empson, *Collected Poems* (Chatto and Windus, 1962) p. 49. P. and A. Gardner mistake Camaralzaman for Prince Hussein in *The God Approached* (Chatto and Windus, 1978) pp. 166–7.

122. 'John Carruthers' was the pseudonym of John Young Thomson Greig. His pamphlet belongs to the well-received series 'Today and Tomorrow' published by Kegan Paul, Trench, Trubner, in association with Dutton, New York, 1927.

123. A back-of-the-book list advertising the 'Today and Tomorrow' series recalls Lahy-Hollebecque's interpretation: '*Les Mille et Une Nuits* sont une "somme" des connaissances du temps' (*Les Féminisme de Schéhérazade*, ch. 5). Scheherazade herself 'had studied philosophy and the sciences, arts and accomplishments' (Burton, Illustrated Library Edition, I, 13). On the motif of the learned slave girl, see Gerhardt, *The Art of Story-Telling* pp. 342–6; and Metlitzki, *The Matter of Araby*, pp. 156–9. A glimpse of the history of Muslim woman at the Abbasid court is provided by Nabia Abbott's *Two Queens of Baghdad* (Chicago: University of Chicago Press, 1946). A more feminist account of the role of women in Arab society and literature is given in Nawal El Saadawi, *The Hidden Face of Eve* (Zed Press, 1980) – on the *Nights*, see esp. pp. 161–7; and Rana Kabbani takes a highly critical view of Scheherazade in *Europe's Myths of Orient* (Macmillan, 1986). Yet Scheherazade introduced the infant De Quincey to a kind of 'Sortes Biblicae'. See *infra*, n. 138.

124. See for instance my essays on Michael Moorcock, in *Twentieth-Century Science Fiction Writers*, ed. Curtis C. Smith (Macmillan, 1981; rev edn 1986) pp. 521–2; and on Brian Aldiss: 'The Helliconia Trilogy', *Foundation: The Review of Science Fiction*, no. 35 (Winter 1985–6) 70–3.

125. *The Other Man: Conversations with Graham Greene*, ed. Marie-Françoise Allain, tr. G. Waldman (Bodley Head, 1981) p. 147.
126. Graham Greene, *Ways of Escape* (1980; Harmondsworth: Penguin, 1986) p. 33.
127. Besides appearing in the current British and American editions of the book, the Preface to *The Golden Notebook* is collected in *A Small Personal Voice*, ed. Paul Schlueter (Vintage Books, 1975) pp. 23–4.
128. It would seem that Beckett, Joyce's secretary and student of Proust, was not unaffected by the fifties renewal of interest in the *Nights*. At any rate, the discovery, made by John Fletcher in his *The Novels of Samuel Beckett* (Chatto and Windus, 1972) p. 184, that the 'jar-man' of *The Unnamable* (1949, 1953) had his origins in an advertising-sign, a menu-holder in the shape of one of the Forty Thieves which stood outside a Parisian eating-house called the 'Ali-Baba', draws one to speculate about the influence of the *Nights* (however oblique) on the hesitant chorus of indistinct presences haunting Beckett's work, presences who are compelled falteringly to rehearse their recursive stories in competition with time. Somewhat different is the use of the *Nights* in Anthony Powell's novel series *A Dance to the Music of Time* (1951–75).
129. The *Nights* are also associated with the powers of darkness in *Monstre Gai* (Methuen, 1955) ch. 3, section vii, and ch. 7, section xiv.
130. Greene, *Ways of Escape*, p. 33, where *In Parenthesis* shares this accolade with Read's *The Green Child*. Moreover, as the *Collected Essays* (1969) shows, Greene has studied, more or less extensively, a number of British writers who have been influenced by the *Nights*. Latin American instances of the Arabesque are most obvious in *Ficciones* by Borges (Weidenfeld and Nicolson, 1962) – to which Greene alludes – but it is also unlikely that he has missed either Borges's sublime revaluation of Scheherazade's passion in terms of Christ's in 'Another Poem of Gifts', *Selected Poems* (Allen Lane, 1972) pp. 218–23, or the role that the *Nights* plays in *One Hundred Years of Solitude* (Jonathan Cape, 1970), the work of his friend Gabriel García Marquéz. Among influential North American writers indebted to the *Nights* are Washington Irving ('*Knickerbocker's*' . . . New York, 1812), Herman Melville (*Moby Dick*, 1851); Mark Twain (*Huckleberry Finn*, 1884), John Barth ('Dunyazadiad', in *Chimera*, 1972), Philip Stevick ('Scheherazade Runs out of Plots, Goes on Talking; the King, Puzzled, Listens: An Essay on New Fiction', *Triquarterly*, 1973), Robertson Davies (*The Deptford Trilogy*, 1975), Joanna Russ (*The Two of Them*, 1978), and Ian Dennis (*Baghdad*, 1985).
131. As there are Sufi elements in Borges – see G. de Garayalde, *Sources and Illumination* (Octagon, 1978) – so there is something Manichean about Greene: see *The Other Man*, p. 165. Manicheanism is among the roots of those Shi'ite esoteric doctrines which have links with Western Sufism, and so the *Nights* – see Henry Corbin, *Spiritual Body and Celestial Earth*, tr. N. Pearson (Princeton, NJ: Princeton University Press, 1977), a work with which Doris Lessing appears to have some acquaintance. However, her knowledge of Sufism plainly owes much

to Idries Shah; see her 'In the World, Not of It', *Encounter*, Aug 1972, pp. 61–4, repr. in *A Small Personal Voice*, pp. 129–37 (see esp. p. 134).

132. On the *Nights'* possible roots in ancient myths and rituals, see *supra*, Preface; also Heath-Stubbs, *infra*, ch. 11.

133. On Lessing's drug-induced dreams, see *A Small Personal Voice*, pp. 58–60, 66–7; on Greene's, *Ways of Escape*, pp. 131–2, 210–11, and *The Other Man*, pp. 127–8, 150. On Greene's memories of the cinema, see *Ways of Escape*, pp. 45–7, 53, and the collected film criticism *The Pleasure Dome* (Secker and Warburg, 1972).

134. See in *A Small Personal Voice* Lessing's comments on the important of black story-tellers (p. 39), her memories of her Persian birthplace (p. 45), and her review of Karen Blixen's *Out of Africa* (pp. 147–51).

135. See my 'Doris Lessing's *Lights of Canopus*: Oriental Sources of Space History', *Foundation: The Review of Science Fiction*. no. 31 (July 1984) 18–30.

136. The captions to these images amount to a veritable digest of some of the most popular of the *Nights*, thus demonstrating in a memorably extreme form the elasticity of the *Nights*.

137. Northrop Frye's observations on the encyclopaedic form, in *The Anatomy of Criticism* (Princeton, NJ: Princeton University Press, 1957), illuminate the way in which the frontispiece of Moorcock's *The Opium General* (Harrap, 1984) mocks the implications of the pseudo-Arabic calligraphy and wording of the poster used by the theatrical group Shared Experience to advertise *Recitals of Mystery, Violence and Desire*, their award-winning dramatisation of the *Nights*. Memories of Mike Alfreds' 1976 experiments with spellbinding theatre narrative have not been effaced even by Michael Hayes's admirable BBC television production of *Tales from the 1001 Nights* (Christmas 1981), though Pasolini's *Il Fiore delle mille e una notte* (1974) remains the finest film ever to be made of the *Nights*; see also *Pier Paolo Pasolini*, ed. Paul Willemen (British Film Institute, 1977) pp. 74–7, and E. Siciliano, *Pasolini* (Bloomsbury, 1987) pp. 341–2.

138. Borges, *Seven Nights*, pp. 50, 57. We are reminded of what it is that fuels 'this marvellous story-machine, the *Arabian Nights*' – Tzvetan Todorov, *The Poetics of Prose* (Oxford: Basil Blackwell, 1977) ch. 5, esp. p. 78 – by Borges's mapping of the common ground between these tales and the world of the archetypes. In his penetrating study 'The Thousand and One Nights', Borges notes De Quincey's 'wonderfully inventive memory'. For 'the idea that the world is made of correspondences', De Quincey said he was indebted to the story of how the wicked North African tracked down the young Aladdin. But 'the fact of the magician putting his ear to the ground and deciphering the footsteps of Aladdin appears in none of these texts. It is an invention of the memory or dreams of De Quincey' (*Seven Nights*, pp. 55–6). This invention seized his mind as a child, becoming, as De Quincey confessed, one of the 'involutes of human sensibility, combinations in which the materials of future thought or feeling are carried imperceptibly into the mind' (*Collected Writings*, I, 128–9), and coming also to haunt his dreams, as Alethea Hayter perceives (*Opium*

and the Romantic Imagination, pp. 128, 207, 247; see also infra, ch. 6).
Paul Jordan-Smith deplores the current neglect of an underlying
metaphysic in tales such as those of the Nights – 'Living Stories',
Parabola: 'Memory and Forgetting', xi, no. 4 (Nov 1986) 54. Cf. the
oriental anticipations of the Jungian insights into the collective
unconscious surveyed by Henry Corbin in Creative Imagination in the
Sufism of Ibn 'Arabi and Spiritual Body and Celestial Earth (both Princeton,
NJ: Princeton University Press, tr. 1966, 1977, respectively); and see
also Corbin, 'Towards a Chart of the Imaginal' and Gilbert Durand,
'Exploration of the Imaginal', repr. in Temenos, i (1981). There is a
spiritual dimension among the more robust elements in the recent
revival of oral narrative by such groups as the Company of Story
Tellers collective; see Jenny Pearson, 'Tales from the Hearth', Sunday
Times, 11 Jan 1987, p. 51.

2

Scheherazade in the Nursery

BRIAN ALDERSON

You have made me as happy as a child with The Arabian Nights
(W. M. Thackeray in a letter to Tennyson, thanking
him for a copy of *The Idylls of the King*)

2   *Image of Old Man prostrate with laughter, from
the Newnes edition (1899)*

There is a telling moment in Maria Edgeworth's story 'The India
Cabinet'.[1] In customary pursuit of a moral lesson – in this instance
the fatigue that results from a surfeit of pleasure – Miss Edgeworth
causes her delightful heroine Rosamond to remark, 'and yet, I
know that listening to the most entertaining things, for a very long

time together, does tire at last. I recollect being once tired of hearing Godfrey read the fairy Paribanon [sic] in the Arabian Tales; and yet *that*, all the time, entertained me excessively.'

The significance of that comment, if we leave aside its uncertain logic, is twofold. First it provides evidence (supplemented elsewhere in the Rosamond stories) that eighteenth-century children enjoyed reading the *Nights*. Second, and more surprisingly, it implies a broad approval of the tales from a lady who, perhaps under the influence of her Utilitarian father, had earlier condemned all fairy tales as sweetmeats which vitiate the taste and spoil the appetite.[2] Given Miss Edgeworth's natural ebullience however, and her love of story-telling in the family circle, it is not really difficult to see how she, like Rosamond, found the Arabian Tales so excessively entertaining.

Indeed, from their earliest appearance among the polite readers of Europe, the *Nights* have been acknowledged as attractive fare for children. As early as 1711 Alexander Pope is to be found recommending Galland's translation (perhaps in French, perhaps in English) to Sir William Trumbull as 'proper enough for the Nursery',[3] and there is no lack of evidence from a variety of memoirs that the tales were one of the great experiences in a child's reading at a time when 'official' children's books had few imaginative delights to offer. Coleridge's account in one of his autobiographical letters to Thomas Poole is, justly, the most famous testimony,[4] but hardly a writer of note, from Johnson to Dickens, does not hint at, or mention, somewhere or other the recollected pleasure of reading the *Nights* in childhood.

More significant than these recollections however is the extent to which Arabian tales came to be thought of as children's stories before all else. At the start of his erudite *Remarks on the Arabian Nights Entertainments* of 1797, Richard Hole comments dismissively that, 'however we may be occasionally amused by the Tales' wild and diversified incidents, they are seldom thoroughly relished but by children, or by men whose imagination is complimented at the expence [sic] of their judgement'. The Revd Edward Forster in introducing his translation of 1802 implies that he was surprised to discover beauties in a work that he had previously regarded as having been merely the delight of his 'boyish days'. And to positive examples such those one may add a kind of negative evidence. Didactic writers for children in the eighteenth century took over the trappings of the 'Persian tale' for their own moralising purposes, finding (as Hannah More did with her adaptation of chapbook formulae for what was to become the Religious Tract Society) that popular forms could provide a disguise – however thin – for conventional morality.[5]

What so much of our evidence regrettably remains silent about, however, is the actual texts of the *Nights* that the children were reading. With cavalier disregard for the needs of future historians and bibliographers, little Rosamond and young Coleridge and the Wordsworths and Thackeray and Dickens give few clues about the nature of the books that so pleased them, and one is left to reconstruct as best one may a sense of the stories and the translations that had so much effect. The dominance of Galland's version for so long makes it almost certain that this is the edition that children would have read (confirmed by such instances as Rosamond's reference to the 'Fairy Paribanon', whose name is frequently misprinted as such in Galland), but early editions of the stories – especially popular editions – are now so scarce that we cannot be sure if children always saw the standard, multi-volume printings. Almost certainly, though, they were confronted with versions – usually unillustrated – that were published for the general reader, and if this is the case then it lends further weight to the view that children were happy to read books primarily intended for adults, so long as the contents were attractive.

This is an object-lesson of relevance to our own times, when a huge industry is devoted to turning out books attuned to what are thought to be the special sensibilities of children and adolescents. For, although Galland – by enlightened modern standards – was a translator who converted his colourful original into an elegant, Europeanised prose, and although his anonymous English follower reduced this to a level which one commentator has called 'Grub Street',[6] the *Nights* that came to children through him were decidedly more free and vigorous than the early imitations and versions that were specially designed for their own use.

James Ridley's *Tales of the Genii* (1764) like Mrs Sheridan's *Nourjahad* (1767), that stemmed from the *contes des fées*, or the invented 'Eastern tales' such as Mrs Trimmer reviewed, or that were incorporated into children's miscellanies, were laboriously didactic: and even when the *Nights* themselves became the basis for a children's book they had to be given an ulterior purpose. This is plainly apparent from the book's title: *The Oriental Moralist; or, the Beauties of the Arabian Nights Entertainments. Translated from the Original and Accompanied with Suitable Reflection Adapted to Each Story*. This volume, which would seem to be the first attempt at rendering down the *Nights* for a child audience, was prepared by 'the Rev'd Mr Cooper' and published by Elizabeth Newbery round about 1791. As is now well known, Cooper was none other than that universal hack Richard Johnson, and in this particular example of his scavenging operations he has – as he put it in his day-book – 'abridged' (not 'translated') his source.[7]

Johnson's Preface gives a credible account of his reasons (other than that of jobbery) for adapting the *Nights*. He tells how he was 'induced' to read through a French edition of the book while staying at an inn, and he likens it to a luxuriant but neglected garden. 'Full of this idea, I determined to turn florist, and to traverse this wild and unweeded spot with a cautious and discriminating eye . . . to cull a pleasing nosegay for my youthful friends.' Selection, abridgement, editorial addition – all are cheerfully admitted. He has 'carefully expunged every thing that could give the least offence to the most delicate reader', and 'not satisfied' with that he has 'added many moral reflections wherever the story will admit of them'.

Now, although Johnson does not entirely live up to those high-minded aims (he was, after all, only a hack and his Preface was only a come-on to the uncertain adult purchaser), his *Oriental Moralist* is a valuable example of the way adults set about trying to construct children's editions of the *Nights*, and the editorial problems which lay in their path.

Most immediate of these problems is, of course, the frame story, if only because its presence is implied by the book's famous title – whether the emphasis is placed on 'one thousand and one', on 'entertainments', or merely on the simple noun 'nights'. What, children might legitimately ask, do these fantastic stories have to do with 'nights', let alone a quantity of them far in excess of the often slim selection of events which they are offered by the publisher? How is Scheherazade introduced, and is any effort made to indicate the passage of nearly three years of story-telling?

Richard Johnson deals with this editorial duty without much enthusiasm. He sees the need to explain how the entertainments came about, and bundles up Scheherazade into an eight-page Preface, where she arrives after the Sultan Shahriar has had his wife – of whom he was 'doatingly fond' – strangled because she had 'betrayed his confidence'. There is nothing of the Sultan's brother, and the main indication of the length of the story-telling marathon lies in the remark about Scheherazade that 'after this amiable lady had passed a thousand and one nights in telling her tales, the Sultan became so much delighted with her, that he renounced in her favour the cruel law', and so on. In fact, she does receive mention now and again as Johnson tells his selection of some eight tales, but she is only a token figure. Moreover, there is a curious discrepancy between the tone of voice of the stories which she is meant to be telling, however stilted, and the sudden interjections of the Revd Mr Cooper. 'We must not quit this chapter without remarking, that in the story of Amine the youthful reader will see what fatal consequences may arise from the most trivial indiscretions . . .' (p. 210).

In the context of their time, these dilutions and interpolations are hardly surprising. (After all, the concept of 'books for children' was still relatively new, and only a few years later the great Establishment arbiter on children's literature, Sarah Trimmer, was to say that 'highly wrought' works of fancy such as 'the Tales of the Genii' and 'the Arabian Nights Entertainment [*sic*]' should not be put into the hands of young people 'till their religious principles are fixed, and their judgement sufficiently strong to restrain the imagination within due bounds'.[8] Nevertheless, at the very start of the sequence of adaptations for children, Richard Johnson's editorial activity points up issues which have only occasionally been satisfactorily resolved by later writers.

If we grant that a full edition – merely because of its length – is highly unpractical for children, we need to establish how far modifications must go to produce a near-ideal abridgement. Without doubt Scheherazade and the frame story in which she figures are essential, although an intelligent method needs to adopted to imply the passing of time as the stories proceed. (Galland himself does not seem to have considered the problem – beginning with laborious repetitions of the nightly formulae and then abandoning the nights entirely at the end of volume vi).

The quantity of stories related ought also to be such that the child reader gains some awareness of the richness and variety of the collection – and indeed of the flexibility of narrative techniques, with stories placed within stories like so many Chinese boxes, and with the interpolated appeals to the audience, to say nothing of the quotations of verse. Above all, some flavour needs to be present of the exoticism of the collection, so different from the language and events that were the staple of the average nursery school-room, and different too from the fantasy of European folktales. It is hardly sufficient, as some adaptors seem to believe, to give the protagonists flowing robes and Mussulmanish names to turn them into orientals. A conscious artistry is necessary, not only to create a consistent diction for the adaptation, which may reflect something of its origins, but also to place that diction within the register of a story-telling rather than a literary tradition. If Scheherazade engaged in the ponderous, Latinate periods that many adaptations give her, her husband would have chopped her head off after Night One.

Needless to say (given the always-marginal status of children's books in the territory of literature), little real thought has been expended on the principles by which a successful adaptation of the *Nights* might be achieved. The scruples and priorities that influenced Richard Johnson are present in his successors and are to be found in one form or another as children's editions of the *Nights* multiplied throughout the nineteenth century. In 1829, for instance, an apparently generous two-volume edition containing nearly thirty stories nails its policy to the title-page with the words *Oriental Tales: Being Moral Selections from The Arabian Nights' Entertainments; Calculated Both to Amuse and Improve the Minds of Youth* (London, for Thomas Tegg). Like the Johnson, it selects from and abridges Galland so that 'the best *moral* can be extracted' and the original 'divested' of the disfiguring 'tautologies and interruptions' – while at the same time appropriate didactic sentiments are added.

Such a policy for the work differs only in its greater explicitness from many of the better-known and widely reprinted editions that were to follow. It would be easy to single out a number of substantial tomes, bound in over-decorated cloth and printed from stereotype plates as books for prizes, to show how the Johnson–Tegg tradition continued.[9] It is also found however in editions of more prestige, such as the two volumes of *Fairy Tales* and *More Fairy Tales from the Arabian Nights*, edited and arranged by E. Dixon (Dent, 1893 and 1895) and the selection from the *Entertainments* made by Andrew Lang (Longmans, 1898), both of which have lasted into the second half of the twentieth century. In the first example the editor confines herself to the remark that her work is for 'virginibus puerisque', and in the second Mr Lang makes jocular play with his omission 'of pieces only suitable for Arabs and old gentlemen', but behind these disavowals there is a casual as well as a protective attitude.

This can be seen partly in the inconsequential treatment of the frame: E. Dixon omits it altogether, and Andrew Lang shuffles through it as fast as possible. It can be seen partly in the thoughtless way that the stories have been chosen. (Both works, for instance, include the story of Zobeide and the two black dogs, but Dixon strips it out of its context, using nothing of the 'Calender' material, while Lang brings in the whipping-incident and the uncovering of Amina's scarred 'neck' but never gives the explanation of these curiosity-arousing matters.) It can also be seen in the failure of both adaptors to find out and control a register for the stories. Dixon takes over the English Galland wholesale, but gives his brisk phrasing a politer, more literary turn; Lang (or, rather, the ladies who worked for him) produces a new translation from the French which veers between an eighteenth-century formality and a more colloquial nineteenth-century tone ('They seem to have pleasant manners, but you have no idea how funny they look. I am sure we should find their company diverting . . .').

The truth of the matter is, of course, that, in all these instances, and in many equivalent ones, we are dealing first and foremost with a commercial operation. The *Nights* may, as the Hon. Mrs Sugden put it, be 'unncessarily prolix', with many details 'disfigured by a coarseness inconsistent with the taste of the present age', but they did provide publishers with a host of good stories – all free of copyright – and as the fashion for 'children's classics' grew they automatically figured high on many publishers' list of options. It did not matter how closely the narratives corresponded to their originals, or whether the language in any way reflected the character of Eastern story-telling; the essential requirement was to provide copy that would be familiar and that could be satisfactorily illustrated.

It is probably not putting the matter too strongly to say that any consideration of the *Nights* as an influence on children from the mid nineteenth century onward must deal in these visual effects before narrative ones. The wide dissemination and the growth in sophistication of the illustrated books and magazines during this period tended to deflect attention away from the images that the reader gained from words. Emphasis was placed more and more on the illustrative interpretation of stories, and even the decorative get-up of books or magazines as objects – cocoa-table books. (An amusing confirmation of this occurs in Heath Robinson's Preface to his *Child's Arabian Nights*, published by Grant Richards in 1903. The book deserves notice in any case for its very personality – it is one of the few attempts at a children's edition that has a distinctive and consistent character, albeit one that comes nearer to farce and parody than serious re-presentation. In his dead-pan Preface, however, where he satirises the way in which adults are inclined to instruct children on how to read their books, he says, 'Fifthly and lastly, you are not to turn up the pictures before reading the stories, or you will be like the boy who picked out all the plums from his cake, and did not care to eat it afterwards.')

In the early children's editions of the *Nights* the plums were very sparsely apportioned and took the form of separately printed engraved plates (there were six in *The Oriental Moralist* [see Plate 2b] and just two frontispieces in Tegg's *Oriental Tales*), and indeed this is an illustrative method that has never died away. One finds some of the hefty Victorian editions containing only separate plates – Mrs Sugden's edition, for instance, or numerous printings of the 'new edition revised, with notes by the Rev. Geo. Fyler Townsend M.A.' published over the decades by Warne's – and the emphasis on plates was paramount in such prominent examples as the three Arabian books made by Edmund Dulac and in editions from other artists who were seen as colour-plate specialists: Charles Folkard, Monroe Orr, Frank C. Papé and others. As late as 1961 the Oxford University Press chose a 'plates only' style for its *Arabian Nights* in the 'Children's Illustrated Classics' – with a text after Lane's edition – a book which heralded the arrival of Brian Wildsmith as a colourist.

Although it can be argued that the low incidence of pictures relative to text in books of this kind keeps the reader's attention focused on the story, it needs to be added that these 'plate-books' rarely do justice to the fluency and kaleidoscopic fantasy of the tales. In their separate existence, divorced from the text, they take on the character of photographic stills or of posed, theatrical scenes, or, in Wildsmith's case, of displaced paintings. (Indeed, in the first of Dulac's volumes, the *Stories from the Arabian Nights* of 1907, the divorce is absolute, for the pictures, on their heavy card mounts, are all packed together at the end of the book.)

A cogent case in favour of highly detailed and atmospheric scene-painting of this kind could rest on the need to build up for the child reader some view of the unfamiliar circumstances of the oriental tale – the artist supplying an imaginative dimension that would otherwise be missing. This indeed seems to have been one of the motives behind William Harvey's massive contribution to the Lane translation of 1839 onward, where the care for details of dress and architecture and the like actually overrides the need to complement the narrative; at times the book seems to be turning into a kind of 'pictorial journal of Lane's travels in the East'. Nevertheless, the emphasis on drawing here, and the integration of pictures with text (see Plate 4), point to an illustrative method of far greater potential than that offered by separate plates.

The most obvious example of a work which followed the direction suggested by Harvey is *Dalziel's Illustrated Arabian Nights Entertainments*, which was issued in parts between 1863 and 1865 to a popular readership that doubtless included many children. As with Harvey, the book strove to capture exotic detail through a mass of wood engravings which were fairly closely linked to the events they pictured; unlike Harvey, though, the emphasis was now heavily on dramatic effects, whose expression was fostered by the creative co-operation of line artists and engravers. The series was undoubtedly a vindication of the Dalziels' faith in this kind of co-operative effort, and it does deserve a place as a memento of the craftsmanship of its period (not least because of the inspired contributions of Arthur Boyd Houghton [see Plates 5–6][10] and Thomas Dalziel). It is going too far however to claim that the work is a wholly satisfactory rendering of its source. Dr H. W. Dulcken's revision and 'emendation' of the text is hopelessly pedestrian (which places it on a par with his translations of Grimm and Andersen), while the spreading of the task of illustration among eight artists leads at times to inconsistencies in the style and texture of the drawings (see Plates 5–8).

The unqualified success of the Dalziels' *Arabian Nights* is its demonstration of the expressive possibilities of line, and it is through the quality of their line drawing that subsequent children's editions of the tales lay claim to attention. The prized editions prepared by Dixon and Lang, already discussed, have probably achieved their eminence as much through the contributions of their illustrators as through anything that their editors have done – although, in both cases, the illustrators were applying well-tried techniques to familiar matter. J. D. Batten (Dixon's illustrator) had achieved success as the artist associated with Joseph Jacobs' various fairy-tale collections, just as Henry Ford was famously associated with Andrew Lang's 'Colour Fairy Books'. Both artists worked best in pen, for reproduction by the relatively new photographic 'process' methods; and both showed much greater gifts for portraying scenes of action – especially if monsters were involved – than for scenes of romantic or domestic charm (see Plates 11–12). (Pre-Raphaelite worship of 'das Ewig-Weibliche' runs a dilute course through most of their work.)

The humour, vigour and controlled design of drawings by Batten and Ford at their best are echoed here and there by other black-and-white artists. W. Heath Robinson's delightful *Child's Arabian Nights* has already been mentioned, and can be singled out for the quality of line as well as for its comedy, but Heath Robinson also contributed some uneven, sub-Beardsley designs to a latter-day imitation of the Dalziel series: *The Arabian Nights Entertainments*, issued in parts by George Newnes and involving four other artists, including Helen Stratton. Here graphic vogue can be seen inconsistently overtaking any serious attempt to reflect the imaginative context of the stories, and, indeed, the facility with which the camera and, later, photolithographic processes could aid the reproduction of artwork led in the twentieth century to a host of characterless, run-of-the-mill children's editions of the *Nights*. As may well have been the case in earlier times too, the stories were kept alive by their raw content of events rather than by distinction in the way the events were set down.

In relation both to the impact of orientalia on children and to the commercial opportunities offered by the fame of the *Nights*, it is important to remember that an alternative mode of presentation has also existed. This is the deliberate excerpting of individual stories which are offered to the reader as part of the large genus 'fairy tale' rather than as an element within the thousand-and-one formula. As such they hardly warrant consideration in terms of the magical influence described by the likes of Coleridge, but they are of some importance, partly because they bear witness to the hospitality of European traditional literature to stories from strange backgrounds, and partly because they show even more clearly than do the host of composite volumes how far the *Nights* have taken on the character of children's stories before all else.

The potential of Galland's collection as an Ali Baba's cave, to be randomly plundered, was already recognised in the eighteenth century. It seems likely that the first story to be separately issued was the *History of Sinbad the Sailor*, of which an Elizabeth Newbery edition is known for 1784,[11] and the story, for many obvious reasons, has continued to be used in anthologies, or as the basis for picture-books to the present times (see Plate 2a). Sometimes its own 'Hindbad' frame is included, sometimes not. Sometimes only two or three of the voyages are dealt with (or there may be severe abridgement – a twelve-page Manchester chapbook of c. 1840 devotes ten lines to the fifth voyage, eight to the sixth, and seventeen to the seventh, including the conclusion). There are also picture-book editions, versions in words of one syllable, and 'movable' adaptations such as harlequinades and pop-up books.

The Voyages of Sinbad the Sailor was also one of the titles chosen for inclusion in the publisher Benjamin Tabart's series of 'Popular Stories for the Nursery', the contents of which were initially published singly as modest paper-covered booklets, accoutred with three engravings which might be plain or hand-coloured. Alongside *Sinbad* were also to be found *Aladdin* and *Ali Baba* (later bound up in volume IV of the 1805 collected edition, together with 'Nourjahad, an Eastern Tale' and 'The History of Jack and the Bean-stalk'). The stories were abridged from Galland – probably by Mary Jane Godwin – and their arrival in the series is important: first, because at this early stage one sees the emergence of the three Arabian tales that were to be outstandingly popular as independent stories; and, second, because Mrs Godwin's text appears to have become the basis for many of the chapbook editions of these tales that were to appear from London and provincial presses in the first half of the nineteenth century – indeed it may well have been the source from which further abridgements were made, such as that by Walter Crane for his elaborate picture book *The Forty Thieves*, which remained in print into the present century.

The truncation of the stories into picture-book editions began in the same publishing-period as that occupied by Tabart, when his highly successful rival John Harris issued *The Little Hunchback* in 1817. This thirty-two-page volume with its four hand-coloured plates takes hold of the anecdote that surrounds the stories of the tailor and the barbers and reduces it into jog-trot verse, converting it into a jest for its late-Regency readership. It is symbolic of the way that material embedded in the *Nights* was to be used for the most diverse purposes. (And this period, too, saw the arrival of *Aladdin* and of *The Forty Thieves* as popular texts for the toy theatre, out of which was to grow their lasting reputation as subjects for pantomine.)

Abridged, adapted, moralised, pictorialised, the tales of Scheherazade thus proved their worth to a book trade that has long
enjoyed refurbishing old lamps to look like new. The publishers
and editors of these children's versions have rarely been able to
make the difficult conjunction of all the imaginative elements that
subsist in their heterogeneous original, but one continues to
wonder what would have happened if they never had tried. For
in all the long registers of editions of the *Nights* that are to be
found in the major libraries of the English-speaking world, only a
small proportion of the entries relate to editions intended for
adults, and it may perhaps be hazarded that almost everyone today
who 'knows' the *Nights* does so, or began to do so, through the
medium of children's books.

And for all their frequent shortcomings the children's editions
are nothing if not persistent. Between the commissioning and
completion of this essay there has appeared a paperback picture-
book edition of *Aladdin* by one of our most praised illustrators,
Errol Le Cain, who has chosen to adapt Andrew Lang's adaptation
of Galland, and whose elaborate paintings hark back to the colour-
plate books of Edmund Dulac and Kay Nielsen. There has also
appeared a selection of *Tales*, put out as 'Shaharzad's' own
favourites, and gaudily illustrated by Victor Ambrus, but retold by
James Riordan, a man sensitive to the tales' origins as told stories.
And there has also appeared what is perhaps the most ambitious
adaptation ever planned for children.

This is a replacement of the old, Lane-based text in the Oxford
Illustrated Classics series, and is *One Thousand and One Arabian
Nights* (1982) by Geraldine McCaughrean, with illustrations by
Stephen Lavis. The less said about these last the better, for they
are an uneven mixture of poor imitations of Henry Ford and
cuttings from a travel agent's brochure, but Miss McCaughrean
proves herself to be the first adaptor ever to face up to the full
implications of her task. Acting on the barest hint from Galland,
with remarkable self-confidence she preserves Scheherazade and
Shahriar as living presences through the telling of the stories and
their episodes, and, casting aside reliance on past translations (or
even on translations of her own), she retells the tales with all the
phrasing and inflection of a story-teller living in the 1980s. Similes,
colloquialisms, sentence rhythms waft the bedroom of the Shah
into some lofty habitation above Regent's Park, but the result is a
freshness and immediacy that has rarely occurred before. It is an

apt confirmation that *The Arabian Nights* still has a place in English literature – even for children.

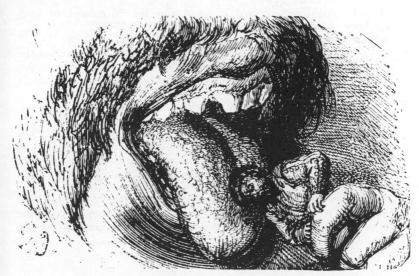

3 *'Supped once more on one of our companions', by Doré for the Cassell edition*

NOTES

Books published in London unless otherwise stated.

1. Maria Edgeworth, 'The India Cabinet', in *Continuation of Early Lessons*, I (R. Hunter, 1816) 227–8.
2. Maria Edgeworth, Preface to *The Parent's Assistant*, quoted from J. Johnson's 1815 edn, p. xi.
3. Alexander Pope, quoted from George Sherburn, 'New Anecdotes', *Notes and Queries*, n.s. v, no. 8 (1958) 345. Trumbull added, however, that the structure of the tales 'makes it beyond the Nurse's Capacity to tack them together and the Child expects always a Conclusion' – pragmatic warrant for future editors!
4. Samuel Taylor Coleridge, letter to Thomas Poole, 9 October 1797, in *Collected Letters of Samuel Taylor Coleridge*, ed. E. L. Griggs, I (Oxford: Clarendon Press, 1956) 208.
5. Juvenile versions of the moralising Eastern tale, perfected for adults in *Rasselas*, abound. See, for instance, Sarah Trimmer's kind words about the Princess of Persia, 'The Adventurers of Mosul, etc.', in *The Guardian of Education*, I (1802).

6. Duncan B. MacDonald, 'A Bibliographical and Literary Study of the First Appearance of the *Arabian Nights* in Europe', *Library Quarterly*, II, no. 4 (Oct 1932) 387–420.
7. M. J. P. Weedon, 'Richard Johnson and the Successors to John Newbery', *Library* (5th ser.), IV, no. 1 (June 1949) 25–63.
8. *The Guardian of Education*, II (1803) 408.
9. Two examples are *The Arabian Nights' Entertainments*, arranged for the perusal of youthful readers by the Hon. Mrs Sugden (Routledge, 1863) and a further Routledge edition which used Thomas Dalziel's illustrations (1865).
10. For a study of the place of the Dalziels' book in Houghton's career, see Paul Hogarth's *Arthur Boyd Houghton* (Gordon Fraser, 1981). Terry Reece-Hackford also devotes space to an analysis of his work in her essay 'Fantastic Visions; British Illustration of the *Arabian Nights*', in *The Aesthetics of Fantasy Literature and Art*, ed. Roger C. Schlobin (Brighton: Harvester, 1981) pp. 143–75. She also puts a strong critical case in favour of Henry Ford and Edmund Dulac.
11. This edition predates Sydney Roscoe's J171 – see *John Newbery and His Successors* (Wormley, Herts: Five Owls Press, 1973) – and is in the collection of Mr Peter Stockham, to whom I am grateful for the reference.

3

English Travellers and the *Arabian Nights*

FATMA MOUSSA-MAHMOUD

In the opening years of the eighteenth century the strange distant East was brought vividly and imaginatively before the eyes of French and English readers with Antoine Galland's translation of the *Nights* into French (1704–17). The French version was immediately translated into English and the tales were so popular that they started a literary fashion on both sides of the Channel, the 'oriental tale' of the eighteenth century.[1] There were so many preposterous imitations of the *Nights* that some genuine translations such as the *Persian Tales* (1710) and the *New Arabian Nights* (1792) were long taken for forgeries. As travelling to the East was difficult and relatively infrequent, readers were very curious about the customs and religion of the infidel inhabitants of those far-off lands. Galland's translation was from the first advertised as a book where 'the customs of Orientals and the ceremonies of their religion were better traced than in the tales of the travellers. . . . All Orientals, Persians, Tartars and Indians . . . appear just as they are from sovereigns to people of the lowest condition. Thus the reader will have the pleasure of seeing them and hearing them without taking the trouble of travelling to seek them in their own countries'. The rich imaginative power of the *Nights* and the dazzling splendour of its descriptions, together with the realistic, homely atmosphere of some of the tales have kept their hold on European imagination to this day.

It soon became part of the task of the travellers to verify the authenticity of the *Nights* and relate them to what they saw. Lady Mary Wortley Montagu was the first English lady to visit Turkey and reside in Constantinople, as the wife of the British Ambassador to the Porte (1716–18). In her letters she gave lively descriptions of Turkish houses, mosques and public baths. She had the chance to penetrate into the harems of the great officials of the Ottoman Court. She wrote in one of her letters, 'This is but too like (says you) the Arabian tales; these embroider'd Napkins and a jewel as large as a Turkey's egg! You forget dear Sister, those very tales were writ by an Author of this Country and (excepting the Enchantments) are a real representation of the manners here.'[2] Lady Mary's letters were widely circulated during her lifetime and some of the details of Turkish life were regarded as being as fabulous as the *Nights*. 'We travellers', she complained, 'are in very hard circumstances if we say nothing but what has been said before us, we are dull. . . . If we tell anything new, we are laugh'd at as fabulous and Romantic' (p. 385).

In 1756 Alexander Russell, resident physician to the English factory in Aleppo, described how oriental men of fashion were lulled to sleep with 'stories told out of the *Arabian Nights Entertainments* . . . which their women were taught to repeat for this purpose'.[3] Patrick Russell's enlarged edition of *Aleppo* (1794) provided more interesting information on the *Nights*, together with more detailed description of the life of the inhabitants among whom he spent many years as his brother's successor. He added a chapter on Arabic literature, and in a note on the *Nights* he testified to their authenticity:

> The Arabic title of our Arabian Nights is Hakayat Elf Leily wa Leily a Thousand and one Nights. It is a scarce book at Aleppo. After much inquiry, I found only two volumes, containing two hundred and eighty nights, and with difficulty obtained liberty to have a copy taken. I was shown more than one complete copy in the Vatican Library; and one at Paris in the King's Library said also to be complete.[4]

He added that he had collected a number of separate tales which he later found in the first and third volumes of the 'Continuation of the Arabian Nights published at Edinburgh in 1792'. His note was quoted by the *Oriental Collections* (Caddell and Davies, 1797, I, 246–7). The editor announced that Jonathan Scott, a retired servant of the East India Company, had acquired a complete manuscript of the *Nights* in five volumes, brought by Edward Wortley Montagu from the East, which he intended to translate.[5] Queries appeared in the *Gentleman's Magazine* as to the two manuscripts and the authenticity of Galland's version. Dr Russell in reply gave a description of his manuscript and again testified to the authenticity of Galland's translation.[6]

In an account of entertainments at coffee houses, Russell's *Aleppo* gives a description of the manner of narration by professional story-tellers that was widely quoted by other travellers and by students of the *Nights*:

> The recitation of Eastern fables and tales partakes somewhat of a dramatic performance. It is not merely a simple narrative; the story is animated by the manner, and action of the speaker. A variety of other story books, besides the Arabian Nights Entertainment (which under that title, are little known at Aleppo) furnish material for the story teller, who by combining the incidents of different tales, and varying the catastrophe of such as he has related before, gives them an air of novelty. . . . He recites walking to and fro, in the middle of the coffee room, stopping only now and then when the expression requires some emphatical attitude. He is commonly heard with great attention, and, not infrequently, in the midst of some interesting adventure, when the expectation of his audience is raised to the highest pitch, he breaks off abruptly, and makes his escape from the room, leaving both his heroine and his audience, in the utmost embarrassment . . . and the auditors, suspending their curiosity, are induced to return at the same hour next day to hear the sequel. He no sooner has made his exit, than the company in separate parties, fall a disputing about the characters of the drama, or the event of the unfinished adventure. The controversy by degrees becomes serious, and opposite opinions are main-tained with no less warmth, than if the fate of the city depended on the decision.   (I, 148–50)

An increasing number of travellers sought scenes from the *Nights* in the crowded bazaars and narrow streets of oriental cities, and their testimonies and experiences were quoted in new editions of the *Nights*. Edward Forster in 1802 quotes Dallaway's book on Constantinople:

> Much of the romantic air which pervades the domestic habits of the persons described in the Arabian Nights, particularly in inferior life, will be observed in passing through the streets of Constantinople. And we receive, with additional pleasure, a

remembrance of the delight, with which we at first perused them, in finding them authentic portraits of every Oriental nation.

James Capper's *Observations on the Passage to India through Egypt* (1783) is cited as recommending the *Nights* as a necessary piece of equipment for a traveller in the East: 'they are in the same estimation all over Asia, that the adventures of Don Quixote are in Spain, and it is presumed no man of genius or taste would think of making the tour of that country without previously reading the works of Cervantes'.[7]

The establishment of the British Empire in India by the end of the eighteenth century, the French Expedition to Egypt (1797–1801) and the continued rivalry between Britain and France for influence with oriental rulers, whose territory lay on the short routes to India, resulted in an unprecedented increase in the number of British travellers to the East. The traveller, whether soldier, diplomat or antiquarian, took notes, preparatory to producing the heavy volumes of travel consumed by a reading public eager for any new information on the East. James Justinian Morier (1780–1849) made two journeys to Persia in 1808 and 1810, as secretary of two successive ambassadors, and, after the signing of a treaty with the Shah to counteract French influence, he resided for some time in Teheran. He published two travel books,[8] but some writers think that his third and most famous book, the *Adventures of Hajji Baba of Ispahan* (1824), is actually a travel book in disguise:

> it is proper to regard [*Hajji Baba*] both as a novel and a book of travel, since in its episodes and characters it follows closely the author's actual experiences as recorded in his *Journeys*, and was intended by him to present facts in a dramatic form that would create a vivid impression on readers completely ignorant of the customs of a Mohammedan Community.[9]

Morier was partly influenced by Thomas Hope's *Anastasius*, an oriental picaresque tale which met great success in 1819, but he only confessed to the influence of Le Sage and the *Nights*. His choice of a barber for his rogue hero is indicative. In the Introductory Epistle, Morier states that for 'delineation of Asiatic manners . . . the *Arabian Nights' Entertainments* give the truest picture of the Orientals . . . because it is the work of one of their own community'.

He adds, however, that 'few would be likely to understand them thoroughly who have not lived some time in the East'. He summarises a story from the *Nights*, an episode of the Three Calenders, where Amina buys wine from the house of a white-bearded Christian without their exchanging a word. He assumes that the explanation would be only understood by someone who had lived in the East. His intention was to write a kind of supplement to the *Nights* that would illustrate the manners and customs of an oriental nation. The reference to the *Nights* was taken up by the *Quarterly Review*:

> We have subjected these little volumes, as far as regards the measure of their agreement to the test of a severe examination . . . we turned over the pages of several of the tales in the Arabian Nights Entertainments . . . it is really curious to observe how exactly . . . [he] has identified the current of the hero's fortunes, the character of his adventures and associates; the customs, feelings and opinions of his country, with the example of everyday Eastern life which may be gathered from those singular chronicles of Asiatic manners.[10]

The triumph of *Hajji Baba* lay in Morier's clever imitation of Eastern style and imagery. The narrative, which is supposed to be in Hajji's own words, keeps up the illusion of the narrator's nationality. When the author wishes to introduce episodes or descriptions of places the hero could not have seen, the tale-within-a-tale is a handy device. As he has no chance of seeing the inside of a grandee's harem or observing how it is run, the fair Zeenab, his sweetheart and the slave of his master the doctor, gives us the details in a most natural way. She takes him on a tour of her mistress's apartment, in the absence of that lady, and the description could have come from the pages of the *Nights*. There were numerous editions of *Hajji Baba* before the end of the century and the book has remained a classic. It was translated into French, German and even Persian. The Persians were understandably furious at the picture of them given in the book, for Hajji Baba, like other picarós, is shown as a mean liar, a coward and a thief; moreover, he was taken by European readers as a typical Persian and a typical oriental. Morier later devoted himself to a literary career. He wrote 'oriental tales' but he never repeated the triumphant success of *Hajji Baba*. In *The Mirza* (1841) he tried to give an imitation of the *Nights*, a series of tales narrated by the court poet (the Mirza), strings of anecdotes and tales within tales he composed for the entertainment of the Shah. The author keeps the outward trappings of the 'oriental tale' and tries to give a picture of manners and customs in three volumes, but the collection is far inferior to *Hajji Baba* and has deservedly sunk into oblivion.

Nineteenth-century interest in the manners and customs of orientals was still fed by publications of various degrees of impartiality or downright bigotry. Missionaries in India provided horrific accounts of the lives and practices of benighted Hindu heathens, but descriptions of the Muslim Near East were much more sympathetic. The popularity of the *Nights* and the 'oriental tale' together with the growing bulk of travel literature explain the difference in attitude. Impartial objectivity in portraying Arab Muslim manners and customs was brought to a peak with E. W. Lane's *Modern Egyptians* (1836). Lane (1801–76) also became famous for producing the first direct translation into English of the *Nights*. He first arrived in Egypt as a young engraver, who had studied Arabic for a year before leaving England. He followed the routine of former travellers who sailed up the Nile to Luxor. He joined a group of artists who were making detailed drawings of Ancient Egyptian monuments. He spent some time in Egypt taking notes on the life of contemporary Egyptians. Though he could not find a publisher for the long account of his travels, the section on contemporary life was accepted by the Society for the Diffusion of Useful Knowledge. He returned for a year and a half in 1833–4 to prepare that section for publication. His *Modern Egyptians* has never been superseded. Lane was fully equipped for his task. On his second visit he assumed Arab dress and lived away from the Frank colony in Cairo. He had native informants and he was steeped in oriental literature, not least the *Nights*. In a note to the Preface to his book he pointed out the importance of the *Nights* as a guide to the customs of the Arabs:

> There is one work, however, which presents most admirable pictures of the manners and customs of the Arabs, and particularly those of the Egyptians; it is 'The Thousand and One Nights; or, Arabian Nights' Entertainments'. If the English reader had possessed a close translation of it with sufficient illustrative notes, I might almost have spared myself the labour of the present undertaking.[11]

His partiality for the *Nights* was obviously no impediment to absolute objectivity. He told his readers in the same Preface, 'I am not conscious of having endeavoured to render interesting any matter that I have related by the slightest sacrifice of truth.'

Lane had two models which he reluctantly admitted in the Preface, Russell's *Aleppo* and Chabrol's 'Essai sur les moeurs des habitants modernes de l'Egypte', published in one of the volumes of the French Institute's *Description de l'Egypte* (1822). Actually Lane modelled the organisation of his material on Chabrol's example, but he had more information to offer than the French writer. Lane, the translator of the *Nights* could give a more comprehensive picture of the life of Muslim Arabs. He could always bring in an incident from the *Nights* to illustrate a custom or an opinion held by the people he so closely observed. When discussing the women's reputation for licentiousness he reminds his readers, 'Some of the stories of the intrigues of women in "The Thousand and One Nights" present faithful pictures of occurrences not infrequent in the modern metropolis of Egypt' (p. 304). On the other hand, his impartiality induces him to translate a note which a sheikh, one of his friends, wrote commenting on a passage on this subject in the *Nights*. The sheikh testifies that many women do not marry a second time after they are widowed or divorced, thus defending his countrywomen against the imputations in the *Nights* (p. 304). In an earlier chapter, describing the customs at mealtime, he is naturally reminded of the constant feasting and drinking in the *Nights* and tries to correct the impression it gives:

> Though we read, in some of the delightful tales of 'The Thousand and One Nights', of removing 'the table of viands' and bringing 'the table of wine', this prohibited beverage is not often introduced in general society . . . by the Muslims of Egypt in the present day. Many of them, however, habitually indulge in drinking wine with select parties of their acquaintance.   (p. 154)

A chapter entitled 'Language, Literature and Science' is immediately followed by a chapter on superstition, 'a knowledge of which is necessary to enable [the reader] to understand their character'. The first elements of superstition are of course the 'Ginn', who naturally bring in the *Nights*. Precautions against offending the 'Ginn' are best understood through certain incidents in the *Nights* (p. 229). When he is told of a wali's head speaking after it was cut off, it brings in the story of the Sage Dooban (p. 241 n. 1). Three chapters are devoted to 'Public Recitations of Romances', including the *Nights*. The manner of recitation, which had excited the curiosity of Russell's readers about forty years before, is again described accompanied by a good engraving (p. 399). Lane finds it necessary to give a summary of a number of the romances recited in the coffee shops, but he expects his readers to be familiar with the *Nights*. He admits, however, that recitations from the *Nights* have become rare, for 'when a complete copy of "The Thousand and One Nights" is found, the price demanded for it is too great for a reciter to have it in his power to pay' (p. 420). One would guess that foreign demand for copies of the *Nights* must have raised the price, for it was the ambition of every European traveller to acquire a copy of the famous tales. In a note to a later edition he cites that the *Nights* and other important books were printed at the government press at Boulak (p. 227 n. 1). It was actually this printed edition that Lane used for his translation of the *Nights*.

When he brought out the third edition of *Modern Egyptians* in 1842, Lane had already published his translation of the *Nights*. He added some notes on songs and anecdotes mentioned in the *Nights*. The story of the ignorant 'fikee' (schoolmaster) on p. 63 is related to a similar anecdote in his translation. He concludes, 'either my informant's account is not strictly true, or the man alluded to by him was, in the main, an imitator; the latter is not improbable, as I have been credibly informed of several similar imitations, one of which I know to be a fact' (p. 63n.). So some of the Egyptians he describes actually imitate the *Nights*! In his account of public festivals, he gives a full translation of a song sung in a 'zikr' (a fervently devotional performance) then adds in a note, 'since the above was written, I have found the last six of the lines here translated with some slight alterations, inserted as a common love song in a portion of the Thousand and One Nights' (p. 454n.).

Lane's translation of the *Nights* (1839–41) was one of the first attempts at a direct translation from Arabic into English. He used the Boulak edition, which supported his view that the tales were originally Egyptian. He dispensed with the division into nights and divided his narrative into chapters. The translation proved a great commercial success, for the text was expurgated to suit family reading. It was elucidated with copious notes written by Lane for the purpose. The tales lost much of their charm under the heavy hand of the scholarly orientalist. In spite of its faults, Galland's version had been powerfully imaginative and had consequently fascinated its readers. Lane's translation had a pronounced biblical tone which did not suit the homely atmosphere of some of the tales or the romantic exaggerations in others. The notes, however, were illuminating. They were later published separately as *Arabian Society in the Middle Ages* (1883). In the Preface to his own unexpurgated translation of the *Nights* (1885), Richard Burton, though contemptuous of Lane's version of the *Nights*, greatly appreciated the notes: 'The student who adds the notes of Lane ('Arabian Society', etc. . . .) to mine will know as much of the Moslem East and more than many Europeans who have spent half their lives in Orient lands.'[12]

Another traveller who toured the Near East at the time of Lane's second visit to Egypt (1833–4) produced a classic of travel literature the opposite of Lane's scholarly *Modern Egyptians*: A. W. Kinglake (1809–91) rewrote the text of *Eothen* (1844) three times. The final version was an intimate account of his personal experience of travelling in the area, addressed to his friend Eliot Warburton, who intended to make the same tour. His excuse for dwelling only on 'matters that happened to interest [him]' was that these countries had 'been thoroughly and ably described and even artistically illustrated by others'. Kinglake was devoted to the *Nights*; he carried a copy in his luggage which he sometimes read in his lodgings in Cairo. He classed it with Homer's *Iliad* as a book dear to him from childhood. While crossing from Smyrna to Cyprus on a Greek ship, he heard a folktale narrated to the mariners in Greek and 'recognised with some alterations an old friend of the Arabian Nights'. Further reading of the *Nights* produced a theory:

> I became strongly impressed with a notion that they must have sprung from the brain of a Greek. It seems to me that these stories, whilst they disclose a complete and habitual *knowledge* of things Asiatic, have about them so much of freshness and life, so much of the stirring and volatile European character, that they cannot have owed their conception to a mere Oriental, who for creative purposes is a thing dead and dry – a mental mummy . . .[13]

As Kinglake's intention, expressed in his Preface, was to steer free from 'all display of "sound learning"' or 'antiquarian research', the problem of the 'European dress' of the translation of the *Nights* he read, still based on Galland, is not mentioned, nor is the subject of frequent borrowings in folk literature.

He sought the *Nights* in the streets of Cairo, though the city was ravaged by the plague. His interests were mainly erotic and supernatural. He visited the open slave market and was not satisfied with the sight of fifty girls, all black. The slave agent promised to show him a Circassian girl as 'fair as the full moon'. This too proved a disappointment, for she was too fat for his taste. She gave him the impression 'of having been got up for sale, of having been fattened or whitened by medicines or by some peculiar diet' (pp. 199–200). Later, he 'thought it worth while to see something of the magicians'. The old man hired by his servants failed to satisfy the inquisitive traveller. However, he bargained to 'raise the devil for two pounds ten, play or pay – no devil, no piastres' (p. 203). The magician did not keep his part of the bargain, for he was carried off by the plague.

Kinglake's fresh, individualistic approach to his subject matter secured him lasting fame as a man of letters. No oriental, however, can easily like *Eothen*, for the Englishman who had come to test his mettle against the hardships of Eastern travel proves his superiority to things Arabic and Islamic at every turn. This attitude was regularly adopted by later travellers, starting with his friend Warburton's *The Crescent and the Cross* (1843).

Richard Burton (1821–90) is most remembered for his translation of the *Nights* (1885–8). It was the crowning work of a long career as soldier, linguist and explorer. It was the outcome, after more than thirty years, of his first visit to the Arab East, his pilgrimage to Makka and Madina in 1853. Burton taught himself Arabic at Oxford and continued studying the language in India, where he served as officer in the army of the East India Company (1842–9). He acquired other oriental languages, both classical and vernacular, learned parts of the Koran by heart and studied Sufism. Burton was familiar with the *Nights* from an early age. His colleagues in India, when engaged on intelligence work, were content with getting information from paid native agents. Burton assumed disguises reminiscent of Harun al-Rashid and his minister in the *Nights*. He pretended to be a rich merchant, half Arab and half Persian, and set up shop in the market as Mirza Abdalla, a name he kept to the end of his life. It is decoratively painted on the first page of his translation of the *Nights*. He was sent home in 1849, ostensibly on sick leave, because his superiors were shocked at the detailed information on male brothels in his reports. The information was later used in his chapter on pederasty in the Terminal Essay in volume x of his translation of the *Nights*.[14] Like Sindbad the Sailor, he could not rest quietly at home, and he obtained financial support from the Royal Geographical Society to explore what he could of Arabia. He intended to make the pilgrimage in disguise as Mirza Abdalla, a Persian. He landed in Alexandria in April 1953 and was advised to change his supposed nationality to Afghan. He travelled to Cairo by steamboat on the Nile and set up in a 'wekallah' or inn, practising as a 'hakim' or physician, which opened many houses before him, giving him the chance to make valuable observations. In his description of Cairo in the first volume of his *Personal Narrative of a Pilgrimage to al Madinah and Meccah* (1855), he cites and corrects Lane on almost every page. Burton stayed in Cairo for some weeks perfecting his pronunciation of Arabic and his knowledge of Muslim customs before joining the pilgrim caravan to Suez. He undertook the strict Ramadan fast in spite of the long days of scorching heat in June. The realities of the traveller's experience and his detailed observations are vividly described (and annotated) without the least attempt at glossing or romanticising. The *Nights*, however, is part of the furniture of his mind. When describing a fellow pilgrim, who at the age of twenty-eight had not yet acquired a wife, the example of Kamer al-Zaman is cited, and he expects his readers to recognise its relevance: 'His parents have urged him to marry, he like Kamer al-Zaman, has informed his father that he is "a person of great age, but little sense".'[15] The caliph Harun al-Rashid is mentioned a number of times in his account of the Hijaz, but it is not the mythical figure of Tennyson's 'good Haroun Al Raschid' in his 'golden prime', but the Abbasid monarch who had many wells sunk on the pilgrim road from Baghdad to Makka (*Personal Narrative*, II, 70, 134).

Burton's great achievement in 1853 was his visit to Makka and Madina and his detailed description of the ceremonies of Haj and Umra, though he was not the first European to do either. His account of the itinerary, together with the crowning visit to the two holy cities of Islam, is full of absorbing details, livened by the sense of danger hanging over 'the pilgrim from the north'. He shows good knowledge of Arab history and literature and of the work of previous travellers, chastising some of them for their erroneous sense of superiority towards customs and literature they did not understand. Harriet Martineau's attack on Muslim harims brings out a defence of marriage customs in the East, which he was later to repeat in the notes of his translation of the *Nights*: 'In quality of doctor I have seen a little and heard much of the harim. It often resembles a European home composed of a man, his wife and his mother. And I have seen in the West many a "happy fireside" fitter to make Miss Martineau's heart ache than any harim in Grand Cairo' (*Personal Narrative*, II, 91). He proceeds to give examples of the importance of love in Arabia, taken from Arabic poetry. Burton retained the same curiosity for marriage customs and sexual practices of different nations that had horrified his compatriots in India. He included some such information in the notes to his travel book, but the publisher suppressed it all as 'garbage'. Burton later used it in the notes to his translation of the *Nights*. Burton was in Aden in 1854, preparing for his second journey of exploration to an Islamic stronghold, the city of Harar in Somaliland, when he conceived the idea of producing a 'full complete unvarnished, uncastrated copy' of the *Nights*.[16] He had a copy of the tales with him when he crossed from Aden to Zayla on the East coast of Africa in October 1854. He had assumed his Arab disguise and from Zayla he travelled inland with a party of nine. It was presumably during this march that 'the wildlings of Somaliland' enjoyed his recitations from the *Nights*, as mentioned in his Translator's Foreword. Two cookmaids who accompanied the party were 'buxom dames about thirty years old, who presently secured the classical nicknames of Shehrazade and Deenarzade'.[17] Another member of the party, 'one-eyed Musa', was dubbed the 'Kalendar'. To his report of the expedition (1856), Burton added an appendix on the sexual customs of the Somalis and an account of the practice of female circumcision (written in Latin). It was torn out by the publisher before the copies were bound, but Burton later used some of the material in a long note in the fifth volume of his *Nights*.

In 1869, after a long career of exploration in Africa and South America, he was finally appointed Consul in Damascus. To him it was again the land of the *Arabian Nights*, 'the land of [his] predilection'. Burton and his wife were very happy in Damascus, and he thought he would spend the rest of his life there. He assumed Arab dress and rode in the Syrian desert. According to his wife, he recited the *Nights* to the bedouins, some of whom 'rolled with pleasure' at some exciting points of the recitation.[18]

He vividly describes the scene in his Foreword to the *Nights*. 'The Shaykks and "whitebeards" of the tribe take their places sitting with outspread skirts . . . round the campfire. . . . The women and children stand motionless as silhouettes with attention' (p. viii). In Syria Burton took up archaeology, one of the typical traveller's interests he had never indulged before. He went on trips to Baalbek and Palmyra and made a visit to Palestine. Burton was unpopular with the Turkish wali (the provincial governor), with his superior the British Consul General in Beirut, and with the British Ambassador in Constantinople, because of his unconventional and sympathetic relations with the Arab population. His position was undermined by the proselytising zeal of his Roman Catholic wife and by the intrigues of money-lenders, who had functioned under the protection of his predecessors, but whose applications for help in extorting debts from poor inhabitants he angrily spurned. He was recalled in 1871 'at the age of fifty, without a month's notice or wages or character'. Burton made two short visits to Egypt and the Eastern coast of Arabia in 1877 and 1878. He had written to the bankrupt Khedive Ismail of Egypt about the possibility of prospecting for gold in Midian in the north-west of Arabia, because of a story he had heard more than twenty years before from Haj Wali, a man he had met in Cairo in 1853. The two expeditions were a failure, Burton lost a lot of money but he produced two volumes with detailed accounts of his travels.[19] He did not realise at the time that he did not need to prospect for gold on desert shores, for he had a goldmine in hand, his translation of the *Nights*. He was working on it when in 1881 he read of John Payne's intention of publishing a complete translation of the *Nights*. Burton wrote to the *Athenaeum* welcoming Payne's project and announcing his own intention of publishing an unexpurgated translation. In the correspondence between him and Payne which followed, he urged the poet to be as literal as possible, but Payne resisted Burton's urging as his intention was basically aesthetic rather than anthropological. When Payne's nine volumes of the *Nights* started appearing in 1882 (dedicated to Richard Burton), the latter saw that there was still a need for *his* translation.

Burton's *Plain and Literal Translation of the Arabian Nights* was privately printed, allegedly for the Kamashastra Society in Benares, a society he invented. It was limited to 1 000 copies for subscribers only, and he made a profit on it of 10,000 guineas. The work is monumental, ten volumes of the original tales with six volumes of

Supplemental Nights from the Wortley-Montagu manuscript in the Bodleian Library. The 'Terminal Essay' in volume x gives a scholarly study and bibliography of the *Nights*, together with a chance for Burton to hit back at his critics with more anthropological data 'to shock Mrs Grundy' to the utmost. The notes to the tales carry details of varied information he collected in his extensive travels. His main point was that previous translations had degraded 'a chef d'oeuvre of the highest anthropological and ethnographical interest and importance to a mere fairy-book, a nice present for little boys'.

Burton's devotion to the *Nights*, which were 'an unfailing source of solace and satisfaction' during his travels, is in great contrast to the attitude of the next traveller of importance in Arabia. Charles M. Doughty spent twenty months in the country, starting from Damascus with the pilgrim caravan in 1876, but he had no use for disguise, for Islam or for the *Arabian Nights*. He was a scientist interested in noting the land formation in the regions he crossed as well as the customs of the bedouins with whom he travelled. He saw parts of Arabia that had not been visited by any European before him, and, when he published his travel book nine years later,[20] he warned his readers 'that nothing be looked for in this book but the seeing of a hungry man and the telling of a most weary man'. His intention in writing was mainly literary 'to redeem English from the slough into which it had fallen since the days of Elizabeth'. The hardships of desert life came over in language suited to Bedouin austerity. The translation of Arabic sentences into biblical or Shakespearian idiom, the Arabic words transliterated into English and the numerous newly coined Anglo-Arabic words all add to the beauty and literary value of the work.

It must be confessed that travellers such as Doughty who had to cope with genuine desert life in the Arabian peninsula at the latter end of the nineteenth century had little occasion or use for the *Nights*. T. E. Lawrence, whose name is associated with Arabia more than any Englishman before him, does not mention the *Nights* in *Seven Pillars of Wisdom* except to show the romantic element in the Arab Revolt:

A second buttress of a polity of Arab motive was the dim glory of the early Khalifat whose memory endured among the people through centuries of Turkish misgovernment. The accident that these traditions savoured rather of the Arabian Nights than of sheer history maintained the Arab rank and file in their conviction that their past was more splendid than the present of the Ottoman Turk. Yet we knew that these were dreams.[21]

Lawrence was right, for he best knew what lay in wait for the Arab Revolt, but the dream persisted with both Arabs and Europeans. Travellers continued to flock into the cities of the Near East changed by the advent of steam and later of the aeroplane. They still looked for the *Nights*, for the flourishing tourist industry adopted them for its own. From Aladdin nightclubs to Harun al-Rashid restaurants, chartered groups are regaled with oriental experience packaged and ready-made. Only the perceptive traveller armed with real knowledge of the *Nights* may suddenly light on an old house with latticed windows and a marble hall of which the fountain is dry, or a row of little old shops in a side street in Cairo, Damascus or Baghdad, and see the scene come alive peopled with the familiar characters of the tales.

NOTES

Books published in London unless otherwise stated.

1. Martha Pike Conant, *The Oriental Tale in England in the Eighteenth Century* (New York: Columbia University Press, 1908).
2. Lady Mary Wortley-Montagu, *The Complete Letters*, I: *1708–1720*, ed. Robert Halsband (Oxford: Clarendon Press, 1965) pp. 385.
3. Alexander Russell, *The Natural History of Aleppo* . . . (A. Millar, 1[7]56; p. 90.
4. *The Natural History of Aleppo*, 2nd edn, rev. and illustrated by Patrick Russell (G. G. and J. Robinson, 1794) I, 385–6.
5. For details of this manuscript, see my 'A MS Translation of the *Arabian Nights* in the Beckford Papers', *Journal of Arabic Literature* (Leiden) VII, (1976) 7–23.
6. *Gentleman's Magazine*, Apr 1798, pp. 304–5, and Feb 1799, pp. 91–2.
7. *The Arabian Nights*, in 5 vols, tr. Edward Forster (William Miller, 1802) I, xli, xliii.
8. *A Journey through Persia, Armenia and Asia Minor* . . . (1812); *A Second Journey through Persia* . . . (1818).
9. *The Adventures of Hajji Baba* . . . , intro. by C. W. Stewart, The World's Classics (Oxford University Press, 1923).
10. *Quarterly Review*, xxx (1824) 200–1.
11. E. W. Lane, *The Manners and Customs of Modern Egyptians*, Everyman edn (Dent, 1908) p. xxi n.

12. Richard Burton, *A Plain and Literal Translation of the Arabian Nights* . . . (Kamashastra Society, Benares, 1885) I. Translator's Foreword.
13. A. W. Kinglake, *Eothen* (Macmillan, 1960) p. 64.
14. Fawn M. Brodie, *The Devil Drives: A Life of Sir Richard Burton* (Eyre and Spottiswoode, 1967) p. 66.
15. Richard Burton, *Personal Narrative of a Pilgrimage* . . . Memorial Edition (New York: Dover) I, 161.
16. In the Foreword to his translation of the *Nights,* Burton erroneously gives the date of the inception of the plan for the translation as 1852. In 1852 he was in Europe, and the visit to Aden after the pilgrimage took place in 1854.
17. Richard Burton, *First Footsteps in East Africa,* Everyman's Library (Dent, 1910) p. 101.
18. Isabel Burton, *Inner Life of Syria, Palestine and the Holy Land,* 2 vols (H. S. King, 1875) I, 128, 353; see Brodie, *The Devil Drives,* p. 254.
19. Richard Burton, *The Gold-Mines of Midian* . . . (1878), and *The Land of Midian (Revisited),* 2 vols (1879).
20. Charles M. Doughty, *Travels to Arabia Deserta* (Cambridge: Cambridge University Press, 1888). See I, 263 for his adverse comments on the *Nights.*
21. T. E. Lawrence, *Seven Pillars of Wisdom,* Penguin Modern Classics (Harmondsworth: Penguin, 1962) p. 344.

4

The Genie and the Albatross: Coleridge and the *Arabian Nights*

ALLAN GRANT

Any student who has read into Coleridge from 'The Rime of the Ancient Mariner',[1] having been exercised by what the poem may be about, is bound to have come across this entry in *Table Talk*:

May 31, 1830

MRS BARBAULD once told me that she admired the Ancient Mariner very much, but that there were two faults in it, – it was improbable, and had no moral. As for the probability, I owned that that might admit some question; but as to the want of a moral, I told her that in my own judgment the poem had too much; and the only, or chief fault, if I might say so, was the obtrusion of the moral sentiment so openly on the reader as a principle or cause of action in a work of such pure imagination. It ought to have had no more moral than the Arabian Nights' tale of the merchant's sitting down to eat dates by the side of a well, and throwing the shells aside, and lo! a genie starts up, and says he *must* kill the aforesaid merchant, *because* one of the date shells had, it seems, put out the eye of the genie's son.[2]

I cannot think that I have been the only student who was puzzled on first reading that note – 'the obtrusion of the moral sentiment so openly on the reader as a principle or cause of action in a work of such pure imagination'.

What I take Coleridge to mean by the remark is that what a poem is, is not a matter of the kind of moral or ideological principle it articulates explicitly, but rather an object produced by the

111

imagination, in that the poem exists in its connectedness, in the organic unfolding of itself according to the definition of the imagination abruptly introduced into chapter 13 of the *Biographia Literaria*:

> The IMAGINATION then I consider either as primary, or secondary. The primary IMAGINATION I hold to be the living Power and prime Agent of all human Perception, and as a repetition in the finite mind of the eternal act of creation in the infinite I AM. The secondary I consider as an echo of the former, co-existing with the conscious will, yet still as identical with the primary in the *kind* of its agency, and differing only in *degree*, and in the *mode* of its operation. It dissolves, diffuses, dissipates, in order to re-create; or where this process is rendered impossible, yet still at all events it struggles to idealize and to unify. It is essentially *vital*, even as all objects (*as* objects) are essentially fixed and dead.[3]

The secondary imagination (which I take to be the poetic imagination at work) is what a poem exemplifies. So that, in order to understand 'The Ancient Mariner', one looks at its structure and its individual elements to see what they yield. A rich and various harvest it is, to judge from the range of interpretations that have offered themselves. However, if one looks further at the analogy Coleridge is making with the *Arabian Nights*, perhaps one finds that the poet might have meant by 'pure imagination' something other than his memorable and recalcitrant formulation.

Mrs Barbauld (1743–1825), who triggered the occasion, has gained a posthumous fame, somewhat like that of the person on business from Porlock, greater than she perhaps deserves. Poet, editor and essayist, her claim on us is as the author of a set of nature studies entitled *Hymns in Prose* (1781), and as one of the originators of pious books for children. She figures prominently in a letter from Lamb to Coleridge of 23 October 1802.

> Goody Two Shoes is almost out of print. Mrs Barbauld['s] stuff has banished all the old classics of the nursery; & the Shopman at Newbery's hardly deign'd to reach them off an old exploded corner of a shelf, when Mary ask'd for them. Mrs B's, & Mrs Trimmer's nonsense lay in piles about. Knowledge insignificant & vapid as Mrs B's books convey, it seems, must come to a child

in the *shape* of *knowledge*, & his empty noddle must be turned
with conceit of his own powers, when he has learnt, that a Horse
is an Animal, & Billy is better than a Horse, & such like: instead
of that beautiful Interest in wild tales, which made the child a
man, while all the time he suspected himself to be no bigger
than a child. Science has succeeded to Poetry no less in the little
walks of Children than with Men. – : Is there no possibility of
averting this sore evil? Think what you would have been now,
if instead of being fed with Tales and old wives fables in
childhood, you had been crammed with Geography & Natural
History?[4]

Lamb's final major point about the relationship between tales in
childhood and their lasting effect is one that we recognise. Most
familiarly in the work of Dickens, no doubt, but equally in
Wordsworth, and, on his own account, Coleridge. In 1797, he
wrote three autobiographical letters to Thomas Poole in the course
of one of which he stated, 'from my early reading of Faery Tales,
& Genii &c &c – my mind had been habituated *to the Vast* – & I
never regarded *my senses* in any way as the criteria of my belief'.[5]
And again, and worth quoting at length:

I took no pleasure in boyish sports – but read incessantly. My
Father's Sister kept an *every-thing* Shop at Crediton – and there I
read thro' all the gilt-cover little books that could be had at that
time, & likewise all the uncovered tales of Tom Hickathrift, Jack
the Giant-killer, &c & &c &c &c –/– and I used to lie by the wall,
and *mope* – and my spirits used to come upon me suddenly, &
in a flood – & then I was accustomed to run up and down the
church-yard, and act over all I had been reading on the docks,
the nettles, and the rank-grass. – At six years old I remember to
have read Belisarius, Robinson Crusoe, & Philip Quarle [Quarll] –
and then I found the Arabian Nights' entertainments – one tale
of which (the tale of a man who was compelled to seek for a
pure virgin) made so deep an impression on me (I had read it in
the evening while my mother was mending stockings) that I was
haunted by spectres, whenever I was in the dark – and I distinctly
remember the anxious and fearful eagerness, with which I used
to watch the window, in which the books lay – & whenever the
Sun lay upon them, I would seize it, carry it by the wall, & bask,
& read – . My Father found out the effect, which these books

had produced – and burnt them. – So I became a *dreamer* – and acquired an indisposition to all bodily activity – and I was fretful, and inordinately passionate, and as I could not play at any thing, and was slothful, I was despised & hated by the boys; and because I could read & spell, & had, I may truly say, a memory & understanding forced into almost an unnatural ripeness, I was flattered & wondered at by all the old women – & so I became very vain, and despised most of the boys, that were at all near my own age – and before I was eight years old, I was a *character* – sensibility, imagination, vanity, sloth, & feelings of deep & bitter contempt for almost all who traversed the orbit of my understanding, were even then prominent & manifest.[6]

What seems to be established beyond doubt from these, and similar, confessions[7] is a powerful association between childhood, fairy tales, including the *Nights*, and a disposition to a dreaminess that reached quite beyond the grasp of the senses on the child's surrounding world, which, in the second quotation, is deliberately exchanged for the imaginary ones supplied with the little yellow- or gilt-covered library. Much later, there appears in the lecture upon Defoe a confirmation of this powerful association between the *Nights* and dreaming:

> Novels are to love as fairy tales are to dreams. I never knew but two men of taste and feeling who could not understand why I was delighted with the Arabian Nights' Tales and they were likewise the only persons in my knowledge who scarcely remembered having ever dreamed.[8]

The connection is amplified in an extended comment preparatory to a judgement of the effect of Defoe's *Robinson Crusoe*:

> The Asiatic supernatural beings are all produced by imagining an excessive magnitude, or an excessive smallness combined with great power; and the broken associations, which must have given rise to such conceptions, are the sources of the interest which they inspire, as exhibiting, through the working of the imagination, the idea of power in the will. This is delightfully exemplified in the Arabian Nights' Entertainments, and indeed, more or less, in other works of the same kind. In all these there is the same activity of mind as in dreaming, that is – an exertion of the fancy in the combination and re-combination of familiar

objects so as to produce novel and wonderful imagery. To this must be added that these tales cause no deep feeling of a moral kind – whether of religion or love; but an impulse of motion is communicated to the mind without excitement, and this is the reason of their being so generally read and admired. . . . The charm of Defoe's works, especially of *Robinson Crusoe*, is founded on the same principle. It always interests, never agitates. Crusoe himself is merely a representative of humanity in general; neither his intellectual nor his moral qualities set him above the middle degree of mankind; his only prominent characteristic is the spirit of enterprise and wandering; which is, nevertheless, a very common disposition. You will observe that all that is wonderful in this tale is the result of external circumstances – of things which fortune brings to Crusoe's hand.[9]

What he says here strongly suggests Coleridge's definition of fancy[10] in chapter 13 of the *Biographia Literaria*, which immediately follows the definition of imagination and is only made a little clearer to the reader by reason of the contrast which Coleridge is establishing between it and the poetic imagination. The same vocabulary is present here – 'association', 'fancy', 'impulse', 'motion', 'will' in a strong chain of connection.

Is the connection strong enough to make one want to suggest that, after all, 'The Ancient Mariner' is Coleridge's *Arabian Nights* tale? Before answering that question, it may be as well to look at 'The Merchant and the Genie' the tale begun by Scheherazade on the first night of her task. In passing, it might be as well to note that this story (like the four immediately subsequent tales in the *Nights*) is an example of what Gerhardt terms the 'ransom frame' in which the act of story-telling itself serves to redeem a human life. Coleridge and Lamb both seem to want to establish a necessary connection between tales and life.

There he found at the foot of a great walnut-tree, a fountain of very clear running water, and alighting, tied his horse to a branch of the tree, and sitting down by the fountain, took some biscuits and dates out of his portmaneau, and as he eat his dates, threw the shells about on both sides of him. When he had done eating, being a good musselman, he wash'd his hands, his face, and his feet, and said his prayers. He had not made an end, but was still on his knees, when he saw a Genie appear, all white with age, and of a monstrous bulk; who, advancing towards him with a scymetar in his hand, spoke to him in a terrible voice, thus; Rise up, that I may kill thee with this scymetar, as you have kill'd my son; and accompanied these words with a frightful cry. The merchant being as much frightened with the hideous shape of the monster, as at those threatening words; answer'd him trembling. Alas! my good lord, of what crime can I be guilty towards you, that you should take away my life? I will, replies the Genie, kill thee, as thou hast kill'd my son. O heaven! says the merchant, how should I kill your son? I did not know him, nor ever saw him. Did not you sit down when you came hither, replies the Genie? Did not you take dates out of your portmanteau, and as you eat 'em, did you not throw the shells about on both sides; I did all that you say, answers the merchant, I cannot deny it. If it be so, replied the Genie, I tell thee thou hast kill'd my son; and the way was thus; When you threw your nutshells about, my son was passing by, and you threw one of 'em into his eye, which kill'd him; therefore I must kill thee. Ah! my lord, pardon me! cried the merchant. No pardon, answers the Genie, no mercy. Is it not just to kill him that had kill'd another? I agree to it, says the merchant, but certainly I never kill'd your son; and if I have, it was unknown to me, and I did it innocently; therefore I beg you to pardon me, and to suffer me to live. No, no, says the Genie, persisting in his resolution, I must kill thee, since thou has kill'd my son; and then taking the merchant by the arm, threw him with his face upon the ground, and lifted up his scymetar to cut off his head.[11]

One thing one notices immediately is the character of the merchant. He is innocent of any positive malice; he is even conventionally a good Muslim, and has not yet risen from prayer when he is attacked by the vengeful Genie. However, Lane points out that the merchant was culpably careless. Before throwing away the date-stone, he should have sought Allah's permission.[12] Coleridge, though, is unlikely to have been aware of this aspect of Islamic belief, as his use of the tale seemingly turns upon the opposite interpretation. Even so, there is a fundamental difference between the merchant's act and the mariner's. That of the merchant (as Coleridge's amused italicisation, mocking the notion of causality, suggests in the earlier quotation from *Table Talk*) was without evil intent, whereas that of the mariner is in a wholly different class. It is inherently a wrongdoing, and the prose commentary to the poem refers to it as 'the crime', and refers to the mariner's inhospitableness in killing the bird. The merchant in the tale, in defending himself to the genie, cries, 'Of what *crime* can I be guilty?' Nevertheless the genie is insistent that the merchant was the agent of his son's death and demands the poor man's life. The merchant is only saved, not merely by the ending of the night, but, in the sequel, by the intervention of two other story-tellers whose stories distract the genie in precisely the way that Scheherazade has distracted the Sultan Shahriar from his intention to kill her.

Even if Coleridge is right, and there *is* no moral, in that, like Robinson Crusoe's, the merchant's fate is 'the result of external circumstances – of things that fortune brings to hand', it is nevertheless quite unlike Crusoe's in that what fortune brings corresponds in no way to his expectations or to his knowledge of what the world is like.[13] Coleridge said he never regarded his 'senses in any way as the criteria of [his] belief'. Perhaps the moral of 'The Merchant and the Genie' is precisely *that* – that one's senses, that the things one can know through the senses, are no guarantee whatsoever of the real shape of the universe and the powers that reside in it.[14]

In *The Road to Xanadu*,[15] Livingston Lowes pursued the clues offered in the notebook employed by Coleridge in the years 1795–7 (and occasionally later on), the so-called Gutch memorandum book, in order to try to illuminate areas of literary reference and allusion embedded in the surface of 'The Ancient Mariner'. A number of these hint at stories, romances and at story-telling – even a possible Arabian tale is mooted for versification.[16] 'Wandering Jew a romance', Thomas Burnet's works, 'Adventures of Christian the Mutineer'[17] – the book contains a stream of unrealised literary projects from which it would be tempting to select those that would help confirm one's view of what 'The Ancient Mariner', the important and undoubted result of all Coleridge's continuous note-taking, is in fact about. The attempt to swallow the contents of the memorandum book whole or to pursue them all in all their chaos can by definition, or by example, of *The Road to Xanadu* itself, simply get you lost on alarming and obscure byways. One entry, however, detains me: 'Moon at present uninhabited owing to its little or no atmosphere but may in Time – An Atheistic Romance might be formed – a Theistic one too. – Mem!' Kathleen Coburn's annotation to this entry in the *Notebooks*[18] safely traces the moon reference to Dr Erasmus Darwin, but makes no comment on the idea of the habitability of the moon as the basis of an atheistic romance – or a theistic one – a utopia or a piece of space fiction, *avant la lettre*. There are other delightfully seductive entries which move straight into 'The Ancient Mariner' or 'Kubla Khan'. I merely observe from the *Notebooks* that the strange and eccentric in human knowledge continually suggest to Coleridge the possibility of a literature of pure imaginings. This notion is obviously related to his own childhood and to the insistence of Lamb and Coleridge upon the nourishment of the imagination by fanciful tales, those from the *Nights* prominent among them, rather than by pious tracts.

Discussing in *Biographia Literaria* the apportionment of the tasks of *Lyrical Ballads*, Coleridge recalled that

> my endeavours should be directed to persons and characters supernatural, or at least romantic; yet so as to transfer from our inward nature a human interest and a semblance of truth sufficient to procure for these shadows of imagination that willing suspension of disbelief for the moment, which constitutes poetic faith.[19]

Between 1798 and 1800 the mock-medieval spellings were modernised in part, and between 1801 and 1817 the commentary was developed.[20] The effect of these changes was to make the telling of the story itself plainer and, at the same time, to add a second framing-device, that of the commentary, to that of the presence in the poem of the story-teller himself. A few pages further on in *Table Talk* from the entry on the moral of 'The Ancient Mariner' and the *Nights* there is an interesting comment on *Pilgrim's Progress*, which, says Coleridge,

> is composed in the lowest style of English, without slang or false grammar. If you were to polish it, you would at once destroy the reality of the vision. For works of imagination should be written in very plain language; the more purely imaginative they are the more necessary it is to be plain.[21]

In the comment 'purely imaginative' again seems to mean 'purely imaginary' rather than relate in any way to the poetic imagination unmixed with fancy. So, like Scheherazade,[22] but for very different reasons, the mariner is compelled to tell in plain language an unlikely story. The unfolding of the story is the explanation of the compulsion which holds the wedding-guest. One need scarcely point to the extraordinary beauty of the language of the poem in its splendidly dramatic progress from the known to the wholly unknown and back again, utterly changed.

Many later critics have agreed with Lamb's response to the poem and his judgement upon it.

I never felt so deeply the pathetic as in that part,

A spring of love gushed from my heart,
And I blessed them unaware –

It stung me into high pleasure through sufferings.

But then later, writing to Wordsworth: 'After first reading it, I was totally possessed with it for many days. – I dislike all the miraculous part of it, but the feelings of a man under the operation of such scenery dragged me along like Tom Piper's magic Whistle.'[23]

There are those who like least the miraculous part, the apparatus of the spirits of the universe who take over the Mariner's destiny: the tone is quite different, and the poem, in part VI, perhaps seems to lose tempo. But Lamb compares the effect to that of magic, thus fastening on an essential element of the poem, the invention of an imaginary universe, that many later critics have preferred to leave out of consideration. That we ought to at least take into account 'all the miraculous part of it' is confirmed by the Latin epigraph of the poem, first published with it in *Sibylline Leaves* (1817), the first publication of the poem under Coleridge's own name. The epigraph is from the 1692 edition of Thomas Burnet's *Archaeologiae Philosophicae*, and the full text is provided in Kathleen Coburn's notes to volume I of the *Notebooks*,[24] where an eighteenth-century translation may also be found. The passages printed in square brackets below are omitted by Coleridge in the epigraph.

I can easily believe, that there are more Invisible than Visible Beings in the Universe: [and that there are more *Orders of Angels* in the Heavens, than *variety of Fishes* in the Sea;] but who will declare to us the Family of all these, and acquaint us with the Agreements, Differences, and peculiar Talents which are to be found among them? It is true, human Wit has always desired a Knowledge of these Things, though it has never attained it. [The Heathen Divines have very much philosophized about the invisible World of Souls, Genii, Manes, Demons, Heroes, Minds, Deities, and Gods, as we may see in *Jamblichus's* Treatise on the *Mysteries of the Aegyptians*, and in *Psellus* and *Pletho* on the *Chaldean Rites*, and everywhere in the *Platonic* Authors. Some Christian Divines have imitated these also, with Reference to the Orders of Angels; and The *Gnostics* have feigned many things in this Matter, under the Names of *Eons* and *Gods*. Moreover, The Cabalists in their *Jetzirah* (or *World of Angels*) range Myriads of Angels under their Leaders *Sandalphon* and *Metatron*, as they who are conversant in those Studies very well know. But of what Value are all these Things? Has this Seraphic Philosophy any Thing sincere or solid about it? I know that *St Paul* speaks of the Angelic World, and has taken notice of many Orders and Distinctions among them; but this in general only; he does not philosophize about them; he disputes not, nor teaches anything in particular concerning them; nay, on the contrary, he reproves those as puft up with vain Science, who rashly thrust themselves forward to seek into these unknown and unsearchable Things.] I will own that it is very profitable, sometimes to contemplate in the Mind, as in a Draught, the Image of the greater and better World; lest the Soul being accustomed to the Trifles of this present Life, should contract itself too much, and altogether rest in mean Cogitations; but, in the mean Time, we must take Care to keep to the Truth, and observe Moderation, that we may distinguish certain Things, and Day from Night.

The poem, in one dimension at least, is some kind of answer to Burnet's questions. (It is notable too, that the passages omitted from Burnet were those concerning 'Genii' and other beings from the 'invisible World', who had their counterpart in the poem itself from its conception, and were more fully augmented in the developing of the prose frame.) It is also a poet's reverie (cf. 'Kubla Khan: or A Vision in a Dream. A Fragment') – the poet does not wish to take responsibility[25] for what follows; what it is requires only 'a willing suspension of disbelief for the moment that consti-tutes poetic faith'. So he can write such a poem without abdicating the human need to 'take Care to keep to the Truth'.

Just as the merchant is totally ignorant of the (passing) genie's son when he casts his date-stones about, so the mariner cannot know what is entailed in shooting the albatross. But he will learn. And what he learns is a purely imaginary way of embodying the possibility that the universe is not at all ordered according to the conception of it that his human senses have perceived. The immediate consequence is an intensity of suffering without equal culminating in a state of total desolation and horror.

> O Wedding-Guest! this soul hath been
> Alone on a wide, wide sea:
> So lonely 'twas, that God himself
> Scarce seemed there to be.

It is only by a terrible chance (of one order) that the Mariner is betrayed into his experience and by a happier chance (of another order) that he survives the game between Death and Life-in-Death aboard the skeleton ship. It is, later, only the forced contemplation of his own desolated existence that brings to his consciousness the possibility that life, of whatever kind, is its own good. Even the water snakes attest to this:

> Within the shadow of the ship
> I watched their rich attire:
> Blue, glossy green, and velvet black,
> They coiled and swam; and every track
> Was a flash of golden fire.

> O happy living things! no tongue
> Their beauty might declare:
> A spring of love gushed from my heart,
> And I blessed them unaware:
> Sure my kind saint took pity on me,
> And I blessed them unaware.

> The self-same moment I could pray;
> And from my neck so free
> The Albatross fell off, and sank
> Like lead into the sea.

Yet the mariner is not released. He is compelled to recount his experience, and the recounting of it is a recurrent horror for the

Ancient Mariner as it is a stunning experience to the unprepared audience. It reveals the uncharted worlds of what Coleridge called 'the sacred horror'[26] of primitive man when he contemplated the possibility of the meaninglessness[27] of the universe in which he existed. Belief was logically necessary to Coleridge, but belief secured within the framework of what was human and known. What drives on 'The Rime of the Ancient Mariner', however, is the urge to *know* something of 'the one Life within us and abroad',[28] the something one and indivisible. Such sublime notions of universal unity cannot be known: they may only be *imagined* as fantasies, or analogies for the necessity of belief; and the source for the fantasies or imaginings is surely in the wild imagining themselves, in 'Jack the Giant-Killer', in *Robinson Crusoe* and, especially perhaps, in the *Arabian Nights*.[29]

NOTES (compiled by DEIRDRE TOOMEY)

Books published in London unless otherwise stated.

1. For convenience I shall refer to the poem henceforth as 'The Ancient Mariner'. The text quoted is taken from *The Complete Poetical Works of Samuel Taylor Coleridge*, ed. E. H. Coleridge, (Oxford: Clarendon Press, 1912) I, 186–209. Other scholars who have considered Coleridge's debt to the *Arabian Nights* include John Livingston Lowes, George Whalley and John Beer. Lowe's account can be followed in *The Road to Xanadu* (Constable, 1927, rev. 1930) pp. 277ff., 415–17. Whalley's 'The Mariner and the Albatross' can be found in *University of Toronto Quarterly*, XVI, no. 4 (July 1947) 381–98. John Beer's argument in *Coleridge the Visionary* (Chatto and Windus, 1959) rests upon his interesting rediscovery of Richard Hole's *Remarks on the Arabian Nights Entertainments* (1797), and he suggests that a source for the poem is the episode, discussed by Hole, of Sindbad's companions' killing of the roc's nestling (pp. 145–9). Beer is, however, somewhat literal in seeking an *Arabian Nights* tale with the complete iconography of ship, mariner and dead bird, and thus somewhat depreciates Coleridge's own emphasis upon a 'tale without a moral'. Hole's work is an attempt to rationalise the *Arabian Nights* by considering not its imaginative aspects, but its utility in the West as a source of anthropological and historical information. Coleridge's own reaction to this book, despite its use of both Purchas and Hakluyt, is surely not likely to have been favourable. John Beer's later interest in the *Nights* can be traced in 'Ice and Spring: Coleridge's Imaginative Education', in *Coleridge's Variety*, ed. Beer (Macmillan, 1974) pp. 54–80, and in *Coleridge's Poetic Intelligence* (Macmillan, 1977). As to possible Grecian sources for the *Nights* Coleridge comments, 'I think it is not unlikely that the Milesian Tales contained the germs of

many of those now in the Arabian Nights; indeed it is scarcely possible to doubt that the Greek empire must have left deep impression on the Persian intellect' – *Coleridge's Miscellaneous Criticism*, ed. Thomas Middleton Raysor (Constable, 1936) p. 194. See also *infra*, p. 126 and n. 14; Lowes, *The Road to Xanadu*, pp. 262–4; *The Notebooks of Samuel Taylor Coleridge*, ed. Kathleen Coburn (Routledge and Kegan Paul, 1973) III (text) 4384. Coleridge returned to the subject in his table talk on 9 May 1830: 'Arabian poetry is a different thing. I cannot help surmising that there is a good deal of Greek fancy in the Arabian Tales' – *Specimens of the Table Talk of the late Samuel Taylor Coleridge*, ed. H. N. Coleridge (John Murray, 1835) I, 123–4.

2. *Ibid.*, pp. 154–6. The conversation is most likely to have taken place around January 1801, as Coleridge had asked Longmans to send her the second *Lyrical Ballads* (*Letters*, I, 654, 15 Dec 1800). Coleridge had first met Mrs Barbauld in summer 1797 and remained on good terms with her until about 1804.

3. *Biographia Literaria or Biographical Sketches of my Literary Life and Opinions*, ed. James Engell and W. Jackson Bate (London: Routledge and Kegan Paul; Princeton, NJ: Princeton University Press, 1983) I, 304. The *Biographia Literaria* is vol. VII of *The Collected Works of Samuel Taylor Coleridge* (sponsored by the Bollingen Foundation).

4. *The Letters of Charles and Mary Anne Lamb*, ed. Edwin W. Marrs, Jr, (Ithaca, NY: Cornell University Press, 1976) II: *1801–1809*, pp. 81–2.

5. *Collected Letters of Samuel Taylor Coleridge*, ed. E. L. Griggs (Oxford: Clarendon Press, 1956) I: *1785–1800*, p. 354.

6. *Ibid.*, pp. 347–8. The tale which frightened Coleridge as a child is 'The History of Prince Zeyn Alasnam, and of the King of the Genii', one of Galland's 'orphan tales' (*Nights*, III, 178–95). This tale essentially divides into two parts and it is the second to which Coleridge refers. Prince Zeyn Alasnam travels to the Island of the Genii in order to obtain a statue, following instructions left mysteriously by his deceased father. Zeyn and his companion are rowed to the island by a monster boatman whose 'head was like an elephant's and his body like a tyger's'. The King of the Genii is a terrifying and unpredictable figure who expresses himself in terms of thunder and lightning: 'The whole island was cover'd with a hideous darkness, a furious storm of wind blew, a dreadful cry was heard, the whole island felt a shock, and there was such an earthquake, as that which Asrafyel is to cause on the day of judgement.' The King of the Genii promises Zeyn his statue on condition that Zeyn bring him a maiden of fifteen, perfectly beautiful, who has neither known, nor desired to know, man: he gives Zeyn a magic mirror which tests purity by clouding in the presence of the slightest impurity. The elements which terrified the child are plain enough. Curiously, no translation until Burton's uses the phrase 'pure virgin'; although the sense is clear, the earlier editions of Galland use 'maiden' or 'maid'. The use of the term 'virgin' suggests that at the time of this letter Coleridge had been rereading this tale in one of the editions (with a modified translation) printed by Longmans from 1778 onwards, in which 'virgin' is used: 'a virgin of your character'

(III, 193). This tale was not forgotten by the mature Coleridge. Its iconography survives in lines 52–111 of 'The Picture', in which we find 'mirror', 'virgin' and virgin reflected in the mirror of the pool. It might be argued that he came to associate elements of this tale with Sara Hutchinson and that in 'Dejection: An Ode' we find a less obvious, more fully processed use of its peculiar imagery: in stanza v we find an emphatic reiteration of Asra's purity, 'O pure of heart . . . save to the pure and, in their purest hour'. In 'The Picture' we have the *virgin*, here we have the *pure*. Perhaps even the 'storm without', with its 'scream/Of agony by torture lengthened out' contains some reminscence of the storm and the 'dreadful cry' of the tale of Zeyn.

7. '"Give me," cried Coleridge, with enthusiasm, "the works which delighted my youth. Give me the *History of St George* and the *Seven Champions of Christendom*, which at every leisure moment I used to hide myself in a corner to read. Give me the *Arabian Nights' Entertainments*, which I used to watch till the sun shining on the bookcase approached it, and glowing full upon it gave me courage to take it from the shelf"' – *Coleridge's Shakespearian Criticism*, ed. Thomas Middleton Raysor, Everyman's Library (Dent, 1930) II, 242. In Essay IV of *The Friend*, Coleridge recalls his 'first entrance into the mansion of a neighbouring Baronet' as being 'long connected in my childish imagination with the feelings and fancies stirred up in me by the perusal of the Arabian Nights' Entertainments'. His own note on this memory runs:

> As I had read one volume of these tales over and over again before my fifth birth-day, it may be readily conjectured of what sort these fancies and feelings must have been. The book, I well remember, used to lie in a corner of the parlour window at my dear Father's Vicarage-house; and I can never forget with what a strange mixture of obscure dread and intense desire I used to look at the volume and *watch* it, till the morning sunshine had reached and nearly covered it, when, and not before, I felt the courage given me to seize the precious treasure and hurry off with it to some sunny corner in our playground.

Quotation from *The Friend*, ed. Barbara E. Rooke (London: Routledge and Kegan Paul; Princeton, NJ: Princeton University Press, 1969) I, 148 and n. *The Friend* is vol. IV of *The Collected Works of Samuel Taylor Coleridge*. See also p. 31n.

The edition of the *Nights* Coleridge used as a child (of either four or five – as he aged, he tended to push this particular piece of his childhood reading further and further back) was either an odd volume of the many English versions of Galland's *Arabian Nights* published since 1706, or possibly an abridged version of the same; it is clear that extracts from the *Nights* were published in the eighteenth century. (See *supra*, Brian Alderson, ch. 2, pp. 90–1, and n. 11.)

As a Grecian at Christ's Hospital, Coleridge owned 'an odd volume of the Arabian Nights' Entertainments in the vulgar tongue', as the

Revd Leapidge Smith, his fag, recalled in 'Reminiscences of an Octogenarian', *Leisure Hour*, 4 Oct 1860, pp. 633–4. The volume would have been one of a translation of Galland's French version. See *infra*, n. 11.

8. *Coleridge's Miscellaneous Criticism*, p. 103.
9. Ibid., pp. 193–4.
10. *Biographia Literaria*, I, 305.
11. The edition in which Coleridge as an adult read 'The Merchant and the Genie' was one of the many English translations of Galland's *Arabian Nights* published since 1706; the edition quoted here is the 1778 English translation, in which 'The Merchant and the Genie' appears at I, 23–40.

The satisfaction that Coleridge took in the tale is well attested in a note of April–May 1816:

> The pompous French Savants' System of the Ante-Adamic Age of the Temple of (?Teuchrea/Teuchira/Tenchira/Tenctira) receiving its mortal wound by the late Traveller's discovery of the chronology, I compared to the Son of the vast Genius killed by a date-shell, that the travelling Merchant cast in his eye – /Ar. Nights. *1 Night* –
> (*Notebooks*, III, 4317)

12. Lane, *The Thousand and One Nights*, 3 vols (1839) I, 29 n. 21.
13. A note of 13 May, 1804, written *en route* to Malta, voices Coleridge's response in extraordinarily similar circumstance.

> Hawk with ruffled Feathers resting on the Bowsprit – Now shot at & yet did not move – how fatigued – a third time it made a gyre, a short circuit, & returned again/5 times it was thus shot at/left the Vessel/flew to another/& I heard firing, now here, now there/& nobody shot it/but probably it perished from fatigue, & the attempt to rest upon the wave! – Poor Hawk! O Strange Lust of Murder in Man! – It is not cruelty/it is mere non-feeling from non-thinking. (*Notebooks*, II, 2090)

However, *both* acts are punished with appalling disproportion by the inhabitants of an unseen, unknown world: perhaps this disproportion caused Wordsworth to note 'that the events having no necessary connection do not produce each other' – *Lyrical Ballads* (1800) pp. 214–15.

If this tale is an influence upon the conception of 'The Ancient Mariner', why does Coleridge so construct the poem as to court the risk of its being read as Mrs Barbauld read it, as an imperfect moral tale? Coleridge's poem depends upon dramatic tensions more frequently found in Greek tragedy than in the *Nights*. The poem is a sort of marchland between Arab, Greek and Christian frames of reference. George Whalley (*University of Toronto Quarterly*, XVI, no. 4, 396) comments that 'there is the sternness and inexorability of Greek tragedy'. The mariner's *act* moves closer to that of Oedipus, who kills

an unknown man and brings upon himself a supernatural punishment
from the Furies.

14. In his exploration of the contrasts between Greek mythology and the
    Islamic supernatural world, which begins Lecture xi of the *Miscellaneous
    Criticism* – the *Nights* was one of its announced subjects – Coleridge
    opined that

> In Asia, probably from the greater unity of the government and the
> still surviving influence of patriarchal tradition, the idea of the unity
> of God, in a distorted reflection of the Mosaic scheme, was much
> more generally preserved; and accordingly all other super or ultra-
> human beings could only be represented as ministers of, or rebels
> against, his will. The Asiatic genii and fairies are, therefore, always
> endowed with moral qualities, and distinguishable as malignant or
> benevolent to man. It is this uniform attribution of fixed moral
> qualities to the supernatural agents of eastern mythology that
> particularly separates them from the divinities of old Greece.
>
> (*Coleridge's Miscellaneous Criticism*, pp. 191–2)

This in effect *is* the supernatural system we see in 'The Ancient
Mariner', for the 'lonesome Spirit', 'from the South-pole', who 'carries
the ship as far as the Line', acts 'in obedience to the angelic troop', but
'still requireth vengeance', having evidently some limited autonomy.
Paradoxically, such is not the case in 'The Merchant and the Genie',
where the genie apparently has complete autonomy, despite the fact
that elsewhere in the *Nights*, as Coleridge was aware, genies are
ultimately subject to Allah's will. He is only stopped from executing
his desires and the merchant by the power of story-telling. See also
Notebooks, ii, 2060.

15. Lowes, *The Road to Xanadu, passim.*

16. *Notebooks*, i, 58 (Gutch 51, 1796): 'The Sister of Haroun – beloved by
    the Caliph – Giafar/Her verses to Giafar – Giafar's answer – good
    subjects'. It is unsurprising that Coburn is unable to find the source
    of this note. The story is not to be found in the *Nights*, but is a
    historical tale, and Coleridge's source (to which Peter Caracciolo
    directed me) was Joseph Dacre Carlyle's *Specimens of Arabian Poetry*
    1796). The work gives Arabic texts, translations and notes. In the
    apparatus to a poem upon the ruin of the Barmecides (pp. 52–6) occurs
    the story of Harun's desire to marry his sister Abassa, 'of whom he
    was passionately fond', to his vizir, Jaafer, in order that he could
    enjoy their conversation together in the harim. The condition was that
    they should never meet but in his presence: this was disobeyed, a
    child was the result, and when Harun discovered this he commanded
    Jaafer's death and the destruction of the Barmecides. The idea of
    verses between Abassa and Jaafer was Coleridge's own. It is clear
    from Coleridge's spelling of the vizir's name that he was reading
    Carlyle at the same time as Galland's translation (which uses 'Giafar').
    Carlyle had been a fellow at Cambridge while Coleridge was an
    undergraduate and became Professor of Arabic in 1795. His book would

have interested Coleridge in many other respects: e.g. discussions of the affective power of a mixture of prose and verse and of translations. The compilation concluding with a speciment of an Arabic song, the whole is obviously another and uncharted road to Xanadu. See also *supra*, Introduction, pp. 7–8.

17. For the Wandering Jew, see *Notebooks*, I, 45 (Gutch 37); for the plan to versify Burnet's *Sacred Theory of the Earth*, see *ibid*, p. 61 (Gutch 54) and also pp. 174 (Gutch 169), 100 (Gutch 94), 189 (Gutch 185) and 191 (Gutch 187). For Coleridge's project concerning Fletcher Christian, see *ibid*, p. 174 (Gutch 22); also pp. 39 (Gutch 31), 46 (Gutch 38) and 159 (Gutch 154).

18. *Notebooks*, I, 10 (Gutch 2).

19. *Biographia Literaria*, II, 6.

20. We can possibly see the beginning of Coleridge's thinking about the prose frame in *Notebooks*, I, 928 (Apr 1801), which includes extensive extracts from Giordano Bruno's *De Monade* and *De Innumerabilibus Immenso*, which anticipate the prose commentary on lines 263–71 of 'The Ancient Mariner'. *Notebooks*, I, 1000 H (see *infra*, pp. 119–20), 1382, 1473, 1996, and II, 2060, all demonstrate how early this matter preoccupied Coleridge. The process continued up to the publication of *Sibylline Leaves* (1817).

21. *Table Talk*, I, 160.

22. In both the poem and the *Nights* this stylistic simplicity is the concomitant of narrative complexity. The growth of the poem's second (prose) frame, of course, elaborates this complexity.

23. Lamb, *Letters*, I, 142 (8 Nov 1798) and 266 (30 Jan 1801).

24. See *Notebooks*, I, 1000 H, and Coburn's note to this.

25. 'A Poet's Reverie' is the subtitle of 'The Ancient Mariner' in the 1800, 1802 and 1805 editions only. Coleridge's dropping of the subtitle in 1817 perhaps suggests a change of attitude to this 'responsibility' and suggests that 'A Poet's Reverie' was a temporary concession to the poem's hostile reception.

26. 'If thou hast mastered this intuition of absolute existence, thou wilt have learnt likewise, that it was this, and no other, which in the earlier ages seized the nobler minds, the elect among men, with a sort of sacred horror. This it was which first caused them to feel within themselves the something ineffably greater than their own individual nature' (*The Friend*, I, 514).

27. See also *Notebooks*, III, 3593, which uses the simile of a ship's crew cast upon an unknown island and also a single castaway 'stunned' and then awakened to embody this awesome question. A more thought-provoking note, however, is *ibid.*, p. 4057.

What a swarm of Thoughts & Feelings, endlessly minute fragments & as it were representations of all preceding & embryos of all future Thought lie compact in any one moment – So in a single drop of water the microscope discovers, what motions, what tumult, what wars, what pursuits, what strategems, what a circle-dance of Death & Life, Death hunting Life & Life renewed & invigorated by Death –

the whole world seems here, in a many-meaning cypher – What if our existence was but that moment! – What an unintelligible affrightful Riddle, what a chaos of dark limbs & trunk, tailless, headless, nothing begun & nothing ended, would it not be! And yet scarcely more than that other moment of 50 or 60 years, were that our all! each part throughout infinite diminution adapted to some other, and yet the whole means to nothing – ends everywhere, and yet an end no where. –

28. 'The Eolian Harp', *Complete Poetical Works*, I, 101.
29. The depth and continuity of Coleridge's interest in the *Nights* can best be illustrated by further samples from his *Notebooks* and *Letters*, which indicate that the stories were a part of his consciousness rather than another mere source for or analogue of his poem. In a letter written in Germany on 6 July 1799 (*Letters*, I, 522) Coleridge describes a story told by an eccentric German collector as 'quite as entertaining tho' not so probable as the story of the Wonderful Lamp [Galland, *Nights*, III, 285 – IV, 87]. *Notebooks*, I, 847 details a dream of 'Friday Night, Nov. 28, 1800, or rather Saturday Morning – a most frightful Dream of a Woman whose features were blended with darkness catching hold of my right eye & attempting to pull it out . . . the Woman's name Ebon Ebon Thalud'. Kathleen Coburn finds a druggist, Ebn Thaher, in the tale of the 185th Night (Galland, *Nights*, II, 126–98): the dream undoubtedly has its source in the *Nights*. In *Opium and the Romantic Imagination* (Faber, 1968) p. 207, Alethea Hayter suggests that Ebon Ebon Thalud is the 'Life-in-Death' figure of Coleridge's poem, but that figure with skin 'white as leprosy', from the earliest (1798) version of the poem, seems unrelated to this *dark* nightmare. Ebon Ebon Thalud seems to have been derived in all but name from Amina, the ghoul-wife (Galland, *Nights*, IV, 102–13).
   Notebooks, III, 4315 (Apr–May 1816) epitomises the problems of the first frame of the *Nights*, and lightheartedly sides with the Genie's mistress's point of view, and sees the episode as 'quite Homeric'. But perhaps the most extraordinary use of the *Nights* in all of Coleridge's prose is to be found in a letter to James Gillman of 9 October 1825:

It is a flat'ning Thought, that the more we have seen, the less we have to say. In Youth and early Manhood the Mind and Nature are, as it were, two rival Artists, both potent Magicians, and engaged, like the King's Daughter and the rebel Genie in the Arabian Nights' Enternts., in sharp conflict of Conjuration – each having for it's [sic] object to turn the other into Canvas to paint on, Clay to mould, or Cabinet to contain. For a while the Mind seems to have the better in the contest, and makes of Nature what it likes; takes her Lichens and Weather-stains for Types & Printer's Ink and prints Maps & Fac Similes of Arabic and Sanscrit Mss. on her rocks; composes Country-Dances on her moon-shiny Ripples, Fandangos on her Waves and Walzes on her Eddy-pools; transforms her Summer Gales into Harps and Harpers, Lovers' Sighs and sighing

Lovers, and her Winter Blasts into Pindaric Odes, Christabels &
Ancient Mariners set to music by Beethoven, and in the insolence
of triumph conjures her Clouds into Whales and Walrusses with
Palanquins on their Backs, and chaces the dodging in a Sky-hunt! –
But alas! alas! that Nature is a wary wily longbreathed old witch,
tough-lived as a Turtle and divisible as the Polyp, repullulative in a
thousand Snips and Cuttings, integra et in toto! She is sure to get
the better of Lady MIND in the long run, and to take her revenge
too – transforms our To Day into a Canvass dead-colored to receive
the dull featureless Portrait of Yesterday; not alone turns the mimic
Mind, the ci-devant Sculptress with all her kaleidoscopic freaks and
symmetries! into clay, but *leaves* it such a *clay*, to cast dumps or
bullets in; and lastly (to end with that which suggested the
beginning –) she mocks the mind with it's own metaphors, metamor-
phosing the Memory into a lignum vitae Escrutoire to keep unpaid
Bills & Dun's Letters in, with Outlines that had never been filled
up, MSS that never went farther than the Title-pages, and Proof-
Sheets & Foul Copies of Watchmen, Friends, Aids to Reflection &
other *Stationary* Wares that have kissed the Publisher's Shelf with
gluey Lips with all the tender intimacy of inosculation! – Finis! –
(*Letters*, VI, 496–7)

The episode in question is a part of the Second Calender's tale, and is
to be found in Galland, *Nights*, I, 143–7. The story encompasses an
extraordinary series of magical transformations in a contest between
Genie and Lady which supplies Coleridge's controlling trope. Many
details which find their way into the supplementary fancy of the
passage, such as the Arabian characters printed on the rocks, are
drawn directly from this source, which also suggests the underlying
darkness of this passage: consumed by her own magic, the Lady is
burned to ashes in this tale.

5

Dickens in Wonderland

MICHAEL SLATER

Writing to thank George Meredith for sending him a copy of
The Shaving of Shagpat: An Arabian Entertainment, Dickens said,
'I . . . shall not be unworthy to enter on its perusal, as one of the
most constant and delighted readers of those Arabian Entertainments of older date that they have ever had, perhaps. A new
Arabian Tale is charming to me in the promise it holds out . . .'[1]
That Dickens was indeed steeped in this favourite childhood classic
of his and that it played an enormously important role in the
development and play of his imagination has long been recognised.
'Except for the plays of Shakespeare,' wrote K. J. Fielding in 1958,
'no other work so stirred his imagination, or is so constantly
referred to in his works.'[2] More recently, Harry Stone has explored
in considerable depth the centrality to Dickens' art of fairy tales,
fables and legends, and he points to the particular appeal that the
Nights would have had for early Victorian children: 'Everything
was exotic, yet somehow believable too, for the stories and all their
trappings came out of a mysterious East where soft fountains
and hanging gardens, harems and pleasure domes, sultans and
scimitars, did most veritably exist.'[3]

A mingling of the exotic and the actual, the casting of a magical
glow over details of everyday life in the London of his day, lies at
the very heart of Dickens' mystery, and, among the tantalisingly
few comments that he made on his own art, one of the most
enlightening is that famous sentence from the Preface to *Bleak
House*: 'I have purposely dwelt upon the romantic side of familiar
things.' We have only to look at his most elaborate tribute to the
Nights to see how strongly instrumental these oriental tales must
have been in forming this very Dickensian *prédilection d'artiste*. The
tribute appears in an essay written for the first Christmas number
of his weekly journal *Household Words*. It is called 'A Christmas
Tree' and is, to my mind, one of the finest essays he ever wrote.

The Christmas tree of the title is an imaginary one carrying in its highest branches, which are full of 'dreamy brightness', Dickens' earliest Christmas memories – first of toys only, then lower down, of books such as the story of Little Red Riding-Hood tripping through her forest; and then

> Hush! Again a forest, and somebody up in a tree – not Robin Hood, not Valentine, not the Yellow Dwarf (I have passed him and all Mother Bunch's wonders, without mention), but an Eastern King with a glittering scimitar and turban. By Allah! two Eastern Kings, for I see another, looking over his shoulder! Down upon the grass, at the tree's foot, lies the full length of a coal-black Giant, stretched asleep, with his head in a lady's lap; and near them is a glass box, fastened with four locks of shining steel, in which he keeps the lady prisoner when he is awake. I see the four keys at his girdle now. The lady makes signs to the two kings in the tree, who softly descend. It is the setting-in of the bright Arabian Nights.
>
> Oh, now all common things become uncommon and enchanted to me. All lamps are wonderful; all rings are talismans. Common flower-pots are full of treasure, with a little earth scattered on the top; trees are for Ali Baba to hide in; beef-steaks are to throw down into the Valley of Diamonds, that the precious stones may stick to them, and be carried by the eagles to their nests, whence the traders, with loud cries, will scare them. Tarts are made, according to the recipe of the Vizier's son of Bussorah, who turned pastrycook after he was set down in his drawers at the gate of Damascus; cobblers are all Mustaphas, and in the habit of sewing up people cut into four pieces, to whom they are taken blindfold.
>
> Any iron ring let into stone is the entrance to a cave which only waits for the magician, and the little fire, and the necromancy, that will make the earth shake. All the dates imported come from the same tree as that unlucky date, with whose shell the merchant knocked out the eye of the genie's invisible son. All olives are of the stock of that fresh fruit, concerning which the Commander of the Faithful overheard the boy conduct the fictitious trial of the fraudulent olive merchant; all apples are akin to the apple purchased (with two others) from the Sultan's gardener for three sequins, and which the tall black slave stole from the child. All dogs are associated with the dog, really a

transformed man, who jumped upon the baker's counter, and put his paw on the piece of bad money. All rice recalls the rice which the awful lady, who was a ghoule, could only peck by grains, because of her nightly feasts in the burial-place. My very rocking-horse . . . should have a peg in his neck, by virtue thereof to fly away with me, as the wooden horse did with the Prince of Persia, in the sight of all his father's Court.

Yes, on every object that I recognise among those upper branches of my Christmas Tree, I see this fairy light! When I wake in bed, at daybreak, on the cold, dark, winter mornings, the white snow dimly beheld, outside, through the frost on the window-pane, I hear Dinarzade. 'Sister, sister, if you are yet awake, I pray you finish the history of the Young King of the Black Islands.' Scheherazade replies, 'If my lord the Sultan will suffer me to live another day, sister, I will not only finish that, but tell you a more wonderful story yet.' Then, the gracious Sultan goes out, giving no orders for the execution, and we all three breathe again.[4]

What is most striking about this passage is first of all the sense of delighted total recall that it conveys: one feels that Dickens could have extended indefinitely his list of common objects that figure significantly in the *Nights*. Almost as striking is the emphasis on the magical transforming power these stories had on the world of everyday things by which the child was surrounded. Everything became a matter for wonder and, as every reader of *Hard Times* knows, the ability to wonder is linked for Dickens with being in a state of moral and spiritual health. Children naturally wonder, and the more they do so the closer they are to God:

There once was a child, and he strolled about a good deal, and thought of a number of things. He had a sister who was a child too, and his constant companion. These two used to wonder all day long. They wondered at the beauty of the flowers; they wondered at the height and blueness of the sky; they wondered at the depth of the bright water; they wondered at the goodness and power of GOD who made the lovely world.[5]

In the autobiographical fantasy, of which this is the opening paragraph, Dickens is looking back, as he so often does, to the lost Eden of his childhood, before the shades of Bayham Street and the still darker shades of Warren's Blacking began to close upon the growing boy. The *Nights* was strongly associated in his mind with the happiness and innocence (of the moral complexities of life) of that period, and this, in turn, related closely to Dickens' religious beliefs. Jesus's words to his disciples, 'Except ye . . . become as little children, ye shall not enter into the kingdom of heaven',[6] were central to Dickens' brand of Christianity, and for him two of the most important aspects of 'becoming as little children' would seem to have been sustaining or reviving in oneself a love for tales of wonder and a substituting of 'innocent' romance for adult sexuality. The strong erotic element in the *Nights* tends to disappear, therefore, in Dickens' fond reminiscences about them. In the passage just quoted from 'A Christmas Tree', for example, a modern reader unfamiliar with the Induction to the *Nights* would assume that the two kings were going to rescue the lady from the giant rather than what is actually the case, that she is about to compel them to satisfy her lust.

A quasi-autobiographical story, 'The Ghost in Master B's Room', that Dickens wrote for the 1859 Christmas number of *Household Words'* successor, *All the Year Round*, is probably the most elaborate illustration to be found in all his work of his association of the *Nights* with an innocent and happy childhood from which he was suddenly and brutally cut off. As I have discussed this story elsewhere,[7] I shall not dwell on it here, except to note that it provides a further example of Dickens' skilful turning of the more erotic aspects of the *Nights* 'to favour and to prettiness'.

For Dickens an ability still to delight as an adult in the wondrous tales that had enchanted one as a child is always a sure sign of a good and kind heart. An amused superiority or careless indifference towards the *Nights* indicates the reverse. This can be neatly illustrated from contrasting Pecksniff and Tom Pinch in *Martin Chuzzlewit*. A mere glimpse of the book in a shop window is enough to bring all his long-lost happy childhood back to Tom:

And there too were the Persian tales, with flying chests, and students of enchanted books shut up for years in caverns: and there too was Abudah, the merchant, with the terrible little old woman hobbling out of the box in his bedroom: and there the mighty talisman – the rare Arabian Nights – with Cassim Baba, divided by four, like the ghost of a dreadful sum, hanging up, all gory, in the robbers' cave. Which matchless wonders, coming fast on Mr Pinch's mind, did so rub up and chafe that wonderful lamp within him, that when he turned his face towards the busy street, a crowd of phantoms waited on his pleasure, and he lived again, with new delight, the happy days before the Pecksniff era.[8]

Tom's transfiguring passion for these stories of his childhood, however, is merely a matter for contemptuous amusement to Mr Pecksniff. His own ludicrous allusion to the *Nights* helps to mark him as a bad man. When he is talking to young Martin Chuzzlewit on the eve of his own departure for London with his family Pecksniff says,

'. . . We leave you in charge of everything. There is no mystery; all is free and open. Unlike the young man in the Eastern tale – who is described as a one-eyed almanack, if I am not mistaken, Mr Pinch?'

'A one-eyed calender, I think, sir,' faltered Tom.

'They are pretty nearly the same thing, I believe,' said Mr Pecksniff, smiling compassionately; 'or they used to be in my time. Unlike that young man, my dear Martin, you are forbidden to enter no corner of this house. . . .'[9]

The beginning of Scrooge's reclamation comes when he is made to revisit his past and vividly to recall his childhood delight in the wonder of the *Nights*:

The Spirit touched him on the arm, and pointed to his younger self, intent upon his reading. Suddenly a man, in foreign garments: wonderfully real and distinct to look at: stood outside the window, with an axe struck in his belt, and leading an ass laden with wood by the bridle.

'Why it's Ali Baba!' Scrooge exclaimed in ecstasy. 'It's dear old honest Ali Baba! yes, yes, I know! One Christmas time, when yonder solitary child was left here all alone, he *did* come, for the first time, just like that. Poor boy! And Valentine,' said Scrooge, 'and his wild brother Orson; there they go! And what's his name, who was put down in his drawers, asleep, at the Gate of Damascus; don't you see him! And the Sultan's Groom turned upside-down by the Genii; there he is upon his head! Serve him right. I'm glad of it. What business had *he* to be married to the Princess!'[10]

(One notices again here that combination of the mundane and the exotic, 'drawers' and 'Damascus', that was clearly such a leading attraction of the *Nights* for Dickens.) It is just a moment after he has relived his childhood experience of the *Nights*, and other tales of wonder such as *Robinson Crusoe*, that Scrooge first exhibits signs of being a morally reformed character ('There was a boy singing a Christmas Carol at my door last night. I should like to have given him something . . .').

Given the strong link that Dickens makes between a sense of wonder cultivated in childhood by reading the *Nights* and goodness of heart in the man to whom the reading child is father, it is not surprising that he always attacks vehemently those who would rationalise the marvels of these exotic tales (indeed, he can hardly bear even linguistic scholarship being brought to bear on them[11]), people such as, in a late essay, he represents generically by Mr Barlow, the indefatigably instructive tutor of Sandford and Merton:

> The incompatibility of Mr Barlow with all other portions of my young life but himself, the adamantine inadaptability of the man to my favourite fancies and amusements, is the thing for which I hate him most. What right had he to bore his way into my Arabian Nights? Yet he did. He was always hinting doubts of the veracity of Sinbad the Sailor. If he could have got hold of the Wonderful Lamp, I knew he would have trimmed it and lighted it, and delivered a lecture over it on the qualities of sperm-oil, with a glance at the whale fisheries. He would so soon have found out – on mechanical principles – the peg in the neck of the Enchanted Horse, and would have turned it the right way in so workmanlike a manner, that the horse could never have got any height into the air, and the story couldn't have been. He would have proved, by map and compass, that there was no such kingdom as the delightful kingdom of Casgar, on the frontiers of Tartary. He would have caused that hypocritical young prig Harry to make an experiment – with the aid of a temporary building in the garden and a dummy – demonstrating that you couldn't let a choked hunchback down an Eastern chimney with a cord, and leave him upright on the hearth to terrify the sultan's purveyor.[12]

Hard Times is, of course, his most formidable and sustained attack on the enemies of wonder. Gradgrind and his pet schoolmaster,

M'Choakumchild, are even worse than Barlow in that they would totally ban such literature as the *Nights*, not merely attempt to explain its wonders away through science. In a famous passage Dickens cleverly uses imagery drawn from the *Nights* to point and sharpen his attack on these fact-grinders, M'Choakumchild is described as going to work

> in this preparatory lesson, not unlike Morgiana in the Forty Thieves; looking into all the vessels ranged before him, one after another, to see what they contained. Say, good M'Choakum-child. When from thy boiling store thou shalt fill each jar brimful by-and-by, dost thou think that thou wilt always kill outright the robber Fancy lurking within – or sometimes only maim and distort him?[13]

We may find elsewhere in Dickens other examples of this 'subversive' use of the *Nights* where the severely factual and determinedly unromantic is described and defined in terms of that to which it is most opposed. There are, for instance, those severe London houses that oppress Arthur Clennam on his return to the city after many years' absence, on that 'gloomy, close, and stale' Sunday evening: 'Ten thousand responsible houses surrounded him, frowning as heavily on the streets they composed, as if they were every one inhabited by the ten young men of the Calendar's story who blackened their faces and bemoaned their miseries every night.'[14]

Generally, however, Dickens uses allusions to the *Nights* in his novels and other writings, and in his speeches, for one of two purposes. The first is to evoke a sense of wonder, beauty, glamour, mystery, sudden and extraordinary terror, and so on. We may judge just how overwhelmed he was by the astonishing nature of Venice when we find him writing to Miss Coutts, 'I never could have believed in, and never did imagine, the full splendour and glory of Venice. That wonderful dream! The three days that I passed there, were like a Thousand and One Arabian Nights, wildly exaggerated a thousand and one times.'[15] Similarly, in his 'Preliminary Word' in the first number of *Household Words*, it is the *Nights* that he invokes when seeking to awaken readers to that 'romantic side of familiar things' which the journal was to specialise in depicting (and we notice, too, how he immediately links these new wonders of technology to a beneficent moral effect): 'The Swart giants, Slaves of the Lamp of Knowledge, have their thousand and one tales, no less than the Genii of the East; and these in all their wild, grotesque, and fanciful aspects, in all their many phases of endurance, in all their many moving lessons of compassion and consideration, we design to tell.'[16]

In the novels there are numerous examples of that use of allusion to the *Nights* to evoke a sense of the marvellous, whether it be charming and beautiful or grim and terrible in its aspect, to which I have already referred. In *David Copperfield*, for instance, there is David's description of the effect on himself of finding his friend Traddles installed in chambers in Gray's Inn surrounded by beautiful young sisters-in-law (like a sort of Gilbert and Sullivan female chorus):

> If I had beheld a thousand roses blowing in a top set of chambers, in that withered Gray's Inn, they could not have brightened it half so much. The idea of those Devonshire girls, among the dry law-stationers and the attorneys' offices: and of the tea and toast, and children's songs, in that grim atmosphere of pounce and parchment, red-tape, dusty wafers, ink-jars, brief and draft paper, law reports, writs, declarations, and bills of costs, seemed almost as pleasantly fanciful as if I had dreamed that the Sultan's famous family had been admitted on the roll of attorneys, and had brought the talking bird, the singing tree, and the golden water into Gray's Inn Hall.[17]

Just before the climactic point in *Great Expectations* when Pip is suddenly disabused of his illusions about the source of his wealth, Dickens uses a powerful image drawn from *The Tales of the Genii*:

> In the Eastern story, the heavy slab that was to fall on the bed of state in the flush of conquest was slowly wrought out of the quarry, the tunnel for the rope to hold it in its place was slowly carried through the leagues of rock, the slab was slowly raised and fitted in the roof, the rope was rove to it and slowly taken through the miles of hollow to the great iron ring. All being made ready with much labour, and the hour came, the sultan was aroused in the dead of the night, and the sharpened axe that was to sever the rope from the great iron ring was put into his hand, and he struck with it, and the rope parted and rushed away, and the ceiling fell. So, in my case; all the work, near and afar, that tended to the end, had been accomplished; and in an

instant the blow was struck, and the roof of my stronghold dropped upon me.[18]

The effect of this particular allusion is twofold, I think. It prepares the reader for the intricate and astonishing nature of the dark mystery by which Pip has been unwittingly surrounded since childhood, and it also serves as an image for the great skill with which Dickens, the Scheherazade–novelist, has laid his plot and prepared the mine which he is now about to explode on his readers.

Eastern-tale imagery, this time from the original Arabian Nights, is again employed in book 4, chapter 4, of *Our Mutual Friend*, when Dickens seeks to create an atmosphere of innocent enchantment around the runaway marriage of Bella and John Rokesmith, which is attended only by Bella's cherubic little father. The marriage feast takes place at a hotel in Greenwich (a place associated for Dickens himself with delightful escapades) and Dickens describes it as follows:

> What a dinner! Specimens of all the fishes that swim in the sea, surely had swum their way to it and if samples of the fishes of divers colour that made a speech in the Arabian Nights (quite a ministerial explanation in respect of cloudiness), and then jumped out of the frying-pan, were not to be recognised, it was only because they had all become of one hue by being cooked in batter among the whitebait.

We notice the satirical parenthesis that Dickens slips into this allusion, mocking the parliamentary pomposity of ministers, and this points us towards the other great use of *Nights* allusions made by Dickens. He will often use some detail from one of the stories to make a satirical point – the totally arbitrary nature of justice in the *Nights*, for example, provides him with a striking satirical image for fashionable 'Byronic' misanthropy in chapter 36 of *Chuzzlewit*:

> Tom was far from being sage enough to know that, having been disappointed in one man, it would have been a strictly rational and eminently wise proceeding to have revenged himself upon mankind in general, by mistrusting them one and all. Indeed this piece of justice, though it is upheld by the authority of divers profound poets and honourable men, bears a nearer

resemblance to the justice of that good Vizier in the Thousand-and-one Nights, who issues orders for the destruction of all the Porters in Bagdad because one of that unfortunate fraternity is supposed to have misconducted himself, than to any logical, not to say Christian system of conduct, known to the world in later times.

Again, in a speech at the Polytechnic Institution in Birmingham in the very year (1844) that he was completing *Chuzzlewit*, he used the *Nights* in his attack on the social injustice of failing to provide proper moral education for the poorer classes but punishing them for turning to crime:

> I hold that for any fabric of society to go on day after day, and year after year, from father to son, and from grandfather to grandson, unceasingly punishing men for not engaging in the pursuit of virtue and for the practice of crime, without showing them the way to virtue, has no foundation in justice, has no foundation in religion, has no foundation in truth, and has only one parallel in fiction that I know of, – which is the case of an obdurate old Genie, in the *Arabian Nights*, who was bent on taking the life of a certain merchant, because he had struck out the eye of his invisible son.[19]

He used the same allusion, to make the same point, eleven years later in the first of a series of three satirical articles entitled 'The Thousand and One Humbugs' published in *Household Words* during April and May 1855.[20] These articles, like his speech to the Administrative Reform Association on 27 June, were part of Dickens' contribution to the anti-Government agitation that had developed as a result of the appalling mismanagement of the Crimean War. Lord Palmerston, who replaced the ineffective Lord Aberdeen as Prime Minister in January 1855, was a particular target for Dickens' criticism, as he seemed to be the very embodiment of a type of aristocratic insolence or 'dandyism' that Dickens detested.

In the first of the articles in *Household Words*, after paying a handsome tribute to Antoine Galland as the man who first opened for Europeans 'this gorgeous storehouse of Eastern riches', Dickens announces with mock solemnity the discovery of a new Arabic manuscript containing stories very similar to those in the *Nights* and introduces his Sultan, Taxedtaurus (or Fleeced Bull), who had been married many scores of times, yet had never found a wife to suit him. Although he had raised to the dignity of Howsa Kummauns (or Peerless Chatterer), a great variety of beautiful creatures, not only of the high nobles of his court, but also selected from other classes of his subjects, the result had uniformly been the same. They proved unfaithful, brazen, talkative, idle, extravagant, inefficient, and boastful. Thus it naturally happened that a Howsa Kummauns very rarely died a natural death, but was generally cut short in some violent manner.

The Sultan's Grand Vizier, 'Parmastoon (or Twirling Weathercock)' seeks to alleviate his master's distress by getting him to listen to the fair Hansardade's legends of previous Howsa Kummauns, and she proceeds to relate stories of 'Scarli Tapa and the Forty Thieves' and of 'The Talkative Barber' (i.e. Palmerston himself).

We may find all this somewhat laboured now as political satire, but it remains brilliant as parody. Dickens must have hugely enjoyed constructing such sentences as 'The breath of the slave, said the Vizier, is in the hands of his Lord, but the Lion will sometimes deign to listen to the croaking of the Frog', or presenting the Speaker of the House of Commons as 'Mistaspeeka, a black mute, the Chief of the officers of the royal Seraglio'. Parodies as good as this can only be written by those who have a real love for, and great inwardness with, the text they are parodying, and I would offer these 'Thousand and One Humbug' articles as a final piece of evidence for the very special place that the *Arabian Nights* possessed in the heart and mind of Dickens.

NOTES

Books published in London unless otherwise stated.

1. *The Letters of Charles Dickens*, ed. Walter Dexter, Nonesuch Edition (1938) II, 773 (10 May 1856).
2. K. J. Fielding, 'The Weekly Serialisation of Dickens's Novels', *Dickensian*, 54 (1958) 135. Fielding goes on to draw attention to the influence of the form of the *Nights* on Dickens' early experiment with framed tales, the stories of Gog and Magog at the beginning of *Master Humphrey's Clock*, and the influence of the figure of Scheherazade on Dickens' conception of his role as a serial novelist as seen in 'Dickens's

constant conviction that like Dinarzade's sister, he kept his position as the favourite of the public only "under the stern condition" that his "inventive capacity must master my whole life"'. Both these aspects of the *Nights'* influence on Dickens have been explored further by Ruth F. Glancy in 'Dickens and Christmas: His Framed-Tale Themes', *Nineteenth Century Fiction*, 35 (June 1980) 53–72.

3. Harry Stone, *Dickens and the Invisible World: Fairy Tales, Fantasy and Novel-Making* (Macmillan, 1979) p. 25.

4. 'A Christmas Tree' is often included in *Reprinted Pieces*, the volume in which, in 1858, Dickens collected a number of items from *Household Words*, including several from the Christmas numbers, but it properly belongs with the collection entitled *Christmas Stories* and is generally found there in modern editions, e.g. the Oxford Illustrated Edition.

5. 'A Child's Dream of a Star', *Household Words*, 6 Apr 1850. Included by Dickens in *Reprinted Pieces*.

6. Matthew 18:3.

7. See Michael Slater, *Dickens and Women* (Dent, 1983) pp. 45–7.

8. *Martin Chuzzlewit*, ch. 5. The 'Persian tales' to which Dickens refers here are *The Tales of the Genii*, a work he always associates with the *Nights* and which he had devoured along with them in childhood. Purporting to be translated from the Persian by Sir Charles Morell, 'formerly Ambassador from the British Settlements in India to the Great Mogul', *The Tales of the Genii* were actually composed by the Rev. James Ridley (1736–65) and published by J. Wilkie in 1764. One of Dickens' earliest literary efforts, a drama entitled *Misnar, the Sultan of India*, was based on one of these tales.

9. *Martin Chuzzlewit*, ch. 6. 'Calendar' means dervish or holy beggar, and the story to which Pecksniff is alluding is the Third Calender's story, evidently a favourite of Dickens's (it contains the description of the dreaded 'loadstone rock' which supplies one of the organising metaphors for *A Tale of Two Cities*). Cf. *infra*, n. 14.

10. *A Christmas Carol*, Stave Two. For a summary of the particular story of Bedreddin Hassan in the *Nights* to which Dickens is referring here see the Penguin English Library edition of *The Christmas Books* (1971) I, 258–9.

11. In 'The Ghost in Master B's Room' he refers to 'the good Caliph Haroun Alraschid' and exclaims, 'let me have the corrupted name again for once, it is so scented with sweet memories!' By this time (1859) E. W. Lane, whose new translation of the *Nights* appeared 1839–41, had taught readers that a more correct way to render the name into English was 'Khaleefeh Hároon Er-Rasheed'.

12. 'Mr Barlow', first published 16 Jan 1869 in *All the Year Round* and later included in *The Uncommercial Traveller*. *Sandford and Merton* by Thomas Day was first published 1783–9 and became a Victorian nursery classic. The morals and behaviour of the naughty little rich boy, Sandford, are contrasted throughout with those of the good boy, Harry Merton, a farmer's son, and their tutor, the Revd Mr Barlow, constantly points the moral that virtue pays.

13. *Hard Times*, book I, ch. 2.

14. *Little Dorrit*, book I, ch. 3. The allusion is to the Third Calendar's story.
15. *Letters of Charles Dickens to Angela Burdett-Coutts*, ed. Edgar Johnson (Jonathan Cape, 1953) p. 255 (8 Dec 1844).
16. 'A Preliminary Word' is reprinted in the volume of Dickens pieces called *Miscellaneous Papers*, ed. B. W. Matz (Chapman and Hall, 1908); also in the *Collected Papers* volume of the Nonesuch Edition of Dickens' *Works*. Dickens uses imagery drawn from the *Nights* again towards the end of the 'Preliminary Word', when he refers to 'the adventurer in the old fairy story, climbing towards the summit of a steep eminence on which the object of his search was stationed . . . surrounded by a roar of voices, crying to him, from the stones in the way, to turn back' (the reference is to the story of the two sisters who envied their younger sister).
17. *David Copperfield*, ch. 59, the allusion is again to the story of the two sisters who envied their younger sister.
18. *Great Expectations*, ch. 38. The story in *The Tales of the Genii* to which Dickens alludes is the story of Misnar, the Sultan of India, the very one he had dramatised as a child (see *supra*, n. 8).
19. *The Speeches of Charles Dickens*, ed. K. J. Fielding (Oxford: Clarendon Press, 1960) p. 60. Dickens goes on to refer to another story 'in the same book of charming fancies', as he calls the *Nights*, in which he compares the Spirit of Ignorance to the genie imprisoned in a casket at the bottom of the sea who would have magnificently rewarded whoever released him but who, when his imprisonment continued for a long time, vowed to destroy whoever should at last free him. As Fielding comments, 'The idea of releasing the Spirit of Ignorance was hardly a happy one', yet the allusion was, according to Dickens' letter to his friend Thompson, the great hit of the evening, being 'applauded to the very echo'.
20. These articles were included by Matz in the *Miscellaneous Papers* volume (see *supra*, n. 16).

6

Wilkie Collins and the Ladies of Baghdad, or the Sleeper Awakened

PETER L. CARACCIOLO

On a first reading of *The Moonstone*, the subtler references to the *Nights* may be scarcely glimpsed amid the flow of explicit allusions to *Robinson Crusoe*. The frequency with which Gabriel Betteredge invokes the name of Defoe's masterpiece emphasises the significance of the role the earlier novel plays in *The Moonstone*. Apart from characterising the kindly, talkative, self-educated steward, and forwarding the religious satire by the mock *sortes biblicae*, the Defoe allusions increasingly evoke a sense of England as Crusoe's isle invested by hostile Indians. Such an impression is an apt reminder of the nature of British overseas settlement, since, wherever the colony, on a Caribbean island or in the Indian sub-continent, the expatriate endeavoured to make a home from home, however precarious.[1] The scores of allusions to Defoe have also the important function of helping to structure Collins' novel, linking Prologue and Epilogue to the main body of the novel which they frame.

However, amidst a steady stream of references to *Robinson Crusoe* there is a break, tellingly at almost the centre of *The Moonstone*. The evangelical spinster, Drusilla Clack (no friend to 'that heathen old man' Betteredge), cherishes a different sacred book, though her Holy Word is not exactly the Authorised Version either. Numerous and meaningful as the Defoe allusions are, paradoxically it is an oblique yet crucially timed appeal to the *Nights* that has the deeper resonance throughout Collins' greatest novel and its precursor texts. The fortunes of the sacred gem in India have been a chronicle of thefts, and when the Moonstone reaches England its fate is no different. A blight falls first upon the lovers. Suspecting

143

Franklin Blake of stealing her diamond, Rachel Verinder accepts the proposal of another cousin, Godfrey Ablewhite, only to realise he too is a suitor whom she cannot trust. When she breaks off this engagement, the father of the man now rejected acts the Victorian tyrant. At this central point intervening between infuriated uncle and misjudged niece, Miss Clack (Rachel's companion and zealous distributor of religious tracts) offers a helpful quotation from 'the correspondence of Miss Jane Ann Stamper – Letter one thousand and one, on "Peace in Families"' (World's Classics edn, p. 289).

The allusion to *The Thousand and One Nights*, like so much else in the novel, evidently springs from the experience of Collins' childhood. As the 'Narrative of Miss Clack' was being dictated, Collins was both in great distress at his mother's approaching death and himself heavily drugged, an acute attack of rheumatic gout having driven him to increased doses of laudanum.[2] Bereavement itself will evoke memories of earlier years. That such recall is intensified by the action of laudanum was an effect noticed by De Quincey, whose 'far-famed *Confessions of an English Opium-Eater*' Franklin Blake is instructed to read (pp. 434–5). De Quincey recollects among the 'Pains of Opium . . . The minutest incidents of childhood, [as] of later years were often revived' (*Collected Writing*, ed. David Masson [Edinburgh: A. and C. Black, 1897] III, 435). Collins' experiences with the drug were similarly phantasmagoric. This is evident in the *dénouement* of the novel, with Ezra Jenning's citations from medical authorities on the unconscious operations of the mind, as well as implied by the Prologue to *The Moonstone*. Among all the memorabilia of the storming of Seringapatam, perhaps the chief icon is the painting of *General Baird Discovering the Body of Tipu Sultan* by Sir David Wilkie; that is, the climax of the dramatic events mirrored in the opening of the novel had been strikingly pictured by Wilkie's godfather and name-giver. But it is a trauma of Wilkie's early life which is most active at the centre of *The Moonstone*. In autumn 1838, at his new boarding school, the fourteen-year-old Wilkie found that the 'captain' of the dorm was a bully and, with his 'satraps',

as fond of hearing stories, when he had retired for the night, as the Oriental despot to whose literary tastes we are indebted for 'The Arabian Nights'. . . . I was the unhappy boy chosen to amuse him. It was useless to ask for mercy, and beg leave to go to sleep. . . . I was warned beforehand to 'be amusing if I wished to come out of it with comfort to myself', . . . In after years I never had an opportunity of reminding the captain that I had served my apprenticeship to story-telling under his superintendence. He went to India with good prospects, and died, poor fellow . . . ('Reminiscences of a Story-Teller', *Universal Review*, 1888)[3]

In the Puttick and Simpson sale catalogue published in 1890 for the auction of Collins' library, there is listed the 'Arabian Nights' Entertainments with signature of W. Wilkie Collins, vols. 2 et 3, 12mo. 1820' (p. 10). This sounds like the 1821 Rivington reprint (whose additional title-pages bear the date 1820) of a translation from Antoine Galland's French, the version by which most English readers of the eighteenth and early nineteenth centuries became familiar with *The Thousand and One Nights*.

Two other items in the sale catalogue (pp. 6, 15) would seem to argue that Collins shared more than a little of the interest in Islamic art which became increasingly common among Victorians. Lots 78 and 242 are, respectively, Washington Irving's *Works* (1853) and John Frederick Lewis's celebrated illustrations of his sojourns in Moorish Spain, *Sketches and Drawings of the Alhambra* (1835). The latter was inherited, it seems, from Collins' father, but obviously the same is not true of the ten volumes by Washington Irving. Among these, *Tales of the Alhambra* (first published 1832) is notable not least for its epistle dedicatory to Sir David Wilkie. The sound advice which the American gratefully acknowledges having received from the old Scottish painter seems also to have been taken to heart by his English godchild:

> You may remember, that in the rambles we once took together about some of the old cities of Spain . . . [we] were more than once struck with scenes and incidents in the streets, which reminded us of passages in the 'Arabian Nights'. You then urged me to write . . . 'something in the Haroun Al-Rasched style. . . .' I call this to your mind to show you that you are, in some degree, responsible for the present work, in which I have given a few 'Arabesque' sketches from the life, and tales founded on popular traditions. (*Works*, [H. G. Bohn, 1853] IV)

Sir David's letters and reminiscences of Spain likewise inspired the family of his closest English friend, eventually rousing William

Collins to take himself, wife and children off on a tour of Italy; his son recalls that at one stage his father was armed with a travel permit 'as all-powerful in its protective influence as an amulet in a fairy-tale' (*Memoirs of the Life of William Collins RA* [1848, repr. Wakefield; E. P. Publishing, 1978] II, 142). Unable to follow his friend further eastward, Collins wrote to Sir David in February 1840 about how gratifying it was for 'our family circle' to receive his news of the Holy Land: 'What you have already seen must afford materials, in your hands, highly attractive to a public, now more interested in eastern matters than during any former period' (II, 175). Sir David's untimely death only intensified his influence over Collins, so that among the paintings Wilkie's father exhibited at the Royal Academy in 1844 was an experiment in the new Eastern manner:[4] 'The oriental robe in which "The Patriarch" is dressed was painted from one brought by Sir David Wilkie from the Holy Land, and presented to Mr Collins by his sister. The picture is in the possession of the painter's family' (II, 253–4).

While young Wilkie's letters joke of coping with a 'seraglio', of how he entertained 'country relations' with stories of the grotesque and supernatural, 'The Monk . . . the Ancient Mariner',[5] it was some time before echoes of that traumatic situation in the dorm began to be heard in his professional work. One could accept, as Sir David had urged, that stories of 'Toledo and Seville . . . should have a dash of that Arabian spice which pervades everything in Spain' (*Tales of the Alhambra*, dedication): it was less easy to see how the cities and landscapes of nineteenth-century Britain also might be better understood if viewed in an oriental light. At first all Wilkie Collins caught were glimpses. His book on Cornwall, *Rambles beyond Railways* (1851), contains a cryptic allusion to the Eastern tales. At one place on the walking tour, his path was obstructed as if it were the task of 'some evil genius of Fairy Mythology to prevent mortal footsteps from ever intruding into the valley' (Westaway, repr., 1948, p. 155) In this passage from 'Legends of the Northern Coast', Wilkie Collins is plainly mindful of Thomas Keightley's *The Fairy Mythology* (1828, rev. 1860). Of greater significance in the longer term was Edward Smedley's *Occult Sciences* (1855), which was sold at the auction of Collins' books in the same lot as the *Nights*. During his encyclopaedic survey of the traditions and superstititions of the past, Smedley glances at Aladdin and other tales from the *Nights*, as well as, interestingly, Tipu's behaviour in defeat. However, it was not the

1   'The Lady of the Glass Case', by R. Smirke for the Forster Edition (William Miller, 1802) vol. I

2(a)   (left)'Sindbad . . . on the Whale's back', from *The History of Sindbad the Sailor*, published by E. Newbery (1784)
2(b)   (right) Sindbad on 'the Island of Serpents', from *The Oriental Moralist* (E. Newbery, c.1791)

3 'Shacabac, the Barber's Sixth Brother', sharing the imaginary meal with the Barmecide, by R. Smirke for *The Adventures of Hunch-back* (William Daniell, 1814)

fought together long and fiercely, till the cat, seeing himself overcome, changed himself into a large red pomegranate, which fell into a pool; but the wolf pursuing it, it ascended into the air, and then fell upon the pavement of the palace, and broke in pieces, its grains became scattered, each apart from the others, and all spread about the whole space of ground enclosed by the palace. The wolf, upon this, transformed itself into a cock, in order to pick up the grains, and not leave one of them; but according to the decree of fate, one grain remained hidden by the side of the pool of the fountain. The cock began to cry and flapped its wings, and made a sign to us with its beak; but we understood not what it would say. It then uttered at us such a cry, that we thought the palace had fallen down upon us; and it ran about the whole of the ground, until it saw the grain that had lain hid by the side of the pool, when it pounced upon it to pick it up; but it fell into the midst of the water, and became transformed into a fish, and sank into the water; upon which the cock became a fish of a larger size, and plunged in after the other. For awhile it was absent from our sight; but at length we heard a loud cry, and trembled at the sound; after which, the Afrite arose as a flame of fire, casting fire from his mouth, and fire and smoke from his eyes and nostrils: the King's daughter also became as a vast body of fire; and we would have plunged into the water from fear of our being burnt and destroyed; but suddenly the Afrite cried out from within the fire, and came towards us upon the raised floor, blowing fire at our faces. The lady, however, overtook him, and blew fire in like manner in his face; and some sparks struck us both from her and from him: her sparks did us no harm; but one from him struck

4 'Transformations', by William Harvey for 'The Story of the Second Royal Mendicant', in Lane's translation (1839–41) I, 174–5 (the page reproduced here is from the single volume edition, 1853)

5(a) (*left*) 'Zobeide prepares to whip the dogs', from 'The History of Three Calenders, Sons of Kings, and of Five Ladies of Bagdad'
5(b) (*right*) 'The journey of Prince Firouz Schah and the princess of Bengal', from 'The Story of the Enchanted Horse'
    Both these are by A. B. Houghton for the 'Dalziel's Illustrated' edition (1863–5)

6 'The Transformation of King Beder', Houghton's 1874 water-colour based on his illustration of the tale recounted in the Dalziel

7 'Zobeidè discovers the young man reciting the Koran', by J. E. Millais, for 'The History of Zobeide' in the Dalziel edition

8 'Sidi Nouman transformed into a Dog', by John Tenniel for the Dalziel edition

9 'The King saves himself by clinging to a plank', by Gustave Doré for 'The Story of the Third Calender' in the Cassell edition (1874–5)

10　'New Crowns for Old Ones', by Tenniel for *Punch*, 15 April 1876

11 'The Slave of the Ring', by J. D. Batten for *More Fairy Tales from the Arabian Nights* (Dent, 1895)

12 'The Giant Enters', by H. J. Ford for Sindbad's Third Voyage in the Andrew Lang edition (Longmans Green, 1898)

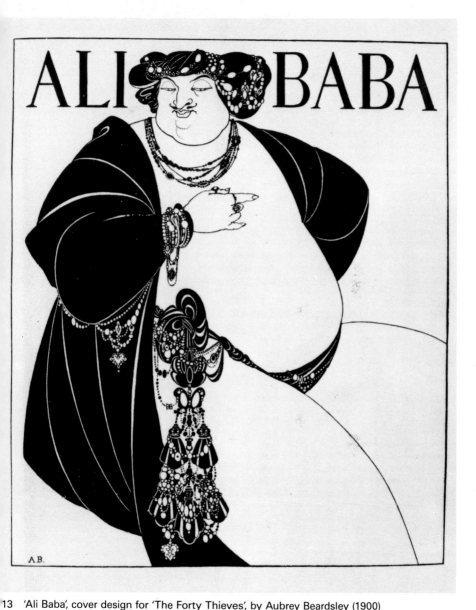

13 'Ali Baba', cover design for 'The Forty Thieves', by Aubrey Beardsley (1900)

14   'Ali Baba in the Wood', by Aubrey Beardsley (1900)

15 'The Damsel upset the Pan', by Edmund Dulac for the continuation of 'The Fisherman and the Genie', in *Stories from the Arabian Nights*, retold by Laurence Housman (Hodder and Stoughton, 1907)

16 'Princess Scheherazade, the heroine of the Thousand-and-one-Nights, ranks among the great storytellers of the world', by Edmund Dulac for the Boots–Hodder and Stoughton edition (1932)

comparative methods of the mythographers so much as the example of the great amateurs of the *Nights* which was immediately useful in showing the young Collins just how to use these oriental tales in his writing as well as in life.

Nearer to home than the models offered by the Brontës (at least intially) were the lessons to be drawn from the art of Scott, Thackeray, above all the increasingly sophisticated Dickens. In his correspondence with Collins one can trace the way Dickens redirected the role-playing of their leisure hours; the fantasising was not allowed to run waste but was channelled anew to fertilise imagination. On 12 December 1855, Dickens wrote to Collins, 'If you are free on Wednesday . . . and will meet me at the Household Words office, half past 5, I shall be happy to start on any Haroun Al-Rasched expedition' (*Letters of Charles Dickens*, ed. Walter Dexter [Nonesuch, 1938] II, 713). Knowing Dickens' fascination with the apparently magical powers of the new Detective Department,[6] and that the tribes of homeless children wandering the city were coming to be known as 'street Arabs', there is a marvellous aptness in Dickens' reference here (as well as in another Haroun reference, in a letter of 11 August 1858 – III, 38) to those persuasively realistic accounts of the extraordinary in the *Nights*, those stories of the great caliph who 'was accustomed to walk abroad in disguise very often by night, that he might see with his own eyes if everything was quiet in the city, and that no disorders were committed in it' (Galland, *Nights* [1821] I, 113).

In his letter of 12 December 1855, Dickens went on to praise 'The Ostler', Wilkie's story for the Christmas number; complained how the other material was generally 'so disappointing, and so impossible to be fitted together or to be got into the frame'; and suggested that Collins look at Dickens' own offering, 'The Boots', 'because I think it's an odd idea, and gets something of the effect of a Fairy story out of the most unlikely materials' (*Letters*, II, 714). Later in the correspondence we come across a reference that suggests how deep was the knowledge they shared of the famous collection. On 4 March 1857, Dickens rejoiced to receive a letter from Collins: 'I immediately arose like the desponding Princes in the *Arabian Nights*, when the old woman – Procuress evidently, and probably of French extraction – comes to whisper about the Princesses they love' (II, 838). According to Nikita Elisséef's analyses in *Thèmes et motifs des Mille et une nuits* (Beirut: Institut Français de Damas, 1949), there is no tale in the collection where a *plurality* of princes communicate with a *plurality* of princesses through the agency of an old woman; and in only a pair of stories are a prince and princess brought into contact by such a go-between (pp. 117–18). That Dickens could expect Collins to recognise the import of his plural implies that the two friends were steeped in Lane. Joseph von Hammer, it is true, gives one of these tales (*Nights* [Henry Colburn, 1826] i, 70–132); but, of the translations available to the mid-Victorians, it is only Lane's that provides some idea of both stories, 'Táj el-Mulook and the Lady Dunya' (i, 523-603) and 'Ardesheer and Hayat en-Jufoos', the latter being dismissed in a footnote 'as . . . little more than a repetition, word for word, of the story of Táj el-Mulook' (iii, 254).[7] Evidence of such an intimate knowledge of these Eastern tales has implications for the younger as well as older writer, highlighting developments in Collins' own art.

Although in collaborations such as their 'Doctor Dulcamara MP' (*Household Words*, Dec 1858) the Arabesque elements may be the work partly of Dickens, around the middle and close of the decade emerge the first clear signs that Collins was beginning to realise how the *Nights* could help him organise his material in the collections *After Dark* (1856) and *The Queen of Hearts* (1859). When the *Athenaeum* described the latter as 'a reprint of the author's contributions to *Household Words*', Collins protested indignantly. This response was not as disingenuous as it might seem, especially if one has a regard to the crypto-autographic manner in which these stories are framed.[8] Both *After Dark* and *The Queen of Hearts* resemble the *Nights* in that they collect tales within tales; the inset stories are told in the evenings, while the outer stories are concerned with gaining time in order to forward a human relationship. As in the *Nights* Scheherazade spins out her tales to save her marriage, her life and the lives of other women from Shahriar, so in *After Dark*, at the instigation of his wife, a portrait painter threatened with blindness recounts nightly the stories he had heard from his sitters, thereby gaining time in which his ailing eyes may recuperate, and (since he is the sole breadwinner of the family) in hopes that, when published, his collection of stories will supply the money necessary for his family's survival. As in the *Nights*, so in *The Queen of Hearts*, sensational stories are told to the person whom they are designed to influence, the listener being a person of the opposite sex. Collins' new frame tale is successful as a quietly amusing take-off of Shahriar and Shahazenan. In Collins, the settled ways of three brothers living apart from womenfolk are disturbed by a beautiful and intelligent young woman, who gradually overcomes the resistance of even the fiercest misogynist. In turn, the head of the household deliberately protracts her visit through the story-telling, so that the lovers can be united at last. In both collections, Collins seeks to give an air of truth to the extraordinary by the more or less middle-class setting of the frame tale – this too is characteristic of the Baghdadian and Cairene elements of the *Nights*.

Needless to say, Collins's frame stories come nowhere near equalling the unforgettable plight of Scheherazade. The trouble with the *Nights*, however, is that the frame is more of a situation than a plot. In this respect at least, *After Dark* and *The Queen of Hearts* may be judged superior; they do have a sustained story-line. Moreover, in Collins' handling of the time-gaining scheme, there is variety in the story-tellers. With *After Dark*, the artist's wife and his doctor encourage the literary efforts of the painter; in *The Queen of Hearts* there are several narrators more psychologically differentiated than those in the previous collection. Again Collins' inset tales are told to a frame audience much more responsive than any to be found at least in printed versions of the *Nights* prior to twentieth-century adaptations. Collins' miniaturisation of the *Nights*, though, is quite in accord with oriental aesthetics. Like compilations such as the *Panchatantra*, the *Nights* can be expanded or contracted as necessary.[9] Further, in a letter of 26 April 1858, Collins seems to have glimpsed the Arabesque possibilities of Dickens' public readings: 'I should not be surprised if stories came to be written in a few years' time for the express purpose of appealing to an audience of *listeners* instead of readers.'[10]

So far Collins' experiments were limited; he had still to emulate earlier British writers and attempt the 'naturalisation' of the immigrant stories within larger Western narrative genres in prose and verse. Regarding the latter, not only was an awareness of Chaucer's oriental debts being communicated to Victorian readers through the researches of Keightley and Lane and others,[11] but Collins possessed also a copy of Crabbe's *Poetical Works*, among which (though on a small scale) 'The Confidant' touchingly echoes the Harun cycle. Eventually other items in his library were to prove even more instructive. A profounder understanding of the encyclopaedic nature of the Arab collection is evident in the structure and motives of *The Antiquary* – 'that masterpiece', as

Collins called it.[12] Likewise in *Hard Times* the covert reminiscences of Scheherazade and her sisterhood operate poignantly among more open allusions. Nowhere among possible models, though, was there anything to match the subtle power with which Emily Brontë sublimates the distinctive elements of the *Nights*. Nevertheless, the fact that *Wuthering Heights'* kinship with the Arabian stories is not so immediately apparent as in *Jane Eyre's* exemplifies a principle in the operation of influence that Collins' readers should bear in mind: the scarcity, or indeed lack, of open references from a later to an earlier work does not necessarily preclude significant filiations of a deeper intertextual kind.[13]

On first consideration Collins' major novels manifest little or no sign of obvious affinities with the *Nights* – not at least until *The Moonstone*. Allusions to other arts, other cultures predominate. In *The Woman in White* (1859–60) the references to Celtic folklore that chiefly inspired *Basil's* (1852) vision of social inequality are translated to an international and age-old arena by the echoes of Dante as well as of Italian opera.[14] *No Name* (1862–3) deploys telling references to English eighteenth-century literature and drama, elaborating and refining a picaresque attack upon the antiquated laws governing legitimacy. *Armadale* (1866) amplifies its concern with problems of fate and free will by a host of allusions to the Bible, the Church Fathers, Greek tragedy, Shakespeare and Goethe. Yet, there are some telling hints of the East in these works; one particularly intrusive instance is the do-it-yourself 'Oriental Cashmere Robe' that in *No Name* gives so much trouble to persons far less innocent than that gentle monster, Mrs Wragge (World's Classics edn, pp. 192, 257, 273, 278, 298, 305, 337–8, 341, 370), the conspiracy of the Captain and Magdelen being as ingenious as any of the impersonations collected among the rogue tales of the *Nights*.[15]

As far as *The Woman in White* is concerned, one of Wendy Doniger O'Flaherty's illuminating comments on certain Indian analogues to the *Nights* seems particularly relevant: 'the double is the narrative equivalent of the framing statement'.[16] The double, indeed the triple, had already been used to memorable effect in the closure of a framed tale that is clearly a prototype for aspects of *The Woman in White*. This ghost story, 'The Bride's Chamber' – as Harry Stone has entitled it – is one of a number of inset tales in *The Lazy Tour of Two Idle Apprentices* (on which Collins and Dickens collaborated in *Household Words*, Oct–Nov 1857).[17] In addition to the parallels between tale and novel noted by Stone, there are overarching Arabian allusions. The day before he is to be haunted by a nightmarish story-teller, one of the tourists, Mr Goodchild, reflects on the origins of Lancaster's prosperity in the slave trade: the 'gain turned to curses, as the Arabian Wizard's money turned to leaves' (the reference is to the story of the Barber's Fourth Brother as it is given in Galland's paraphrase). That night Mr Goodchild hears from a ghost how a cruelly mercenary husband, having imprisoned his white-clad bride in a decaying mansion isolated in a wall-enclosed wilderness, finally drove the maddened woman to her death, only to find himself eventually exposed by a young man who had worshipped the wife from afar. These prefigurings of *The Woman in White* are reinforced by 'the tourist's' next adventure, when, himself falling madly in love with a fashionable beauty glimpsed at the great St Leger, the unhappy Goodchild yearns in 'the desert of his heart' to be with his beloved for ever – a wish that leads him to call on the help of 'Slave of the Lamp, or Ring', and then what sounds something like an echo of the adventures of Hasan of El-Basrah in search of *his* lost love (Lane, *Nights*, III, 384–517): 'Arab drums powerful of old to summon Genie in the desert'.[18] In *The Woman in White* the identification of the Victorian with the Arabian wilderness is rendered inescapable in a passage that acts as a kind of microcosm for the novel's far-ranging oriental reminiscences, a paragraph where the use of epanalepsis (a device not unknown to Arab poets) calls out for attention.[19] In the course of his investigations, the artist Walter Hartright finds himself in a desolate new country town; wittily the enfolding gloom is further suggested by the paragraph's envelope pattern, the repetition of phrases in parallel emphasising that this modern wasteland is worse than 'the deserts of Arabia . . . the ruins of Palestine' (World's Classics edn, p. 445). Restrospectively one recognises in the description of Blackwater, the family seat of the callous English husband, another desert in the making: the lake, Sir Percival complains, is 'a blot on a gentleman's property . . . has a curse on it, like the Dead Sea' (p. 208; see also pp. 184–5).

From this oriental angle, Marian Halcombe's journal looks increasingly like further statements for the defence of womankind against man's inhumanity. Like Scheherazade's story-telling, Marian's record is interrupted at dawn. True, when fever-stricken she desists, the ominous response of the 'sincere friend' who adds the 'postscript' (p. 307) is more loquacious than the Sultan's (even after hearing his own story as Count Fosco has just done); but, as his confession reveals, Fosco is to be identified with Shahriar: both are in Keightley's phrase 'Bluebeard Sultans' (*Tales and Popular Fictions*, p. 72), living embodiments of what is institutionalised in a patriarchal legal system – a cruelly sexist threat to the wives of a whole nation (*The Woman in White*, p. 570). Not for nothing is it that Fosco is twice compared with Henry VIII (p. 196); acting the Sultan to Madame Fosco, wearing 'Nankeen trousers' and 'morocco slippers' (p. 205), he has designed a 'pagoda-cage' for his white mice (pp. 198, 199, 207, 208, 209, 211, 213, 214, 544, 554, 555); when serenading the sisters, Fosco brazenly chooses Rossini's 'Moses in Egypt . . . Prayer of the Israelities at the passage of the Red Sea' (pp. 286–7); as his own titles declare, the Count lays claim to much the same territories as shah and caliph, being 'Perpetual Arch-Master of the Rosicrucian Masons of Mesopotamia' (p. 557). Like his Eastern predecessors, Fosco is outwitted more by narrative than by legal means, as Hartright puts his case to the court of public opinion.

'The aesthetics of the Old Bailey' were what the author of *Basil* was charged with adopting. Yet, as if Owen Jones were discovered to have cast a crypto-Moorish influence on the architecture of the Central Criminal Court,[20] the stream of oriental images disclosed in *The Woman in White* throws into a strangely exotic relief what has been previously regarded as a wholly European fusion: Collins' use of criminal conspiracy, detection and the formal procedures of the judiciary with its deposition of testimony. A major source for *The Woman in White* has been shown by Clyde K. Hyder to lie in an actual French trial recorded in a volume of law reports Collins had picked up off a Paris bookstall.[21] However, were these records and Collins' memories of the law courts he had visited the only forces helping him to shape his first masterpiece? Since it is plain that the *Nights* continued to be an important item in his reading from childhood on, that Collins had used the oriental frame technique in three earlier groupings of stories (the last as recently as 1859), that *The Woman in White* functions partly through a system of Arabesque allusions, surely it is more than possible that the example of the Arabian collection swayed Collins into using features of criminal justice as part of his manner no less than of his subject? Beside the police investigations and courts of law in the *Nights* (for instance, the story of Ali Cogia, that old favourite about the street-wise child whose detective skills are superior to those of his elders and betters),[22] the structures themselves of the collection derive in large degree from the processes of Islamic law. Originating in the need to verify the sayings of Mohammed, the system of a chain of witnesses affected Arab narrative literature. Thus, at the start of his own tale, the Second Calender in Forster's version recalls learning 'all the traditions received from the mouth of our prophet by those illustrious men who were his contemporaries' (1839, p. 39). To the failed lawyer as much as to the ambitious writer in Collins, the witnessing system must have appealed for the sense of authenticity, variation and drama that the device creates.

A *tour de force* in Collins' synthesis of tale within tale, testimony of witness, teasing allusion and word-play is found in *Armadale*. Its theme has much in common with the interaction of free will and fate in the Arab stories, and its nomenclature echoes the rhyming names of the *Nights* – 'Armadale' confusing friend and foe somewhat more than 'Abu Kir and Abu Sir'. Such information on these matters as Collins gathered from Lane and other translations could have been reinforced through his acquaintance with Layard and Burton. Both the 'excavator of Nineveh and Babylon' and 'the pilgrim to Mecca' moved, like Collins, in the Monckton Milnes circle).[23] In augmentation of similar tendencies in English usage, a characteristically oriental concern with tell-tale names and the ludic possibilities informing the triliteral roots of Arabic words, elaborate paronomasia of this Arabesque sort may have helped to inspire a bizarre episode in *Armadale*.[24] While one origin of the passage in question seems to lie in the history of theatrical hoaxes (the notorious 'Bottle Conjuror', 1749), a related source is surely to be found in a pun. Collins plays on memories of the oriental jugglers (who first captivated his father's teacher – see *Memoirs*, I 35–6) and the physical constraints upon sword-swallowing, i.e. the vital difference between *juggler* and *jugular*. Near the beginning of the main narrative of the novel, young Allan Armadale tells a weird Arabian tale-within-a-tale. Against the advice of his friend the Rector, Allan insists on being allowed to act the Good Samaritan to a mysterious and sick destitute who will turn out to be not merely his namesake, but, in the eyes of a third relative, Allan Armadale's potential supplanter. Allan protests,

Deuce take the pounds, shillings and pence! I wish they could all three get rid of themselves like the Bedouin brothers at the

show. Don't you remember the Bedouin brothers . . . ? Ali will
take a lighted torch, and jump down the throat of his brother
Muli – Muli will take a lighted torch, and jump down the throat
of his brother Hassan – and Hassan, taking a third lighted torch,
will conclude the performances by jumping down his own throat,
and leaving the spectators in total darkness. (Dover edn,
pp. 48–9)

In *Armadale* the Bedouin brothers' joke clearly has more than a
local function; one is reminded how at the circus or in pantomine
an act displaying genuine physical agility will be followed by a
clownish parody. In the novel too, there are implications wider
than just dismissal of the cash nexus. Unbeknown to Allan, the
joke assumes an ambiguous significance. The Good Samaritan
empathises with the man fallen among thieves. Still, is there not
something potentially suspect in this ability to project one's
personality into another's? Such an identification is related to the
impersonation of the actor, and, moving down the moral scale,
the confidence trickster. Actors with ulterior motives are plentiful
in Collins's *oeuvre*, as they are in the *Nights*. In *No Name* Magdalen
Vanstone is a militant Cinderella with a fairy godfather in Captain
Wragge, and that swindler is always appreciative of an alias,
keeping lists of the deceased headed 'Skins to Jump Into' (Dover
edn, p. 269). Again, though Allan is innocent of them, the Bedouin
joke has nuances of aggression and bungling. Such ambiguities
work proleptically within and even go beyond the novel's confines.
There is a lethal genie in a bottle at the climax of *Armadale*, and
how far he is circumvented emerges from a concatenation of self-
sacrifice as gripping as any of the substitutions in the *Nights*.

Still, one is left feeling that the grotesqueness of Allan's joke is
out of proportion to the novel in which is appears, as if the Bedouin
brothers might end up swallowing *Armadale* itself. *Mise en abîme*,
André Gide's coinage,[25] seems particularly illuminating here, for
the joke on the one hand is a microcosm of the rivalry and
friendship running from one generation to the next in *Armadale*,
and on the other hand creates the effect of a sudden magnification
of perspective. The Bedouin brothers connect with a whole range
of cultural phenomena from the popular to the intellectual: bawdy,
folk art, fairy tale, symbols of wisdom, forms of infinity, riddles,
magical teases to theories of narrative, and hypotheses about the
workings of the mind, nesting toys like Russian dolls and Chinese

boxes, the serpent eating its tail, the self-swallowing sets of the logician, a neo-Freudian description of the Unconscious as 'Infinite Sets', and not least *The Thousand and One Nights* themselves.

Like *Armadale*, *The Moonstone* turns out to have a uroboric form.[26] 'The Bedouin Brothers'' connection with narrative structure becomes yet clearer as one notes how Allan's joke anticipates episodes in *The Moonstone* (1868). Here are found instances of things *mises en abîme* – literally dropped into the abyss of the Shivering Sand. The peculiar horror of this quicksand is that it is pictured as a monstrous man-eating face. Having known the infernal depths of Victorian society, the wretched servant girl Rosanna is fatally mesmerised by the horrid sand:

> The broad brown face of it heaved slowly, and then dimpled and quivered all over. . . . 'It looks as if it had hundreds of suffocating people under it – all struggling to get to the surface, and all sinking lower and lower in the dreadful deeps!' (World's Classics edn, p. 28)

Before being driven to commit suicide there by Franklin Blake's rejection of her love, Rosanna has used the quicksand as a cache in which to store her knowledge of who took the stolen diamond. The fact that Rosanna's secret concerns the suspiciously libidinous action of a sleep-walker suggests that the Shivering Sand acts as an image of the unconscious where what is shameful gets repressed. This idea is reinforced by the language Blake employs to describe his subsequent probing of the sand. Kneeling as he must on the brink of the South Spit, it is as if he were about to kiss the 'false brown face' of the Sand: 'a horrible fancy that the dead woman might appear . . . to assist my search – an unutterable dread of seeing her rise through the heaving surface of the sand, and point to the place – forced itself into my mind' (pp. 342–3).

The raising of the box containing her letter wrapped in a man's nightgown transforms Rosanna into a deeply disturbing presence. What Blake discovers is reminiscent of a number of stories in the *Nights*. Repeatedly in the Arab collection one encounters a container, the disclosure of its contents proving dangerous and not merely to the finder: one obvious instance is the malignant jinni in the bottle pulled up by the fisherman – of which there seems to be a faint echo in an episode near the opening of the central action of Collins' novel. This is the first scene on the beach, where Betteredge has the premonition that a 'quiet English house [is to be] suddenly invaded by a devilish Indian Diamond' (p. 36) released from the 'little sealed paper parcel' (p. 31) which Franklin Blake has pulled from his pocket. A more strongly felt influence from the *Nights* upon this and later beach scenes in *The Moonstone* is that frequent variant on the motif of the dangerous container which discloses a fateful woman (or boy): in the *Nights'* frame tale, the lady in the glass case by the seashore who forces herself upon the two kings; the mutilated corpse in a basket fished out of the river and presented to Harun in 'The Three Apples'; indeed, with 'The Porter and the Ladies of Baghdad' the story of each royal calender concerns a prince who, chancing upon a well-equipped underground hiding-place, contributes to the destruction of its sexually erring occupants.[27] To Rosanna, who fell in love with him at first sight, Franklin Blake was 'like a prince in a fairy story' (p. 349), and they meet on the beach where ultimately she is to hide her secret, and then herself (pp. 28, 174–5, 343–5).

An *aperçu* of Todorov's is brought to mind by the way Rosanna's haunting tale at once contains the dark secret of lovers and is itself contained, being buried literally in her grave as well as inset within Franklin's narrative. In *The Poetics of Prose* (ch. 5), the structure of the *Nights* is seen as 'narrative-men' embedded in other 'narrative-men', Yet, useful as is Todorov's insight, a more illuminating approach to *The Moonstone*'s Chinese-box structure is suggested by an observation of Borges:

> *The Thousand and One Nights.* This collection of fantastic tales duplicates and reduplicates to the point of vertigo the ramifications of a central story in later and subordinate stories. . . . None is more perturbing than that of the six hundred and second night, magical among all the nights. On that night, the king hears from the queen his own story. He hears the beginning of the story which comprises all the others and also – monstrously – itself.   ('Partial Magic in the *Quixote*', *Labyrinths* [Harmondsworth: Penguin, 1964] p. 230)

Payne (*Nights* [1883] v, 333–6) and Burton (*Nights* [1885] vi, 199–201) seem to have been the first fully to translate (or, at least, to publish such a rendering of) 'The King's Son and the Afrit's Mistress', Lane (iii, 177) giving only an abstract of the *mise-en-abîme* structure to which Borges refers. None the less early-nineteenth-century versions of the Arabian collection contain several stories that tease the reader with much the same threat against which Borges here alerts us: the vertiginous possibility that the *Nights* is about to become 'infinite and circular'.[28]

A comic variant on this unsettling prospect opens up during that episode, central to *The Moonstone*, at which I glanced in beginning this essay. Interposing herself between outraged uncle and defiant niece, Miss Clack thrust before the gaze of this Victorian domestic tyrant.

> Letter one thousand and one, on 'Peace in families' . . . 'Manna in the wilderness, Mr Ablewhite! Dew on the parched earth! . . . the blessed, blessed, blessed words of Miss Jane Ann Stamper.' [At which] this monster in human form shouted out furiously, 'Miss Jane Ann Stamper be ——!' (pp. 289–90)

Like 'the martyr' (p. 290) whose epistle she cites, Miss Clack is revealed as a burlesque Scheherazade: a role 'this Rampant Spinster' (p. 291) plays not just in the confrontation with Uncle Ablewhite but also in the wider context of the novel's structure. She is giving her account of what resulted from the diamond's disappearance, and the tale she tells is at the behest of Franklin Blake. The constraints which as editor he imposes on Drusilla Clack drive her to interrupt the story as she vainly strives to protect 'our Christian hero' Godfrey (p. 283). Significantly her first name associates Clack with the Middle East, though less as a native than as wife of a corrupt colonial governor (see Acts 23–4). Clack proves to be a not wholly reliable link in a chain of witnesses, one of a number of narrators who piece together the larger story of the crime. But, whereas Clack's testimony contains within it a story of apparent innocence – the career of the 'Godly' Ablewhite – Franklin Blake's narrative discovers a tale of seeming guilt. In her letter from the grave, Rosanna accuses the man she loves, and her accusation is corroborated by Rachel Verinder; both reformed thief and ex-fiancé identifying as the chief suspect – Franklin Blake. Such instructive inversions and surprises recall the *Nights*.[29] As with the Sultan and Caliph, so Blake gets to hear his own damning story. Happily the feverish ramblings of Candy suggest a line of defence; but then, to persuade Rachel, Blake must arrange a recapitulation. The half-caste doctor Ezra Jennings sets up an experiment to reconstruct the circumstances of the theft. Rachel is convinced by the evidence, but what of the world? So, yet again, servants and masters put pen to paper to explain what each personally knows of the mystery. The extension of narratives continues on into the future. In the Prologue to the novel there are legends and chronicles: an honest English officer describes the misconduct of a comrade, tells of rumours concerning the sacred diamond, of Muslim then British conquest, until yet again 'the Moonstone' is no lawful prize of war. Completing this framework in the Epilogue, a 'celebrated Indian traveller', disguised like Burton as an oriental pilgrim, witnesses how this story in the Book of Fate is apparently closed by the restitution of the numinous diamond to its lawful owner. Yet is this 'The End'?

So the years pass and repeat each other; so the same events revolve in the cycles of time. What will be the next adventures of The Moonstone? Who can tell?   (p. 522)

Who indeed? Mr Murthwaite's statement is dated 1850 – the very year when, having passed through the hands of a succession of potentates from gods to men, Hindu, Muslim, Sikh, Indian and non-Indian, the Koh-i-noor ('mountain of light') came into the possession and eventually the regalia of Victoria. Before the decade was out, the sepoys were to mutiny and attempt to expel the British who had acquired so ill-fated a diamond as that which helped inspire Collins' novel. Borges's remark about those nesting toys, the 'generations of Russian dolls', seems applicable here: that it is 'as if the distances of the past and the future were reducing them and as if there were incalculable others besides the six or seven visible – others imperceptibly minute, others imperceptibly gigantic, concealed by their enormity' (*Discusión* [Buenos Aires, 1932] p. 155).[30]

One person in the hierarchy of narrators composing *The Moonstone* who, I hope, has been made a little more visible is Wilkie Collins himself: a somnambulist, drugged, feverishly reliving that adolescent trauma, now irrevocably parted from his mother, once more the Victorian Scheherazade dictating his story against the clock – and how suggestive of the executioner is the jargon of publishing – desperately meeting the deadlines of each instalment in Dickens' *All the Year Round*. Not that Collins is the only Scheherazade who may go unperceived by the modern reader. The circumstances of serial publication and the vast popularity of

The Moonstone created in 1868 a multitude of tellers and listeners in family circles, among friends rich and poor, at home or in the Empire.[31]

In other respects Collins' situation here is much less usual. *The Moonstone* comes almost into a class of its own with the novel's subject, its sources, the way they are used. Collins develops a new sub-genre, the detective novel, to investigate the insidious effects of empire upon the morality of the British class-structure. While *The Moonstone* is not the first novel in the language ambitious to place the nation's life in its global context of colonialism, before Collins' work there had been only a handful of such attempts.[32] From *Robinson Crusoe* onwards, Defoe was concerned to explore the consequences as well as opportunities of British overseas expansion. Apart from Swift, though, whose parody of *Robinson Crusoe* ended up being misread by many as an adventure story, Defoe's few British literary successors are found mainly in the nineteenth century. The most important of these was Scott, who, at one point, looked set to extend his scrutiny of English conquest by despatching his muse to India: not only does *The Surgeon's Daughter* allude to Aladdin's palace, but the latter half of the plot takes place around Seringapatam, where the father of Tipu Sultan, though hostile to the English, acts the role of the disguised Haroun (ch. 14; Border edn, pp 472–3, also pp. 334–5). Thus yet another intimate of Collins' father glances at a subject close to the historical material on which is based the Prologue to *The Moonstone*. Moreover, while *The Surgeon's Daughter* is far from being numbered among 'the Author of Waverley's' finest achievements, Scott, like Sir David Wilkie, does seem to have suggested how the problems of imperial aggrandisement could be viewed more clearly from an angle that was at once familar and exotic.[33]

An anniversary issue of the *Spectator* (14 July 1866) remarked that even after the 1857 Mutiny most Englishmen got their knowledge of the Orient from the Bible and *A Thousand One Nights*.[34] In the case of the sub-continent this was not altogether surprising. 'From time immemorial India has been a conquered country', as J. Talboys Wheeler explains in his *Madras of the Olden Time* (Madras: Higginbotham, 1861–2) – adding ironically, such was the 'dryness' of the Mughal chronicles, that 'until some historical romancer can be found with sufficient boldness to . . . confine himself to Arabian Nights-like stories . . . the history of Delhi will be a blank to the general reader' (i, 12–13).[35] One consequence was that the British tended to view imperial politics in terms of the *Nights*. As J. Timbs noted in 1851, from the moment that it arrived in England as the spoil of the Sikh Wars, 'no small share of the lustre of *The 1001 Nights* [had played] about' the notorious history of the Koh-i-noor.[36] And in his 1860 lecture on diamonds the great mineralogist Maskelyne argued that, while his London audience might not believe it to be 'the talisman of oriental empire', they must recognise the Koh-i-noor's historical importance, for, among other vicissitudes, it had been wrested from the Hindus by 'Ala-ud-din . . . the first Pathan sovereign of Delhi'; moreover in the course of estimating its original weight Maskelyne also refers explicity to '*The Arabian Nights*' (*Chemical News*, 7 Apr 1860, pp. 208–13). Much of this lecture was borrowed by C. W. King, an acknowledged source for *The Moonstone*.[37] In the 1867 version of his work on gems, *The Natural History of Precious Stones and Precious Minerals*, before tracing 'the malign powers' of the Koh-i-noor in the Crimean War and the Mutiny (p. 74), King writes of having 'wandered lovingly through the true Aladdin's garden of Eastern literature plucking its fruits which be all manner of precious stones' (Preface, pp v–vi).

The same trope was used by Dickens' close friend Emily Eden of the magnificent jewellery presented by her brother Lord Auckland to Runjeet Singh, the great Sikh ruler who in 1838 (when he showed the celebrated diamond to Miss Eden) was among the last Indian possessors of the ill-fated Koh-i-noor. At Lucknow, a name later famous in the Mutiny, she was delighted to find the palace was 'quite as *Arabian-Nightish* as I meant it to be',[38] while the gardens brought back memories of Abou Hassan the Sleeper Awakened (p. 62); subsequently the reported discovery of magnetic stones may also have struck a chord recalling the shipwreck of the Third Calender in 'The Porter and the Ladies of Baghdad'. For Emily Eden seems to have had almost by heart G. S. Beaumont's translation of Galland; but, then, in the Governor General's retinue there was not only Torrens, one of the finest of the translators of the *Nights*, but also William Hay Macnaghten, who in 1838 had just published his edition of *Alf laila wa-laila*. Unfortunately, accomplished orientalists as the pair were, Torrens and Macnaghten share a heavy responsibility for the annihilation of a British army on the North-West Frontier. And eventually the Eden journals are overwhelmed by the horrors of the Afghan campaign. In a letter of 24 August 1842, Wilkie too notes the widespread criticism of Lord Auckland's government of India.[39]

The retreat from Kabul was linked by an outraged De Quincey with comparably disastrous expeditions against Kandy, the 'fierce little Lilliputian kingdom' of Ceylon. Although the sympathetic attitude towards Indians in *The Moonstone* is opposed to the colonial propaganda voiced by De Quincey in his 1843 *Blackwood's* essay on Ceylon, Collins' interest in the works of the Opium Eater is indicated by the contents of the novelist's library as well as by the explicit references in the novel. When De Quincey's essay was reprinted in 1859, Collins clearly did not miss the way Sri Lanka, this 'gorgeous jewel in the imperial crown' (paradoxically too 'this Pandora of islands'), is associated with not 'the hardships of Robinson Crusoe' but the treasures won by the resourceful 'Sindbad and Ali Baba' (*Collected Writings*, vii, 430, 433, 437, 449–50, 453–4). Moreover, on their 1853 Italian tour Dickens had introduced Collins to Sir James Emerson Tennent, who repeatedly links Serendib with the *Nights*, especially the adventures of the Third Calendar, the Eldest Lady and Sindbad, in his authoritative *Account of Ceylon* (London: Longman, 1859; 5th edn, 1860, i, 6, 443, 526, 540, 596–8, and ii, 400–1, 538, 640), selections from which (finely illustrated by C. O'Brien) were published in 1864.[40]

Considerations of this nature, which must have weighed with an author such as Collins seeking background information, were given additional force by the fact that, during the composition of *The Moonstone*, the newspapers were full of old and new versions of the 'Eastern Question', some coming dangerously near home.

During this period, as Collins notes in a letter to his mother, there was also a state visit from the Sultan of Turkey accompanied by the Viceroy of Egypt.[41] One of the lavish entertainments mounted in July was marred. Monckton Milnes wrote to his wife, 'You will see in the papers the grim ending of the "Arabian Night". Madam Musurus attacked at the Sultan's supper table . . . she was never conscious again . . . he was a tutor in the family . . . the Sultan [said] his nerves were quite overcome by this event' (T. W. Reid, *Life, Letters and Friendships of R. Monckton Miles, First Lord Houghton* [London: Cassell, 1890] ii, 177). Just a month or so after this sensational act of violence, in a letter of 30 September, Anne B. Proctor told Houghton that their mutual friend Collins 'is working hard at a new book to appear in *All the Year Round* about

January next' (II, 182). As recently as August 1864, Collins had been again a guest at Fryston, Lord Houghton's North Country seat near Wakefield (II, 127). Did gossip about this 'Arabian Nights' murder in the Houghton circle give Collins the idea of showing muscular, evangelical Christianity helpless before an oriental curse which imperial plunder brings down upon a Yorkshire country-house party?[42] *The Moonstone* presents a view of things not far removed from that of the Indian Mutiny Correspondent of *The Times*, another friend of Dickens. In 1860, alarmed at the vengeful colonial cry of 'open sesame!', anguishing over the spoliation of 'the fairy city of Lucknow', W. H. Russell warned, 'our Christian zeal in Exeter Hall will not atone for . . . violence and fraud in the Upper Provinces of India' (*My Diary in India in the Years 1858–9* [London: Routledge, 1860] I, 63–4, 254, 356).

Over-zealous proselytising of the sort mocked in the missionary campaigns of Miss Clack was both one of the causes of the Mutiny and an explanation advanced by many newspapers to account for Constance Kent's dismaying confession in 1865 to a murder beyond her physical powers. In giving *The Moonstone* (which incorporates elements of this notorious Victorian crime) a shape close to *Oedipus Tyrannus*, Collins would seem to have anticipated Yseult Bridge's comparison of the Road Hill House case with 'Greek Tragedy' (*Saint with Red Hands?* [London: Jarrolds, 1954] p. 17). In other respects, the murder of Constance's half-brother resembles more a tale from the *Nights*. The author of *The Moonstone* seems to have found the Road Hill House case suggestive of the Haroun 'Story of the Three Apples'; in both cases, the initial police inquiries bungled, the investigation proceeds under the critical eye of higher authority, the solution emerging from a mixture of collective effort and luck. In a cloacal spot is found a body in a box, the victim from an outwardly respectable middle-class family; the womenfolk are unjustly suspected; the provocation for the murder is a child's involvement with evidence of apparent adultery; the guilty person turns out to be the man of the household, though a close relative endeavours to shield him by making a false confession.

In *The Moonstone* (pp. 432–5) Ezra Jennings' citation of medical authorities is instrumental in unravelling the mystery. Among the evidence on the workings of the unconscious mind that is assembled by Dickens' friend Dr John Elliotson, there are the important testimonies of several writers with whom Wilkie Collins's father was well acquainted.[43] In his *Human Physiology* (5th edn

[London: Longman, 1840] pp. 615–16, 622–3) Elliotson passes from the circumstances in which Coleridge composed *Kubla Khan*, through a discussion of lunatic hallucinations 'of being . . . an emperor', to mention 'a curious instance of the discovery of legal papers by a dream in Sir Walter Scott's notes to *The Antiquary*.' While this particular anecdote is reminiscent of a folktale as well known in Europe as in Arabia, tellingly in Scott's novel Mr Oldbuck entertains an Arabesque ambition related to such acts of 'double consciousness'; 'were I caliph for a day, as honest Abou Hassan wished to be' (ɪ, ch. 13, p. 164 – Border Edition) – an allusion to 'The Sleeper Awakened' that not only helps characterise the Antiquary himself but also is elaborated so as covertly to structure the Lord Glenallan sub-plot. The subtlety with which the finest of the *Waverley* novels are constructed was not lost on Collins. Believing him to be 'the model for all fiction-writers', Collins advises, 'Study Walter Scott. . . . Get *The Antiquary* and read [it] over and over and over again.'[44]

Collins' admiration for *The Antiquary* (and also *The Bride of Lammermoor* with its eloquently kaleidoscopic reference to the Arabian story) helps account for his own exploitation of 'The Sleeper Awakened'; for elements of the psychology and plot concerning Franklin Blake's apparent guilt and vindication are inherited from Abu Hassan. Both Arab and English protagonists are drugged into believing that matters of state are their responsibility (Abu Hassan, the caliphate; Franklin, the Indian diamond); in the process of deceit and delusion, both victims are instructed by their consequent loss of status; both tricksters are oriental potentates incognito (at least figuratively): as Harun masquerades as a merchant, so the doctor in *The Moonstone* bears no English name – 'Candy' ('Kandy') being the territorial title and capital of the rebellious mountain kingdom in central Ceylon from which, half a century before *The Moonstone*, the British had punitively removed the palladium – as De Quincey points out, not a gem but the Buddha's tooth – *Collected Writings*, vɪɪ, 450–1).[45] Tellingly, Collins splits the Harun role between the mischievous Candy and his very different assistant, whose gypsy looks recall 'the ancient people of the East' (*The Moonstone*, p. 358). This half-caste also bears a potent name, 'Ezra' (Hebrew 'help'), alluding to the priest and scribe whose book in the Old Testament records how, having circumvented malicious enemies and the forgetfulness of an alien administration by causing a search to be made of the archives, the post-exilic Jews were able to restore to Jerusalem the temple treasures pillaged by Nebuchadnezzar, thus renewing the covenant between Israel and Yahweh (see not only Ezra but also Nehemiah).[46]

The Moonstone's associations with the plundered East are further activated by our remaining alert to the way in which Collins continues to use De Quincey, whose *Confessions* (it will be recalled) also figure prominently among the medical testimonies cited by Ezra Jennings (pp. 434–5). Asia constantly threatens the English Opium Eater: 'I fled from the wrath of Brahma . . . Vishnu hated me' (*Collected Writings*, III, 442). Often this menace assumes Arabian guise: De Quincey as infant reader is appalled by the evil magician's ability to hear from afar Aladdin's footsteps (I, 128); at an older age the runaway De Quincey finds an undelivered letter as burdensome as Sindbad's Old Man of the Sea (III, 303); and recognising 'The Dream Fugue' – originally part of 'Suspiria de Profundis' – helped inspire the description of Rosanna Spearman's death in the quicksands (Hayter, *Opium and the Romantic Imagination*, p. 266, compares *The Moonstone*, pp. 172–7, with, *inter alia*, De Quincey's *Collected Writings* XIII, 320–1). It becomes significant that in 'The English Mail Coach' the one-eyed psychopomp of a driver evokes in De Quincey a mingled 'vision of sudden death', Waterloo and 'one of the Calenders of the *Arabian Nights*' (XIII, 306). Similarly the relationship between Franklin Blake, Rosanna and the Shivering Sand (patterned after the structure latent in the tales of the Three Calenders) alerts the reader to other borrowings. As useful to Collins' purpose is the companion story of 'The Eldest Lady'; Zobeide tells of a trading expedition from a westerly port to an Indian kingdom, whose capital has been devastated by an occidental power, i.e. Magian culture overwhelmed by Islam. In the palace of the City of Statues is first discovered a huge luminous diamond the size of a bird's egg; secondly, associated with this precious stone, an attractive and learned young prince. Homeward bound, these prizes are ill-fated; family jealousies part the lovers, though eventually a supernatural power restores the treasure at least to its rightful owner.

The resemblance between Zobeide's tale and *The Moonstone* grows more apparent when her story and those of the Three Calenders are placed in their *Arabian Nights* context as constituents of 'the Porter and the Ladies of Baghdad'.[47] If one sets aside the Prologue to *The Moonstone*, the first person one meets in both novel and frame tale is a servant, amiable, forward yet discreet, self-educated, always ready with a quotation, fond of his drink and women; indeed, though he is single, his relationship with the lady who employs him is almost hypergamous. In both cases the mistress has two (or more) sisters; at supper one evening the family are surprised by oriental visitors, who are not all that they seem. The strange goings-on in the house invite questions from high-ranking law officers in plain clothes – at which the ladies of the household take umbrage, and, as the atmosphere grows occult, their visitors must account for themselves. Further police investigation elicits the stories of the ladies: Zobeide's cryptic narrative about the price of Eastern conquest is followed by Amina's record of marital suspicion; the echoes and reflections within the Arabian frame tale stimulate in Collins' invention a greater mingling of the political and sexual, human and supernatural. In 'the Porter and the Ladies of Baghdad', almost all the protagonists speak for themselves the best they can, as do the characters in *The Moonstone*; there is one important exception in both frame tale and novel – the Third Lady and Rachel Verinder do not tell their own tales. Common to both works is a necessary re-enactment of a crucial episode in the case, and the wish expressed by an important legal authority that a record be kept of this extraordinary affair. Similarly telling is the interplay between free will and destiny, scepticism and belief, reason and the irrational, as (listener or reader) one follows the quest for justice in these related labyrinths of testimony. Not least of the likenesses between Arabian and English master-pieces is the way that, in both, legendary and public events are focused upon a domestic stage.

Significantly, though, in *The Moonstone* Collins beats the oriental storyteller at his own game of inversion, turning 'The Porter and the Ladies of Baghdad' inside-out. This difference in the ordering of the bourgeois and the exotic material whereby the epic events in India frame the more domestic action in England emphasises the degree to which home affairs are shaped by imperial history. Registering in the Prologue how Muslim conquest preceded the East India Company's aggrandisement, Collins is able to transcend a simplistic attack on the Raj.[48] This historical perspective (to which reflections of *The Arabian Nights* add further dimensions) extends the critique of empire backwards from British to Mughal and, it is surely implied, earlier invasions. However, while 'The Porter and the Ladies of Baghdad' is one of the most coherent, realistic and subtle of the framed collections within the *Nights*, for these enthralling narratives to be transformed into a novel greater complexity and inwardness were required.

As can be seen, Collins found in the *Nights* themselves some means of securing the richness and depths of characterisation necessary to amplify the psychological and moral consequences of an overseas empire and a caste system at home. In Arabeque fashion shaping a new frame out of 'the Eldest Lady's Tale', Collins telescopes the remaining tales, the erstwhile container and contents of 'The Porter and the Ladies'. Upon the resulting congeries he superimposes related narratives from the Haroun cycle. Memories of the detective story of 'The Three Apples' tie in with the Road Hill House tragedy, but stronger are the echoes of 'The Sleeper Awakened'. Doubtless the link between the disturbing psychological study of Abu Hassan and 'The Porter and the Ladies' was another porter celebrated in the medical literature on somnambulism – the case Ezra Jennings quotes of 'an Irish porter . . . who forgot, when sober what he had done when drunk; but, being drunk, again recollected' (p. 433). In both the medieval Baghdadian and Victorian patients the double consciousness produced by waking from a drugged state is part of the process of self-understanding.

In this context of psychic discovery we can see a further connection between the diamonds and delusions of *The Moonstone* and the *Nights*. Like the hero of the best known among these Arabian teaching-stories, Franklin Blake is educated into a profounder awareness of things, both he and Aladdin being initially ignorant of the true significance of the jewels they handle. As 'precious stones . . . constitute a sort of *Leitmotiv*' in the story of 'The Wonderful Lamp' (Gerhardt, *The Art of Story-Telling*, p. 324), so in *The Moonstone* – where the sacred diamond partakes of the general symbolism of treasure – the right disposal of such riches signifies moral and intellectual growth. As an outward sign of the irradiant, adamantine centre of things, the Moonstone represents that gnosis in which there is no shunning of one's fellow.[49] Such suggestions (found also, to some degree, constellated in Smedley's *Occult Sciences*) help illuminate the changing fortunes of both the hero and the diamond in *The Moonstone*. Among their other functions in the novel, autobiographical, characterising, atmospheric, structural, poetically anatomising a whole society, the allusions to the *Nights* tease us to recognise how Franklin Blake achieves self-integration through meeting his *alter ego* Ezra

Jennings – a stage in the complex process by which, at least momentarily, the Englishman and the Indian diamond are each restored to their proper place in the community.

In his comparison of *The Eustace Diamonds* and *The Moonstone* (*Studies in Philology*, xxxvi [1939] 651–63) H. J. W. Milley argues that the many affinities between the two novels arise from the fact that Trollope is parodying Collins. Persuasive as Milley's explanation is, he does not reckon with what is the most intimate of these ties, a remark let drop by Lizzie which (for all the satirist's irony) indicates that a not wholly unsympathetic Trollope had glimpsed the import of Collins' symbolism, not least the manner in which Collins' Arabesque devices help expose the thoughtless Western reader's own complicity in the theft of the sacred diamond:

'I do feel so like some naughty person in the Arabian Nights,' she said, 'who has got some great treasure that always brings him into trouble; but he can't get rid of it, because some spirit has given it to him. At last, some morning it turns into slate stones, and then he has to be a water-carrier, and is happy ever afterwards, and marries the king's daughter.' (*The Eustace Diamonds*, Penguin edn, pp. 323–4)

NOTES

Books published in London unless otherwise stated.

1. At times the strain was too much: 'I feel all Robinson Crusoe-ish. I cannot abide India', writes Emily Eden – *Letters from India* (Richard Bentley, 1872) I, 148. True, Crusoe never manages to re-create a Palladian residence on his West Indian island – at least, not to the degree to which Miss Eden, sister of the Governor General, contrives to find desirable lodgings on her arduous journey from Calcutta to the Himalayas; nevertheless, Pat Rogers concludes from his acute survey of 'Crusoe's Home', *Essays in Criticism*, xxiv (1974) 375–90, Defoe's novel tells 'the story of a Caribbean nabob who makes a little England in remote surroundings'. The horror was all the greater, therefore, when such domesticity was threatened: 'it is considered quite a shocking thing to have a robbery in India – pilfering is commendable and rather a source of vanity, but the robbery of an European is a sort of high treason in all native states, and the town pays for that loss' (*Up the Country* [Virago edn] pp. 150–1). Although Emily Eden's observation here is dated 2 July 1838, her letters were not published until the second half of the 1860s (see *infra*, n. 38); yet

in the sense of outrage Eden conveys, hindsight recognises feelings more global and of longer standing than just a premonition of the Great Sepoy Mutiny of 1857. Writing *The Moonstone* in the tenth anniversary of the Indian uprising against abuses at once religious and racial, Betteredge's creator teases us to remember how in *The Further Adventures*, during his ramble from the West to East Indies, then on through Central Asia back home, Crusoe himself is guilty of the desecration of an oriental shrine. This act of irresponsible bigotry endangers the caravan with which Crusoe is travelling when the merchants find themselves besieged by enraged tribesmen (Collins Classics edn, pp. 440–9).

2. Kenneth Robinson, *Wilkie Collins* (Bodley Head, 1951) pp. 212–14; Nuel Pharr Davis, *The Life of Wilkie Collins* (Urbana: University of Illinois, 1956) pp. 255–6.

3. E. R. Gregory, 'Collation of Manuscript with Printed Version of "Reminiscences of Story-Teller"', in Dorothy L. Sayers, *Wilkie Collins; A Critical and Biographical Study* (Toledo, Ohio: University of Ohio, 1977) Appendix.

4. On the changing attitudes of eighteenth- and nineteenth-century European painters and designers towards North Africa, the Near East and the Middle East, see Patrick Conner (ed.), *The Inspiration of Egypt* (Brighton Council, 1983); Michael Darby, *The Islamic Perspective: An Aspect of British Architecture and Design in the Nineteenth Century* (World of Islam Festival Trust, 1983); and Mary Anne Stevens (ed.), *The Orientalists* (Royal Academy, 1984). On the artistic as well as scholarly response of the British to India during this period, especially Emily Eden's *Portraits of the Princes and Peoples of India* (L. Dickinson, 1844), see Mildred Archer and Ronald Lightbown, *India Observed* (Victoria and Albert Museum, 1982). Collins enthuses over the orientalist painter Horace Vernet in a letter to his mother (Pierpont Morgan Library, A1 MA3150 (20), Paris, 6 Oct 1845).

5. Pierpont Morgan Library, A1 MA3150 (10), n.p., n.d. [c. July 1844?], Collins to his mother; A1 MA3155, London, 24 Aug 1842, to his father.

6. Philip Collins cites a *Household Words* description of Inspector Field in a thieves' den, 'the Sultan of the place' – *Dickens and Crime*, 2nd edn. (Macmillan, 1964) p. 207.

7. 'Inventory of Contents of 1 Devonshire Terrace, May 1844', *Pilgrim Letters of Charles Dickens*, ed. Kathleen Tillotson and Nina Burgis, IV (Oxford University Press, 1977) 715, lists among the books Jonathan Scott's version of the *Nights* (1811). See also J. H. Stonehouse's edition of the *Catalogue of the Library of Charles Dickens* (Piccadilly Fountain Press, 1935) p. 8. However, John Forster possessed three different translations: Edward Forster, 2nd edn (1810); Lane (1839–41); and George Lamb's rendering of von Hammer's selection, 2nd edn (1829) – see *South Kensington Museum: [John] Forster Collection: Catalogue of the Printed Books* (1888) pp. 9–10. To all three, Professor Tillotson informs me, it may be assumed Dickens would have had access.

8. Robinson, *Collins*, p. 123. At this time Collins found himself in a situation where, like the story-teller of *After Dark*, weak eyesight

persuaded him to abandon thoughts of being a painter; see Kirk H. Beetz, 'Plots within Plots', *Wilkie Collins Society Journal*, iv (1984) 31–4.

9. See *supra*, Introduction, pp. 5, 16, 37, 59–60 and n. 136.

10. The Madding Victoriana Collection (M 30), Department of Special Collections, Stanford University Libraries.

11. Thomas Keightley, *Tales and Popular Fictions* (Whittaker, 1834) pp. 39–41, 74–6; Lane, *Night*, ii, 548; also G. Moir Bussey, Introduction to Forster, *Nights* (Joseph Thomas, 1839) p. xxviii. On Crabbe's use of the *Nights*, see *supra*, Introduction p. 11 and n. 38.

12. Robinson, *Collins*, p. 329. Collins possessed not only the 'Illustrated' *Waverley Novels* (Edinburgh, 1859) but also the *Poetical and Prose Works* with the Turner vignettes (1833–4), lots 86–9 in Puttick and Simpson's sale catalogue (1890). Crabbe's *Poetical Works* (1834) are lot 28; lot 194, Balzac's *Oeuvres complètes*, 45 vols (Paris, 1859–69), is a reminder that Collins could also have been inspired by 'Les Mille et une nuits de l'Occident'. See Collins' 'Portrait of an Author', *All the Year Round*, i, no. 8. (June 1859) 184–5, 205–10, repr. in *My Miscellanies* (1863) pp. 205–49. On Yeats's debt to Balzac's Arabesques, see *infra*, Warwick Gould, ch. 10, p. 265 and n. 55.

13. For a fuller discussion of the subtle use of the *Nights* by Wordsworth, Scott, the Brontës and Dickens, see, *supra*, Introduction, and Michael Slater, ch. 5.

14. 'All Mannions come from Manannan', Yeats's line in 'Three Songs to the One Burden' in *Last Poems and Plays* (Macmillan, 1940) p. 52, illuminates *Basil*; on *The Woman in White* see my 'Wilkie Collins's "Divine Comedy"', *Nineteenth Century Fiction*, xxv, no. 4 (Mar 1971) 383–404.

15. Prominent among the models for *No Name*, Smollett's fiction partly derives from Moorish Spain, the picaresque being influenced by Islamic culture. Cervantes' acknowledgement of this debt pervades *Don Quixote*, not least in Clavileño's burlesquing of the Arabian flying horse (pt ii, ch. 40). For Aurengzeb's encounter with an enchanted wooden horse, see Thomas Keightley, *A History of India* (Whittaker, 1846–7) p. 38; on the possible origins of the picaresque in the *maqáma*, see for example W. M. Watt and P. Cachia, *A History of Islamic Spain* (Edinburgh: Edinburgh University Press, 1965) p. 159.

16. Wendy Doniger O'Flaherty, *Dreams, Illusion and Other Realities* (Chicago: University of Chicago Press, 1984) p. 99.

17. Harry Stone, *Dickens and the Invisible World* (Macmillan, 1979) p. 296.

18. *The Lazy Tour of Two Idle Apprentices* (Chapman and Hall, 1890) chs 3 and 4 (pp. 65, 94).

19. Echoes of a similar kind are a favourite device of Abu Nuwás, who figures so prominently in the *Nights* that it might be said that, within the Haroun cycle, this 'famous poet . . . has a miniature cycle to himself' – Mia Gerhardt, *The Art of Story-Telling: A Literary Study of the Thousand and One Nights* (Leiden: Brill, 1963) p. 456. For an examination of such envelope structures, see Andras Hamori, *On the Art of Medieval Arabic Literature* (Princeton, NJ: Princeton University Press, 1974) pp. 68–9, 113–14, 119–21. An instance well known to nineteenth-

century England occurs in 'Habib and Dorathil-Goase . . .', *The Arabian Tales* . . . (Edinburgh: Bell *et al.*, 1792) III, 320–3; see *infra*, n. 23. Collins here also echoes J. L. Stephens, whose *Incidents of Travel in . . . Arabia Petraea* (Richard Bentley, 1838) alludes to the *Nights* (chs 2 and 13).

20. In the early Victorian period Owen Jones's attempts at basing a style for the nineteenth century on Islamic aesthetics found their most memorable expression in the Crystal Palace. Although by the 1860s Jones was falling from favour, his influence persisted into the twentieth century via the work of such designers as Christopher Dresser: see *supra*, Introduction, pp. 18, 58; also Darby, *The Islamic Perspective*, esp. section 3.

21. Clyde K. Hyder, 'Wilkie Collins and *The Woman in White*', *PMLA*, LIV (1939) 297–303, repr. in *Victorian Literature: Modern Essays in Criticism*, ed. Austen Wright (New York: Galaxy, 1961) pp. 128–35. The oriental roots of the detective story are traced in varying degrees in Dorothy L. Sayers, *Great Short Stories of Detection, Mystery and Horror* (Gollancz, 1928) pp. 9, 51–6; Régis Messac Le *'Detective Novel'* (Paris: Bibliothèque de la Revue de la littérature comparée, 1929) pp. 17–46; A. E. Murch, *The Development of the Detective Novel*, rev. edn (Peter Owen, 1968) pp. 24–7. See also *supra*, Introduction, pp. 37–8.

22. 'Ali Cogia' is one of the tales collected by Galland and Scott that is omitted by Lane but reinstated by Burton (*Supplemental Nights*, III).

23. Collins himself could have had some direct contact with an Arab story-teller. In late August 1851, to illustrate the 'Diorama of the Holy Land, at the Egyptian Hall, Piccadilly', there was imported a troupe of 'musicians, singers and performers from Syria . . . Among them a [hunchback] . . . said to know by heart every tale in the Arabian Nights, and whose mode of recital [was] grotesque in the extreme' – *Theatrical Journal*, XII (1851) 283; see also Richard D. Altick, *The Shows of London* (Cambridge, Mass.: Harvard University Press, 1978) pp. 182–3 and esp. pp. 460–1. Such details of what was 'the single most popular topic of panoramas in the Crystal Palace Year' are likely to have been kept alive in Collins' memory less by those pantomimes which increasingly in the 1860s burlesqued the *Nights* – see the reminiscences of Collins' friends the Bancrofts, *On and off the Stage* (Richard Bentley, 1888) p. 94 – than by the work of certain Pre-Raphaelites with whom the novelist was intimate, e.g. William Michael Rossetti, who had posed for the much-travelled Holman Hunt's illustration to Tennyson's 'Recollections of the Arabian Nights': head-piece to the poem in the Moxon edition of 1857; watercolour version c. 1866 – see *The Pre-Raphaelites*, ed. Leslie Parris, catalogue for the Tate Gallery exhibition (1984) p. 302. However, Sir John Everett Millais's contributions to Dalziel's *Illustrated Arabian Nights* published in parts (1863–5) are not as persuasive as Arthur Boyd Houghton's realistically oblique suggestions of the magical: see Plate 5 and *supra*, Introduction, pp. 33–4; also Terry Reece Hackford, 'Fantastic Visions: Illustration of the *Arabian Nights*', in *The Aesthetics of Fantasy, Literature*

and Art, ed. R. C. Schlobin (Notre Dame, Ind.: University of Notre Dame Press; and Brighton: Harvester, 1982) pp. 144–55.

24. On the use of puns in medieval Arabic rhetoric see Torrens, *The Book of the Thousand and One Nights* (Calcutta: Thacker, 1838; London: W. H. Allen, 1838) I, v–vi; Lane, *Nights* (1839) I, xvii–xviii; Idries Shah, *The Sufis* (1964) p. 384; Hamori, *On the Art of Medieval Arabic Literature*, ch. 5.

25. André Gide, *Journal 1889–1939* (Paris, 1948) p. 41.

26. Another analogue for 'the Bedouin brothers' is found in 'The History of Habib and Dorathil-Goase, or the Knight', *The Arabian Tales: Being a Continuation of the Arabian Nights Entertainments* (1792) III, 277, 285, 294, 297 – the story used by Wordsworth in *The Prelude*, v (see *supra*, Introduction, p. 9), and to which A. Loiseleur-Deslongchamps, *Essai sur les fables indiennes* (Paris: M. Robert, 1838) p. 175, and T. Benfey, *Das Panchatantra* (Leipzig, 1859) I, 123, drew the attention of Continental readers. This episode, deriving from the Vikrama cycle, in which a genie repeatedly manifests his power of entering other persons' bodies, had been accessible also in a Hindu form since the early nineteenth century in M. le Baron Lescallier, *Le Trône enchanté* (New York: J. Desnoues, 1817); an English translation appears in Mary Frere, *Old Deccan Days* (John Murray, 1868) pp. 71–92. See Maurice Bloomfield, 'On the Art of Entering Another's Body: A Hindu Fiction Motif', *Proceedings of the American Philosophical Society*, LVI (1917) 1–43. On the serpent eating its tail, see Patrick Hughes with George Brecht, *Vicious Circles and Infinity* (Harmonsworth: Penguin, 1978) esp. plates 11–12 and note. On the symbol of uroboros and its relation to 'the treasure hard to attain', see Erich Neumann, *The Origins and History of Consciousness* (Princeton, NJ: Princeton University Press, 1970). Freud comes close to using the simile of 'a Chinese box' in *Psychotherapy of Hysteria* (Harmondsworth: Penguin, 1974) p. 378, also pp. 374–5; on Freud and the *Nights*, see also *supra*, ch. 1, pp. 38, 71 and n. 84. Ignacio Matte Blanco, in *The Unconscious as Infinite Sets* (Duckworth, 1975), supports the view of those such as Anton Ehrenzweig, in *The Psychoanalysis of Artistic Vision and Hearing* (New York: George Braziller, 1965) pp. 108–10, who hold that the unconscious, far from being a chaos, plays a creative role – e.g. 'mirror' and 'crab' reversals. On the relationship between the use of *mise en abîme* in literature, mathematics and logic, see Lucien Dällenbach, *Le Récit spéculaire* (Paris: Editions du Seuil, 1977) pp. 144–5; also, on its reflection of the nature of human thought-processes, Claude Lévi-Strauss, *The Raw and the Cooked* (Jonathan Cape, 1969) pp. 10–11, 340–1. In *Gödel, Escher, Bach: An Eternal Golden Braid: A Metaphorical Fugue on Minds and Machines in the Spirit of Lewis Carroll* (Harmondsworth: Penguin, 1980) Douglas R. Hofstadter introduces aptly an infinity of 'Genies of the Lamp' (pp. 108–16; see also pp. 15, 127–52, 183–5, 643–5, 688–9); see also Wendy O'Flaherty's critique in *Dreams, Illusion and Other Realities*, pp. 202, 252–9. Cf. Collins' fusion of the Bottle Conjuror and the Genie in the Bottle with Melville's conflation in *Moby Dick* (1851)

ch. 112; also ch. 50, which itself draws from the *Spectator*, no. 578 (9 Aug 1714), a paraphrase of a tale in Ambrose Phillips's *1001 Days* (1714–15).

27. Hamori, *On the Art of Medieval Arabic Literature*, p. 173.

28. See for example 'The False Khaleefeh' (Lane, *Nights*, ɪɪ, ch. 13). As for that story which disturbingly echoes the frame tale of the *Nights*, 'The King's Son and the Afrit's Mistress', it is probable, given its presence in the second Calcutta text (1839–42), that it figured in the conversation of a chain of acquaintances running from the editor, Sir William Macnaghten, and the translator, Torrens, through Emily Eden to fellow enthusiasts in the Dickens circle; see *infra*, pp. 160, 173 and n. 38.

29. Hamori comments on 'The Porter and the Three Ladies of Baghdad', 'the tale is a series of echoes and reflection . . . periodicity is [more than just a] device for holding the audience's attention' (*On the Art of Medieval Arabic Literature*, p. 172); 'the story-teller constantly has his characters puzzled by problems of justice' (p. 178). See also Gerhardt, *The Art of Story-Telling*, pp. 50–5; and Tzvetan Todorov, *The Poetics of Prose* (Oxford: Basil Blackwell, 1977) p. 78.

30. Cited in A. M. Barrenechea, *Borges, the Labyrinth-Maker*, tr. R. Lima (New York: New York University Press, 1965) p. 41. *Discusión 1932* was volume 1 of *Colección de nuevosescritones argentinos*.

31. On the ways serial publication of Victorian novels affected their authors and audience, see Malcolm Andrews' note in *Reading the Victorian Novel*, ed. Ian Gregor (Vision Press, 1980) pp. 243–7; Kathleen Tillotson, *Novels of the Eighteen-Forties* (Oxford University Press, 1954) pp. 21–53; Emily Eden, *Up the Country* (Virago, 1983) pp. 157–8, 265. Perceptive as is Alethea Hayter's recognition, in *Opium and the Romantic Imagination* (Faber, 1971) p. 259, of 'the Chinese box intricacy' of *The Moonstone*, an insight amplified by Sue Lonoff in *Wilkie Collins and his Victorian Readers* (New York: AMS Press, 1982) pp. 187–8, 200–1, both fail to register the *Arabesque* implications of the novel's genesis, structure and serial reception by listeners no less than readers.

32. Martin Green's otherwise enlightening study of this area, *Dreams of Adventure, Deeds of Empire* (Routledge and Kegan Paul, 1980), ignores *The Moonstone*. See also *supra*, Introduction, pp. 25–6, 30, 31.

33. See Robinson, *Collins*, pp. 18, 32.

34. Cited in Christine Bolt, *Victorian Attitudes to Race* (Routledge and Kegan Paul, 1971) p. 202, the *Spectator* echoes Mrs Charlotte Speir's pre-Mutiny comment on her fellow-countryman's first impressions of India: 'his mind well informed with all that the hints and story-telling of classics and Indian history afford . . . [he] feels transported into . . . dreams of Arabian Nights or passages from Scripture – *Life in Ancient India* (Smith, Elder, 1856) pp. 32–3.

35. In 1867, Wheeler's *History of India* (Trubner) had not got beyond the Vedic period.

36. See '. . . The Mountain of Light', *The Illustrated Year Book of 1850*, ed. J. Timbs, p. 74.

37. According to the extant documents concerned with the genesis of *The Moonstone*, Collins derived some knowledge of diamonds from

Encyclopaedia Britannica, 8th edn, and more from C. W. King's *The Natural History . . . of Precious Stones and Gems . . .* (Bell and Daldy, 1865); yet plainly the process of gathering material did not stop at the notes preserved in Princeton University Library (AM13435). The 1865 version of King's much reworked popularisation is silent about the suggestive legends concerning the Koh-i-noor (pp. 33, 36), whereas in King's *Antique Gems* (Bell and Daldy, 1860) p. 68, or more accessibly in his *Natural History of Precious Stones and of Precious Metals* (Bell and Daldy, 1867) pp. 70–6, there is much to inspire a novelist.

38. Emily Eden, *Up the Country*, (Virago edn), p. 61. When published in 1866 (reissued 1867; another selection 1872 – see *supra*, n. 1), these letters from India were quickly recognised as a classic account of life in the sub-continent; additionally the letters have great literary and political interest. It is noteworthy that Eden anticipates Collins in viewing India in the light of both *Robinson Crusoe* and the *Nights*.

39. Pierpont Morgan Library, A1 MA 3155; it is in this letter that Collins pictures himself as a male Scheherazade entertaining 'country relations' – see *supra*, pp. 146, 168 and n. 5.

40. See Collins' letter from Rome, 13 Nov 1853, to his brother Charles: Pierpont Morgan Library, A1 MA 3152 (2). Dickens had a presentation copy of Tennent's handsomely illustrated book (1859); see *The Catalogue of the Library . . .* [at] *Gadshill*, ed. J. H. Stonehouse (Piccadilly Fountain Press, 1935) p. 109.

41. Pierpont Morgan Library, A1 MA 3150 (105), London 18 July 1867.

42. *The Times*, 14–26 July 1867, records that, during the course of receptions, repeatedly described as like something out of the *Nights* (in the case of the Ball at India House as further decorated with the magnificent loot taken from Tipu Sahib), and in the presence of not only His Imperial Turkish Majesty but at times members of the British royal family, the Maharajah Duleep Singh (heir of Runjeet, the last Indian owner of the Koh-i-noor) and Sir Robert Peel (long a benefactor of the Collins family), there came a convergence of alarming reports about the Abyssinian captives, the execution of Maximilian by the Mexican Indians, lastly the fatal assault on Madame Musurus, the wife of the distinguished Turkish ambassador – see esp. *The Times*, 22 July 1867, p. 9, and 26 July, p. 10. Already in November 1862 the hospitality extended by the eccentric Milnes at Fryston had occasioned Laurence Oliphant's notable satire on the evangelical excesses of Exeter Hall, and upper-class hypocrisy; serialised first in *Blackwood's Magazine* (1865), with its Indian from Bombay intruding on an English country-house party, a reformed criminal as servant, the allusions to Kant, and not least the hero playing 'the part of a bountiful prince in the Arabian Nights' (p. 278), *Piccadilly* (Blackwood, repr. 1870) prefigures much in *The Moonstone*. Many of Collins' contemporaries had similarly viewed the 1865 Jamaican negro revolt in terms of the Indian Mutiny (Bolt, *Victorian Attitudes to Race*, pp. 77, 105). But Collins' likely attitude to Governor Eyre, who suppressed the revolt, may be gauged from 'Pray Employ Major Namby', *All the Year Round*, I, 6 (4 June 1859) 136–41, esp. p. 137, repr. in *My Miscellanies* (1863).

43. See Robinson, *Collins*, pp. 15, 65, 164, 280.

44. Cited *Ibid.*, pp. 328–9.
45. On the 1817 rebellion, the theft and recovery of this 'great palladium', see Tennent, *Account of Ceylon*, II, 91–2. Although in the nineteenth century enshrined at Kandy (in a sixfold casket symbolising the diamond at the heart of the lotus), the relic had formerly been kept at Anuradhapura, the famous ruined city of Ceylon where, adjacent to the Temple of the Tooth, are the so-called 'moonstone' doorsteps (Tennent, *Ibid.*, II, 619, illustrates). *Adaluria* abounds but contrary to Arabian geographers, no true diamond is mined in Ceylon (I, 38). However, legend associates this precious stone with the Tooth relic, British memories of which were again stirred both in 1859–60 by Tennent (I, 388; II, 198–9) and, contemporaneously with *The Moonstone*'s genesis, by James Fergusson's archaeological displays at the Crystal Palace, the Great Paris Exhibition, Fergusson's June lecture and writings on Buddhist sculpture. See his 'Description of the Amravati Tope', *Journal of the Royal Asiatic Society*, III (Autumn 1867) 132–66, and *Tree and Serpent Worship* (W. H. Allen, 1868) pp. iv, 82, 159–60, 195–6; note also ch. 38 of *The Pilgrimage of Fa Hian to the Buddhist Kingdoms*, tr. Remusat, Klaproth and Landresse (Paris, 1836), J. W. Laidley (Calcutta, 1848), James Beal (1869). Perhaps in some degree because of his oriental sympathies, indeed Singhalese friends, Milnes was one of the jurors at the Paris Exhibition (Reid, *Life, Letters and Friendships of R. Monckton Milnes*, II, 167–8).
46. R. P. Laidlow comments on the significance of Jennings' first name 'Since the biblical Ezra was charged with the reconstruction of the new Jerusalem, [this] adds a certain Nabokovian ironic dimension to one's response to Betteredge's trifling objections' to the reconstruction of the crime – 'Awful Images and Associations', *Southern Review*, IX (1976) 226 n. 5.
47. I abbreviate the full title, which even in Forster is 'The Porter, the Three Royal Calenders, and Three Ladies of Baghdad'; on the way in which R. L. Stevenson likewise exploits what is perhaps the most novelistic of the Arabian tales in *The Master of Ballantrae* (1889), see *supra*, Introduction, pp. 25, 27, 29, 30, 31, and *infra*, Leonee Ormond, ch. 7, p. 192. Significantly, the story of Zobeide, the Eldest Lady, also inspired three Victorian poets: Christina Rossetti, 'The Dead City . . . 9 April, 1847', *New Poems*, ed. W. M. Rossetti (Macmillan, 1896) pp. 342–53; George Meredith, 'The Sleeping City', *Poems* (J. W. Parker, 1851) pp. 16–21 (see *infra*, Cornelia Cook, ch. 8, p. 201); James 'B. V.' Thomson, 'The Doom of a City . . . November 1857', III. ii, *Natural Reformer*, 18 Aug 1867 – see *Poems and Some Letters*, ed. A. Ridler (Centaur Press, 1963) p. 260.
48. In his otherwise valuable account of Collins' novel, 'English Imperialism and the Unacknowledged Crime of *The Moonstone*', *Clio* (University of Wisconsin), II (1973) 281–90, John R. Reed fails to reckon with the Muslim conquest of Hindu and Buddhist India; see the shrewd comment of Kirk H. Beetz in *Wilkie Collins: An Annotated Bibliography* . . . (Scarecrow Press, 1978) p. 122.
49. See entries on 'Centre' and 'Diamond' in J. E. Cirlot, *A Dictionary of*

Symbols, 2nd edn (Routledge and Kegan Paul, 1971); and C. G. Jung, *Aion; Researches into the Phenomenology of the Self*, 2nd edn (Routledge and Kegan Paul, 1968) *passim*. The full implications of insights such as 'the diamond mandala' or 'the elusive mystic centre of *The Moonstone*', glimpsed by, respectively, Laidlow (*Southern Review*, IX, 211–27, esp. p. 217) and Blair ('Wilkie Collins and the Crisis of Suspense', *Reading the Victorian Novel*, p. 45), emerge only when the symbolism of Collins' sacred diamond is placed in a more comprehensive history of ideas than that provided by Theodore Ziolkowski, 'The Mystic Carbuncle: Transmutations of an Image', *Varieties of Literary Thematics* (Princeton, NJ: Princeton University Press, 1983) pp. 34–85. Even Mark M. Hennelly Jr's very perceptive account of the role of Indian gemology in *The Moonstone*, 'Detecting Collins's Diamond', *Nineteenth Century Fiction*, XXXIX, no. 1 (June 1984) 25–47, wants more historical and incongraphical exactitude. For the years surrounding the composition of *The Moonstone* witnessed a convergence of mythographic and psychological studies: although the great series 'Sacred Books of the East' did not commence until 1879, already by 1868 its editor, in his collected essays, *Chips from a German Workshop* (Longman) had helped to publicise Western scholarship's recovery of ancient oriental literature. Besides the early translations of the great religious texts, such *hautes vulgarisations* as R. Spence Hardy's *Eastern Monachism* (Partridge, 1850) and Mrs Charlotte Speir's 'very interesting and lucid account' of Hinduism and its great rival (1856) caught Max Muller's eye. In these works, the chief aims of the Indian religions, whether the Hindu relation of Atman to Brahma (Speir, *Life in Ancient India*, pp. 184, 192; Muller, *Chips from a German Workshop*, I, 71) or the emulation of the Buddha, his teaching and priesthood are to be seen traditionally symbolised in terms of precious stones, especially the diamond (Hardy, *Eastern Monachism*, pp. 166, 209; Muller, *Chips from a German Workshop*, I, 274). James Fergusson is informative about the evolution of Buddhism from the Hinayana school of Ceylon to the Mahayana of the North-West Frontier (*Tree and Serpent Worship*, p. 65), its iconography and psycho-theology (pp. 199, 221), its influence on Western folklore (p. 73). The Mahayana Buddhism practised throughout the Himalayas and Trans-Himalayas is the esoteric form known as Vajrayana or Diamond Vehicle: see Deborah E. Klimburg-Salter (ed.), *The Silk Route and the Diamond Path* (Los Angeles: UCLA Art Council, 1982) p. 19. Among the five Buddha families of this sect there are the Gem and Vajra (i.e. diamond) elements (p. 72). The pervasive use here of the term *vajra* has psycho-sexual connotations (p. 77), Mahayana inconography frequently borrowing features from the Hindu pantheon (pp. 106, 113). The goal of these tantric rituals is to achieve wakefulness, learning to co-operate with one's own mind, liberating oneself from personal confusion and ceasing to harm others. The resultant global vision, whereby events are seen within their larger contexts, presents a psychological analogue to the perspectives of the oriental framed tale (pp. 207, 227). In *The Moonstone*, note that Miss Clack's pivotal allusion to *The Thousand and One Nights* (p. 289) is slightly preceded by her reference to 'the Grand Lama of Thibet' (p. 271); eventually, the restoration of the sacred diamond to the Hindu god is witnessed by Mr Murthwaite disguised as a 'Hindoo-Buddhist' (p. 519). The Dalai Lama as reincarnated saviour has the power to be 'The Lord of Mysteries', the Diamond Buddha – a potential we all share 'though unaware of it': H. Zimmer, *The Art of Indian Asia*, rev. edn (Princeton, NJ: Princeton University Press, 1968) I, 184, 195, 205. The great Mahayana text *The Diamond-Cutter Sutra* was translated by Samuel Beal in the *Journal of the Royal Asiatic Society*, I (1864). Likewise the Hindu *Vedanta Sutra* (tr. 1845, 1850) to which Speir refers (*Life in Ancient India*, p. 192) images spiritual development in the allegory of a man distressed at the loss of a jewel, who discovers it on his own person. Marjusri's celebrated mantra on the diamond at the heart of the lotus, *'om mani padme hum'* (p. 330), could also have suggested *The Moonstone*'s affecting linkage of 'The Last Rose of Summer' and the Koh-i-noor (see also Speir on Ceylonese roses and lotuses, p. 15). Although he omits mentioning it in the Princeton notes drawn from King's *Natural History . . . of Precious Stones and Gems* (1865) there Collins must have read of the attempt made to shape 'the Nizam's Diamond' into 'the mystic *Yoni*' (p. 36). By his recourse for help to the Bombay Civil Service (Davis, *Life of Wilkie Collins*, pp. 250, 331), apparently through a contact of the Eden family (see Princeton University Library, A1 AM 13435, Wyllie to Eden), Collins was exceptionally well placed to obtain the most advanced information that Europeans had concerning Indian culture. Likewise the novelist seems thoroughly briefed respecting psychological discoveries. The notable affinities between this science and oriental myths are not fortuitous. The need to awaken from delusion (*maya*) being a psychological imperative, the growth of psychology in the eighteenth and nineteenth centuries owes much to Eastern ideas about the mind: see for instance Lancelot Law Whyte, *The Unconscious before Freud* (Tavistock, 1967), pp. 64–5, 116, 140–1, 154–5; H. Zimmer, *Philosophies of India* (Routledge and Kegan Paul, 1952) pp. 331, 354–5, 414. Both Zimmer, for example in *Myths and Symbols in Indian Art and Civilisation* (Princeton, NJ: Princeton University Press, 1972) p. 221, and Joseph Campbell, in *The Hero with a Thousand Faces*, 2nd edn (Princeton, NJ: Princeton University Press, 1968) pp. 65–8, 74–7, 226–8, 230, recognise in collections such as the *Nights* a repertoire of 'teaching-stories'. Collins himself makes explicit mention of these 'oriental apologues' in 'A Sermon for Sepoys', *Household Words*, XVII (27 Feb 1858) 244–7. Collins' rooted if not unchanging faith in the supernatural is evident not merely in novels such as *Armadale* but also in earlier letters now preserved at the Huntington Library. During the 1850s, the young writer contributed to a radical weekly, the *Leader*. In his correspondence with Edward Pigott, the editor (and, as he came to be, the novelist's longstanding friend), Collins avows a faith in Christianity that is remarkable for an author so often supposed to be an atheist. As Kirk H. Beetz also has perceived, further and 'more subtle interpretations of the religious themes' in Collins's work are required: 'Wilkie Collins and *The Leader'*, *Victorian Periodicals Review*, xv, no. 1 (Spring 1882) 20–9. The Pigott correspondence offers evidence in support of Chesterton's view that there is in Collins a strain of mysticism: see *The Victorian Age in Literature* (1913; last repr. Oxford University Press, 1966) p. 57; also my study of the use of Dante in *The Woman in White* (see *supra*, n. 14).

7

Cayenne and Cream Tarts: W. M. Thackeray and R. L. Stevenson

LEONEE ORMOND

Thackeray's affinity with the eighteenth century is well-known and amply demonstrated in his work. It is, incidentally, an affinity which he shared with Robert Louis Stevenson. Less obvious, yet important, is Thackeray's association of the *Arabian Nights* with his fictional picture of the Augustan Age. In *Henry Esmond* and *The Virginians* we see English readers becoming acquainted with the *Nights*. Esmond has not read the work in the mid 1690s, whereas his grandson, Harry Warrington, later finds a 'translation [presumably Galland's] of an Arabian Work of Tales, very diverting' (x, 249). Harry's friends, the Lambert family of Tunbridge Wells, have a copy of *The Persian Tales*, translated from the French by Ambrose Philips in 1714. This collection imitated the *Nights* in exploiting the appeal of the exotic and unusual.

Thackeray's first encounter with the *Nights*, probably in Galland's French version, came on a school half-holiday. In contrast to Coleridge, whose first reading was associated with terror, Thackeray always recalled his with pleasure, as a relief from a loathed classical education. The memory returned, more than twenty years later, on a visit to Smyrna: 'how often and often have you tried to fancy this, lying out on a summer holiday at school' (v, 629). Another twenty years on, in Thackeray's last novel, *Denis Duval*, the hero borrows a copy from the local rector, and becomes absorbed in the voyages of Sindbad the Sailor, passing 'delightful nights . . . in the company of Robinson Crusoe, Mariner, and Monsieur Galland and his Contes Arabes' (xii, 532).

A more complex reference to this early experience comes in *Vanity Fair*, where Thackeray transfers the memory to William

Dobbin, 'who was lying under a tree in the playground, spelling over a favourite copy of the *Arabian Nights* which he had – apart from the rest of the school, who were pursuing their various sports – quite lonely, and almost happy' (I, 37). Dobbin, Thackeray says,

> had for once forgotten the world, and was away with Sindbad the Sailor in the Valley of Diamonds, or with Prince Ahmed and the Fairy Peribanou in that delightful cavern where the Prince found her, and whither we should all like to make a tour; when shrill cries, as of a little fellow weeping, woke up his pleasant reverie; and, looking up, he saw Cuff before him, belabouring a little boy.   (I, 37)

The little boy is George Osborne, who, as a worthless but attractive young man, is to marry the girl Dobbin loves, Amelia Sedley. In the context the reference to the *Nights* is an apt one. Thackeray mentions two separate stories. One is the well-known Second Voyage of Sindbad the Sailor. Sindbad, carried by a fantastic bird, the roc, is dropped into a valley of diamonds, guarded by huge snakes. With his usual ingenuity, Sindbad escapes with a hoard of diamonds. The other story is that of Prince Ahmed and the Peri Banou. The Prince follows his arrow into a cave, and finds a magnificent palace and a lady, richly dressed and covered in fabulous jewels. The fairy marries Prince Ahmed and keeps him happily in her cavern, until his desire to see his father again exposes him to danger and intrigue. In the end, however, true love triumphs and Prince Ahmed becomes the Sultan of India. These two stories ironically reflect Dobbin's 'inferior' status as the son of a grocer in the city. Sindbad the Sailor, a figure of romance, is also a tradesman, and even the aristocratic Prince Ahmed sets out on his journey in the guise of a merchant. This is a glorious fantasy for Dobbin. The *Nights* indicate a culture where the merchant is valued. On a deeper level, they offer a significant contrast to Dobbin's subsequent career in India. The romantic relationship of the Peri Banou and Prince Ahmed, in which he offers to be her slave, and she makes a marriage proposal within minutes of his arrival, is an equally far cry from Dobbin's unrequited love for Amelia. Dobbin's shyness and self-sacrifice contrast poignantly with the precipitancy of the fairy's approach.

These aspects of the *Nights*, evoking a world of impossible daring

and extremes of wealth and happiness, were part of its delight for
Thackeray, whose own adult life was, like Dobbin's, scarcely cast
in an exotic mould.[1] The fact that happiness so often eluded
Thackeray made the recollection of this dream-world of childhood
all the more precious. He told Tennyson in 1859 when congratula-
ting him on the first *Idylls*, 'You have made me as happy as I was
as a child with *The Arabian Nights*.'[2] This is not only high praise, it
also suggested that the delight of the *Nights* belonged to childhood
and was not to be re-experienced in adult life. For Thackeray, as
for Dickens, the *Nights* recalled a joyful period before much later
unhappiness. Another indication of this comes in *The Newcomes*.
Here the adult Clive recalls Ethel's first appearance in his life,
again setting the ideal of the fairy princess against the cold-hearted,
fickle reality of the adult world, where Ethel vacillates cruelly:

> *Clive:* I remember one of the days, when I first saw you, I had
> been reading the 'Arabian Nights' at school – and you
> came in in a bright dress of shot silk, amber and blue -
> and I thought you were like that fairy princess who
> came out of the crystal box – because –
>
> *Ethel:* Because why?
>
> *Clive:* Because I always thought that fairy somehow must be
> the most beautiful creature in the world – that is 'why
> and because'.   (VIII, 493)

It is appropriate that Clive should compare the flirtatious Ethel
with the 'fairy' in the 'crystal box', another fickle woman who
appears in the opening frame tale of the *Nights*. This conversation
between Clive and Ethel also raises a question which can be asked
of Stevenson as well as of Thackeray: how far does the appeal of
the *Nights* arise from a nostalgic recollection of childhood, as
opposed to its intrinsic literary qualities? Stevenson's adult life,
even with illness, was never as tragic as Thackeray's, but his
nostalgia was far more pronounced.

Escapism, fantasy, adventure: such feelings have been aroused
by the *Nights* since its first European publication. In poems and
essays, Stevenson writes of the vivid imaginative life which reading
it gave him. The *Nights* was associated with the liberating effect of
an older cousin, Bob (R. A. M. Stevenson), who came to stay when
Robert Louis was six. Bob invented games which drew upon the
stories in the book:

Here is the sea, here is the sand,
Here is simple Shepherd's Land,
Here are the fairy hollyhocks,
And there all Ali Baba's rocks.
(xiv, 50)

In the essay 'Child's Play' Stevenson recalls eating calves'-foot jelly
and imagining that 'sooner or later my spoon would lay open the
secret tabernacle of the golden rock. There, might some miniature
Red Beard await his hour; there, might one find the treasures of
the *Forty Thieves*, and bewildered Cassim beating about the walls'
(ii, 402).

At this time, in November 1856, Robert Louis first received his
Skelt's model theatre. In his 'roll-call of stirring names' (ix, 116) it
is 'Aladdin' which has pride of place among his plays. In 'A Penny
Plain and Twopence Coloured' he pictures himself in the third
person, coming home with a new cardboard drama:

> a little late for dinner, the lamps springing into light in the blue
> winter's even, and *The Miller*, or *The Rover*, or some kindred
> drama clutched against his side – on what gay feet he ran, and
> how he laughed aloud in exultation! I can hear that laughter
> still. Out of all the years of my life, I can recall but one home-
> coming to compare with these, and that was on the night when
> I brought back with me the 'Arabian Entertainments' in the fat,
> old, double-columned volume with the prints [the Revd Edward
> Forster's translation]. I was just well into the story of the
> Hunchback, I remember, when my clergyman-grandfather (a
> man we counted pretty stiff) came in behind me. I grew blind
> with terror. But instead of ordering the book away, he said he
> envied me. Ah, well he might! (ix, 118)

Stevenson's final comment is an important one. In the essays and
poems, he constantly stresses the division between adulthood and
childhood. This is not a Wordsworthian lament. Stevenson's point
is that childhood is different from adulthood, not that it is
necessarily better. 'The regret we have for our childhood is not
wholly justifiable' is the opening line of 'Child's Play' (ii, 394). The
child needs props and stimuli to invention. Lacking the resources
of memory, his world is one of 'dim sensation, play is all in all.
"Making believe" is the gist of his whole life, and he cannot so

much as take a walk except in character' (II, 401). Stevenson tells how the *Nights* helped him overcome a lack of natural enthusiasm for football:

> I knew at least one little boy who was mightily exercised about the presence of the ball, and had to spirit himself up, whenever he came to play, with an elaborate story of enchantment, and take the missile as a sort of talisman bandied about in conflict between two Arabian nations.   (II, 402–3)

This association with the imaginary and fantastic was not forgotten by either writer, although both attempted to rationalise their enthusiasm in adult life. Thackeray, appropriately enough, raised the subject when describing a visit to the Middle East. He told his readers that he liked the *Nights* for its lack of tragedy, for the absence of worrying realism in its account of violent events:

> The beauty of that poetry is, to me, that it was never too handsome; there is no fatigue of sublimity about it. Schacabac and the little barber play as great a part in it as the heroes; there are no uncomfortable sensations of terror; you may be familiar with the great Afreet, who was going to execute the travellers for killing his son with a date-stone. Morgiana, when she kills the forty robbers with boiling oil, does not seem to hurt them in the least; and though King Schahriar makes a practice of cutting off his wives' heads, yet you fancy they have got them on again in some of the back rooms of the palace, where they are dancing and playing on dulcimers. How fresh, easy, good-natured is all this!   (V, 629)

Since *Vanity Fair* is subtitled 'a novel without a hero', we should note the reference to characters who lack heroic qualities, but who are, for Thackeray, as important as the heroes. The astrologer-barber is a leading figure, eventually the story-teller, in one of the most sustained and ingenious sequences of the *Nights*, 'The Tale of the Hunchback'. The barber tells the stories of his six brothers, of whom Schacabac is the sixth. Thackeray frequently refers to the story of Schacabac, which evidently appealed to his wry sense of humour. The near-starving Schacabac is entertained to dinner by an old man, a Barmecide (or member of the Barmak family) who offers him a fabulous meal of which nothing ever appears.

Schacabac joins in with the old man's elaborate mime, and finally when the 'wine' is served, gets 'drunk', and strikes his host, whose anger he appeases by confessing to drunkenness, as imaginary as the meal and the wine. Amused, the old man offers him a real meal and a home.

References to the 'Barmecide banquet' turn up throughout Thackeray's published writings and letters. As late as *Pendennis* in 1850, he was inventing the Barmecide Club at Oxbridge, whose members presumably expected to feed on more than air. Reviewing *Coningsby* by Disraeli in 1844, Thackeray dismissed it as 'a cheap Barmecide entertainment',[3] and he used the expression more appropriately a year later when reviewing a cookery book by Joseph Bregion and Anne Miller, under the title 'Barmecide Banquets':

> In default of substantial banquets even imaginary ones are pleasant. I have always relished Alnaschar's [a mistake for his brother, Schacabac's] dinner, off lamb and pistachio-nuts, with the jolly Barmecide, and could, with an easy and thankful heart, say grace over that light repast. [He goes on to compare the sensation to that of reading about the meals in the *The Iliad*, in Ariosto, and in Scott's *Ivanhoe* and *Quentin Durward*.] The very thought of these meals, as recalling them one by one, I note them down, creates a delightful tickling and longing, and makes one quite hungry.[4]

In 'Memorials of Gourmandising', written in Paris in 1841, Thackeray tells the story of Schacabac in more detail, as an illustration of his own advice to keep your dinner bills. He equates fate with the Barmecide, and sees the ability to slap fate's face, in this instance by recalling good meals eaten in the past, as a source of strength in adversity:

> Is not that dinner in the 'Arabian Nights' a right good dinner? Would you have had Bedreddin [another understandable mistake for Schacabac] to refuse and turn sulky at the windy repast, or to sit down grinning in the face of his grave entertainer, and gaily take what came? Remember what came of the honest fellow's philosophy. He slapped the grim old prince in the face; and the grim old prince, who had invited him but to laugh at him, did presently order a rich and substantial repast to be set before him. . . . Thus should we, my dear friends, laugh at

Fate's beard, as we confront him – thus should we, if the old master be insolent, fall to and box his ears. He has a spice of humour in his composition; and be sure he will be tickled by such conduct.   (v, 628)

The Barmecide incident had appealed to earlier writers. Joseph Addison retold the story in the *Guardian* in 1713, reading into it the moral that one should live at ease with oneself and with others. Although Thackeray is never as explicit about his interpretation of the story as Addison, he seems to have seen it in a far less moralistic light. For Thackeray, this story was an illustration of the pre-eminence of the imagination and of its power to alleviate deprivation through dream or fantasy. This interpretation is even further from the original than Addison's, since there is nothing in the *Nights* to suggest that the dinner finally eaten is in any way inferior to the one already eaten in the imagination. On the contrary, the text implies that the second meal lives up to the claim of the first. That this interpretation is probably the right one is confirmed by Thackeray's comments on Smyrna, which thrilled him for just two hours: 'The first day in the East is like that. After that there is nothing. The wonder is gone, and the thrill of that delightful shock, which so seldom touches the nerves of plain men of the world, though they seek for it everywhere' (v, 628).

Accounts of eating and drinking and of fabulous banquets are one of the perennial delights of the *Nights*, where characters equally often experience extremes of hunger. Two stories which particularly captured Thackeray's imagination both relate closely to this theme. The first is the tale of Sidi Numan, who marries Amina, a witch with a ghoul lover. Where the Barmecide banquet represented the triumph of the imagination for Thackeray, this story of Sidi Numan became a type of the unnatural and the depraved. The unlikable Agnes Twysden in *Philip* is compared to Amina, and, reviewing the Royal Academy Exhibition of 1844, Thackeray described P. F. Poole's painting of starving *Moors Beleaguered in Valencia* as 'A clever hideous picture in the very worst taste':

Why do young men indulge in these horrors? . . . Don't let us have any more of these hideous exhibitions – these ghoul festivals. It may be remembered that Amina in the 'Arabian Nights', who liked churchyard suppers, could only eat a grain of rice when she came to natural foods. There is a good deal of sly satire in the apologue which might be applied to many (especially French) literary and pictorial artists of the convulsionary school. (XIII, 438)

On other occasions, Thackeray associated the tale of Amina with the affected excesses of young girls. Ottilia, in *The Fitzboodle Papers*, is drawn from one girl whom he met as a young man in Weimar, and whom he discovered overate: 'I do not dislike', he begins, 'to see a woman eat comfortably. . . . No! a woman who eats a grain of rice, like Amina in the "Arabian Nights", is absurd and unnatural; but there is a *modus in rebus*: there is no reason why she should be a ghoul, a monster, an ogress, a horrid gormandiseress – faugh!' (IV, 338–9). The 'absurd and unnatural' is part of the affectation of Blanche Amory in *Pendennis*:

> When nobody was near, our little sylphide, who scarcely ate at dinner more than the six grains of rice of Amina, the friend of the Ghouls in the *Arabian Nights*, was most active with her knife and fork, and consumed a very substantial portion of mutton cutlets: in which piece of hypocrisy it is to be believed she resembled other young ladies of fashion. (II, 364)

Another story to which Thackeray was particularly attached was that of the barber's fifth brother, Alnaschar. Like the story of Schacabac, it concerns the power of the imagination. On inheriting one hundred pieces of silver from his father, Alnaschar buys some glassware. In a rapidly accelerating daydream of wealth and success, he contemplates his marriage to the Grand Vizier's daughter. Fantasising about how he will spurn the girl's mother with his foot, he kicks the glass over. If he enjoyed eating glorious meals in the imagination, Thackeray also frequently recognised himself as Alnaschar, telling a friend on one occasion that he was having 'Alnaschar visions'[5] about magazines which would employ him, a situation which he described in the words of Arthur Pendennis: 'What an Alnaschar I am because I have made five pounds by my poems, and am engaged to write half-a-dozen articles for a newspaper' (II, 324). Leaving home for Cambridge, Henry Esmond, seen through the eyes of his older self, suggests the same comparison: 'be sure that there are other folks who build castles in the air, and have fine hopes, and kick them down too, besides honest Alnaschar' (VII, 96). Thackeray's interpretation is again subtly different from Addison's. For Addison the story illustrated the unreasonableness of hope 'misemployed upon temporal objects . . . at a great distance from us'.[6] Thackeray may think such fantasies hopeless, but he can understand and delight in them.

Taking up the story again in *Pendennis*, Thackeray approaches it from a different angle, that of the grasping Vizier's daughter. Writing to propose to Blanche Amory, Pen draws an elaborate comparison between the Alnaschar story and the theme of Bulwer Lytton's play *The Lady of Lyons*. He presents the former as truer to life, with its unromantic account of what happens to a penniless suitor, whereas the latter speaks of love triumphing over penury:

> Alnaschar, who kicked down the china, was not a married man; he had cast his eye on the Vizier's daughter, and his hopes of her went to the ground with the shattered bowls and tea-cups. Will you be the Vizier's daughter, and refuse and laugh to scorn Alnaschar, or will you be the Lady of Lyons, and love the penniless Claude Melnotte?   (II, 708)

In fact, it is Blanche who first draws an analogy to the *Arabian Nights*, when she fancifully tells Pen that her money could bring him a 'seat in Parliament as backsheesh to the sultan! . . . my songs will amuse my lord's leisure' (II, 644). Pen replies to her with a reference to the stories of Ali Baba, rescued from certain death by his wily slave Morgiana:

> 'And if thieves are about the house,' said Pen, grimly pursuing the simile, 'forty besetting thieves in the shape of lurking cares and enemies in ambush and passions in arms, my Morgiana will dance round me with a tambourine, and kill all my rogues and thieves with a smile. Won't she?' But Pen looked as if he did not believe that she would.   (II, 644)

In his relationship with Blanche, Pen is destined to be an Alnaschar (although it was Ali Baba's son who actually married Morgiana). In *Vanity Fair*, it is Becky, with her vivid imagination and her memories of the *Nights*, who shares the novelist's customary self-identification with Alnaschar. She dreams of marrying Jos Sedley, whom she has never seen:

> she had built for herself a most magnificent castle in the air, of

which she was mistress, with a husband somewhere in the background (she had not seen him as yet, and his figure would not therefore be very distinct); she had arrayed herself in an infinity of shawls, turbans, and diamond necklaces, and had mounted upon an elephant to the sound of the march in 'Bluebeard', in order to pay a visit of cermony to the Grand Mogul. Charming Alnaschar visions! it is the happy privilege of youth to construct you, and many a fanciful young creature besides Rebecca Sharp has indulged in these delightful day-dreams ere now!   (I, 18)

The reference to Bluebeard perhaps established Jos Sedley as a comic Shahriar, while Becky becomes a would-be Scheherazade (she *is* a character gifted at talking her way out of trouble). In a slightly later passage, after she has actually met Jos, the husband-hunting Becky, pretending to love all things Indian, asks for some curry. Already 'suffering tortures with the cayenne pepper' (I. 21), she eats a chilli, thinking that it will be cool, and then cries out desperately for water. Having temporarily lost control of the situation, Becky quotes the *Nights* to re-establish her dominance. Forcing herself to appear good-humoured, she says: 'I ought to have remembered the pepper which the Princess of Persia puts in the cream-tarts in the "Arabian Nights". Do you put cayenne into your cream-tarts in India, sir?' (I, 21). Becky is coquettishly recalling the story of Noureddin Ali and Bedreddin Hassan, where Bedreddin's mother, the daughter of the Vizier of Egypt, makes excellent cheesecake flavoured with pepper, a skill enabling her to trace the long-lost son and reunite him with his wife. At the end of the evening, Joseph Sedley goes off to see Miss Decamp perform Morgiana's dance in *The Forty Thieves*, carrying the *Nights* motif right through the third chapter.

Ethel Newcome, who compares herself to an Arabian maiden, put onto the market, again invokes the cheesecake story, when she hands a plate of her aunt's currant-and-raspberry tarts to Lord Farintosh (whose nocturnal prowlings are later comically compared to those of Harun al-Rashid). When Lord Farintosh congratulates the cook, Ethel asks him,

> 'Don't you remember the princess in the "Arabian Nights" who was such a stunner for tarts, Lord Farintosh?'
> Lord Farintosh couldn't say that he did.

> 'Well, I thought not; but there was a princess in Arabia, or
> China, or somewhere, who made such delicious tarts and
> custards that nobody's could compare with them: and there is
> an old lady in Brighton who has the same wonderful talent. She
> is the mistress of this house.'   (VIII, 448)

Farintosh's ignorance of the *Nights* is a point against him, while
Ethel's reference to a tart-making princess mocks his snobbish
dismay at a hostess who does her own cooking.

Unlike Thackeray, Stevenson rarely makes explicit reference to
specific episodes in the *Nights*, but he is more reponsive than
Thackeray to its structural qualities, approaching it more directly
as literature. If the experience of Smyrna led Thackeray to define
the appeal of the book, Stevenson approached the *Nights* through
a discussion of literary 'Romance' in 1882:

> There is one book, for example, more generally loved than
> Shakespeare, that captivates in childhood, and still delights in
> age – I mean the 'Arabian Nights' – where you shall look in vain
> for moral or for intellectual interest. No human face or voice
> greets us among that wooden crowd of kings and genies,
> sorcerers and beggarmen. Adventure, on the most naked terms,
> furnishes forth the entertainment and is found enough.   (IX,
> 141)

While Thackeray delighted in an absence of heroes and of tragedy,
Stevenson, again defining by negatives, rejoices in what he saw
as the lack of moral and intellectual interest, and in the absence of
the human. The adventure is naked; it has no basis in probability.

In his essay 'Child's Play' Stevenson again disassociates the
Nights from the intellectual or sorrowful thoughts which dog the
adult mind.

> Our day-dreams can no longer lie all in the air like a story in the
> 'Arabian Nights'; they read to us rather like the history of a
> period in which we ourselves had taken part, where we come
> across many unfortunate passages and find our own conduct
> smartly reprimanded.   (IX, 400)

In Stevenson's work, morality, although apparently questioned
and even flouted, remains a major presence and issue. Nor was

his discussion of varieties of adventure an entirely academic one. Writing about a favourite novel, *The Vicomte de Bragelonne* by Dumas the younger, Stevenson asked, 'What other novel has such epic variety and nobility of incident? Often, if you will, impossible; often of the order of an Arabian story; and yet all based in human nature' (IX, 129). Significantly, in *The Wrecker*, Stevenson's narrator, Loudon Dodd, marks the movement from one area of the narrative to another by telling us that the first part of the plot was 'the romance of business', while the second, and more fantastic, half 'was its Arabian tale' (XIII, 351).

Both Thackeray and Stevenson made use of narrators and frame tales, Thackeray in *Esmond* and *The Virginians*, Stevenson in *Dr Jekyll and Mr Hyde* and *The Master of Ballantrae*, to take only the most obvious examples. In this context, we should perhaps reconsider the apparently unsatisfactory and rambling shape of *The Virginians*, where event follows event until a point of monotony is reached. One of Stevenson's first published works, *The New Arabian Nights* of 1882, places a series of modern adventures into a narrative framework which consciously echoes the structure of the original. He does not bring in a Scheherazade figure, but the battle of wits between Prince Florizel of Bohemia and the President of the Suicide Club provides a loose framework for the series of stories.

Both story groups in *The New Arabian Nights*, 'The Suicide Club' and 'The Rajah's Diamond', are punctuated by passages like those in the *Nights* where one character or theme is jettisoned, leaving the way open for the narrative to go on to the next. As a story-telling device, Stevenson often uses this affectionate parody for the purposes of irony. After the young man has escaped from the Suicide Club,

> *Here* (says my Arabian author) ends THE STORY OF THE YOUNG MAN WITH THE CREAM TARTS, *who is now a comfortable householder in Wigmore Street, Cavendish Square. The number, for obvious reasons, I suppress. Those who care to pursue the adventures of Prince Florizel and the President of the Suicide Club, may read* THE STORY OF THE PHYSICIAN AND THE SARATOGA TRUNK. (IV, 37)

These switches come, as they often do in the *Arabian Nights*, at the most tantalising moments, where one tale opens abruptly out of another, or where a character answers a question by beginning a different story. In *The New Arabian Nights* such changes of direction often lead into an account of a new character:

STORY OF THE PHYSICIAN AND THE SARATOGA TRUNK

Mr Silas Q. SCUDDAMORE was a young American of a simple and harmless disposition. . . .   (IV, 37)

Scuddamore discovers a dead body in his bed, packs it into his trunk (an episode borrowed from the story told by the purveyor to the Sultan of Casgar in the *Nights*), and takes the trunk to London, only to drop out of the story in his turn when a new figure appears.

The New Arabian Nights is set in London and Paris. Several sequences recall the twisting and tortuous streets of Baghdad. For the young Stevenson, Baghdad must have transposed itself into Edinburgh, of whose alleys and wynds he often writes with such concentrated descriptive power. In *The New Arabian Nights*, Lieutenant Brackenbury Rich is asked to a party in a luxurious suburban villa. He eventually learns that everything has been moved in for the occasion, and then watches the whole interior (furniture, flowers, waiters, music, food, guests) being dismantled, like Aladdin's magic palace.

A prominent feature of the *Nights* is the precise but incomprehensible set of instructions which must be obeyed. Both Aladdin, and Agib in 'The Three Calenders' are ordered to carry out a complex set of tasks, with certain prohibitions attached. In the same way, Francis Scrymgeour in Stevenson's 'Rajah's Diamond' is told that he will receive £500 a year if he marries as his unknown benefactor wishes, and fulfils these instructions:

You must be in Paris by the afternoon of Sunday, the 15th; there you will find, at the box-office of the Comédie Française a ticket for admission taken in your name and awaiting you. You are requested to sit out the whole performance in the seat provided, and that is all.   (IV, 129)

In the unlikely context of 'An Autumn Effect' (1875), an essay on the Chiltern Hills, Stevenson included a striking image which reveals how much this aspect of the *Nights* meant to him. He describes a sudden glimpse of a family group seen through a lighted window, recalling a similar effect in Brussels:

Night after night I found the scene rivet my attention and keep me awake in bed with all manner of quaint imaginations. Much of the pleasure of the 'Arabian Nights' hinges upon this Asmodean interest; and we are not weary of lifting other people's roofs, and going about behind the scenes of life with the Caliph and the serviceable Giaffar. It is a salutary exercise, besides; it is salutary to get out of ourselves and see people living together in perfect unconsciousness of our existence, as they will live when we are gone.   (xxII, 121)

This is Stevenson as Harun al-Raschid. It confirms that there was an element of wish-fulfilment, not only in Prince Florizel, but in another early hero, Prince Otto. Chapter 2 of *Prince Otto*, headed 'In which the Prince plays Haroun al-Raschid', describes how Otto leaves his small German court in order to mingle with his subjects, and to hear their unflattering views of himself. Florizel and Otto have other folk and literary antecedents. They are the archetypal kings in disguise.

Florizel in *The New Arabian Nights* is considerably cosier than any of his Eastern or Western counterparts, and was believed by some to represent the Prince of Wales. In the first group of stories, 'The Suicide Club', he and his faithful companion, Colonel Geraldine, meet a young man intent upon giving away a tray of cream tarts, before he joins the Suicide Club. This is a sinister institution whose members, weary of life, draw lots to discover which shall be victim and which murderer. The cream tarts come from that same story of Noureddin Ali and Bedreddin Hassan to which Becky Sharp refers, but here they serve the purpose of parody. To gain admission to 'strange societies' the stout Prince Florizel disguises himself with 'false whiskers and a pair of large adhesive eyebrows' (IV, 6). Pointedly, his final metamorphosis turns him into a cigar merchant in Rupert Street: 'a recent revolution hurled him from the throne of Bohemia, in consequence of his continued absence and edifying neglect of public business' (IV, 166).

Much of the fun of *The New Arabian Nights* comes from relating ancient formulae to modern times. Like Dickens with his 'Thousand and One Humbugs', Thackeray tried direct parody of the *Nights* in his *Sultan Stork: Being the Thousand and Second Night*, where a king and his vizier are turned into storks. Thackeray's immediate source here was an earlier parody, 'The Caliph Turned Stork' by the German writer W. Hauff.[7] Thackeray's intention was social satire, particularly aimed at unrealistic writers, but, compared with Stevenson, he fails to maintain the sparkling humour.

Not everything in *The New Arabian Nights* is light-hearted. Stevenson's characteristic ability to create dark and evil characters is present in this early work. Both the President of the Suicide Club and old John Vandaleur appear in disguise in unexpected places, like the rogues, djinns and evil spirits of the *Nights*. Another of Stevenson's recurring themes is that of the double, often associated in his work with ideas of metamorphosis. Here again there are parallels in the *Nights*: Sindbad, the fabulously wealthy, befriends the impoverished porter, Hindbad; the fates of Abu Kir, the rascally dyer, and Abu Sir, the saintly barber, are sharply contrasted. Doubling is hinted at in *The New Arabian Nights*, but explicitly introduced in Stevenson's *The Master of Ballantrae*. Here he presented 'all I know of the devil'[8] in the elder brother, James, contrasting him to the younger, Henry. The result was far more complex and ambiguous than Stevenson's statement implies. By the end of the novel it is hard to see which is the 'good' and which the 'evil' brother. 'If there is any hell to go to [James is] gone to hell; and I forgive him',[9] Stevenson wrote later.

In an incomplete account of the genesis of the novel, Stevenson wrote of the two ideas which came together in it. The first was that of a 'buried and resuscitated fakir, which I had been often told by an uncle of mine'.[10] The second was the story of the usurpation of an older brother by a younger, of which Stevenson knew an actual instance. The first idea gave him the final section of the book, which the master apparently dies and is disinterred a few days later by his Indian servant, Secundra Dass. The plan to restore him to life, which nearly succeeds, recalls a number of characters in the *Nights* – for example, the hunchback who is resuscitated after apparent death, and the prince, in the tale of the First Calender, who goes into his tomb to enjoy an incestuous relationship with his sister, but is killed by a thunderbolt instead. Stevenson told Henry James: 'The elder brother is an *INCUBUS*: supposed to be killed at Culloden, he turns up again and bleeds the family of money.'[11] Stevenson's stress on the word 'incubus', and his reference to the devil in his letters about the novel, suggest that the Master is an evil spirit, perhaps already dead when he appears in Scotland with Secundra Dass. The Durie brothers cannot exist without each other. Their deaths are simultaneous.

There is one direct reference to the *Nights* in the novel. The

Irishman, Burke, gives a tantalising glimpse of James in India. Burke describes his meeting with Ballantrae during a skirmish in the Anglo-French war. A sudden British attack finds Burke in the streets 'without shoes or stockings';

> In short, I was for all the world like one of those calendars with whom Mr Galland has made us acquainted in his elegant tales. These gentlemen, you will remember, were for ever falling in with extraordinary incidents; and I was myself upon the brink of one so astonishing that I protest I cannot explain it to this day.   (xii, 147)

Burke climbs a wall into a garden, and finds Ballantrae, whom he knows, seated 'cross-legged, after the Oriental manner' (xii, 148). He 'never moved a muscle, staring at me like an image in a pagoda' (xii, 149). James pretends not to speak English, and Secundra Dass carries on his side of the conversation. While Burke demands food and money, blusters and threatens, James says not a word. The flight into a mysterious garden might indeed come from the *Nights*, but the underlying effect of this scene is very different. True, it serves to introduce James's relationship with his servant, whom we might identify as an attendant spirit or genie, but, at bottom, James remains a malevolent Scotsman: 'The Sahib would be glad to know if you are a dam low Irishman' (xii, 150), he makes Secundra Dass ask Burke. This ambivalence between the supernatural and the exotic, and something far more mundane and savage, is an essential part of the novel's effect.

There is a similar mingling of the exotic and the threatening in Stevenson's late story 'The Bottle Imp', collected in *Island Nights' Entertainments*, and apparently a darker version of the story of 'Aladdin and the Wonderful Lamp', fused with 'The Fisherman and the Jinni'. The lavish benefits of Aladdin's lamp are happily accepted by the characters in the original story, but, in 'The Bottle Imp', a young Hawaiian, Keave, risks damnation by buying the bottle. The bottle imp has the power to bestow whatever the recipient wishes, but, should the owner die while still in possession, he goes to hell. The story has a complicated literary history. Stevenson himself had the idea from the comedian O. Smith (Richard Smith), and there is a derivation from an Orkney tale, later written down by Edwin Muir. But there is no imp in the

Orkney bottle, and it is the imp which leads one back to Aladdin and the fisherman.

The usual series of apparently meaningless prohibitions are involved here. Keave is told that, if he is to sell the bottle, it must be for less than he paid for it, a problem which becomes increasingly desperate. The bottle imp is far nastier than the huge jinni who appears when Aladdin rubs his lamp, is more akin to the fisherman's jinni. Keave's friend, Lopaka, demands to see him: 'Now as soon as that was said the imp looked out of the bottle, and in again, swift as a lizard; and there sat Keave and Lopaka turned to stone' (XVII, 285). Like Aladdin, Keave asks the bottle for a palace, but, where Aladdin, after considerable trials, can enjoy good fortune, Keave's request has unhappy consequences. He has his house, but only because his uncle and nephew are killed at sea. Vowing not to use the bottle again, Keave sells it to Lopaka. As in 'Aladdin', problems arise when Keave falls in love. Unlike Aladdin, he is able to woo and win the girl without the aid of the imp, but then he finds, in a moment of chilling horror, that he has leprosy, and must buy the bottle back in order to be cured. His happiness with his wife is blighted by fear of hell, until she, Alcestis-like, takes the burden of damnation upon herself. The couple are only extricated when an evil man steals the bottle.

What did this story mean to Stevenson? It has an obvious anti-materialistic message, close to that with which Scheherazade glosses the story of Aladdin. She tells Schahriar that Aladdin has the right intentions, while the evil magician seeks to acquire wealth by wicked methods, and is unworthy to enjoy it. 'The Bottle Imp' can be read as a story of redemption through love. Keave is abstemious with the bottle, but it becomes a terrible burden, clearly associated with a very northern sense of sin. Mia Gerhardt writes of the theme of predestined luck in the Aladdin story, associated with the rational and sensible behaviour of the hero.[12] In comparison, Keave is almost entirely in the hands of his evil fate.

Even these limited explanations imply a moral clarity which the Stevenson story does not have. Aladdin is at first very lazy and sponges on his mother. Keave is a good, hard-working man, who succumbs out of curiosity. The transaction retains the apparently arbitrary air of an event from the Arabian Nights, but, once it has happened, there is no turning back, no shifting of responsibility, except through the power of love, and, ultimately, through another man's evil. This story typifies Stevenson's use of his memories of the *Nights*. Unlike Thackeray, for whom the work retained its purity and innocence, Stevenson works his memories of the *Nights* into a painful moral allegory, taking over the dark and mysterious elements, and carrying them far beyond their original narrative function. A year later, he began on an even darker story, *The Ebb Tide*, the first chapter of which introduces one of Stevenson's most telling references to the *Nights*. Three derelicts lie sick on the beach at Papeete. The most imaginative, Robert Herrick, amuses the others by describing his meeting with a magician from the *Nights*. The Arab has a magic carpet, like that in the tale of Prince Ahmed and the Fairy Peribanou. The carpet, its pocket full of double eagles, could transport them all to London in nine hours. This fantasy releases nostalgic dreams of going home, an oblique expression of Stevenson's own yearnings in the troubled last years of his life. Through a boyhood recollection, the starving Herrick momentarily rouses his two disreputable companions to innocent gaiety. Not long afterwards, having stolen a ship, they set out to rob another Englishman of a fabulous collection of pearls. The riches of the East have become the object of late-nineteenth-century materialism and greed. The ironic resonance of the tale spreads far beyond the first chapter, and suggests that the influence of the *Nights* upon Stevenson must be rated higher than that upon Thackeray, because it is more widespread, harder to isolate, and more pervasive.

NOTES

Books published in London unless otherwise stated. References in the text are to W. M. Thackeray, *Works*, ed. A. T. Ritchie (Smith, Elder, 1898–9) and to R. L. Stevenson, *Works*, Swanston Edition (Chatto and Windus, 1911–12).

1. Thackeray, born in India in 1811, lived for most of his adult life in London.
2. Thackeray, *Letters*, ed. G. N. Ray (Oxford University Press, 1945–6) IV, 152.
3. Thackeray, *Contributions to the Morning Chronicle*, ed. G. N. Ray (Urbana, Ill.: University of Illinois, 1955) p. 40.
4. Thackeray, *Works*, Smith, Elder edn (1891) xxv, 74–5.
5. *Letters*, I, 459.
6. *Spectator*, 13 Nov 1712, in J. Addison, *Works*, ed. R. Hurd (Bohn's British Classics, 1864) IV, 55–60.
7. For a fuller account see R. Hawari, 'A Study of the Exotic East in the

Works of Thackeray, with Reference to the Cult of the Oriental in Eighteenth and Nineteenth Century England' (PhD thesis, University of London, 1967) pp. 215–39.

8. *Letters of R. L. Stevenson*, ed. S. Colvin (Methuen, 1899) ɪɪ, 102.
9. Ibid., p. 181.
10. Stevenson, 'The Genesis of *The Master of Ballantrae*', *Works*, Tusitala Edition (William Heinemann, 1923–4) x, xxiii.
11. *Henry James and Robert Louis Stevenson*, ed. J. Adam Smith (Rupert Hart-Davis, 1948) p. 171.
12. Mia Gerhardt, *The Art of Story-Telling: A Literary Study of the Thousand and One Nights* (Leiden, 1963) pp. 324–8.

8

The Victorian Scheherazade: Elizabeth Gaskell and George Meredith

CORNELIA COOK

The *Arabian Nights* were 'the tales of our childhood' to Elizabeth Gaskell, and indeed the *Nights* in England were over a century old when the Victorian novelist was born. The great Victorian translations, Lane's (1839–41) and Burton's (1885), which frame the period of the *Nights'* most widespread popularity were presented to a reading public steeped in Scheherazade's lore. Already several generations had grown familiar with a tradition that included *The Arabian Nights Entertainments* and the numerous imitations, excerpts and pseudo-translations which had multiplied from the early eighteenth century. Weber's unsurpassed collection of this literature was available from 1812,[1] and by the mid nineteenth century an English habit of Eastern allusion was well established. The 'Story of the Eastern King' from Petis de la Croix's *Turkish Tales* (1708) mentioned in Gaskell's *North and South* had long ago reached a wide audience in a *Spectator* essay on notions of Time (*Spectator* no. 94).[2] The motif of 'Alnaschar-dreams', the castles-in-the-air building of the barber's fifth brother, introduced into *Mary Barton*, had, too, been excerpted by Addison (*Spectator*, no. 535) as an exemplum of false hopes and worldly ambition. Meredith's Eastern tale *The Shaving of Shagpat* (1856) betrays genetic links throughout the tradition: it looks back to the resilient barber of the picaresque *Hajji Baba* (1824) as well as to the garrulous barber of the Hunchback tale; it recalls Beckford's *Vathek* and is directly indebted to Southey's *Thalaba* (1801), itself an offspring of the *New Arabian Nights* (1792).

Casual allusions to the *Nights* in Victorian texts, like the contemporary popularity of its familiar structures (the story collection, frame tales, travel stories), pay an almost unconscious homage to the skill and influence of the obscure Arab story-tellers whose sophisticated narrative forms had become 'our very nursery tales and romances'.[3] In some writers the old forms became the impetus for distinctively 'modern' practices in fiction. George Meredith's innovatory narratives were the likely achievement of one who as a boy had passed 'dreary church services' inventing 'tales . . . of the kind found in the Arabian Nights, of which he was very fond'.[4] But in these Victorian years – especially given Dickens' lead – there was probably not a writer of serial or part-published fiction who did not recall with sympathy Scheherazade's predicament, or who did not at some time borrow her narrative strategies.

Dickens addressed Elizabeth Gaskell in 1851 proleptically as 'my dear Scheherazade'; she had not then begun to publish serially or he, as editor of Household Words, to act as her Schahriar. But Gaskell was tellingly to incorporate Scheherazade's performance into her own studies of English life. That Gaskell considered the Nights – like her own novels – to be pre-eminently an experience of the educated classes is established in the texts. Cynthia Kirkpatrick, a self-confessed light reader and follower of fashion, and Lady Harriet, a cultured modern woman of leisure, are the Nights readers in Wives and Daughters. More importantly, Nights allusions underline the cultural contrasts at the centre of Gaskell's Manchester fictions. 'Of all shops a druggist's looks the most like the tales of our childhood', the narrator of Mary Barton tells us, 'from Aladdin's garden of enchanted fruits to the charming Rosamond with her purple jar'. But she adds of the working man, 'No such associations had Barton' (ch. 6).

In North and South a Nights metaphor assists the southerner Mr Hale to comprehend the wonders of steam-driven machinery.

> Thornton . . . explaining to Mr Hale the magnificent power, yet delicate adjustment of the might of the steam-hammer, which was recalling to Mr Hale some of the wonderful stories of subservient genii in the Arabian Nights – one moment stretching from earth to sky and filling all the width of the horizon, at the next obediently compressed into a vase small enough to be borne in the hand of a child.   (ch. 10)

The equation which distinguishes between the experiences of Hale and Thornton enables the reader, who is more likely to share Hale's background, to share as well in his awed glimpse of the wondrous industrial world.

Gaskell also exploits Arab narrative forms. The 'entertaining'[5] frame became a simple unifying device, collecting some of her periodical essays as a set of inset tales partially framed by the introduction, 'Round the Sofa' (1856). In a more subtle echo of the frame device, the unusual and effective shape of *North and South*, with its oblique opening and delayed resolution, derives from North being practically framed in South.

Gaskell's first serial fiction, *Cranford*, may be argued to engage most carefully with the *Nights*. Cranford memorialises a class of village society – 'the holders of houses above a certain rent . . . gentle folks' – whose way of life was already an anachronism in the 1830s. Remote from the busy commercial life of medieval Arabia celebrated in the *Nights*, Cranford's tale establishes a counterpart. Mary Smith's Cranford appears a harem without a sultan. The fear and suspicion of the opposite sex rife among the Cranford ladies amusingly recall the King of Tartary's obsession. Mary Smith's affectionate and leisurely account of passing times and people could not be more different from Scheherazade's desperate enterprise and the variety of her stories. But Gaskell's novel exploits contrast. Just as *Cranford* captures its transitional moment in a synthesis of poised Johnsonian diction and Pickwickian episode, it gains significance and colour from a quiet but consistent interaction between the English exotic of Cranford life and the Eastern exotic of the *Nights*.

Miss Matty picking at her peas 'as Aminé ate her grains of rice' is thwarted not by gruesome surfeit but by Mr Holbrook's two-pronged fork. Matty is an innocent Amina – not the lover of a ghoul, not even a wife. The comic and pathetic aspects of the comparison illuminate the quality of Cranford life – its spinsterish worries, its hidden tragedies. Mr Holbrook, however, resembles Sidi Numan in having been denied marital happiness by a spectre's power over his would-be wife. The social snobbery which declared that '*Mr* Thomas Holbrook, yeoman . . . would not have been enough of a gentleman for the rector and Miss Jenkyns' leaves an abiding sorrow in Miss Matty's homely, much valued life. Oblique presentation of the story's facts and persons through the medium of Mary Smith promotes growth in our sympathetic understanding of characters whose ways are, at the time of the narrative, formed and unchanging. And she herself becomes the audience for significant inset stories told by Miss Matty, Miss Pole and Signora Brunoni. These inset tales provide a context for the present relation, injecting glimpses of the past, and a sense of the world outside Cranford. Several of *Cranford*'s inset tales notably concern the lost Peter Jenkyns and thus shape an outlandish history of Peter which ultimately converges with the main tale in his surprising and rewarding reappearance. Through Peter Jenkyns the atmosphere of the *Nights* actively invades *Cranford*: 'Their quiet lives were astonishingly stirred up by the arrival from India – especially as the person arrived told more wonderful stories than Sindbad the Sailor; and, as Miss Pole said, was quite as good as an Arabian Night any evening' (ch. 16). Peter's history has its Sindbad elements – captivity and escape, habituation to a foreign life – and this 'favourite at Cranford' is more revered the more fantastic and Sindbad-like his stories grow. 'I don't think the ladies at Cranford would have considered him such a wonderful traveller if they had only heard him talk in the quiet way he did to [the Rector]. They liked him the better, indeed, for being what they called "so very Oriental".'

Peter's return thus highlights an ever-present attraction in the ladies to the exotic (often linked with 'the masculine gender'), elsewhere glimpsed in encounters with an exotic rendered suitably 'respectable' (and harmless) in the forms of fashion (Matty's desired 'sea-green turban'), literature (Miss Jenkyns' selection of Johnson's Eastern tale as a riposte to Pickwick), or public entertainments (Signor Brunoni's conjuring performance). The magnificent impression ('like a being of another sphere') created by Brunoni's Turkish garb is overshadowed subsequently by the pathos of his family's misfortunes. These open to Mary Smith the novel's most wonderful history, of Signora Brunoni's desperate trek through India to save her child, which unexpectedly reveals the where-abouts of the lost Peter, the 'kind Aga Jenkyns' of Chunderabaddad.

Peter's arrival satisfies, in a way appropriately chaste, the ladies' needs and the novel's. Peter returns to provide the Cranfordians the masculine guidance and protection they have lacked and the exotic they desire. In the Aga Peter, sitting amongst them cross-legged (an attitude that strikes the ladies as elegant and patriarchal, indeed reminiscent of the Prophet), the harem has found its Sultan. At the end of *Cranford*, as at the end of Scheherazade's stories, an accommodation between the sexes is achieved.

The 'formative' influence of the *Nights* which George Meredith acknowledged[6] is manifest throughout his writings. Meredith's poems include two after *Nights* subjects, and a series of Arab lyrics. Neither 'The Sleeping City', based on the story of Zobeide, nor 'Shemselnihar', from 'The History of Aboulhassan, Ali Ebn Becar and Shemselnihar, Favourite of the Caliph Haroun Alraschid', attempts to retell the Arabian story; both explore the heroine's reactions in the situation described by the tale, varying the emphasis widely from the *Nights* to suit Meredith's thematic concern. The scene in 'The Sleeping City' (1851) and 'the princess's' reactions to it correspond closely to Galland's descriptions; the poem's rhythm and the fountain and balustrade of the third stanza probably recall Tennyson's 'Recollections of the Arabian Nights'. The princess's awed discovery of a record of human passion in the 'lifeless immortality' of the enchanted stone figures is Meredith's addition to his source, promoting his own musings on the arrested life of nocturnal London.

'Shemselnihar' is a striking lyric addressed by the favourite of Harun al-Rashid to her secret lover, lamenting her dual slavery to the possession of the Caliph and to his generosity. The favourite's dilemma foreshadows Clara Middleton's desperation in *The Egoist*, and Semselnihar's is the obverse of the speaker's agony in *Modern Love*,[7] that other work deriving from a Shahzenan plight, with which this poem was published in 1862.

All the elements of 'Shemselnihar' are consistent with the source story, though its vivid imagery is not local to the tale. Fountain, lemon-groves and the darkling song of the bulbul are Tennysonian.[8] A Keatsian richness colours the waning 'gloom' of the departing night of love, and echoes of Keats's Nightingale Ode acquire an Eastern tinge as they in turn lend a sense of dangerous desire. The Sun of Day which is Shemselnihar's emblem (as it translates her name) becomes her enemy, the light a dark token revealing at dawning her two worlds of slavery to love and slavery to him 'whose I am', of the impossible and the necessary. This poem probably benefits from Lane's translation, for its imagery echoes the tale's crucial songs, first included there.

It is evident from his familiarity with the Victorian translations that Meredith not only recollected the *Nights* of his childhood but studied them in maturity. Indeed when George Eliot reviewed his first novel, *The Shaving of Shagpat* (1856) – subtitled 'An Arabian Entertainment' – she called it 'an admirable imitation of Oriental tale-telling, . . . less an imitation of the "Arabian Nights" than a similar creation inspired by a thorough and admiring study'.[9]

The Shaving of Shagpat is a comic and partly parodic tale of a heroic barber and of social revolution – wearing, as Meredith put it, 'a sort of allegory . . . not as a dress-suit; rather as a dressing-gown, very loosely' (*Letters*, II, 1095), employing Arab settings, motifs and characters. Its allegory, urging the destruction of Illusion, the perennial enemy of personal and social liberty, owes little to the *Nights* and is yet faithful to that text's morality. The novel's shape acknowledges the Arab model, comprising successive episodes in a quest framed by introductory and concluding comments, enlivened and illuminated by interpolated narratives.

Meredith claimed to imitate 'the style and manner of the Oriental Storytellers';[10] his tale has been called 'the finest Eastern Story outside the *Arabian Nights*' (*Letters*, I, 27) and a remarkably faithful approximation to the tone of the original.[11] Meredith formed his style on the language and manner of the best Victorian translation, the single volume of Henry Torrens, 'Irishman, Lawyer . . . and Bengal Civilian'. According to Burton, Torrens' 'copy was carefully moulded upon the model and offered the best example of the *verbatim et literatim* style'.[12] In Torrens' colourful mispronunciations and his predilection for oaths, exclamations, and the activating interjections 'Now' and 'And', Meredith discovered an imitable exuberance of expression suiting his comic mode. The tones of Meredith's Baba Mustapha, uncle to Shibli Bagarag, and of Shibli himself are heard in the Barber of Torrens' translation.

Then said he, 'Oh! my Lord, I do not think you are aware of my rank; surely my hand presses the heads of kings, and men of power, and ministers, and men in command, and learned men, and the poet said on me the verse;–

"Like knots in the way other callings appear,
But this fellow's the shaver that pares the path clear
Above every craftsman he takes his stand,
And the heads of kings are under his hand!" . . .

Restrain your spirits, for hastiness is of Satan, and the bequeather of repentence, and disappointment, and he has said, on whom be blessings and peace, "The matter's good on which thou makest delay"; but I, Wullahy! have some doubt about your affair, for I am much afraid that it is something else than that which is good, and it wants now three hours to prayer time.'[13]

In approximating not simply to the *Nights* but to Torrens' rendition, *The Shaving of Shagpat* becomes more precise in its orientalism. The novel recalls the most familiar *Nights* stories, introducing the roc, the jinni who serves and defies his mistress, and a wondrous perspective glass. Original features, however, acquire authenticity and significance through their likeness to *Nights* elements, a likeness which often contains an echo of Torrens. The horse Garraveen ('black to look on . . . silver-hoofed, fashioned in the curves of beauty and swiftness – *Shagpat*, pp. 160–1) recalls the 'noble steed, dark as in the blackness of night' (Torrens, p. 155) who punishes the Third Calender for his impetuous curiosity and vanity. Koorookh, Shibli's avian ally, probably derives his name from Torrens' spelling of 'Rookh' (p. 150). The dish of pomegranate grain into which Noorna whips a soporific drug for Shagpat is that confection familiarly known to Galland's readers as 'cream tarts' but correctly translated (and annotated) by Torrens (pp. 235, xxv n. 121).

It is even likely that Torrens taught Shibli his pride in barbercraft. Meredith has noted the content of the Barber's speech above, and of Torrens' note, 'The barber is looked upon by most Mussulman nations as a person of considerable importance, arising from . . . the charge (as boasted by the barber of the tale) which he has of the head, the most noble part of even the most noble' (p. xx n. 152) In Shibli's tale of Rumdrum the Barber, the eponymous hero reminds the treacherous king that 'there is nought like confidence in thy kind; and he that dishonoureth the barber is in turn dishonoured, seeing that it is a craft made familiar with the noblest part of man (*Shagpat*, pp. 176–7).

Most importantly, Torrens showed Meredith the role of verse in the Arab prose tale. The only translator at the time of *Shagpat*'s writing to have rendered the original verse into English poetry, Torrens is still considered the best.[14] Burton judged that Torrens' 'verse, always whimsical, has at times a manner of Hibernian whoop which is comical when it should be pathetic'.[15] It is lucky that on these grounds Torrens' verse would rather have appealed to Meredith than the reverse; just as Torrens' faithfulness promoted Meredith's orientalism, his comicality usefully became, on occasion, Meredith's burlesque. The rescue of the comic from the pathetic is, in a sense, the continuous project of the manner *and* action of *The Shaving of Shagpat*.

'Eastward', Meredith famously opined in his *Essay on Comedy*,

> you have total silence of Comedy among a people intensely susceptible to laughter, as the Arabian Nights will testify. Where the veil is over women's faces, you cannot have society, without which the senses are barbarous and the Comic spirit is driven to the gutters of grossness to slake its thirst. . . . There has been fun in Baghdad. But there will never be civilization where Comedy is not possible; and that comes of some degree of social equality of the sexes.[16]

No wonder Meredith found deeper tragic material in Shemselni-har's story than the pathos of fatal fidelity, and no wonder his favourites appear to be those ladies of magical power who are above the slavery of circumstance and who often influence the fate of men in the *Nights* – the sorceresses and fairies. Noorna, in *The Shaving of Shagpat* is akin, in her condition of sorceress, to such a figure as the Peri Banou, whose magic made her more than equal to her husband and made her husband a sultan. Noorna is guide, comrade and lover of the man who will master the Event.[17] But Noorna is victim as well – 'ensorcelled' (the word is Torrens'[18]); she needs the help of her elected champion Shibli to liberate her from a deforming transformation by the powerful servants of oppression and illusion.

Noorna and Shibli join one battle: he to defeat illusion within himself and in society; she to defeat oppression which robs her identity and exploits her energy. Ian Fletcher, noting Meredith's feminism, still expresses surprise that the epic pattern of noble friendship between men 'is replaced by love and comradeship between man and woman', where 'woman is still the prize, but not the toy, whether of men or gods'.[19] In appealing to the conventions of romance epic, Fletcher ignores the authority and flexibility which the *Nights* gives to Noorna's role and even to the argument equating female and social liberation. One of the striking aspects of the *Nights* is the extent to which its veils are lifted (I do not allude simply to the aspect which occasions Scheherazade's enterprise). Women in Scheherazade's tales are glimpsed every-where, in virtually all their differing social roles and moral tenden-cies: slaves, princesses, wives, companions, clever, powerful, envious, selfless, victims, heroines. In embracing this multifarious aspect of the *Nights*, Meredith's comic formula exceeds his narrow reading of Arab culture in the *Essay*, and emerges both oriental, and consistent in its argument.

Noorna guides Shibli to mastery of the Event through her command of magic and her common sense, the virtue Meredith associates fundamentally with Comedy. Noorna's sense joins Shibli's growing command of 'thoughful laughter', the palpable expression of 'the first-born of common-sense, the vigilant Comic' (*Essay*, p. 32), to accomplish illusion's defeat. These capacities Meredith injects into the Arab dough of *The Shaving of Shagpat* to make the 'fun' rise into 'Comedy', able to 'touch and kindle the mind'.

The Shaving of Shagpat does not violate the naturalism or spontaneity of the Arab mode; it incorporates elements of romance not unknown in the *Nights* – the questor Shibli's moral growth, the tale's steady progress towards the defeat of Shagpat/Illusion and the consequent marriage of Shibli and Noorna – to dignify the fun and enforce its relevance. And the vitality of the oriental tale never falters in the language, imagery, the sheer story-telling craft of this 'similar creation inspired by a thorough and admiring study'.

Shagpat's opening establishes the slightest imaginable entertainment frame, with the reader as audience. In two opening paragraphs the impersonal narrator calls attention to the business of story-telling and to the story of Shibli Bagarag – and then the framed recital begins: 'Now, things were in that condition with Shibli Bagarag, that on a certain day he was hungry and abject . . .' (pp. 1–2). A concluding paragraph alludes to the matter of other chronicles and their entertainment value. The episodic tale itself frames the inserted narratives which George Eliot called 'pleasant landing places on the way' and whose relationship to the main narrative is one of amplification.

In the first edition *Shagpat*'s inserted stories number five. Three exemplary tales, 'Bhanivar the Beautiful', 'Khipil the Builder' and 'Rumdrum the Barber', provide respectively a foil for the main story, a caution against dilatoriness, and an instructive instance of the worth of barbers. 'The Story of Noorna' fills in the crucial antecedent events in Noorna's history, and 'The Recital of the Vizier Feshnavat' describes events in the city of Shagpat during the time of Shibli's preparatory ordeal. In later editions Meredith removed Shibli's story of Rumdrum, an exquisite anecdote, akin to the story of the Grecian King and the Physician Douban, and the Vizier's painful and wordy recital. Their removal leaves three balanced and relevant insertions by the leading executors of the revolutionary Event – Shibli, Noorna and the Vizier.

The story of Rumdrum is a ghost in the revised editions, alluded to but not recounted, enhancing the sense, so alive in this novel as in the *Nights*, that the world is full of stories, and that the common and appropriate destiny of experience is to be rendered into tales. Countless stories in the *Nights* witness themselves being 'put in writing' for posterity by kings, sultans, viziers and Harun himself. Shibli Bagarag is well aware that he will inhabit a tale; he approaches the climax of his adventure exclaiming, ' 'Tis well! The second chapter of the Event is opened; so call it, thou that tellest of the Shaving of Shagpat. It will be the shortest' (*Shagpat*, p. 319). The emphasis on fictionality which blurs the lines of demarcation between text, author and reader achieves striking effects in Meredith's later works.

That the story of Shibli exists before his malnourished appearance on the first page is clear; this is but the arbitrary beginning of Shibli's greatest adventure. Earlier tales stand in the stretch of time from Shibli's birth with its auspicious auguries to his meeting with Noorna, and this past becomes the entertainment of the future as Shibli promises Noorna, 'Wullahy! many adventures were mine, and if there's some day propitiousness in fortune, O old woman, I'll tell thee of what befell me in the kingdom of Shah Shamshureen: 'tis wondrous, a matter to draw down the lower jaw with amazement!' (p. 5). King Shamshureen's is a recurrent and ever-wondrous ghost-tale. Shagpat's hair is measured against the King's – 'not even King Shamshureen, after a thousand years, sported with such mighty profusion! Him I sheared: it was a high task!' (p. 11) – and Shibli's majesty realises itself in the possession of a head cook who rivals Shamshureen's own.

The conclusion of Shibli's tale reaches the end neither of Shibli, nor of tales. The frame reasserts itself, alluding to a future – already accomplished and chronicled – in which tales of the past will be told and the promises of the present fulfilled.

Now, of the promise made by the Sons of Aklis to visit Shibli Bagarag before their compulsory return to the labour of the Sword, and recount to him the marvel of their antecedent adventures, and of the love and grief nourished in the souls of men by the beauty and sorrowful eyes of Gulrevaz, that was named the Bleeding Lily, and of her engagement to tell her story, on condition of receiving the first-born of Noorna to nurse for a season in Aklis; and of Shibli Bagarag's restoration of towns and monuments destroyed by his battle with Karaz; and of the constancy of passion of Shibli Bagarag for Noorna, and his esteem for her sweetness, and his reverence for her wisdom; and of the glory of his reign, and of the Songs and Sentences of Noorna, and of his laws for the protection and upholding of women . . . – of all these records, and of the reign of Baba Mustapha in Oolb, surely the chronicles give them in fulness; and they that have searched say of them, there is matter therein for the amusement of generations.   (pp. 383–4)

By this device, telescoping the processes of time and opening out towards past and future, the open-endedness of Arabic tale-telling coexists with the closure of Shibli's quest.

The episodes in Shibli's adventures embed Meredith's theme in the familiar scenes, images and conventions of Scheherazade's tales. Metamorphosis, a chief wonder of the *Nights*, becomes a varied agency of theme and drama in *The Shaving of Shagpat*. (Even Meredith's style transforms itself with magic flexibility, the stylistic burlesque of the incongruous and the over-elaborated mingling with the dramatic, the dramatic with the moralising.) Several kinds of transformation are exploited: the genie Karaz menaces in successive animal forms; Noorna battles with Goorelka's lightning-quick transformations which recall the fatal battle of the sorceress and genie in the Second Calender's tale, also the model of *Shagpat*'s apocalyptic conclusion.

The most significant transformations, however, directly promote the tale's lesson of humility and self-knowledge. Meredith recalls the *Nights* convention of men transformed through evil agency or their own weakness, in order to invoke as an antidote the Comic Spirit, the genius of thoughtful laughter itself. The process is twice witnessed – in the enchanted birds of Goorelka (men who can be liberated only by exercising the human 'privilege' of laughter) and in the transformed beasts of Aklis. Noorna wonders at the birds' helplessness: 'my breast melted with pity at their desire to laugh . . . for could they think of their changed condition and folly without laughter?' (*Shagpat*, p. 210). Noorna's loss of beauty is itself a saving transformation: 'Surely I grew humble with the loss of beauty, and by humility wise' (pp. 219–20).

The counterpart of Noorna's probation as a hag is Shibli's humiliating near-transformation in Aklis. Vanity wins Shibli a jewelled crown of asses' ears and monkeys' skulls and with it the homage of less lucky men transformed to these animals. 'Of a surety', observes Shibli, 'if these sitters could but laugh at themselves there would be a release for them' (p. 281). Virtually all Meredith's heroes undergo the ordeal of seeing themselves as ridiculous, often with the aid of such an ignominious mirror. The capacity for critical self-recognition issuing in 'thoughtful laughter' distinguishes those, such as Harry Richmond, Evan Harrington and Shibli, who reap the rewards of self-knowledge, from the diverse likes of Willoughby Patterne, Richmond Roy and Victor Radnor – captives all to the enchantment of egoism.

Ian Fletcher remarks in *Shagpat* 'shifting patterns of parallelism, anticipation and echo'; Barbara Hardy has explored Meredith's effective departure from the Jamesian priorities of ' "organic" serial patterns' and the aspiration to 'unity and order' in *Harry Richmond*,[20] the novel outside *Shagpat* most tellingly informed by the *Nights*. Meredith, Hardy observes, 'uses repeated figures in his scenes and his characters, and these figures are often correlatives of the theme'. These narrative features widely exploited in Meredith's fiction are quintessentially Arab, and may remind us that for James (in his Preface to *The Aspern Papers*) the antithesis of 'singleness', unity, or 'roundness' *was* the *Nights*.

Signal amongst the repeating figures in the carpet of *Harry Richmond* is the *Nights*. Harry Richmond, as princely in endowments and expectations as a Camaralzaman, tells the tale of his growing-up. What complicates the tale and gives it its colourful episodic plot is the influence in Harry's life of his father, an incorrigible dreamer of Alnaschar dreams. Roy, too, begs or cozens his money of others, but, where Alnaschar buys glass, Roy straightaway prosecutes what he himself sees as an *Arabian Nights* life.

Roy takes his Harry into the *Nights* literally and figuratively. The pleasant entertainment of reading the *Nights* together, with Roy acting out the famous incidents, promotes the habit of living the fantasies.

An omission to perform a duty was the fatal forgetfulness to sprinkle pepper on the cream-tarts; if my father subjected me to an interrogation concerning my lessons, he was the dread African magician to whom must be surrendered my acquisition of the ring and the musty old lamp. We were quite in the habit of meeting fair Persians. He would frequently ejaculate that he resembled the Three Calendars in more respects than one. (*Harry Richmond*, pp. 38–9)

Roy uses the *Nights* to enliven and explain an itinerant and uncertain mode of living to his child; the 'Arabian Life' provides Harry with a rationale for a baffling reality: 'During this Arabian life, we sat on a carpet that flew to the Continent, where I fell sick, and was cured by smelling at an apple; and my father directed our movements through the aid of a telescope, which told us the titles of the hotels ready to receive us' (p. 40).

A failure to distinguish between fantasy and reality is appropriate, consoling, even endearing in a child, but degrading and destructive in an adult. It soon becomes clear that what is for Harry an entertainment is for Roy a way of life. The same man who plays the egregious barber, shaving a hired actor for a convalescent boy's amusement, later provides, at his son's expense, society balls and dinners, which are 'Princely entertainments' to the enraptured Bulsteads, 'Arabian Nights!' To Julia their host is 'Aladdin's magician if you like, . . . only – good!' (p. 473). Roy embraces the role without perceiving the irony that Julia's qualification signals. 'You will find I am a magician, and very soon' (p. 550) announces his great scheme's near-success and necessary failure, and Harry recognises in horrified admiration, 'my father was indeed a magician' (p. 555).

The presence of the Aladdin story typifies Harry Richmond's exploitation of the *Nights* to interpret the natures and relationship of Richmond father and son. The Arab tales help to structure the *Bildungsroman* and to enlarge its significances. The frequent innocent-seeming Aladdin references remind us that the African sorcerer who presented himself to the orphan as a lost uncle – a pseudo-father – pursued Aladdin's destruction, having initiated his good fortune. Such parallels with the story of Harry's deluded progenitor suggest what becomes clear – that Richmond Roy is unsound and doomed. Perhaps inevitably, the end of the misguided, as of the evil, magician is incineration; Roy is claimed by the conflagration at Riversley caused by his own well-meant excesses – 'lamps, lights in all rooms . . . illuminations along the windows . . . extraordinary decorations fitted up to celebrate our return in harmony with my father's fancy' (p. 684): probably his final *Arabian Nights* entertainment.

More telling and pervasive in *Harry Richmond* than Aladdin's story is the tale of Prince Ahmed and the Peri Banou. Immediately before Harry's description of 'this Arabian Life', supplying its allusions to magic carpet, telescope and apple, the tale works to reconcile the boy to the possibility of his beloved father's remarriage: 'I could think earnestly of Prince Ahmed and the kind and beautiful Peribanou, whom I would not have minded his marrying' (p. 39). Marriage with 'the sweetest fairy ever imagined' is not one of Roy's roles, however, and the allusion only acquires a lingering resonance ironically, in the postponed revelation that his livelihood throughout the book's period and his temporary rescue (with that of Harry's inheritance) are owing to the secret providence of the 'dear lady' Dorothy Beltham who has loved but *not* married him.

The Ahmed role shifts to Harry in the course of the 'Arabian Life' travels when he adopts as his 'Peribanou' an older young lady, Clara Godwin. Clara will prove but one among Harry's good-fairy protectresses in the book, along with his Aunt Dorothy, the gipsy Kiomi, the Princess Ottilie and Janet Ilchester, whom he survives his illusions to value and win. Again, Meredith's use of the tale is approximate. Harry's situation superficially resembles the Princess Nouronnihar's, beset by three irreproachable suitors. Harry's merit, despite the blemishes of youth, egoism and impetuousness, wins over Kiomi, Ottilie and Janet, a trustworthy trio of constant witnesses to the worth of his character who jointly promote his happiness. Such structural resemblance to the fairy-tale-like story of Ahmed places the young man's often elliptic presentation of his own awakening to sexuality and self within a readily assimilable fabular convention.

Most significantly for *Harry Richmond*, the story of Ahmed is not only the tale of prince and fairy. It is also a tale of father and son. Ahmed loves and is beloved of his father, and his exile from the Sultan in the Peri Banou's realm is the only source of regret in a surpassing happiness there. Assured of his love and assuring her protection, the Peri Banou releases her husband to visit his father at intervals. Ahmed's mysterious appearances, betraying limitless wealth and power, provoke an unreasonable fear and jealousy in his misguided father, who plots his son's ruin. The course of jealousy is irreversible; the Sultan's jealousy of Ahmed *brings about* the result it feared. Making increasing demands on Ahmed's loyalty and Peri Banou's magical powers, the Sultan alienates his son and ultimately summons his own nemesis: the fairy's brother kills the Sultan and Ahmed becomes ruler of the Indies. Love and uncalculated betrayal, jealousy and overthrow, mark the tale's discernibly Oedipal pattern.

Harry Richmond does not duplicate the tale's plot, but may be interpreted in its light. The boy Harry, seeing his intermittently absent father as the fortunate Ahmed, inhabits for a time the position of jealous one (p. 40). But Harry outgrows jealousy. His father's increasing demands on his loyalty and his fortune create for him an Ahmed role and the ambivalent attitudes of shame, pity, embarrassment and desire to please that go with it, in the perception of parental indiscretion. The Sultan's refrain, 'I not only desire you to preserve the good understanding between us we have lived in hitherto, but that you would use your credit with the fairy to obtain for me a little of her assistance which I stand in need of . . . ',[21] is hardly more naked in its opportunism than Roy's schemes. Roy, having secured by his own marriage the wealth he enjoys through Harry's indulgence, embarks on a project to choose and bestow upon his son the fairy who will supply his remaining and obsessing deficiency, royal rank. Harry supports his prodigal father with a natural and near-tragic loyalty. Ahmed-like oscillations between his home (here the maternal home where kindly Aunt Dorothy and his destined fairy Janet preside) and his father mark Harry's growth from boyhood dependence to manhood and self-knowledge. Harry does not, in his sad triumph over his father's dishonour or upon the deluded man's subsequent death, preside as conqueror in either sphere; home and father are both destroyed. The poles of Harry's inheritance are incorporated in his self-knowledge and surpassed in the enforced independence with which he watches all trace of his progenitors eliminated in the Riversley fire. Meredith shrewdly seized as a guiding motif for Harry Richmond the story of Ahmed, in which the hero's departure from childhood is initiated by a father's scheme leading to the discovery of mature fulfilment outside the paternal plan, and where the youth claims his sexual and individual inheritance through alienation from, defeat and death of the father.

A further stamp of the *Nights* marks the very point at which Harry's childhood confidence in his father gives way to maturer vision and inevitable disillusionment. The image which generates this shock in the chapter entitled 'The Statue on the Promontory' is a bronze equestrian statue which moves, to reveal the greatest yet of Roy's impostures. Such an image occurs in more than one tale of the *Nights*. In the Third Calender's tale there is, atop the magnetic mountain, a dome of brass where 'stands a horse of the same metal, with a rider on his back . . . fatal to all that have the misfortune to come near it',[22] as the youth discovers. The story of the City of Brass (in Lane) shows another statue on a promontory – the brass horseman on the hill whose spearhead guides the Emir to the City's awful lesson of mortality and the vanity of worldly ambition.

Harry and the other onlookers experience wonder: 'the statue was superb – horse and rider in new bronze polished by sunlight . . . I had always laughed at sculptured figures on horseback. This one overawed me' (*Harry Richmond*, p. 193). The statue's grotesque awakening signals the end of more than the immediate illusion. The artifact is an imposture, the father–hero is mortal: 'I knew it was my father, but my father with death and strangeness, earth, metal about him' (p. 197). Fatal statues and hero fathers belong to fantasy or to childhood's vision and are destined to cruel exposure in the sunlit arena of experience.

The *Bildungsroman* acquires pathos as it becomes clear that, in growing beyond the marvellous and pathetic Richmond Roy, Harry leaves behind a father more a child than himself. The first-person narrative, presenting Roy as he exists in Harry's experience, creates a marvellous figure to rival those tales with which he is associated, who lives untarnished in the teller's memories of childhood. Richmond's pathos emerges through the narrator's maturer vision which sees his failure to distinguish between Scheherazade's fictions and the facts of place, time, necessity. Through the associations surrounding Roy, as well as in the novel's systematic undermining of the 'royal' Richmond, Meredith evokes childhood's loss. *Harry Richmond* is as fantastic in its variousness and coincidences as an Eastern tale. It preserves for its reader's entertainment the structure and rewards of the Arabian fantasy which, for that reader's edification and its hero's, it marks as a childhood dream.

Evan Harrington's hero, like Harry, 'had read Arabian tales' (p. 313) and, like Shibli, rises from tradesman's origins to realise publicly an innate princeliness. Meredith exposes his society's materialism and snobbery in a novel which nevertheless allows its hero, defying plausibility, to triumph over that society's despised priorities, on a pattern that belongs more to the wonders of the *Nights* than to the legitimate expectations of nineteenth-century individualism.

However deserving, Shibli and Evan benefit from good fortune which can only be – and is – called magical. That Evan is, like Aladdin, a poor tailor's son (with a similar disrelish for the trade) may alert us to the archetype which informs *Evan Harrington* and legitimises the blatant fantasy of its outcome. Evan 'had read the Arabian Tales and could believe in marvels; especially could he believe in the friendliness of a magical thing that astounded without hurting him' (p. 313).

The story of *Evan Harrington* develops out of the shifting, blurring relations of propertied or titled and commercial classes from the Napoleonic era, and elaborates with ironic brio bourgeois sensitivity to gradations of rank, from tailordom to merchant princes. The novel's canvas of social prejudice and economic change, as well as its bold side-glances at the tyranny of the marriage laws (anticipating the centrality of this issue in Meredith's late fictions) set a fantasy amidst the real social conditions of England in the generation after the Regency.

Evan is explicitly cast as an Aladdin: 'he was clutched by a beneficent or a most malignant magician' (p. 313). The magician whose crabbed beneficence is Evan's good fortune is Tom Cogglesby, elsewhere glimpsed as 'a grim old genie' (p. 564). But Tom more strikingly recalls the caliph Harun, as he appears in so many of his exploits of disguise. Meredith's view of Harun is hinted in *Beauchamp's Career* when Cecilia's allusion to the Caliph economically hits off the intemperate, good-hearted tyrant Everard Romfrey: 'She suggested the Commander of the Faithful, the Lord Haroun, who likewise had a turn for buffooneries to serve a purpose, and could direct them loftily and sovereignly' (p. 230). Dispensing justice and rewards according to his generally sound lights, Tom Cogglesby is, like Harun, not above having fun with his beneficiaries first. His practical jokes puncture illusion and carry an embedded lesson of humility, democratically embracing the Harrington, Cogglesby and Jocelyn families.

The mirrorings and repetitions of Arab story-telling again mark *Evan Harrington*. Distorting mirrors offer numerous foils for the hero – in old Tom Cogglesby, who has mastered his pride, in young Harry Jocelyn's weak impetuousness, in Ferdinand Laxley's

egoism and in the Great Mel himself, the 'embodied protest against
our social prejudice' whose stupendous and legendary snobberies
discover the genuine gentility through which his son actively
conquers that prejudice. John Raikes, 'a born buffoon' (and something of a latter-day Aboulhassan) illustrates by contrast the
developing strength of Evan's character. Raikes's Aladdin aspir-
ations offer Evan 'a burlesque of himself' evoking salutary Mere-
dithian laughter. Evan 'smiling at himself in the mirror of John
Raikes' is engaged in a divergent progress which makes him a
gentleman and installs Raikes in the tailor's shop.

The Hindbad–Sindbad relationship of these young men may
remind us that Evan, like Sindbad, 'did not attain to this happy
condition, without enduring . . . trouble of body and mind for
several years':[23] that he deserved his good fortune. But Evan's
England, like the world of the *Nights*, is full of Hindbads and
Sindbads, locations where the change of a letter would signify the
opposed condition. This emerges in the superb chapter 22 ('In
which the Daughters of the Great Mel have to digest him at
Dinner'), where a Miss Carrington and a Mrs Barrington assist at
the ordeal of the erstwhile Misses Harrington. It is as if the former
are placed by a mere consonant in the elect class.

Repetition and correspondence expand the significance of events
in the novel and contract its world of action in a comic fatality.
The novel's emphasis on repeated stories suggests that all stories
participate in a structure of recurrences, and have an infinite
capacity to rebound effectively in real experience. Virtually all the
stories in the Countess de Saldar's repertoire have been told or
duplicated elsewhere and their use to deflect discovery clashes
entertainingly with their capacity to evoke dangerous memories.
Anecdotes of the Great Mel rehearsed by tradesman Barnes and
Grossby are retold by Mr George Uploft at Lady Jocelyn's dinner
table, where what is an echo to the reader becomes a blow and a
chastisement to the Harringtons. Throughout *Evan Harrington*, the
mirrorings of Arab narrative become 'the correspondences which
make images, scenes, and characters co-operate in pointing a
theme'.[24]

The *Arabian Nights* is a monument of and to narrative, a fabular
triumph embodying a myth of narrative effectualness. Meredith
measures his authorship against both aspects. A self-mocking
allusion to Ahmed's tale signifies the author's dream of success in
Beauchamp's Career:

I shoot my arrows at a mark that is pretty certain to return them to me. And as to perfect success . . . I should believe that genii of the air fly above our tree-tops between us and the incognizable spheres, catching those ambitious shafts they deem it a promise of fun to play pranks with.   (p. 7)

The pursuit of effective narrative fiction informs Meredith's plea for a new realist fiction 'veraciously historical, honestly transcriptive' discovering that 'the sight of ourselves is wholesome, bearable, fructifying, finally a delight' (*Diana of the Crossways*, p. 15). A 'cycle of years' had brought the modern English novelist to seek the vitality and openness of the medieval Arab tale. The Victorian who had read Arabian tales knew that such a materialist fiction expressing a coherent social idea and delight in human nature had existed long ago in the East and could fertilise with its manner the ground of modern fiction.

Meredith's modernism retains the primacy of *story* – as evident in *Modern Love* as in *Evan Harrington* – and of stories, often interpolated directly or by allusion to enrich his fictions. (In *Diana of the Crossways* the novels of that Scheherazade appear as facts in her career *and* as alternative versions of her story, analogues to the main tale mirroring the novel's preoccupation with narrative subjectiveness.) The aphoristic wit which had appropriated and parodied the Arab manner in *Shagpat* continues characteristic of the author's mannered style and certain characters' humour.

In *Shagpat* a fusion of West and East first asserted Meredith's continuing effort to disrupt the patterns and premises of contemporary fictional convention – to question narrative authority and social consensus. In his late novel *The Amazing Marriage* a co-operative effort of direct and oblique narrators disguised as a conflict produces the tale and an exploration of the motivations generating it. Meredith's success emerges from such synthesis – of story and 'philosophy', of the fantastic and the familiar and factual – in an effective fiction which announces its fictionality and demands to be taken as substantial experience. The 'brain' which Meredith required of fiction appeals – as did Scheherazade – to the reader's desire to know, and proposes no tale as final. Meredith's work, like Scheherazade's, is a series of autonomous tales and a larger endeavour to influence the conduct of the kingdom.

NOTES

Place of publication London unless otherwise stated.

1. Henry Weber, *Tales of the East; Comprising the Most Popular Romances of Oriental Origin, and the Best Imitations by European Authors*, 3 vols (Edinburgh: John Ballantyne; London: Longman, 1812).
2. See Angus Easson's edition of *North and South* (Oxford University Press, 1973) p. 438n.
3. George Eliot, *Leader*, vii (1956) 15.
4. *Letters of George Meredith*, ed. W. M. Meredith, 2 vols (Constable 1912) i, 3.
5. The categories are Mia I. Gerhardt's in *The Art of Story-Telling: A Literary Study of the Thousand and One Nights* (Leiden, 1963).
6. *The Letters of George Meredith*, 3 vols, ed. C. L. Cline (Oxford: Clarendon Press, 1970) iii, 1556. Cited in the text as *Letters*.
7. See *Modern Love*, ii.12–16 'A star with lurid beams, she seemed to crown/The pit of infamy: and then again/He fainted on his vengefulness, and strove/To ape the magnanimity of love,/And smote himself,/a shuddering heap of pain.' Cf. also the imagery of ii.14–15, v.15, xlix.3–4, 6.
8. R. Hawari, 'The Arabian Background of Tennyson, Thomson and Meredith' (B.Litt. thesis, Oxford University, 1962) 354.
9. *Westminster Review*, n.s. ix (1856) 638.
10. George Meredith, *The Shaving of Shagpat: An Arabian Entertainment* (Chapman and Hall, 1856) p. v. Subsequent references in text.
11. Hawari, 'Arabian Background', pp. 369, 395, 397.
12. *The Book of the Thousand Nights and a Night*, tr. Richard F. Burton, 10 vols (Benares, 1885) i, xi.
13. *The Book of the Thousand Nights and One Night*, tr. Henry Torrens (Calcutta: W. Thacker; and London: W. H. Allen, 1838) i, 311–12. Subsequent references in text.
14. Gerhardt, *The Art of Story-Telling*, pp. 88–9.
15. Burton, *Nights*, i, xi.
16. George Meredith, *Works*, Memorial Edition (1910), *Essay: On the Idea of Comedy and the Uses of the Comic Spirit*, pp. 30–1. All subsequent references to Meredith's works, except *The Shaving of Shagpat*, are to the Memorial Edition (Constable, 1910–11) and are given in the text.
17. Meredith's small masterpiece the inset tale of 'Bhanivar the Beautiful' significantly reverses the main tale. The sorceress who serves evil pursues power and beauty, not right love; the tale looks backward – 'What thou hast been thou art' (*Shagpat*, p. 121) – to better times marred by evil ambition, counter to the forward motion and promise of Noorna's restoration to a beauty matching her virtues: '"Thou art that Thou art" . . . "Not so, but that I shall be"' (p. 10) and Shibli's progress to the Event.
18. Torrens' use in 'The Tale of the Ensorcelled Youth' (elsewhere 'The Young King of the Black Islands') is overlooked by the *Oxford English Dictionary*. Meredith's use of the word, the first documented after the

sixteenth century, is followed by similar examples from the *Nights* translations of Burton and Payne.

19. Ian Fletcher, *'The Shaving of Shagpat:* Meredith's Comic Apocalypse', in *Meredith Now,* ed. Fletcher (1971) p. 36.
20. Barbara Hardy, '"A Way to your Hearts through Fire or Water": The Structure of Imagery in *Harry Richmond'*, *Essays in Criticism,* x (1960) 163.
21. Weber, *Tales of the East,* p. 449.
22. Ibid., p. 52.
23. Ibid., p. 69.
24. Hardy, in *Essays in Criticism,* x, 163.

9

The Genie out of the Bottle: Conrad, Wells and Joyce

ROBERT G. HAMPSON

I

Cedric Watts begins his extremely valuable book on *Heart of Darkness* with a short account of the convention of the tale-within-a-tale.[1] He notes that the history of the format 'can be traced back via *The Canterbury Tales* and *The Decameron* to *The Odyssey* and *The Iliad*' (p. 22). He suggests that the 'abundance of shorter narratives' (p. 22) using this convention in the mid to late nineteenth century was partly a consequence of the huge market for shorter narratives provided by periodicals, and partly a consequence of developments in communications, foreign trade and empire building – which meant that there were more travellers with tales to tell. Cedric Watts's map of the convention misses out what is probably the most famous example of tales-within-a-tale, *The Arabian Nights*, and what he misses from his suggested causes for the popularity of this convention is the immense popularity of the *Nights* in precisely the period he indicates. The British Library Catalogue includes thirty different editions of the *Nights* published between 1850 and 1890.[2] For writers, the *Nights* provided a pool of images and allusions and a compendium of narrative techniques.

In *The Art of Story-Telling*, Mia Gerhardt gives an account of some of these techniques.[3] About a quarter of the shorter pieces in the *Nights* use 'oblique presentation': the story is told 'obliquely, through one of the characters' (p. 385). A character is given the function of 'witness' to a story in order to validate it, but this witness can develop into something more than just a reporting and authenticating device. Gerhardt comments on 'The Lovers from the Tribe of Udhra', 'The adventure becomes more interesting by being seen through the eyes of Jamil and coloured by his reactions' (p. 385). The emotional involvement of the narrator with

218

the characters makes the tale not merely the tale of the lovers but also the tale of the lovers *as experienced by the narrator*. There is a model here for the epistemological concerns embodied in Conrad's use of Marlow in *Heart of Darkness*, *Lord Jim* and *Chance*.

The second technique Gerhardt mentions, that of inserted stories, occurs when a character interrupts the progress of the story in which they appear in order to relate another, subsidiary story. This produces the Chinese-boxes pattern of the first part of the *Nights*, a series of stories within stories within stories, or it can lead to the grouping of parallel situations around the centre provided by the main story. Again, there are obvious parallels in Conrad's work: the narrative structure of *Chance*, with its succession of witnesses, or the presentation and exploration of Lord Jim's position and personality through the use of various parallel and contrasting characters.[4] (As I shall show, Joyce uses a conciser version of this technique in *Ulysses* and *Finnegans Wake*.) The frame story, however, is the characteristic narrative technique of the *Nights*: the story of Scheherazade and Shahriar acts as a container for the entire collection of tales. The frame story, however, is not just a container: at its most interesting, there is an interaction between the framed story and its frame.[5] Conrad's handling of Marlow involves a variety of such interactions.

In 'Youth', there is a fairly simple interaction between the framed story and the frame. Conrad alternates between Marlow's older and younger selves to counterpoint past and present and to articulate a nostalgia for lost youth: 'I remember my youth and the feeling that will never come back any more – the feeling that I could last for ever, outlast the sea, the earth, and all men; the deceitful feeling that lures us on to joys, to perils, to love, to vain effort – to death. . . .'[6] Nostalgia, here, shades into an awareness of mortality, and the fact of death is used to provoke a questioning of values. This is the implication of one of the narrative climaxes: the sinking of the *Judea*. It is also the force of the final return to the frame story, where Marlow asks his audience whether their youth at sea wasn't the best time of their lives: 'And we all nodded at him: the man of finance, the man of accounts, the man of law . . . our faces marked by toil, by deceptions, by success, by love; our weary eyes looking still, looking always, looking anxiously for something out of life, that while it is expected is already gone' (p. 42). Conrad uses the device of frame and framed story as the vehicle of a dual vision: it juxtaposes youthful optimism and middle-aged disillusionment. At the same time, Conrad exploits the 'vocational convention' to suggest that various activities that might seem productive of value are ultimately valueless.

In *Heart of Darkness*, there is a more complex relationship between frame and framed story. Again, Conrad uses the interaction between them to produce a radical questioning of values. This time, the reality disclosed at the heart of the framed story stands revealed as the reality underlying the world of the frame story: the African experience flows back to question London society psychologically, politically and philosophically. In part, the greater complexity of *Heart of Darkness* derives directly from a more complex interaction between inner and outer narratives: interruptions of Marlow's tale, for example, suggest a gulf of incomprehension between narrator and audience, a clash of values that is a way of challenging the 'civilised' complacency of *both* of Marlow's audiences, while, at the same time, distancing Conrad from Marlow.[7] Another development from 'Youth' is that Marlow's story, in *Heart of Darkness*, is not primarily about himself: it is, rather, about himself in relation to Kurtz. The thrust of the narrative is towards Kurtz and Kurtz's experience: the centre it points towards is Kurtz's story. After the first section, Kurtz becomes the focus of interest, and the repeated references to Kurtz's 'eloquence' contain the implicit promise that Kurtz, with his 'gift' of 'expression' (p. 147), will articulate the secret and will provide the solution to the moral, psychological and philosophical problems that the journey has presented. The embedded irony is that Kurtz does not tell a tale: his 'supreme moment of complete knowledge' produces only the words 'the horror, the horror' (p. 149). The real 'absence' at the heart of *Heart of Darkness* is this promised tale that isn't told.[8] There is a deliberate anti-climax in relation to Kurtz that expresses the story's radical scepticism about ultimate values.

II

The closest parallel to Conrad's narrative method in *Heart of Darkness* is to be found in H. G. Wells's first novel, *The Time Machine*. First of all, the form of the novel is that of a frame story: the frame presents the Time Traveller as story-teller, a naturalistically represented environment, and an audience to whom the tale is told. This frame story functions primarily as an authenti-

cating device for Wells's 'scientific romance': however scientific the
basis and inspiration of the framed tale, it is, nevertheless, like the
Arabian story or the Gothic novel, a tale of wonders and marvels.
Secondly, as in *Heart of Darkness*, the audience for the tale consists
of a nameless first-person narrator, who plays only a very minor
role – his main function is as our representative in the frame story –
and other characters designated mainly by their professions: 'the
Psychologist', the 'Provincial Mayor', and so on. This audience
serves to authenticate the framed story partly because their professional identities point towards a recognisable, everyday world – and
partly, paradoxically, because of their incredulity. Their disbelief is
used as a way of engendering our belief.

In his review of *The Time Machine* Israel Zangwill wrote, 'Mr
Wells's *Time Machine* . . . traverses time . . . backwards or for-
wards, much as the magic carpet of *The Arabian Nights* traversed
space.'[9] The 'time machine' is an example of what Todorov calls
'the instrumental marvellous': that species of the marvellous which
resides in technological feats which were not possible at the time
of writing.[10] In other words, the 'instrumental marvellous' of the
Nights can be seen as an early version of science fiction – a genre
in which both Wells and Conrad were pioneers.[11] However, there
are closer connections between Wells and the *Nights* than this. For
example, in 1895, the same year as *The Time Machine*, Wells also
published a collection of short stories.[12] One of these stories, 'The
Lord of the Dynamos', makes a punning allusion to the jinn
imprisoned in bottles by Solomon. Wells gives Azumi-zi's view of
the dynamo he has come to worship:

> it lived all day in this big airy shed, with him and Holroyd to
> wait upon it; not prisoned up and slaving to drive a ship as the
> other engines he knew – mere captive devils of the British
> Solomon – had been.[13]

We can compare this with Conrad's account of the African fireman
in *Heart of Darkness*:

> He squinted at the steam-gauge and at the water-gauge . . . a
> thrall to strange witchcraft . . . what he knew was this – that
> should the water in that transparent thing disappear, the evil
> spirit inside the boiler would get angry . . . and take a terrible
> vengeance. (pp. 97–8)

In *Almayer's Folly*, Conrad comments on the 'little brass cross' worn by Mrs Almayer:

> That superstitious feeling connected with some vague talismanic properties of the little bit of metal, and the still more hazy but terrible notion of some bad Djinns and horrible torments invented, as she thought, for her especial punishment . . . were Mrs Almayer's only theological luggage.[14]

Similarly, in 'Karain', one of the short stories included in Conrad's 1897 volume, *Tales of Unrest*, Hollis remarks, when he gives Karain a Jubilee sixpence as a charm against his ghost,

> This is the image of the Great Queen, and the most powerful thing the white men know. . . . She is more powerful than Suleiman the Wise, who commanded the genii, as you know. . . . She commands a spirit, too – the spirit of her nation: a masterful, conscientious, unscrupulous, unconquerable devil. . . .   (p. 49)

The context, in all four passages, is the meeting of the ideas and artifacts of the West with a 'more primitive' culture: this is a version of the 'instrumental marvellous' that relates not to different times but to different cultures. These passages reveal a trope, associated with the *Nights*, that appears in various authors. Poe's story 'The Thousand-and-Second Tale of Scheherazade' is governed by this trope: Scheherazade's account of Sindbad's further adventures describes nineteenth-century technological developments (such as the printing-press and the telegraph) within a linguistic and conceptual framework appropriate to the medieval Arabian world.

'Aepyornis Island', another story in Wells's 1895 collection, takes the argument a step further. This story is a comic-scientific variant of Sindbad's Second Voyage (crossed with *Robinson Crusoe*). In the *Nights*, the story of the Second Voyage begins with Sindbad left behind on a desert island and finding a roc's egg. The narrator of Wells's story refers explicitly to the Sindbad story. He mentions a giant bird, the Aepyornis, and remarks that 'Sindbad's roc was just a legend of 'em' (p. 261), before proceeding to his own story of being shipwrecked on an island and discovering a giant egg. This story was written in 1894. The Library Edition of Richard Burton's translation of the *Nights* was published in the same year.

Burton's footnotes to 'The Second Voyage of Sindbad the Seaman' include one on the roc, which begins by noting other mythical birds and suggesting a common source for them in memories of 'gigantic pterodactyls and other winged monsters'. Burton then adds, 'A second basis, wanting only a superstructure of exaggeration . . . would be the huge birds but lately killed out. Sindbad may allude to the Aepyornis of Madagascar . . .' (*Nights*, IV, 358). In a letter to his mother in December 1894, Wells described his existence during that year as 'writing away for dear life', and his autobiography records his consequent vigilance for ideas for articles or stories at that time.[15] If this footnote provided one of those ideas, there are further implications. *The Time Machine* started life as a short story, 'The Chronic Argonauts', which was published in the *Science Schools Journal* in April, May and June 1888. In this version, the story was divided into two parts: 'The Story from an Exoteric Point of View' and 'The Esoteric Story based on the Clergyman's Depositions'. Wells reworked the story several times. In the penultimate draft, which appeared in W. E. Henley's *National Observer*, as late as March–June 1894, the form still remained little more than a set of miscellanies on the theme of time-travelling.[16] Did a reading of the *Nights* lead Wells to the frame-tale structure of *The Time Machine*? And was Wells's use of the 'vocational convention' influenced by the presence of stereotypical characters (the merchant, the fisherman, the tailor, and so on) in some of these tales?

III

If this suggests that the *Nights* played a significant part at the start of Wells's writing career, there is clear evidence that it remained an important source for him. *The History of Mr Polly*, for example, contains a reference to the *Nights* as a whole, an allusion to a particular story, and a further reference to a motif from the tales. One of the books Mr Polly buys is a copy of the *Nights*. Literature, in this novel, functions as a sign of life's possibilities, as a sign of something beyond the constrictions of conventions and circumstances. Wells uses this reference to the *Nights* as part of this pattern, but he uses the other references to express the opposing repressive forces. Mr Voules, for example, almost embodies the constrictions of conventionality, and, to describe his blossoming at Mr Polly's ill-fated wedding, Wells draws on 'The Tale of the Fisherman and the Jinni': 'It was in the vestry that the force of Mr Voules' personality began to show at its true value. He seemed to open out, like the fisherman's Ginn from the pot, and spread over everything.'[17] Similarly, it is significant that one of Mr Polly's 'principal and most urgent creditors' is a 'Mr Ghool' (p. 186).

Two of Wells's novels make particularly interesting use of the *Nights*. *The Sleeper Awakes* (1898) echoes the title of the tale 'The Sleeper Awakened', and that echo represents Wells's acknowledgement of the source for various elements of the novel. In 'The Sleeper Awakened', Abu Hassan, a merchant's son, is the victim of a trick played upon him by the Caliph, Harun al-Rashid. He is drugged and transported to the Caliph's palace; when he awakens, he is treated as if he were the Caliph; then he is drugged again and returned home. When he next awakens, his experiences at the palace seem like enchantment or a dream. In *The Sleeper Awakes*, Wells uses falling asleep not as part of a trick but as a method of time-travelling. When the Sleeper awakens, he has been asleep for over 200 years. Where Abu Hassan awoke to find himself Caliph, Graham gradually discovers that he is 'King of the Earth' – not through magic or trickery but through capital accumulation. At this point, the parallel with Abu Hassan breaks down. Abu Hassan was tricked into believing he was Caliph: Graham really is 'King of the Earth'. Wells now uses the Caliph himself as his model for Graham. Graham, like Harun, has his Grand Vizier. Like Harun, he wanders in disguise through the streets of his city by night. Chapter 20 begins, 'And that night, unknown and unsuspected, Graham, dressed in the costume of an inferior wind-vane official keeping holiday and accompanied by Asano in Labour Department canvas, surveyed the city' (p. 400). 'The Sleeper Awakened' had itself started with a chance meeting between Abu Hassan and the disguised Harun al-Rashid on one of the bridges over the Tigris; 'behold, up came the Caliph and Masrur, the Sworder of his vengeance, disguised in merchant's dress, according to their custom'.[18] Harun's 'custom' is motivated in some stories by insomnia, it is a period of insomnia that precedes Graham's extended sleep.

The Research Magnificent (1915) provides an interesting comparison with *The Sleeper Awakes*. First of all, in the 'Prelude', Benham's 'research', which gives the novel its title, its direction and its central theme, is defined by means of a reference to the *Nights*:

at first it seemed to him that one had only just to hammer and will; and at the end, after a life of willing and hammering, he was still convinced there was something, something in the nature of an Open Sesame . . . which would suddenly roll open for mankind the magic cave of the universe, that precious cave at the heart of all things in which one must believe.   (p. 7)

In this novel, Wells draws on the *Nights* for imagery to suggest a potential for wonder and significance in life that is not realised in the world as it is currently organised. Benham's quest ends in what Wells, elsewhere, terms 'the open conspiracy': the idea of an intellectual elite ruling a world state. Benham dreams of the kind of power that Graham awoke to find himself possessing, and this dream culminates, in the final chapter, in the figure of Benham wandering through the world 'kingly, unknown' (p. 370). This final chapter is called 'the New Haroun al-Rashid'. Wells explains, 'At last he was, so to speak, Haroun al-Rashid again, going unsuspected about the world, because the palace of his security would not tell him the secrets of men's disorders' (p. 370). Here Wells makes explicit use of the model that was implicit in *The Sleeper Awakes*, when Graham wandered 'unknown and unsuspected' through the city.

Two further examples show the continuing imaginative vitality of the *Nights* for Wells. In his *Experiment in Autobiography* (1934) Wells wrote of his flight to Moscow, 'In 1900 . . . this would have been as incredible a journey as a trip on Prince Houssain's carpet.'[19] A more interesting example occurs in Wells's penultimate work, *The Happy Turning* (1944). Wells begins by describing a recurring dream: 'I dream I am at my front door starting out for the accustomed round. I go out and suddenly realise there is a possible turning I have overlooked' (p. 2). This turning takes him to a land where his 'desires and unsatisfied fancies, hopes, memories and imaginations have accumulated inexhaustible treasure' (p. 2). Wells describes the start of this dream of plenitude as 'a sort of Open Sesame' (p. 1).

IV

When *An Outcast of the Islands* was published in March 1896, one of the most favourable reviews was that in the *Saturday Review*.

Conrad wrote to the reviewer, who turned out to be Wells. Two years later, in September 1898, Conrad wrote to Wells,

> For the last two years (since your review of the *Outcast* in the *Saturday Review* compelled me to think seriously of many things till then unseen) I have lived on terms of close intimacy with you, referring to you many a page of my work, scrutinising many sentences by the light of your criticism.[20]

The Sleeper Awakes (1898) testifies to this close relationship. In chapter 7, Graham is left alone in a room, one wall of which is covered with rows of cylinders, this future's equivalent of books. Graham deciphers three titles: Kipling's *The Man Who Would Be King*, James's *The Madonna of the Future*, and Conrad's *Heart of Darkness*. He has not heard of the last two and assumes they are by 'post-Victorian authors' (p. 239). We might fail to notice what I take to be a private joke here: *The Sleeper Awakes* was published in 1898; *Heart of Darkness* wasn't published until 1899.

If Conrad was indebted to *The Time Machine* for the narrative methods of *Heart of Darkness*, he also seems to have had direct contact with the *Nights*. There was a Polish translation published in Warsaw in 1873. Conrad left Poland in 1874, but it is more likely that, if he knew the *Nights* at this time, he had come across them in French.[21] It is also likely that, given Conrad's interest in Burton as an explorer and his interest in Islam (dating from his time in Malaysia), he would later have been drawn to Burton's edition.[22] There are a number of possible allusions to the *Nights* in Conrad's letters written in the years immediately after the publication of the Library Edition.[23] Karl and Davies have noted the allusion to Sindbad's Fifth Voyage in a letter of 4 September 1897, where Conrad writes of his difficulties with 'The Return': 'It is an old man of the sea to me. I can't shake it off.'[24] He repeats this image in a letter to Cunninghame-Graham (31 Jan 1898): 'I am like the old man of the sea. You can't get rid of me by the apparently innocent suggestion of writing to your brother.'[25] More significantly, in 1899, in a letter to Ford, Conrad described *Heart of Darkness* as growing 'like the geni out of the bottle'.[26] This suggests the possibility of a direct debt to the *Nights* for the narrative methods of *Heart of Darkness*: certainly the two works are associated in his mind. Also, since the 'geni' released by the fisherman was fearful rather than benevolent, this might suggest a certain anxiety in Conrad about where *Heart of Darkness* was taking him.

I have already mentioned some of the allusions in Conrad's work during this period (1895–7). The clearest references to the *Nights* occur in two works of 1904–5. In 'Autocracy and War' (1905), Conrad describes Russia as 'This dreaded and strange apparition, bristling with bayonets, armed with chains, hung over with holy images; that something not of this world, partaking of a ravenous ghoul, of a blind Djinn grown up from a cloud, and of the Old Man of the Sea.'[27] In *Nostromo* (1904), when Gould Senior is first given the San Tomé Concession, Conrad remarks, 'He became at once mine-ridden, and as he was well-read in light literature it took to his mind the form of the Old Man of the Sea fastened upon his shoulders. He also began to dream of vampires' (pp. 55–6); and, when Charles Gould, his son, inherits the mine, Conrad repeats the motif: 'With advancing wisdom, he managed to clear the plain truth of the business from the fantastic intrusions of the Old Man of the Sea, vampires and ghouls, which had lent to his father's correspondence the flavour of a gruesome Arabian Nights tale' (p. 58).

Initially, Conrad uses *Nights* references to underline the fact that the San Tomé Concession is an economic trap, a means of extracting money from Gould Senior, and to show how this preys on his mind. As the novel continues, however, these references come to suggest the stranglehold of 'material interests' on both Goulds. We are told later, 'the mine had got hold of Charles Gould with a grip as deadly as ever it had laid upon his father' (p. 400). Similar imagery is used in relation to Nostromo, the other character whom Conrad described (in the Author's Note) as 'captured by the silver of the San Tomé mine' (p. xi). When Nostromo sets out with the lighter-load of silver, he describes this task as 'taking the curse of death upon my back' (p. 259), and he repeats this image later: 'I felt already this cursed silver growing heavy upon my back' (p. 268). The earlier references to the Old Man of the Sea provide a base against which these images resonate: unlike Sindbad, neither Gould nor Nostromo is able to free himself from his burden.

In *Nostromo*, Conrad uses the *Nights* subliminally to suggest forces operating within the individual or within history. It is also noticeable that Conrad conflates the Arabian and the Gothic. There is a similar conflation in *Lord Jim*. The floating derelict against which the *Patna* strikes is described as 'a kind of maritime ghoul on the prowl to kill ships in the dark' (p. 159), but the description goes on, 'Such wandering corpses are common enough in the North Atlantic, which is haunted by all the terrors of the sea, – fogs, icebergs, dead ships bent upon mischief, and long sinister gales that fasten upon one like a vampire . . .' (p. 159). This conflation of the Arabian and the Gothic, of ghouls and vampires, points to an important difference between Wells and Conrad in their use of the *Nights*: where Wells generally associates the *Nights* with potentiality or plenitude, Conrad uses *Nights* references to express oppressive forces.

Ghouls seem to have taken a particularly firm grip on his imagination. In *Romance* (1903), when Kemp is trapped in a cave with Castro and Seraphina, he refers to their captors as 'the miserable band of ghouls sitting above our grave' (p. 385). In *Under Western Eyes* (1911), Razumov refers to the 'red-nosed student' who persecutes him with his attentions as a 'silly, hypnotized ghoul' (p. 302); Sophia describes Russia as being 'watched over by beings that are worse than ogres, ghouls and vampires' (p. 254); and Madame de S——, who is 'like a galvanized corpse out of some Hoffmann's tale' (p. 215), 'extended a claw-like hand, glittering with costly rings, towards the paper of cakes, took up one and devoured it, displaying her big false teeth, ghoulishly' (p. 217). Similarly, in 'The Inn of Two Witches' (1913), a Gothic tale about two old women who prey on travellers, Byrne shudders at the notion of 'the two miserable and repulsive witches busying themselves ghoulishly about the defenseless body of his friend' (p. 157), while, in *The Arrow of Gold* (1919), Theresa's self-righteous preying on her sister is expressed by reference to her 'piously ghoulish expression' (p. 246).

Conrad's responsiveness to ghouls might be related to his fascination with cannibalism. There are the cannibal crew-men in *Heart of Darkness*; Singleton is compared to a cannibal chief in *The Nigger of the 'Narcissus'* (p. 6); Stevie's remains, in *The Secret Agent*, are described as 'an accumulation of raw material for a cannibal feast' (p. 86). In 'Falk', cannibalism is the central issue.[28] 'Falk' begins, like *Heart of Darkness*, with a group of men who form the audience for an oral tale. This audience has been 'dining in a small river hostelry' (p. 145) and this frame situation is permeated (like the account of Heat's investigation of Stevie's remains) with the language of food and taste. Food is the connection between frame and framed tale. Also, as Tony Tanner has pointed out, this opening establishes a link between eating and narrating – the controlling motifs of this story.[29] Thus the start of the story invokes the beginnings of culinary and narrative arts, 'when the primeval man, evolving the first rudiments of cookery from his dim consciousness, scorched lumps of flesh at a fire of sticks in the company of other good fellows; then, gorged and happy, sat him back among the gnawed bones to tell his artless tales of experience' (pp. 145–6). The framed story that follows (of the narrator, 'my enemy Falk, and my friend Hermann' – p. 147) contains other stories inserted within it: Schomberg's false account of Falk; Hermann's false account of the narrator as Falk's rival: and, finally, Falk's account of his experiences. One of the mysteries about Falk concerns food: Schomberg is indignant that Falk doesn't eat meat but only 'rice and a little fish' (p. 174), which he eats in private. The mystery is solved when Falk at last breaks his silence and confesses to cannibalism. There is a curious parallel here to the story of Sidi Numan: Sidi Numan is puzzled when his new bride eats only a few grains of rice at meal-time. This mystery is solved when he finds his wife in the cemetery 'seated with a Ghul' and realises that she is 'a cannibal and a corpse-eater' (*Nights*, x, 182). The starting-point for Sidi Numan's story-telling was his cruel treatment of his mare: his tale ends by revealing that the mare is his wife, magically transformed. Falk, for his part, is imagistically transformed: he is likened to a centaur, and he is presented later as 'like a good-tempered horse when the object that scares him is removed' (p. 197). Falk's story-telling, however, is more like that of the Ancient Mariner – not just because it is a tale of guilt set in the Antarctic, but also because it forces on its audience the vision of a different reality.[30]

V

Conrad and Wells, in rewriting certain elements of the *Nights*, demonstrate that principle, restated by Shklovsky, that 'The work of art arises from a background of other works and through association with them.'[31] Joyce's mature artwork is the epitome of such intertextuality: Kenner described the 'mythic method' of *Ulysses* as the creation of a 'grammar of generative plots' through the superimposition of the *Odyssey*, *Hamlet*, *Don Giovanni* and the events of Joyce's own life.[32] The *Nights* also contributed to that grammar. Victor Bérard's *Les Phéniciens et l'Odyssée*, which provided *Ulysses* with the general outline of the Odyssean adventures and its episodes, could also have drawn Joyce's attention to the *Nights*. Bérard not only notes the obvious connection between the *Odyssey* and Sindbad's voyages, but also relates Proteus to Harun al-Rashid.[33] The merchant Sindbad is arguably a necessary step between the aristocratic Greek and the democratic Bloom, and the Harun stories are as urban and perambulatory as *Ulysses*.

Joyce's knowledge of the *Nights* is well documented. Joyce owned an Italian translation in Trieste. When he moved to Paris, he replaced it with the Burton Club Edition.[34] The *Nights*, like the *Odyssey*, was one of the works which was permanently part of Joyce's library. *Ulysses*, however, points to another important *Nights* source. In 'Telemachus', Stephen's memories of his mother include a reference to 'old Royce' singing 'in the pantomime of Turko the terrible' (p. 9). *The Pantomime of Turko the Terrible* was performed at the Gaiety Theatre, Dublin, at Christmas 1873, but Royce also played Turko the Terrible in December 1892 as a part inserted into *The Pantomime of Sinbad the Sailor*.[35] Joyce incorporates reviews of this pantomime into 'Ithaca' when Bloom considers 'What had prevented him from completing a topical song. . . . If Brian Boru could but come back and see old Dublin now . . . to be introduced into the sixth scene, the valley of diamonds . . . of the grand annual Christmas pantomime *Sinbad the Sailor*' (p. 555). David Hayman has written of Joyce's use of pantomime in *Ulysses*, 'pantomime clowns, pantomime effects and the pantomime theme come into their own in "Cyclops" and persist through "Nausicaa", "Oxen of the Sun" and "Circe" as concomitants of the disintegrating realistic surface'.[36] Bloom's apotheosis at the end of 'Cyclops', Rudy Bloom's appearance at the end of 'Circe', and the conclusion of 'Ithaca' have been related to the 'transformation scene' that concluded the traditional pantomime.[37] Joyce's notes for 'Cyclops' refer to the 'transformation scene' and to 'Finn MacCool and Brian Boru, an Irish pantomime'.[38] This points forward to *Finnegans Wake*, whose form and content are both deeply indebted to the pantomime. There are repeated references to 'Thorker the Tourable' (132:18), *Sinbad* and many other pantomimes. *Finnegans Wake* includes Joyce's own pantomime, 'The Mime of Mick, Nick and the Maggies', complete with 'a Magnificent Transformation Scene showing the Radium Wedding of Neid and Moorning' (222:16–17).

Finnegans Wake is itself a 'punnermine' (519:13) with its puns, riddles, rhymes, songs, dances, cross-talk comedians and final transformation scene: the death of ALP in part IV is not just the passing of the river into the sea but the transformation of the story-telling night into morning.[39]

One of the first direct references to the *Nights* in *Ulysses* occurs in 'Proteus', when Stephen recalls a dream from the previous night: 'Open hallway. Street of harlots. Remember. Haroun al Raschid' (p. 39). This dream resurfaces in 'Scylla and Charybdis', after Bloom passes Stephen and Mulligan in the Library:

> Last night I flew. Easily flew. Men wondered. Street of harlots after. A creamfruit melon he held to me. In. You will see – The wandering jew, Buck Mulligan whispered with clown's awe. Did you see his eye? He looked upon you to lust after you. I fear thee, ancient mariner.   (p. 179)

Here Stephen's failure to 'recognise' Bloom is expressed through the juxtaposition of a passage associating Bloom with Harun with another passage that implicitly associates him with Sindbad. In 'Circe', part of Stephen's dream comes true. Among the various transformations of this episode, one of Bloom's recurrent identities involves that familiar trope of Harun al-Rashid, wandering in disguise through his city. Thus, after the election of Bloom/Dick Whittington as Lord Mayor of Dublin, Bloom/Caligula appoints his 'faithful charger Copula Felix' as 'Grand Vizier' (p. 394). Similarly, shortly after Stephen recalls his dream again ('It was here. Street of harlots'), Bloom intervenes to rescue him, and is challenged about his identity: 'Bloom . . . draws his caliph's hood and poncho and hurries down the steps with sideways face. Incog Haroun Al Raschid' (p. 478).

Another dream in *Ulysses* has a related structural function: this is Bloom's dream of the East. In 'Calypso', Bloom indulges in a fantasy:

> Somewhere in the east . . . Wander through awned streets. Turbaned faces going by. Dark caves of carpet shops, big man, Turko the terrible, seated crosslegged, smoking a coiled pipe. . . . Dander along all day. Might meet a robber or two. . . . Night sky, moon, violet, colour of Molly's new garters. Strings. Listen. A girl playing one of those instruments what do you call them: dulcimers.   (p. 47)

The nostalgia that the captive Odysseus felt finds its equivalent in Bloom's thoughts of the Middle East. These are focused, in this episode, on the Agendath Netaim plantation with its orange-groves and melon-fields. However, as Bowen notes, Bloom's reference to Turko the Terrible echoes Stephen's earlier allusion and acts as the first overt connection between Bloom and Stephen: significantly, Stephen associates Turko with his mother, Bloom with his wife.[40] Also, as *Ulysses* proceeds, Agendath Netaim becomes part of a more generalised 'Eastern' fantasy that is, ultimately, an erotic fantasy about Molly. Thus the passing reference to 'Molly's new garters' grows into the following apparition in 'Circe': 'Beside her mirage of datepalms a handsome woman in Turkish costume stands before him. Opulent curves fill out her scarlet trousers and jacket, slashed with gold' (p. 359).[41] Molly's birthplace, in 'Moorish' Gibraltar, facilitates her incorporation into this fantasy.

In 'Ithaca', the other half of Stephen's dream is realised when he is entertained by Bloom. At the same time, Bloom's dream is fulfilled in both its nostalgic and sexual aspects. After Stephen has left, Bloom retires to bed, where he kisses 'the plump mellow yellow smellow melons' (p. 604) of Molly's rump. As Gilbert said, *à propos* Bloom's interest in the melon-fields of Agendath Netaim, 'The melon . . . is a fruit for which Mr Bloom has, on *a posteriori* grounds, a marked predilection' (p. 138).

In the final chapters of *Ulysses*, Bloom is identified explicitly with Sindbad rather than with Haroun. In 'Eumaeus', the focus is on Odysseus as traveller and teller of tales: Sindbad too is both traveller and teller of tales. Joyce complicates his Homeric correspondences through D. B. Murphy. In the Linati outline, Joyce called Murphy 'Ulysses Pseudoangelos': Murphy, who tells tall stories and claims to be a returned sailor, is the equivalent of the disguised Odysseus, who stays in the hut of the swineherd Eumaeus and tells him a false story about his identity, parentage and travels. The source for this device – the splitting of Ulysses into Ulysses/Bloom and false-Ulysses/Murphy – is to be found in the frame tale for the voyages of Sindbad, where Sindbad of the Sea entertains Sindbad of the Land. In the 'Eumaeus' section of *Scribbledehobble*, Joyce noted 'there are two sinbads' (p. 153). In *Ulysses*, Joyce refers to Murphy as 'friend Sinbad' (p. 520), and Murphy describes 'The Arabian Nights Entertainment' as his favourite book. At the end of 'Ithaca', Bloom is lying in bed with Molly, his day's journey completed:

He rests. He has travelled.
With?
Sinbad the Sailor and Tinbad the Tailor and Jinbad the Jailer
and Whinbad the Whaler and Ninbad the Nailer. . . .

(pp. 606–7)

The leading theme of this final section of *Ulysses* is the return of the
wanderer. The list of companions reminds us of the constellation of
figures that is gathered around the Bloom/Sindbad/Odysseus core:
'ancient mariners' such as St Brendan, Enoch Arden, the Flying
Dutchman; and 'awakened sleepers' such as Rip Van Winkle.
'Tinbad' and 'Whinbad', however, are not merely arbitrary transformations of Sinbad: as Robert M. Adams discovered, Tinbad and
Whinbad were characters in the pantomime *Sinbad the Sailor*.[42]
Bloom thus ends where he began with thoughts of the pantomime.

In *Ulysses*, various literary and mythic patterns are superimposed
to create the 'deep structure' of the novel's narrative language. In
'Ithaca', Bloom/Odysseus returns to his family, while
Bloom/Sindbad creates a pseudo-familial relationship with an
unrelated male. (Bloom's hospitality to Stephen corresponds to
Sindbad's hospitality to Sindbad the porter.) Where the *Odyssey*
underwrites the domestic resolution, Bloom's return to Molly,
'Sindbad', with its urban resolution, points to Joyce's deeper
theme, the renewal of Dublin. In *Finnegans Wake*, superimposition
occurs at the lexical, as well as the syntactical, level. This linguistic
condensation affects characterisation: the main figures are 'fluid
composites, involving an unconfined blur of historical, mythical
and fictitious characters'.[43]

Finnegans Wake is an extension of *Ulysses* and of all Joyce's
previous work. The workbook which Joyce started in 1922, from
which *Finnegans Wake* was constructed, is divided into sections,
which correspond to each of Joyce's previous works and to the
separate episodes of *Ulysses*.[44] This workbook testifies to the
importance of the *Nights* for *Finnegans Wake*. The section entitled
'The Sisters' begins 'Arabian nights, serial stories, tales within
tales' and alludes to 'Scharazads feat' (p. 25). This suggests that
the title of the *Dubliners* story might allude to Scheherazade and
Dinarzade. Certainly the structure of the story is a version of the
frame tale with inserted tales: an account of old Cotter with his
'endless stories' is followed by an account of Father Flynn and his
'stories' and the climax is Eliza's story of her brother. (It is perhaps

significant that Eliza's sister, Nannie, seems 'about to fall asleep' when Eliza tells her tale.[45]) In *Finnegans Wake*, the 'two girls' in the park are explicitly related to the frame tale of the *Nights*. When they first appear, they are introduced as 'inseparable sisters, uncontrollable nighttalkers, Skertziraizde and Donyahzade' (32:7–8). A later passage repeats this identification, with obscener implications, and ends, 'Not the king of this age could richlier eyefeast in oreillental longuardness with alternate nightjoys of a thousand kinds but one kind. A shahryar cobbler on me when I am lying!' (357:17–19). If Dickens plays down the erotic aspects of the *Nights*, Joyce exploits them to the full.[46]

Finnegans Wake, like the *Nights*, is a night-book.[47] Clive Hart has suggested that two particular *Nights* tales underlie the dream structure of *Finnegans Wake*: 'The Sleeper Awakened' and 'The Two Lives of Sultan Mahmoud'.[48] In the first case, Abu Hassan 'is a type of Shaun, the Son who aspires to the condition of the Father. After a sleep he awakens on a new plane, having symbolically become the Father' (p. 107). Abu's mock death and speech from under his shroud prefigure Finnegan's revival and outburst from his bier, while Abu's 'oscillations from one world to another' (p. 107) parallel the spatial oscillations of Finnegans Wake. The second tale is alluded to early in *Finnegans Wake*: 'one yeastyday he sternly struxk his tete in a tub for to watsch the future of his fates but ere he swiftly stook it out again, by the might of moses, the very water was eviperated and all the guennesses had met their exodus' (4:21–4). In this tale, a lifetime passes in an instant: the tale provides a source for the compression and expansion of time in *Finnegans Wake*. Together, the two tales relate to space and time, which Joyce personifies as Shaun and Shem or, later, as 'the old woman in the sky' and 'the old man of the sea' (599:34–5).

There is also evidence to suggest that a third tale, 'The Hunchback's Tale', is involved in *Finnegans Wake*. This is a tale of death and revival (like the ballad of Tim Finnegan), but it is also one of the most brilliantly handled frame tales. The accidental death of the hunchback initiates a chain of events. When the end of the chain is reached, the characters are reintroduced in reverse order and each has to tell a tale in order to avoid execution. Joyce describes the motivation of these inserted tales in the 'Sisters' section of his workbook: 'desperate storytelling, one caps another . . . 1001 Nights, Decameron, Interpreters = at point of death' (p. 25). The anticipation of death is the controlling frame of

Finnegans Wake.[49] The last of these tales is told by a tailor. With a narrative exuberance characteristic of the *Nights*, the tailor's tale introduces a barber, who tells his own story and the stories of his six brothers. In Joyce's workbook, the section entitled 'An Encounter' begins 'Barber's story (1001 N.) self and onanism: on booby trap' (p. 37). This probably refers to the barber's first brother, a booby who is the victim of a succession of tricks. One trick leads to his turning a mill-wheel all night. This echoes the onanist in 'An Encounter' whose 'mind was slowly circling round and round in the same orbit' (p. 29) and Patrick Morkan's horse walking round and round 'King Billy's statue' (p. 258) in 'The Dead'.

In *Finnegans Wake*, there are 'sordidly tales within tales' (522:05): the various versions of the incident in Phoenix Park, or recurring stories such as that of Buckley and the General or the tailor and the Norwegian captain. Like *Heart of Darkness* or *The Time Machine*, *Finnegans Wake* is a quest for truth that problematises truth by locating narratives within narrators. At the same time, Joyce also collects and superimposes similar stories in an attempt to write Vico's universal history: an ideal history in which all the actual histories of all nations should be embodied. The *Nights* is acknowledged as the model for a collection of stories ('one thousand and one stories, all told' – 5:28–9) and for the deeper structure of Joyce's 'millwheeling vicociclometer' (614:27): 'arubyat knychts, with their tales within wheels and stucks between spokes' (247:03–04).[50]

'The Hunchback's Tale', however, has particular relevance. With its Christian broker and Jewish doctor, it testifies to the cosmopolitanism of the Arab cities – a cosmopolitanism which finds its counterpart in Joyce's language and theme. This tale also looks forward to the *Wake*'s geographical ambiguities: in Burton's edition, the Islamic world of the tale is found 'in a certain city of China', and Burton notes that other versions read 'at Bassorah' or even 'at Bassorah and Kájkár', which is 'somewhat like in Dover and Sebastopol' (*Nights*, I, 234). Finally, we should not forget that HCE is himself a hunchback, and that 'The Hunchback's Tale' involves the transmission of guilt: all the characters attempt to deny their guilt by disposing of the hunchback's body, but all in turn are forced to acknowledge their guilt.[51]

Finnegans Wake is even more of an 'Aludin's cave' (108:27) than *Ulysses*: allusions to the *Nights* are heterogeneous, clear and extensive. One of HCE's avatars, for example, is 'Haroun Childeric

Eggeberth' (4:32), and the disguised Harun, appropriate to the changing identities of Finnegans Wake, makes a number of disguised appearances. The history of Earwicker's name makes reference to an anonymous figure 'stambuling haround Dumbaling' (33:36; 34:01) – a subsequent reference to the 'commender of the frightful' (34:05) confirms our suspicions. Similarly, chapter 11 includes a glimpse of someone 'Rambling. Nightclothesed, arooned' (355:18/19). The story of HCE, the two girls and the three soldiers is presented, at one point, as if it were a Nights tale: 'the hardly creditable edventyres of the Haberdasher, the two Churchies and the three Enkelchums' (51:13–15).[52] Elsewhere, Joyce parodies one of the conventional endings for Nights tales: 'And they leaved the most leavely of leaftimes and the most folliagenous till there came the marrer of mirth and the jangtherapper of all jocolarinas and they were as were they never ere' (361:26–8). Compare the end of 'Ma'aruf the Cobbler and his Wife Fatimah':

> So they abode awhile in all solace of life and its delights, and their days were serene and their joys untroubled, till there came to them the Destroyer of delights and the Sunderer of societies, the Depopulator of populous places and the Orphaner of sons and daughters. (Nights, VIII, 50).

Two chapters are of particular interest. Chapter 9, which describes the children playing before bedtime, uses the 'playhouse' as a framing device: this brings in references to various pantomimes, including Aladdin, Ali Baba and Sinbad. Of these, Sinbad is used structurally: Shem's three attempts to answer Isabel's riddle are presented with reference to Sindbad's voyages. Shem's exile, after his first attempt, leads to the production of his 'jeeremyhead sindbook' (229:32), Ulysses. Shem's return for his second attempt is described as the return of 'sin beau . . . the seagoer' (233:5–11). After his third attempt, we are told that 'Singabed sulks before slumber' (256:33–4).[53] In chapter 13, Shaun with his postman's lamp is identified with both Diogenes and Aladdin: ' 'twas his belted lamp! Whom we dreamt was a shaddo, sure, he's lightseyes, the laddo!' (404:13–14). Later, Shaun is shown 'vigorously rubbing his magic lantern to a glow of full-consciousness' (421:22–3), and the wizard's cry 'New worlds for old' (412:02) has an obvious appropriateness to the start of a new cycle. Aladdin provides a shifting point of reference throughout the chapter.[54]

Todorov has described the *Nights* as a 'narrative machine'.[55] Conrad, Wells and Joyce, in their response to the *Nights*, deepen the meaning of that phrase.

NOTES

Books published in London unless otherwise stated.

1. Cedric Watts, *Conrad's 'Heart of Darkness': A Critical and Contextual Discussion* (Milan: Mursia International, 1977) p. 22.
2. See Introduction.
3. Mia Gerhardt, *The Art of Story-Telling: A Literary Study of the Thousand and One Nights* (Leiden: Brill, 1963).
4. In *'Chance:* The Affair of the Purloined Brother', *Conradian*, VI (June 1981) 5–15, I have discussed the narrative structure of *Chance*, with its succession of witnesses, and compared it to that of the detective story as exemplified by Poe's 'The Murders in the Rue Morgue'.
5. 'Sindbad the Sailor' is of particular interest. (See Gerhardt, *The Art of Story-Telling*, pp. 236–63 and 396–7.)
6. 'Youth', *Youth: A Narrative and Two Other Stories*, pp. 36–7. All references to Conrad's works are to the Uniform Edition (Dent, 1923–8).
7. Ian Watt has noted that the first Marlow story, 'Youth', was also the first story that Conrad wrote with a particular group of readers in mind: the readers of *Blackwood's Magazine*. Conrad reproduced his relationship with his readers in the fictional situation of Marlow and his audience (*Conrad in the Nineteenth Century*, [Chatto and Windus, 1980] p. 212).
8. 'The Hunchback's Tale' provides an analogue to this reading of *Heart of Darkness*: the tailor's story features a loquacious barber, but, when this barber finally appears in person, he resists the invitation to tell his story and insists on the appropriateness of his name 'the Silent Man' (*Nights*, I, 234–324). All references to the *Nights* are to *The Arabian Nights' Entertainments*, tr. Sir Richard Burton. Library Edition (1894).
9. 'Without Prejudice', *Pall Mall Magazine*, VII (Sep 1895) 153–5; repr. in *H. G. Wells: The Critical Heritage*, ed. Patrick Parrinder (Routledge and Kegan Paul, 1972), pp. 153–5.
10. Tzvetan Todorov, *The Fantastic* (1973) p. 56.
11. See Elaine L. Kleiner, 'Joseph Conrad's Forgotten Role in the Emergence of Science Fiction', *Extrapolation*, XV (1973) 25–34.
12. *The Stolen Bacillus and Other Incidents* (1895).
13. *The Short Stories of H. G. Wells* (Ernest Benn, 1948) p. 287. For jinn imprisoned by Solomon, see 'The Fisherman and the Jinni' (*Nights*, I, 34–41) or 'The City of Brass' (V, 1–36).
14. *Almayer's Folly*, p. 41. Almayer's 'dream of wealth and power' (p. 3) is analogous to Alnaschar's vision ('The Barber's Tale of his Fifth Brother', *Nights*, I, 309–17).

15. *Experiment in Autobiography* (Victor Gollancz and Cresset Press, 1934) I, 375 and 398–9.
16. For a brief account of the different stages of the text, see Bernard Bergonzi, *The Early H. G. Wells: A Study of the Scientific Romances* (Manchester: Manchester University Press, 1961) pp. 38–40. For W. E. Henley, see *supra* pp. xiv, xvi, xxi, n. 1, xxiii n. 13 and ch. 1, pp. 36–7).
17. *The History of Mr Polly*, p. 137. All references to Wells's novels are to the Atlantic Edition (T. Fisher Unwin, 1924–7).
18. *Nights*, IX, 2. See my article 'H. G. Wells and *The Arabian Nights*', *Wellsian*, VI (Summer 1983) 30–4, for a more detailed discussion.
19. *Experiment in Autobiography*, II, 799; 'Prince Ahmad and the Fairy Peri-Banu', *Nights*, x, 244–97.
20. G. Jean-Aubry (ed.), *Joseph Conrad: Life and Letters* (William Heinemann, 1927) I, 248.
21. Conrad's father, Apollo Korzeniowski, was a student of oriental languages at St Petersburg University. Tymon Terlecki, 'Conrad w kulturze polskiej', *Conrad Żywy* (B. Świdevski, 1957), notes that oriental exoticism played a considerable part in the literature of the 'Young Poland' movement of the 1870s.
22. 'Geography and Some Explorers', *Last Essays*, mentions Burton; Conrad refers to Burton's *Personal Narrative of a Pilgrimage to El-Medinah and Meccah* (1855–6) in a letter of 4 Dec 1898 (*Conrad: Life and Letters*, I, 258–9); John Lester, 'Conrad and Islam', *Conradiana*, XIII, no. 3 (1981), notes close correspondences between Burton's *Pilgrimage* and Conrad's novels; Hans van Marle, 'Conrad and Richard Burton on Islam', *Conradiana*, XVII, no. 2 (1985) 137–42, has demonstrated, through a comparison of Burton's *Pilgrimage* and English translations of the Koran, that 'only recourse to Burton' explains the specific Islamic terms Conrad uses; Norman Sherry, *Conrad's Western World* (Cambridge: Cambridge University Press, 1971) suggests that Conrad used Burton's *Letters from the Battle-Fields of Paraguay* (1870) as a source for Decoud. (Leonard Smithers, who published the Library Edition, was in contact with Conrad during 1896: Smithers published the *Savoy*, which printed Conrad's story 'The Idiots' in October 1896.)
23. See my article 'Conrad, Guthrie and *The Arabian Nights*', *Conradiana*, XVIII, no. 2 (1986) 141–3.
24. *The Collected Letters of Joseph Conrad*, ed. F. R. Karl and L. Davies (Cambridge: Cambridge University Press, 1983) I, 380. Conrad's slip, in his letter of 5 April 1897, when he refers to Kipling's 'Slaves of the Lamp' as 'Slaves of the Ring', suggests that the story of Aladdin was in the back of his mind. Laurence Davies has drawn my attention to another Aladdin reference in a letter to Gissing (21 Dec 1902). In 'The Planter of Malata', the editor uses the pen name 'the Slave of the Lamp' (*Within the Tides*, p. 49) and Renouard, in a dream, sees himself 'carrying a small bizarre lamp' through 'an empty and unfurnished palace' (p. 31). (It was the Slave of the Lamp who built Aladdin's palace.) In a letter to Lady Ottoline Morrell (17 Feb 1914), Conrad describes himself as 'the slave of the desk'.

25. *Joseph Conrad's Letters to R. B. Cunninghame-Graham*, ed. Cedric Watts (Oxford University Press, 1969) p. 71. Cunninghame-Graham travelled to Morocco in 1897 disguised as 'Mohammed el Fasi'. His account of this journey, *Mogreb-el-Acksa* (1898), was known to Conrad.
26. Z. Najder, *Joseph Conrad: A Chronicle* (Cambridge: Cambridge University Press, 1983) p. 250.
27. *Notes on Life and Letters*, p. 89. (See also pp. 93 and 113.)
28. *Typhoon and Other Stories*, pp. 143–240. ('Falk' was written in 1901.)
29. Tony Tanner, '"Gnawed Bones" and "Artless Tales" – Eating and Narrative in Conrad', in Norman Sherry (ed.), *Joseph Conrad: A Commemoration*, (Macmillan, 1976) pp. 17–36.
30. See *supra*, Allan Grant, ch. 4.
31. Viktor Shklovsky, 'The Connection between Devices of *Syuzhet* Construction and General Stylistic Devices', *Twentieth Century Studies*, VII–VIII (1972) 48–72. I am quoting the translation given in *Russian Formalist Criticism: Four Essays*, ed. L. T. Lemon and M. J. Reis (Lincoln, Nebr.: University of Nebraska Press, 1965) p. 118.
32. Hugh Kenner, *The Pound Era* (Faber and Faber, 1975) pp. 169–70.
33. Victor Bérard, *Les Phéniciens et l'Odyssée* (Paris, 1902), confines himself to the similarity between Proteus in Menelaus's story and the Old Man of the Sea of Sindbad's voyages. He also makes an arbitrary connection between Proteus and Harun al-Rashid (11, 50–1). For Bérard's contribution to *Ulysses*, see Stuart Gilbert, *James Joyce's 'Ulysses'* (Faber, 1930), and Michael Seidel, *Epic Geography* (Princeton, NJ: Princeton University Press, 1976). For Joyce's own version of Sindbad–Odysseus correspondences, see *James Joyce's Scribbledehobble*, ed. T. E. Connolly (Evanston, Ill.: Northwestern University Press, 1961) p. 153.
34. *Le mille e una notte*, tr. Armando Dominicis (Florence, 1915), *The Arabian Nights*, tr. Sir Richard Burton, Luristan Edition (c. 1919). See 'Joyce's Library in 1920' in Richard Ellmann, *The Consciousness of Joyce* (1977), and Thomas E. Connolly, *The Personal Library of James Joyce* (Buffalo, NY: University of Buffalo Studies, 1955).
35. W. Thornton, *Allusions in 'Ulysses'* (Durham, NC: University of North Carolina, 1968) p. 10; R. M. Adams, *Surface and Symbol: The Consistency of James Joyce's 'Ulysses'* (New York: Oxford University Press, 1962) pp. 76–82. All *Ulysses* references are to the Bodley Head edition of 1986.
36. David Hayman, 'Forms of Folly in Joyce: A Study of Clowning in *Ulysses*', *ELH*, XXXIV (June 1967) 274. We might notice here Bloom's mother's appearance in 'Circe' wearing 'pantomime dame's stringed mobcap, widow Twankey's crinoline and bustle' (p. 358) as an allusion to *Aladdin*, while 'Ali Baba Backsheesh' is among the viceregal houseparty in 'Cyclops'. Pantomine was an early-eighteenth-century dramatic innovation; up to 1860, the *commedia dell'arte* was the dominant influence. *Nights* themes also began to appear with Henry Woodward's *The Genii . . . An Arabian Nights Entertainment* (1752) and John O'Keeffe's *Aladdin* (1788). (*Nights* material was used in other dramatic forms in this same period: there was the 1789 farce *The Little Hunch-back; or, A Frolic in Bagdad*, or the 1793 entertainment *Abon*

Hassan.) In the period 1800–1850, the tradition of the Christmas pantomime became established. Harlequin still dominated the pantomime, but the shape of things to come is suggested by some titles of the period: *The Valley of Diamonds; or, Harlequin Sinbad* (1814); *The Silver Arrow; or, Harlequin and the Fairy Peri Banon* (1819); *Harlequin and the Talking Bird, The Singing Trees and the Golden Waters* (1824); *Forty Thieves; or, Harlequin Ali Baba and the Robbers' Cave* (1845). By 1850, *Sinbad* and *Aladdin* were firmly established: there were performances of *Sinbad* in 1805, 1812, and 1820, and performances of *Aladdin* in 1810, 1811, 1813, 1826, 1830 and 1833. (*Ali Baba* had appeared in 1806.) Gradually, the *commedia dell'arte* was displaced by the *Nights*: there was at least one *Aladdin* every year from 1872 to 1899 and one *Sinbad* from 1874 to 1896. See Allardyce Nicoll, *A History of English Drama, 1660–1900* (Cambridge: Cambridge University Press, 1952); and Gerald Frow, *'Oh, Yes, It Is!': A History of Pantomime* (BBC, 1985).

37. David Hayman, 'Cyclops' (pp. 271–3), Hugh Kenner, 'Circe' (p. 359), A. Walton Litz, 'Ithaca' (p. 403), in *James Joyce's 'Ulysses': Critical Essays*, ed. Clive Hart and David Hayman (Berkeley, Calif.: University of California Press, 1974).

38. British Library Add. MS 49975.

39. For a fuller account, see J. S. Atherton's excellent article 'Finnegans Wake: "The Gist of the Pantomime"', *Accent*, xv (Winter 1955) 14–26. See also J. S. Atherton, *The Books at the Wake* (Faber, 1959) pp. 149–51 for a discussion of Joyce's use of drama and the theatre in *Finnegans Wake*.

40. Z. Bowen, *Musical Allusions in the Works of James Joyce* (Albany, NY: State University of New York Press, 1974) pp. 67 and 84. Is there also a memory of Ali Baba behind the thought of caves and robbers?

41. As Bowen has pointed out (p. 255), this image of Molly is also the culmination of a series of allusions to the song 'The shade of the palm'.

42. Adams, *Surface and Symbol*, p. 80. A. Walton Litz discusses the end of 'Ithaca' in relation to the transformation scene of pantomime: 'Molly has merged into her archetype, Gea-Tellus, while Leopold Bloom has become the archetype of all human possibility' (*James Joyce's 'Ulysses'*, ed. Hart and Hayman, p. 403). Just as the content looks forward to *Finnegans Wake*, so too does the technique: the transformations of 'Sinbad' look forward to the sound-repetition-and-variation that is a major device in *Finnegans Wake*. (See Kathleen Wales, 'The "Ideal Reader" of *Finnegans Wake*: Making "soundsense and sensesound kin again" (121.15)', *VIII International James Joyce Symposium* (1982).

43. Roland McHugh, *The Sigla of 'Finnegans Wake'* (Edward Arnold, 1976) p. 10.

44. *James Joyce's Scribbledehobble.*

45. *Dubliners* (1914) p. 17.

46. Richard Brown, *James Joyce and Sexuality* (Cambridge: Cambridge University Press, 1984), discusses Joyce's intertextual relationship with contemporary sexological writings (including Burton's *Nights*).

47. Andrew Gibson has drawn my attention to Mary and Padraic Colum, *Our Friend James Joyce* (Gollancz, 1959):

> And because *Finnegans Wake* dealt with night life he wanted to know about other books that proceeded from night life. One was *The Arabian Nights* . . . the framework has to do with nights, and, we are told, the art of the collection originated in 'night-walkers' stories'. Joyce wanted *The Arabian Nights* read by someone who would tell him some of its features, so he sent over to my apartment a sixteen-volume set of Burton's translation. The first thing I reported interested him: back of the Arabian stories were Persian stories: in fact, the names of the storyteller and her sister were Persian. The fact of one culture leading into another was always fascinating to Joyce, and he wanted to know if there was a parallel between the Persian stories giving rise to the Arabian and the Celtic stories giving rise to the stories of the Arthurian cycle. And what did the names of the storyteller and her sister mean? I read the sixteen volumes with great delight, naturally (I had read only Lane's four volumes previously), and talked to Joyce about various features in them. The Caliph walking about at night with his Vizier must appear on some page of *Finnegans Wake*, but the only lines I am sure derived from my reading are those about the 'nighttalking sisters'. (pp. 161–2)

48. Clive Hart, *Structure and Motif in 'Finnegans Wake'* (Faber, 1962) pp. 104–8; 'The Sleeper and the Waker', *Nights*, ix, 1–28; 'sleeper awakening', *Finnegans Wake* (597:27). 'The Two Lives of Sultan Mahmoud' is not in Burton but is included in Mardrus (vol. 13). This tale first appeared in English in 'The History of Chec Chahabeddin', *Turkish Tales* (1708). This was retold by Addison (*The Spectator*, no. 94, 18 June 1711). Joyce might have known it from C. R. Maturin, *Melmoth the Wanderer*, ii, ch. 8; from Dickens, *Hard Times*, book ii, ch. 1; or from Gaskell, *North and South*, i, ch. 3. There is an allusion to it in the 'Oxen of the Sun' section of *Ulysses*: 'the lord Harry put his head into a cow's drinkingtrough in the presence of all his courtiers and pulling it out again told them all his new name' (p. 328). He certainly knew it from Heinrich Zimmer, *Maya. Der indische Mythos* (Berlin, 1936). The copy of this in his personal library contains three pages of notes (made by one of Joyce's readers) which make reference to the 'Story of Shiek [sic] Schahab-al-Din', and the appropriate pages (pp. 64–9) are pencil-marked. (See *The Personal Library of James Joyce*, p. 46.) Zimmer tells the story in his chapter on 'Vischnus Maya'. Hinduism, like the *Wake*, has a cyclic view of history: at the end of each cycle, the world is destroyed and only Vishnu survives. Vishnu then sleeps and the world is created during his sleep. Zimmer writes, 'Gestalten durchgeistern die Welt, die dem göttlichen Träumer innen geworden ist, wie Traumgestalten unsern Leib im Schlaf durchwandeln' – *Gesammelte Werke* (Zurich, 1952) ii, 44. Hence the concept of *maya* (the illusory nature of the phenomenal world). Zimmer ends his retelling of the story of the

Sheik, 'Was ist das Wirkliche? Ist, was wir wachend und bewusst an uns und um uns zu greifen meinen, die ganze Wirklichkeit? . . . Ist unser Wachen eine Art Träumen, ausgeworfen von unserer unbewussten Tiefe als eine besondere Form, in der wir uns als uns selbst verfangen?' (p. 55).

49. 'As Joyce informed a friend later, he conceived of his book as the dream of old Finn, lying in death beside the river Liffey and watching the history of Ireland and the world – past and future – flow through his mind' – Richard Ellmann, *James Joyce* (Oxford University Press, 1965) p. 557.

50. This structure is determined by Vico's cyclic view of history: part I is his divine age; part II his heroic age; part III his human age; part IV the *ricorso* before the cycle begins again. In addition, this cycle is repeated within parts II and III, and twice in part I. There are numerous word-plays on 'Arabian Nights' and 'hasard and worn' (107:21) nights. 1001 is one of *Finnegans Wake*'s magic numbers: ALP has 1001 children; HCE (10) with ALP (01) make 1001 – 'Ainsoph, this upright one, with that noughty beside him zeroine' (261:23–4) – and so on.

51. Margot Norris, *The Decentred Universe of 'Finnegans Wake'* (Baltimore, MD: Johns Hopkins University Press, 1976) suggests that *Finnegans Wake* attempts 'to plumb the conflict of the individual, confronted by primordial guilt, who is tempted to deny and confess, to evade and embrace responsibility for an involuntary, non-volitional sin' (p. 39), but 'the question of guilt is insoluble in *Finnegans Wake* precisely because of its circularity' (p. 76). Another entry in *Scribbledehobble* suggests Joyce's detailed knowledge of 'The Hunchback's Tale'. Joyce notes 'cabbaging . . . (tailor steals cloth) pejorative' (p. 175). A note to 'The Barber's Tale of his First Brother' reads, 'The tailor in the East, as in Southern Europe, is made to cut out the cloth in presence of its owner to prevent "cabbaging"' (*Nights*, I, 296).

52. Cf. 'The Porter and the Ladies of Baghdad and the Three Royal Mendicants' (*Nights*, I, 79–170), and notice that HCE later appears as Mr Porter.

53. *Sinbad* is also used in the first part of chapter 11, which tells the story of the Norwegian captain and the Dublin tailor. The captain (identified with HCE because of his humped back) is also associated with Sinbad and other sailors. He marries Tina-bat-Talur (327:04), the tailor's daughter. Sailor and tailor tend, however, to merge: Tinbad the Tailor (from the pantomime) eases the merger; it is cemented by 'Tinker, tailor, soldier, sailor', that list of potential identities that is one of *Finnegans Wake*'s motifs; it is held fast because each is a 'seamer' (613:32) and a 'teller' (310:30).

54. References to *Aladdin* reappear in chapter 16. An early mention of 'alladim lamps' (560:19) leads to the picture of ALP 'looping the lamp' (578:18). ALP, 'the slave of the ring', is also the rubber of the lamp (580:26), and rubbing the lamp suggests here (as it did to Jung) sexual excitation. In *The Psychology of the Unconscious* (Kegan Paul, 1916) Jung

discusses masturbation using this image: 'Aladdin rubs his lamp and the obedient genii stand at his bidding' – pp. 187–8.
55. Tzvetan Todorov, *The Poetics of Prose* (Oxford: Basil Backwell, 1977) p. 78.

10

'A Lesson for the Circumspect': W. B. Yeats's Two Versions of *A Vision* and the *Arabian Nights*

WARWICK GOULD

I

Then said the yellow youth: 'O guests, the tale of this yellow colour is so strange that, were it written with needles on the corner of an eye, yet would it serve as a lesson for the circumspect. I pray you to give me your best attention.' 'Our best attention is yours,' they answered. 'We are impatient for you to begin.'

At this point, Shahrazād saw the approach of morning and discreetly fell silent.[1]

Shahrazād by means of this formula establishes the nightly exchange from tale to more marvellous tale. My present essay, however, depends upon a story which has not been told and which cannot be summarised here, depending as it does upon unpublished research into the folkloric origins of Yeats's fantasies and fictions.

Far from supplying merely incidental local colour and the odd source for a poet with an abiding interest in Eastern religions, folklore and history (an interest well served by scholars and critics),[2] the *Arabian Nights* provided Yeats with a structural principle for linking his abundant and seemingly self-propagating fictions. The principle is implicit in the *Nights*: Yeats shares with Shahrazād a simple need – time-gaining.

The great majority of the fictions of the 'Robartes set'[3] were published as notes and plays between the reinvention of Robartes shortly after Yeats's marriage in 1917 and the publication of *A*

244

Vision [A] in 1925.[4] A further set appeared in 1931 to hold ground for the second version, published in 1937. The method of such fictions had been established as early as 1899 when Yeats published in *The Wind Among the Reeds* some forty-four pages of folkloric essays to support some sixty-two pages of lyrics (*YO*, p. 230). The Robartes set reached back to embrace the stories of 1896, 'Rosa Alchemica', 'The Tables of the Law' and 'The Adoration of the Magi', wherein the 'personages' who were also to act as 'principles of mind' (*VP*, p. 803) in *The Wind Among the Reeds* made their first appearance. The set has evident connections with *The Speckled Bird* and many other papers not published in Yeats's lifetime.

Yeats first 'walked upon Sindbad's yellow shore' (*Au*, p. 52) in 1872, and the *Nights* in several versions provided his syncretic mind with folkloric materials over a lifetime.[5] Such is his familiarity with the *Nights* that he frequently cites it in strategies of allusion which have escaped the attention of his commentators. Two examples must suffice here. The first is his affirmation of declaration itself as a mythic method in *Per Amica Silentia Lunae*.

> At one time I thought to prove my conclusions by quoting from diaries where I have recorded certain strange events the moment they have happened, but now I have changed my mind – I will but say, like the Arab boy that became Vizier: 'O brother, I have taken stock in the desert sand and of the sayings of antiquity.' (*Myth*, p. 343)

That desert sand is, perhaps inattentively, read as some Thebaid, a reading which does not seem at odds with the defence Yeats undertakes of tradition and folklore and the disavowal of ordinary evidences. But its source, the story of 'King Wird Khan, his Women and his Wazirs' confirms that what Yeats has in mind here is the concept of geomancy, used in 'Ego Dominus Tuus' – the proem to *Per Amica* – written in 1915. In Burton's version a king in disguise inquires of a boy how he comes to know intimate state secrets, and receives the following reply:

> 'O brother, I know this from the sand wherewith I take compt of night and day and from the saying of the ancients: – No mystery from Allah is hidden; for the sons of Adam have in them a spiritual virtue which discovereth to them the darkest secrets.' Answered Wird Khan, 'True, O my son, but whence

learnedest thou geomancy and thou young of years?' Quoth the
boy, 'My father taught it me. . . .'   (*B*, IX, 117)[6]

Learned in divination, the youth is also sagacious, as Wird Khan
discovers, and his reward is the wazirship.

Yeats's reference is studiedly vague. Of course, he implies, the
story of Wird Khan is so well known that it is shared between
reader and writer. Such vagueness is entirely congruent with the
point Yeats is making: dispensing with documentation is liberating.
Since the occult philosophy of 'Anima Mundi' comes from above
and beyond, its burden of proof rests with an immanent authority.
In his desire to found his thought upon an unchallengeable basis,
Yeats found, *via* the *Nights*, ways in which occult learning and
experience could be irrefutably presented in fable, folklore or
invented folklore. To do this on any scale was to employ the
enclosing narrative structures of the *Nights* to support poems until
the projected systematisation of his thought could appear. Like
the metaphysicians of Tlön, Yeats saw metaphysics as but 'a branch
of fantastic literature'.[7]

I take, secondly, 'Desert Geometry or The Gift of Harun Al-
Rashid' as it was entitled in *A Vision [A]*. It disappears from *A
Vision [B]*, though reference to it in that book (*AV[B]*, p. 54)
retains it within the penumbra of works upon which that book
acroamatically depends. It is increasingly forgotten that the poem
is a fiction dependent upon the *Nights*. Modern scholarship worries
the 'biographical allegory' of the poem, and yet ignores that the
words of Harun concerning the murder of Jaffer which it quotes
are from the *Nights* themselves.[8] In Mathers' translation:

> Al Rashid's face grew dark, and he pushed her away, saying:
>   'My child, my life, my sole remaining happiness, how would
> it advantage you to know the reason? If I thought that my shirt
> knew, I would tear my shirt in pieces.'   (*M&M*, IV, 712)

For Burton, the quoted phrase (in his terminal essay) runs 'My
dear life, an I thought that my shirt knew the reason I would rend
it in pieces!' (*B*, X, 141). Yeats's lines are

> 'If but the shirt upon my body knew it
> I'd tear it off and throw it in the fire.'
>   (*AV[A]*, p. 122)

Mardrus and Mathers enclose the lore found in Burton's terminal essay into a new story for Shahrazād. Her introductory formula tells us that the 'historians and annalists are far from being agreed as to the cause of this catastrophe' and she offers us the alternate possibilities of 'the events which may be supposed to have led up to' Jaffer's murder (*M&M*, IV, 712–13).

Yeats, in order to make room for his new *Arabian Nights* tale, leaves Jaffer's death a mystery, which suggests that he too probably returned to Burton's terminal essay to check the various accounts. The poem hangs upon a note which accompanied its first publication in *The Dial* in June 1924. Further, both poem and note depend upon the Harun al-Rashid cycle, yet the note functions not merely as a foundation for the poem, but also as a frame tale announcing another dependency. This time it is upon a letter of Owen Aherne's which will be published in *A Vision*. The implication is that the poem is a reconstruction of materials which have been assessed by Aherne, master of schism and heresy, and, in composing the extract from Aherne's letter, Yeats indulges a scholar's delight in the alternate possibilities which sketchy evidence allows. This has always been read in a reductive way as biographical disingenuousness, but, without denying the facts of Mrs Yeats's mediumship, it is possible to suggest that poem and note offer something more than camouflage for the facts of their origin. An examination of the many stories in the Harun cycle which the poem imitates, alludes to, and depends upon, reveals an interest in legend and in the spawning of fictions which shows Yeats at his most Borgesian. Such is the dependence of poem and note upon the *Nights* that the *Nights* are never mentioned. Both are, as it were, contained by the *Nights*: 'We know Harun ar Rashid through the *Arabian Nights alone* [emphasis added] and there he is the greatest of all traditional images of generosity and magnanimity' (*Ex*, p. 448).

Yeats therefore imitates not only the *Nights* themselves, but also the oriental, accretive methods of Mardrus, who himself disclaimed 'all scholarly pretensions' and insisted that his version was only 'a literary work of art', written for a 'congenial public'.[9] Yeats even has Kusta Ben Luka, whom he introduces into the court of Harun al-Rashid with a fine display of 'poetic licence' (*AV[B]*, p. 54), see the process of turning scholarly detail into fantasy[10] as inevitable:

> In after time they will speak much of me
> And speak but fantasy.
>
> (VP, p. 462)

In doing so Yeats seems to have seized upon framing and boxing as the instinctive principle of propagation. Stallworthy conjectures from the surviving drafts of the poem that 'Yeats wrote this poem in two parts, roughly corresponding with a picture and its frame.'[11] Certainly, all of Yeats's narrative poems – 'The Wanderings of Oisin' being the outstanding example – show a most sophisticated grasp of narrative enclosure and the principle seems to have been learned from the Nights.[12]

One might say for the characters in the Nights, who use the protective formula 'But Allah knows all', that the will of Allah, the 'Book of Destiny' (M&M, II, 789) is the one 'total book on some shelf of the universe'. In his discussion of the enigma of the 602nd night, Borges rephrases Carlyle to conclude, 'the history of the universe is an infinite sacred book that all men write and read and try to understand, and in which they are also written'.[13] The Nights, in all versions, but especially in that of Mardrus and Mathers, records its own contribution to some total book of human experience. Tales which are told by Shahrazād of Harun al-Rashid frequently conclude with the Caliph's order that the adventures be written in splendid calligraphy, carefully documented, and added to his library. Yeats's poem is not only a dramatic epistle to inform its recipient of an extraordinary experience. It contains orders that the story be placed within the 'great treatise' of Parmenides within the Caliph's library. Its concern with writing is not merely in imitation of the method of the Nights; it is also an extension of it.

> Carry this letter
> . . .
> And pause at last, I was about to say,
> At the great book of Sappho's song; but no!
> For should you leave my letter there, a boy's
> Love-lorn, indifferent hands might come upon it
> And let it fall unnoticed to the floor.
> Pause at the Treatise of Parmenides
> And hide it there, for Caliphs to the world's end
> Must keep that perfect. . . .
>
> (AV[A], p. 121; VP, p. 461)

The fate of Sappho's poems, typically preserved in fragments in the works of grammarians, is used retrospectively to justify Kusta's decision to bury his letter in Parmenides. The contribution it will make to human wisdom is unquantifiable, but assured, and it is not for Kusta to judge his experience, but to marvel. Such is the attitude of al-Rashid in the *Nights*: his chroniclers must fill his library with the case lore of the remarkable.[14]

So, far from being a poem struggling to escape the influence of Browning's 'Karshish',[15] 'The Gift of Harun Al-Rashid', as it was later entitled, pays accomplished homage to the *Nights* through the link between love and wisdom which it celebrates. The earlier title in *A Vision [A]*, 'Desert Geometry or the Gift of Harun Al-Rashid', implies a link between geomantic power and magnanimity and that link is made through love. The conclusion to Mardrus's version of the *Nights* exemplifies the significance of documenting just such another love story. After Shahrazād's account of the various reasons offered for Jaffer's murder, she tells Shahryar one last tender tale of 'Prince Jasmine and Princess Almond' before revealing to him his three children. The double wedding celebrated, the 'most renowned annalists and proficient scribes from all quarters of Islam' are 'ordered to write out the tales of Shahrazād from beginning to end, without the omission of a single detail' (a task[16] which implicitly taxes Shahrazād with a retelling). Copies of the thirty volumes are disseminated to the 'four corners of the empire', but the 'original manuscript' is 'shut in the gold cupboard of his reign' and Shahryar makes his 'wazīr of treasure responsible for its safe keeping' (*M&M*, IV, 745). Yeats for his part has Kusta ben Luka instruct Abd al-Rabban to bury the letter in the 'Treasure House' where 'books of learning from Byzantium/ Written in gold upon a purple stain' (*AV[A]*, p. 121; *VP*, p. 461) are kept, and where (as we learn in *AV[B]*) Yeats has also stored the 'lost egg of Leda, its miraculous life still unquenched' (p. 51).

Just as Kusta's letter will be secure within the treatise, so is Yeats's poem secure within the *Nights*, which is a huge testament to the power of Shahrazād's 'pure, holy, chaste, tender, straightforward, unassailable, ingenious, subtle, eloquent, discreet, smiling, and wise' love, which has turned Shahryar's own irrationality into magnanimity (*M&M*, IV, 739).

Enclosed within Kusta's letter is the tale of Harun's generosity according to Yeats, Kusta's love and his wife's wisdom, and within *that* tale is the tale of Yeats's marriage to *his* Shahrazād, and her tales and truths 'without father',

> truths that no book
> Of all the uncounted books that I have read,
> Nor thought out of her mind or mine begot,
> Self-born, high-born, and solitary truths,
> Those terrible implacable straight lines
> Drawn through the wondering vegetative dream,
> Even those truths that when my bones are dust
> Must drive the Arabian host.
>
> *(AV[A], p. 125)*

Since this prophetic future is a past already enacted, as well as a future which will re-enact a completed cycle of the past, the system of enclosures within the poem and its surrounding precursor fictions in the *Nights* is vertiginous.

Read as a modern contribution to the composite art of the *Nights*, designed to utilise their method and harness their fictions in the service of a philosophy (*AV[A]*, p. 252), the poem takes on new dimensions from endlessly forming and reforming patterns. Many stories[17] of the *Nights* use wise girls as geomancers, but Yeats's poem offers a wise bride who sleepwalks to the edge of the desert to mark the sand with her 'white finger' (*AV[A]*, p. 126). In geomantic terms the scene is strictly unnecessary; she does not need the desert to dance in, as do the 'Four Royal Persons' of *A Vision [A]*. The incident is comprehensible however as Yeats's implied *riposte* to 'Amina the Ghoul Wife', entitled in the Mardrus and Mathers version 'The Master of the White Mare' (*M&M*, IV, 179–97). Amina leads Sidi Numan to the edge of the town, to the cemetery, where she joins another ghoul for a feast of human remains. Kusta's bride, on the other hand, returns good for evil magic whilst still announcing in her sleep catastrophe to the world. Her divination, which involves a degree of daimonisation, dominates both versions of *A Vision* and I turn now to examine each of them.

II

Since Yeats himself admitted that his Robartes fictions were a time-gaining operation which would enable him to publish poems rooted in the system before he had finished its exposition, arousing at the same time curiosity about what was to be a very strange book, the idea seems current that the fictions merely serve to delay exposition of that system. Some critics have sought to read the fictions in the light of the system; other see them as the comic manipulation of the form of a printed book.[18] No one has tried to read the system by the light of the fictions. Yet, since they were the bridge Yeats used between doctrine and its concrete embodiment in lyrics, it is worth asking whether the fictions might serve for the reader not as some temporary scaffolding, but as a permanent, necessary and integral part of Yeats's work, conterminous with plays and poems on the one hand and with abstract thought on the other.

Yeats, it will be noted, never abandoned them. From 1918 until 1925, and again until the publication of *A Vision [B]* in 1937, and possibly even beyond it,[19] the 'Robartes set' kept growing. Yeats's excuse that he had been 'fool enough to write half a dozen poems that are unintelligible' without the frame tales, themselves 'unnatural' and in need of rewriting (*AV[B]*, p. 19), has been accepted. Yet such rewriting merely reunifies the material whilst apparently disavowing it. I start the examination of *A Vision [A]* not with the Robartes story and the quarrel over the book's authorship which provides the second frame – the outermost being Yeats's[20] – but with the innermost 'box' or fictive frame, the pastiche *Nights* story entitled 'The Dance of the Four Royal Persons', which is the crux of a 'tangled hierarchy'.[21]

This new 'night' introduces a wise man (not, of course, found in the *Nights*)[22] who responds in a wily fashion to his Caliph's wish so to be instructed in 'human nature' that he will 'never be astonished again' (*AV[A]*, p. 9). The Caliph is rapidly bored by Kusta's attempt to instruct him 'with his book of geometrical figures' and banishes him from the palace, declaring that all 'unintelligible visitors' are to be 'put to death'.

Unaccountably, the King, Queen, Prince and Princess of the Country of Wisdom arrive a few days later with the 'intention to reveal all in a dance', since 'a certain man has pretended that wisdom is difficult' (p. 9). The Caliph finds the dance 'dull . . . nobody has ever been more unintelligible' (p. 10) and orders their execution. Before they can be garrotted, the dancers ask leave to rub out the marks their feet have made in the sand. Kusta is summoned after their execution to explain the marks. The dancers were in fact his students, demonstrating his philosophy in the full knowledge that death could follow – 'he that dies is the chief person in the story' (AV[A], p. 10; cf. VPL, p. 309). The myth they die into concerns the origin of the name 'The Dance of the Four Royal Persons' which tradition has assigned to the 'first figure drawn by the Judwali elders for the instruction of youth', which is 'identical' with the 'Great Wheel' of Giraldus (AV[A], p. 10).

This story is the frame of the next two doctrinal books of A Vision [A]: there is also a sense in which it is an unclosed frame for the entire doctrinal section of the system. Surviving manuscripts of the story show that it was plainly written after 'The Gift of Harun Al-Rashid' (though itself of uncertain date). Yeats abandoned a version[23] with al-Rashid as hero, proposed but cancelled Shahryar, substituted the historically identifiable El-Mukledar, but finally settled for the more capacious 'A Caliph who reigned after the death of Harun . . . [when] Kusta ben Luka [was] . . . a very old man' (AV[A], p. 9). Folkloric technique offered this 'poetic licence' and obviated the necessity of Owen Aherne's attempting as editor to verify the story in Arab history. Other attempts to imitate the Nights found in the manuscripts came to nothing.[24]

'The Dance of the Four Royal Persons', which frames[25] the system, is itself virtually unreadable except as framed by the Nights themselves. It therefore links the system to the outer fictions and yet yokes the whole book to a larger, older body of lore. Even if Yeats had not considered Shahryar as his Caliph's name, it would have been clear that he sought to imitate the frame tale of the Nights. His unnamed Caliph seeks wisdom. He had

> discovered one of his companions climbing the wall that encircled the garden of his favourite slave, and because he had believed this companion entirely devoted to his interests, [he] gave himself up to astonishment. After much consideration he offered a large sum of money to any man who could explain human nature so completely that he should never be astonished again
> (AV[A], p. 9)

The choice of such a frame tale begs every question about A Vision, from those concerning the choice of the frame of divided authorship to those concerning the meanings of its doctrines. The briefest answer is that Yeats sought an 'appropriate form' for an account of human life which, in its multitudinousness, demanded encyclopaedic expression. Too often Yeats's prophecies have dominated the reading of a book which, for all its fearful glimpses into the future, is based upon grand comic energies of reincarnating and cyclical patterns. One recalls Robartes, the system in his head, asserting 'things move by mathematical necessity, all changes can be dated by gyre and cone, and pricked beforehand upon the Calendar' (AV[A], p. xvi). The system functions *via* the encyclopaedic codifications of personality and history which are conterminous with the fictions which enclose them, and are in their turn enclosed by such larger compilations as the *Nights*. If we can for the moment ignore the imminence of the new dispensation (of which *A Vision* is the catastrophe theory), and concentrate upon the immanence of its topology, or grand design, we can come to trust not only the 'system' *in* the fictions,but also the hermeneutical exercises which the fictions prompt when they are considered in relation to these larger fictional structures, on which they ultimately depend. In this case we have an arbitrary, cruel, cuckolded Caliph, who enacts his vengeance upon the dancers (who accept that theirs is a part in a text already scripted), and a wise man who wins the Caliph to partial understanding of himself and the world. Kusta's wisdom converts irrational authority into magnanimity: such is the lesson of the *Nights* as a whole. Shahrazād's time-gaining tales slowly convert haughty cruelty into generosity and the acceptance of the interaction of Chance and Choice: such too is the lesson of the Harun cycle, as the author of 'The Gift of Harun Al-Rashid' seems to have endorsed.

I turn briefly to the connection between 'The Dance of the Four Royal Persons' and the rest of the 'Robartes set'. The folktale (for that is what Yeats wants it to seem) tells of the origins of a diagram found in Judwali religion and in a sixteenth-century mythography of Giraldus. This bifurcated stemma of invention converges in the 'Robertes set' which forms Aherne's supposed introduction. Here also converge the fictions of Robartes' return from the East (and from the dead, for his end had been portrayed in 'Rosa Alchemica'), his wanderings and doctrinal discoveries, his quarrels with Aherne and Yeats, his travels in Ireland with Aherne, and the outcome of the whole difficulty of putting his philosophy – 'no man had ever less gift of expression' – into a form for publication. The structural principle of the book is mapped out by Aherne and it is a structure built upon an irresolvable division between Aherne and Yeats over the system of the now absent philosopher.

> Mr Yeats consented to write the exposition on the condition that I wrote the introduction and any notes I pleased. . . . Mr Yeats's completed manuscript now lies before me. The system has grown clearer for his concrete exposition of it . . . .
>
> (AV[A], pp. xxii–xxiii)

'The Dance of the Four Royal Persons' is placed immediately after 'The Phases of the Moon' and both appear after the rubric of book I – 'What the Caliph Partly Learned'. The poem offers a concrete image of the doctrine the Caliph cannot master, but which Robartes manages to communicate to an unusually receptive Aherne. Robartes, commanded to sing 'the changes of the moon once more;/True song though speech: "mine author sung it me"',[26] does so by rote, turning that knowledge into a joke played upon Yeats, who, extinguishing the light in his tower, ends the poem. There is a 'tangled hierarchy' here too, with characters apparently exulting in a wisdom withheld from their author, who allows them their freedom. It is an apt image of the hierarchical arrangements of the fictions as a whole. We pass to the story to learn what it is that has given the book its rubric. If one can trust the characters, one cannot, it would seem, trust the author to have got the system right.

Yeats has framed this oriental tale with an occidental gloss by Aherne, who offers both Robartes' recension and a respectful, if doubting, scholarly frame. The gloss (from Yeats's point of view) is intended to be misleading. Aherne's doubts express themselves in terms of an alternate possibility: the Dance might be 'a later embodiment of a story that it was the first diagram drawn upon the sand by the wife of Kusta ben Luka' (AV[A], pp. 10–11). Aherne, however, reserves his position for his 'own book upon the philosophy and its sources'. Taking no responsibility for the tale, he helps us to read it, inviting us to see its philosophy as

> a series of fragments which only display . . . their meaning, like one of those child's pictures which are made up out of separate cubes, when all were put together. The object of this was . . . to prevent the intellect from forming its own conclusions, and so thwarting the Djinn who could only speak to curiosity and

passivity. I cannot, however, let this pass without saying that I doubt the authenticity of this story, which Mr Yeats has expanded into the poem 'Desert Geometry or The Gift of Harun Al-Raschid', at least in its present form, and that an almost similar adventure is attributed in one of the Robartes documents to a Mahometan grammarian of a much later date. I will . . . discuss all these matters at length in my own book . . . .　　(AV[A], p. 11)

The clue is no sooner supplied than withdrawn. It reappears in *A Vision [B]*, when Yeats calls his system and its periods 'stylistic arrangements of experience comparable to the cubes in the drawings of Wyndham Lewis and to the ovoids . . . of Brancusi' (*AV[B]*, p. 25). In both versions, *A Vision* seeks to 'thwart' the intellect, to defy, if not to defeat, analysis, incorporating its occidental substructure of doctrine, system and footnotes as a massive apparatus to its Eastern tales. The comedy of Aherne's scholarly frame is reserved for readers of Burton, Clouston or Jacobs, because, just as Yeats's system is set within a pseudo-scholarly frame, so that frame must be read with reference to the wider folkloric debate. Aherne creates fictions as fast as he disavows them.[27] To the reader who views the 'Robartes set' in the context of the *Nights*, the real life of the book seems to have been missed by those who are detained by the question of its biographical origins and the assumption that its fictions are an exotic disguise. The story of the boy who became vizier endorsed for Yeats the virtues of ignoring biographically verifiable fact.[28]

'The Dance of the Four Royal Persons' is a 'wisdom' frame tale. Kusta ben Luka fulfils the role accorded to such men in *The Seven Sages*[29], *The Ten Wazirs* and, oldest of all, the *Panchatantra* (which Yeats owned, certainly from 1932 onwards). Further, it explores an Arabesque duality in its conception of reality as 'a congeries of beings' and as 'a single being' which human reason, 'subject always to one or the other [conception], cannot reconcile' (*Ex*, p. 305). It borrows from the *Nights* a witnessing and recording system for its cavalcade of human types.

It surely follows that we can indeed read *A Vision* both as Menippean *satura* (as Korkowski suggests), and as an encyclopaedic romance of infinite (and therefore comic) possibility, as a cycle of incarnations. The book for the moment all but realised, his imagination dwelling upon a copy of the Mardrus and Mathers *Nights*, Yeats offers in his dedication an extraordinary meditation.

A 'new intensity' has come into 'all visible and tangible things', which is the 'very self' of 'wisdom'. By means of this intensity he can pass easily from his philosophy to its restored mythology, and see into and share the life of things. The 'living world' has become his 'text' (*VP*, p. 324).

> Yesterday when I saw the dry and leafless vineyards at the very edge of the motionless sea . . . or felt the warm sunlight falling between blue and blue, I murmured, as I have countless times, 'I have been part of it always and there is maybe no escape, forgetting and returning life after life like an insect in the roots of the grass.' But murmured it without terror, in exultation almost.   (*AV[A]*, p. xiii)

Working in a wisdom tradition to place a finite shape upon an infinity of potential experience, *A Vision* is encyclopaedic, its 'limitlessness' springing from what Katharine Slater Gittes calls 'the most unusual feature of the medieval frame narrative – open-endedness'.[30] The content of Yeats's 'multitudinous' vision determines not only the structural conventions of *A Vision*, but also those of the whole 'Robartes set' of informing (and yet ultimately dependent) fictions.[31] Once the presence of the *Nights* has been detected as the acroamatical basis for the mode of the frame tales and its *cante-fable* structure, one sees traces of its philosophy everywhere in its structure. Robartes is not so much an absent witness as a departed djinn, who leaves Yeats and Aherne to 'thwart the intellect' by presenting differing accounts to the reader as if to kadi or caliph. Yet Yeats's name is on the title page; so, remarkably, are those of Kusta ben Luka and Giraldus. Yeats's face stares at us from the Dulac portrait, ostensibly a mediaeval woodcut of Giraldus from the *Speculum*. Illusion is created only to be broken.

In the outermost frame, the dedication to 'Vestigia', Yeats emphasises the spiritual quest of their shared youth, laying out clearly the beliefs upon which the whole testimony will be based. '[T]ruth cannot be discovered but may be revealed.'[32] Such a belief has been expressed in 'a phantasy that has been handed down for generations . . . now an interpretation, now an enlargement of the folk-lore of the villages' (*AV[A]*, p. xi). The practical object Yeats sets himself is the creation of 'a system of thought that would leave my imagination free to create . . . and yet make all that it created . . . part of the one history, and that the soul's. . . . What I have found is indeed nothing new . . . but . . . I am the first to substitute for Biblical or mythological figures, historical movements and actual men and women' (pp. xi–xii).

Yeats's proudest boast is of the poetry the system 'seems to have made possible', but, besides the realisation which comes with the force of a mystical vision that 'I have been part of it always', there is also the hope that 'the curtain may ring up on a new drama' if Yeats's old fellow students will 'master what is most abstract' (p. xii). This outermost frame is itself a wisdom frame, and yet but a testament in some larger cycle of testimonies from 'the folk-lore of the villages'. So it is quite unexceptional to pass from this level into Aherne's scholarly delving among discarded fictions of the 1890s, and his treatment of Robartes as if he were 'already a part of history' (p. xxiii). Displaced, 'The Dance of the Four Royal Persons' then gratifies the curiosity aroused by the poem and section title which precede it[33] and we are ready for the intricately sectioned doctrine of 'The Great Wheel'. Each of its twenty-eight embodiments is an abstract of a complete life or lives. All phasal types, incarnate and discarnate, are represented. Forty-eight named witnesses are called, plus 'many beautiful women', 'an unnamed friend', 'the idiot of Dostoieffsky perhaps' and others, before we return to the level of the tale which encloses the entire section. Since all of this lore (and its laws) are what the Caliph 'partly learned', this section and its successor 'What the Caliph Refused to Learn', emerge as huge, disguised, occidental footnotes. In this section Yeats summons more witnesses, and with its taxing jargon of tinctures, Will, Mask, Creative Mind and Body of Fate (functioning as a new expression of Allah's will), its 'dangling categories'[34] and the rest, we feel that the Caliph has had a long and difficult dīwan. Narrative design and scholarly designs run a parallel course here: the abstract is partially embodied. 'Expression' is for Yeats a part of 'study' (*L*, p. 922). Equally, history becomes myth as the 'real men and women' are stylised into essences and take their place alongside characters drawn from the Tarot, from literature and legend. The sections hover between abstract outline and historical drama as Yeats passes some sort of Last Judgment upon his own inner world. The sudden endnote, 'Finished at Thoor, Ballylee, 1922, in a time of Civil War' (*sic*) (*AV[A]*, p. 117) disturbs the hierarchy of enclosing sections of the volume, and brings us by a 'strange loop'[35] back to the outermost frame. The device distances the reader, and reminds him that the whole 'congeries' of beings he has had placed before him is but the contents of one mind, one man's tale.

Book II is of similar pattern. The Caliph refuses to learn that which is first imaged in 'Desert Geometry or The Gift of Harun Al-Raschid'. Graham Hough argues that the solid geometry of 'gyres and cubes and midnight things' is all too much and he endorses the judgment of the Caliph.[36] Baroque, complex and proliferating, the symbolisms of this section are cut back in *A Vision [B]*, but what the Caliph cannot learn is *in fine* a theory of history which ends with a prophecy:

> A woman's beauty is a storm-tossed banner;
> Under it wisdom stands, and I alone –
> . . . Nor dazzled by the embroidery, nor lost
> In the confusion of its night-dark folds,
> Can hear the armed man speak.[37]

The Caliph is dazzled and lost; yet, while much is bewilderingly abstract, and much is unembodied, the section does adumbrate a world view which would seem to excuse, if it does not quite justify, the 'night-dark' intricacies of doctrine. A Caliph who would be 'never astonished again' must learn that

> there can be no philosophy, nation or movement that is not a being or congeries of beings, and that which we call the proof of some philosophy is but that which enables it to be born. The world is a drama where person follows person, and though the dialogue prepares for all the entrances, that preparation is not the person's proof, nor is Polonius disproved when Hamlet seems to kill him. Once the philosophy, nation or movement has clearly shown its face, we know that its chief characteristic has not arisen out of any proof, or even out of . . . any visible cause whatever, but is unique, life in itself. There can be neither cause nor effect when all things are co-eternal.
>
> (*AV[A]*, pp. 171–2).

Owen Aherne is silent throughout book II, while Yeats draws out (somewhat spectacularly and indulgently) this central metaphor of *Theatrum Mundi*.[38] The title is not only a self-criticism; for we have been warned in the dedication that this particular section is not for those who 'come to this book through some interest in my poetry alone' (AV[A], p. xii). The title therefore reflects also upon a Caliph who sought perhaps some 'unexplained rule of thumb' (AV[B], p. 81) rather than necessarily complex wisdom.

In books III and IV the frame of 'The Dance of the Four Royal Persons' is ostensibly abandoned: here A Vision [A] is inconsistently structured. Fleeting echoes of the story remain, so that the overall design is subliminally recalled in the dance of King and Queen, Sun and Moon (AV[A], p. 182 and n.).[39] Other patternings are indicated: the period before Christ is contrasted with the future. In the former 'myth becomes a biography' (p. 185) while in the latter 'history [has] grown symbolic, the biography [has] changed into a myth' (p. 214).

Moving forward in time, Yeats places the Baghdad Caliphate in the system not in the ninth century, but in what Yeats imagines to be the period of its chronicling, in the later Middle Ages. A diametric opposition between the Caliphate and Byzantine Christianity gives shape and vividness here, and Yeats chooses one passage of the Nights to stand for the Caliphate:

> Harun Al-Raschid looked at the singer Heart's Miracle, and on the instant loved her . . . [and] covered her head with a little silk veil to show that her beauty 'had already retreated into the mystery of our faith'. (AV[A], p. 197)

Heart's Miracle, 'Lieutenant of the Birds and queen of all earthly lute players' (M&M, IV, 430–73 [468]), recalls the guitar player of 'Discoveries' (1907; E&I, pp. 268–70), and therefore Yeats's early aesthetic. Here, she symbolises the origin of Romance as a genre, because she represents a beauty 'which [is] its own sanctity' (AV[A], p. 197).

Displacing the Caliphate from its historical to its symbolical period also enables Yeats to compare it to 'the Homeric period some two thousand years before' (AV[A], p. 198). Romance corresponds for him with Romanesque architecture of 'overflowing ornament . . . where all is more Asiatic than Byzantium itself' (p. 198). The tale of Heart's Miracle has been somewhat 'bent' to fit the system here, for the mystery of the faith into which she retreats is less the expression of the sanctity of her own beauty than it is of the Caliph's power. Mardrus and Mathers actually wrote,

The Khalīfah rose from his throne and, going down to the girl, very gently returned the little silk veil to her face, as a sign that she belonged to his harim, and that the fairness of her had already retreated into the mystery of our Faith.   (iv, 440)

Two further points remain about book iii. Again it returns to a date and place (see n. 31) in order to bring the reader back to the outermost frame of the book, which is Yeats brooding at Capri. The second is that just as the *Nights* as acroamatic substratum now contain the system as footnotes to Yeats's new tales, 'The Gift of Harun Al-Rashid' and 'The Dance of the Four Royal Persons', so the system as historical schema now contains the *Nights*, as represented by Heart's Miracle. There is more than an echo of the problem of the 602nd night here, but Yeats, 'absorbed in drama' (*E&I*, p. 443), is undetained by it.

Book iv is another long movement of Yeats's own thought, which functions as a footnote to book ii, just as book iii can be seen as an addendum to book i. Each comments upon aspects of doctrine a caliph may have become bored by. 'The Fool by the Roadside', which begins book iv, brings us back to the personal gyres of reincarnation, 'forgetting and returning life after life', but with the emphasis upon forgetting inside 'The Gates of Pluto'. Aherne returns with footnotes when Yeats discusses beatitude, linking Yeats's redaction of Robartes' doctrines to those of the Syrian Gnostic Bardesanes. Again the book returns to the outermost frame, this time to Syracuse. Yet the last pages contain a reverie which significantly amplifies and qualifies the solipsism of 'All Souls' Night' with which the whole volume ends, so that, if Yeats seems in this final closure to be 'wound in mind's wandering' until he needs 'no other thing', then at least we are aware of the immensity of his inner possessions. Significantly headed 'Mythology', this last reverie runs,

A book of modern philosophy may prove to our logical capacity that there is a transcendental portion of our being that is . . . immortal, and yet our imagination remain subjected to nature as before. The great books . . . beget new books, but life goes on unchanged. It was not so with ancient philosophy. . . . That we may believe that all men possess the supernatural faculties I would restore to the philosopher his mythology.

(*AV[A]*, pp. 251–2)

That Yeats should do his thinking on such a stage in eternity, seeing the life of even modern books as a process parallel to that of natural reproduction, is a startling enough vision. It is even more remarkable that he should so consciously opt for fictional enclosure to inaugurate his grand restoration of mythology to philosophy. His doctrine stands in a dependent relation to his pastiche *Arabian Nights* tales, which themselves depend upon the *Nights*, and upon some further fictions concerning the origins of the book the reader holds in his hands. Doctrine then is wrapped in fiction, fiction in fable, and fable, of course, in ultimate structure. How this helps us understand the doctrine is a question to which the following is a tentative answer.

Theatrum Mundi, Yeats's underlying metaphor, is expressed in two ways. The system gives it abstract expression, while the fictions and narrative reveries, such as the twenty-eight embodiments and the historical survey and the section upon life after death, give it concrete, but not dramatic, embodiment. *A Vision* remains in perpetuity a potential drama. Its realisation would be all history, and all personality, considered from every perspective. Considered as a scenario for 'what is past, passing and to come', and one for which the chief structural principle is enclosing narrative, it can be viewed in a way which reconciles the rival readings currently advanced for it,[40] including that which sees the book as the exoteric expression of an unpublished private philosophy.

Yeats's private philosophy finally envisaged death as a series of judgements passed upon experience and culminating in the dissolution of all sensuous images and the soul's final reunion with 'pure unified experience' (*L*, 916–17). *A Vision* conceals such a doctrine in something 'like an old faery tale'.[41] It is a series of provisional statements, and if accepted as such ceases to trouble the reader who anxiously seeks some overall key. He may even come to marvel the more at the mythology being built up from each new deposition. The *Nights* provided the model for such pattern formation, which links the system to its embodiment via codified experience. Neither wholly theoretical nor wholly symbolical, but endlessly[42] reforming itself in 'ghostly paradigms', *A Vision* is a far less abstract book than is usually thought.

III

A Vision [B] (1937), apparently dismantles much of the fictive structure of its predecessor. It is more accurate, perhaps, to argue that Yeats adds to the fictions in substance, while himself deconstructing them, for, far from loosening the connection with the *Nights*, he strengthens it and subtilises it. The understatement of detail, the seeming off-handedness of the narrative and the increased strategies of disavowal show not embarrassment with the earlier fictions of *A Vision [A]*, as Yeats pretends, but a deeper commitment and one of a different kind. In the *Stories of Michael Robartes and his Friends: An Extract from a Record Made by his Pupils* (hereafter the *Stories*), Yeats moves from imitative pastiche of the *Nights* into modern – even Modernist – *hommage*. He relies even more heavily upon their being read as dependent fictions, and on the whole this dimension has been missed, even when their framing function has been noted.[43]

A Vision [A] filled Yeats 'with shame' (*AV[B]*, p. 19). On the whole his geometrical and philosophical reasons do not concern us,[44] but he was also disarming about its fictions.

> [A]s my wife was unwilling that her share should be known, and I to seem sole author, I had invented an unnatural story of an Arabian traveller which I must amend and find a place for some day because I was fool enough to write half a dozen poems that are unintelligible without it.   (p. 19)

The statement is disingenuous. The Mardrus and Mathers version of the *Nights* had given Yeats a new interest in their style, and possibly even after *A Vision [B]* was published he might have been still writing Robartes stories. It is worth asking if the relation between the Robartes stories and this version's doctrine is similar to that between the stories and the first version's doctrine.

The forematter is entitled *A Packet for Ezra Pound* and is a revision of a book of the same title published by the Cuala Press in 1929. A sketch of life at Rapallo with Pound is followed by 'Introduction to "A Vision"',[45] a letter to Pound and Yeats's transcription of Pound's 'The Return'. *A Packet* was a self-conscious book, and an epigraph from *A Tale of a Tub* reveals Yeats's time-gaining intention: 'This way of publishing introductions to books, that are God knows when to come out, is either wholly new, or so long in practice that

my small reading cannot trace it' (AV[B], p. 8). Yet the quotation
may have a new relevance on its reappearance in the 1937 text.
The agglomeration of discretely published sections seems casual
and even arbitrary by comparison with the fake-scholarly A Vision
[A]. Yet a A Vision [B] is thus the more convincing witness to the
truth that books record the process of their own creation. Yeats in
fact seems relieved by the sense that no final testament or doctrine
is possible or indeed concomitant with life itself. A Vision [B] is
therefore the 'moving image' of a dynamic or vitalist cosmo-
conception, and arguments about whether its form is or is not
'organic'[46] must engage this 'multitudinousness' of form and
philosophy. Like the Nights, A Vision [B] is a composite work of
art: yet unlike them it is by one author.[47]

Yeats said that his system enabled him to 'hold in a single
thought reality and justice'.[48] The buried allusion to Blake's

> Every Time less than a pulsation of the artery
> Is equal in its period & value to Six Thousand Years,
> For in this Period the Poet's Work is Done, and all the Great
> Events of Time start forth & are conceiv'd in such a Period,
> Within a Moment . . .[49]

alerts us to the ways in which the flux of thought defeats the
finality of print. It was some such conception that lay at the heart
of Yeats's new design.

Perhaps A Vision [A] had come to seem the teaching of that
'unexplained rule of thumb'; perhaps wisdom seemed to have
retreated before its onslaught. In A Vision [B] a deeper relation
between mythology, and philosophy is essayed to show the
'multitudinousness' (VPl, pp. 932–3) of even a single thought: the
'wheel is every completed movement of thought or life . . . a single
judgment or act of thought' (AV[B], p. 81). A pluralistic shape (and
title) had been allowed by the prospect of a new de luxe edition of
Yeats's works in 1930: Discoveries (as A Vision was to have been
called) was but one of several plural titles in the series.[50]

So A Packet, with its introduction to an introduction to an as yet
unwritten book, becomes in itself the introduction to the published
book. Preserving in its own dated layers a manifold story, this
little congeries has at its heart the 'incredible experience' of the
marriage and the automatic writing in Ashdown Forest. It proceeds
to a final defence of enclosing structures for the externalising of

an 'arbitrary, harsh, and difficult symbolism'. 'One remem-
bers . . . the diagrams in Law's *Boehme*, where one lifts a flap
of paper to discover both the human entrails and the starry
heavens . . .' (*AV[B]*, pp. 23–4). *A Packet* is so convincing an
introduction for the 'hard symbolic bones' of the system because
by means of it they are embodied in the strangest of all marriage
tales. Although the tale of Yeats and *his* Shahrazād displaces 'The
Gift of Harun Al-Rashid' from *A Vision [B]*, it but confirms the
poem's miracle. It is a 'true' tale which overwhelms the reader
with 'miracle'. Its author describes his blessed state which succeeds
its completion, in which the 'mountain road . . . seems like something in my own mind, something I have discovered' (*AV[B]*, p. 7).
To Pound he promises that the completed book will 'proclaim a
new divinity' (p. 27).

Suddenly a complete disjunction of method appears. '[T]he new
version of the Robartes stories', Yeats told Olivia Shakespear,
would invest Michael Robartes with 'an energy and a dogmatism
and a cruelty' of which Yeats felt himself incapable in his 'own
person'. Such he felt were appropriate for discussing the deductions
he saw as following from the proof of 'the immortality of the soul'
(*L*, p. 768). These new features are deployed in the style, the
abrupt transitions and narrative enclosures of the *Stories*. Finished
and published by All Hallows, 1931, they were augmented before
1937[51] by the addition of Denise de L'Isle Adam's story, the
frankest piece of writing in the volume. As that piece is essentially
indistinguishable in other respects from the 1931 stories, certain
passages from Yeats's letters of 1935 may be safely applied to the
Stories.

> The best Arabian Nights, and even certain parts of Balzac have
> as little psychology as [the birds I observe] eating bread on the
> windowsill.   (*LMR*, p. 37)

> Our traditions only permit us to bless, for the arts are an
> extension of the beatitudes. Blessed be heroic death (Shake-
> speare's tragedies), blessed be heroic life (Cervantes), blessed be
> the wise (Balzac). Then there is a still more convincing reason
> why we should not admit propaganda into our lives. I shall
> write it out in the style of *The Arabian Nights* (which I am reading
> daily). There are three very important persons (1) a man playing
> the flute (2) a man carving a statue (3) a man in a woman's arms.

Goethe[52] said we must renounce, and I think propaganda – I wish I had thought of this when I was young – is among the things they thus renounce. . . . I have found a quotation[53] in the Powys Mathers translation . . . which would serve for a motto to . . . a book on the education of children. . . . Sherazada tells her king that she is about to tell three anecdotes which she thinks moral but others think profligate. The king suggests that they send away her little sister who is playing among the cushions. 'No,' says Sherazada, 'it is not shameful to talk of the things that lie beneath our belts.' (*L*, p. 832).

Shakespeare, Balzac, the *Nights* and the rest were 'serious literature' (*L*, pp. 832–3) for those whose 'passion is reality' (*Myth*, p. 331). Each of the cited works was valued for its encyclopaedic quality. When asked about books, Yeats replied in terms profoundly selective and yet profoundly inclusive:

'Lionel Johnson held that a man should have read through all good books before he was forty and after that be satisfied with six.' . . . I said I wanted six authors not six books. . . . 'First comes Shakespeare,' I said. 'Then the *Arabian Nights* in its latest English version, then William Morris, who gives me all the great stories, Homer and the Sagas included, then Balzac, who saved me from Jacobin and Jacobite.' (*E&I*, p. 447)

A desire for 'all the great stories' was neither new in 1934, nor remote from Yeats's own aims as a writer of fictions.[54] That passion for reality, for energy, dogmatism, even cruelty of style resulted in an imitation not only of the *Nights* but also of the 'Western Thousand and One Nights'.[55] The much-admired *Les Comédiens sans le savoir*[56] lies behind the abrupt transitions of Yeats's *Stories*, and, in the edition in which Yeats read the story, George Saintsbury had even commented upon the agreeably *'Arabian Nightish'* quality of it.

Mr Stevenson took his idea of *New Arabian Nights* from Balzac . . . and I do not know that Balzac himself was ever happier in his 'Parisian Nights', as we may call them, than here. The artists and the actresses . . . and all the rest, appear and disappear in an easy phantasmagoric fashion . . . there is nothing so good as a fairy tale.[57]

The passion for reality demanded not realism, but its opposite, a fictional form in which the characters were the 'unconscious mummers' of some greater drama: in Yeats's system all 'actual men and women' are *dramatis personæ*. Unflinching expression of the system's geomantic prognostications was also demanded.

> Dear predatory birds, prepare for war. . . . Test art, morality, custom, thought, by Thermopylae; make rich and poor act so to one another that they can stand together there. Love war because of its horror, that belief may be changed, civilisation renewed. We desire belief and lack it. Belief comes from shock and is not desired. . . . Belief is renewed continually in the ordeal of death.   (*AV[B]*, pp. 52–3)

Robartes departs for the desert with Aherne and Mary Bell to hatch the third egg of Leda, and thereby usher in the new dispensation. His sect believes that civilisations do not end, but are transformed, just as the soul survives the body (p. 50). Robartes never reveals to us his proofs of these doctrines, except via his extraordinary ability to foretell the immediate future of each of his followers, which gift is utilised to bring them all to his caravanserai and temporary academy in Regents Park. There, they are commanded to tell each other their stories, and these enfolded narrative depositions serve to prove Michael Robartes' gifts to each of them and to the reader. Daniel O'Leary's apparently spontaneous protest at the theatre has either been foreseen[58] (or mysteriously instigated) by Robartes. O'Leary (and each of the others) becomes the unconscious mummer of Robartes' will. The jerkiness[59] of the plot illustrates this sense of a higher understanding of destiny than can be found in either the lesser characters or the reader. The same magus-like powers had been in evidence in the occult romances of the nineties, in which Robartes and his order sought a control over others which they could not finally implement over the unnamed narrator: nothing indeed, has changed but the style, and stylistic change, as is vigorously pointed out in John Aherne's document which concludes the *Stories*, is but a small manifestation of the necessity of alternation in eras or dispensations.

John Aherne, by reiteration and disavowal, manages to unify restrospectively the entire 'Robartes set', from the nineties romances, through the various poems and plays and notes, the now discredited stories of *A Vision [A]*. Aherne manages to make all of this material part of the same narrative: self-swallowing is the principle by which the set propagates itself.

The Stories open with a poem which shows Yeats engaged in the spendthrift invention of new characters. His personal testament involves cheerful manufacture:

> Huddon, Duddon and Daniel O'Leary
> Delighted me as a child.[60]
> I put three persons in their place
> That despair and keep the pace
> And love wench Wisdom's cruel face . . .
> Hard-living men and men of thought
> Burn their bodies up for nought,
> I mock at all so burning out.
>   (AV[B], p. 32)

'Burning out' is of course the master trope of stories and doctrine, the approaching transformation of civilisation at the end of the age. It is used in several places (pp. 16, 50, 55), to cover every aspect of the expiring age, even down to its prose style. It will be asked whether in the hierarchy of A Vision [B]'s ordering Yeats stands outside these tales in unchallenged supremacy as their creator. The hierarchy is thoroughly tangled, so that the Stories do not provide a neat closed box for the doctrine of A Vision which follows. Yeats is both author and something of a character. Although he does not appear in any of the travellers' tales, it is clear from John Aherne's concluding letter to him that he is in effect an estranged fellow student of the 'real' Robartes and that the former appearance of Robartes and Aherne in Yeats's stories was a crude fiction on Yeats's part. Such disclaimers extend fiction rather than merely disavow it. In their midst, the portait of Giraldus by Dulac stares out at us with Yeats's eyes, as a glaring icon of his existence inside and outside his texts.

The severe economy of the tales makes them impossible to précis. They accommodate doctrine and plot formidably: Yeats establishing via his narrator, or recorder, John Duddon, that appreciation of the record of this esoteric group is of necessity dependent upon possession of various other stories. Placed in this penumbra is Axël: Denise de L'Isle Adam's story of her life requires that we know that play. Huddon, Duddon and O'Leary recall a fairy tale; John Bond and Mary Bell recall two nearly eponymous poems of

Blake.[61] When Denise's 'full and admirable' tale – the forecommen-
dation is Robartes', but might well be Dunyazād's – is over,
Robartes' peroration begins. It places the history of Leda's third
egg in a few sentences of now specific, now unspecific detail.
These details gesture back (and so retrospectively unify) Yeats's
Harun al-Rashid story. The egg 'was for a time in the treasury of
Harun al-Rashid', just as Kusta ben Luka's letter was. By such
means Robartes links his doctrine not only to Yeats's previous
thought, but also to most of the mythology and folklore Yeats
himself has used for the authority he has conferred upon his
doctrines.

> 'I bought it from an old man in a green turban at Teheran; it
> had come down from eldest son to eldest son for many gener-
> ations.' 'No,' said Aherne, 'you were never in Teheran.' 'Perhaps
> Aherne is right,' said Robartes. 'Sometimes my dreams discover
> facts, and sometimes lose them, but it does not matter. I bought
> this egg from an old man in a green turban in Arabia, or Persia,
> or India. He told me its history, partly handed down by word
> of mouth, partly as he had discovered it in ancient manuscripts.
> It was for a time in the treasury of Harun Al-Rashid and
> had come there from Byzantium. . . . Its history before that is
> unimportant for some centuries. During the reign of the Anton-
> ines tourists saw it hanging by a golden chain from the roof of a
> Spartan temple.   (*AV[B]*, p. 51)

The 'sometimes eloquent, often obscure' discourse on the Judwalis
and Giraldus is summarised here, but even small references
are enough to revivify the doctrine in the reader's mind. The
endorsement of war as providing the renewal of belief is given
before riddle and incoherence close John Duddon's record. But the
whole of the five doctrinal books depends from these two pages,
and from John Aherne's closing letter, like long footnotes. The
Stories (including John Aherne's letter) therefore stands in the same
relation to the doctrinal sections of *A Vision [B]* as does 'The Dance
of the Four Royal Persons' to the doctrine of *A Vision [A]*. It is
usually said that the *Stories* are a new version of Owen Aherne's
Introduction to *A Vision [A]*, but, while this is true of their
substance, it is not true of their framing function. In the earlier
volume, the Robartes material frames 'The Dance of the Four Royal
Persons', which open-endedly frames the first two doctrinal books,

'What the Caliph Partly Learned' and 'What the Caliph Refused to Learn'. With a greater sense of design and economy, Yeats now has all his doctrinal books depend as occidental documentary glosses to the *Stories*. Yeats is no longer the *redacteur* of Robartes' doctrine, but the conveyor of a system ascribed unequivocally to his wife's mediumship. John Aherne, interested but not astonished by Yeats's work, can find 'no essential difference' between it and the records of the Robartes sect, which he may someday publish (*AV[B]*, pp. 53–5). What now is the relation of Yeats and Robartes?

John Aherne is an honest broker, and his invention, or his employment by Yeats at this juncture, is a masterstoke of tidying-up. He first appeared, seemingly by accident, in the 1919 preface to *The Wild Swans at Coole*,[62] probably as a slip for Owen Aherne. His invention soon proved useful, for he can intervene between the 'reinvented' Robartes and Aherne, and Yeats-as-character in his own fictions. Indeed this neutral brother accounts for the whole matter of this independent reality of Yeats inside his own tales,[63] his poems and stories about Robartes, his miraculous draught of doctrine. Yeats himself becomes one of the unconscious mummers. Subsequently he thought of making this connection between himself and his characters even closer.[64] But, since the doctrine that Yeats and his wife externalise is broadly comparable in John Aherne's judgement to that Robartes, we are left (at this stage) to infer that he is just another, estranged and rather brighter fellow student. His 'Packet' of doctrine therefore just takes its place in the heap of depositions. Hierarchy, threatened by the invention of which the introductory poem has seemed to be evidence – 'I put three persons in their place' – is not toppled and we can read the line not as declared invention but as the admitted substitution of reality for legend. But such is perhaps a provisional reassurance.

Another improvement over *A Vision [A]* is that now there is no hierarchical break between the various books of the system. Gone, too, are Aherne's qualifying footnotes. If anything, Aherne's role has been taken over by Frank Pearce Sturm.[65] The result of these two reformulations is that we now have a perfectly self-swallowing set, all of which disappears into the section entitled 'The End of the Cycle', before being re-enclosed into the reverie 'All Souls' Night'. This is in a sense the 602nd night of the whole book: the whole work, fictions, system and all, is swallowed back into Yeats's testimony, itself but a contribution to some total book.

Thus the personal shape of *A Vision [B]*, which seems to shrink the claims of the work, in fact enlarges them. The 'congeries' of reality is a huge text; equally it is one man's testimony which endeavours to swallow that text. Yeats's own metaphor for self-swallowing may well be that great 'egg that turns inside-out perpetually without breaking its shell' (AV[B], p. 33), with which Robartes liked to tease his students.[66] Yeats's testimony frames the Stories, while the Stories apparently underpin that frame independently, drawing together and hierarchically rearranging all that remains of Yeats's previous and temporary efforts to make sense of his miraculous experience through his wife's mediumship. The Stories are the key to all previous sets, and that rearrangement which is forced upon all of Yeats's previous work forces us to read A Vision in the context of that work, rather than to use it merely as an 'unexplained rule of thumb', a key to all that work.

The suggestion that the Stories replace 'The Dance of the Four Royal Persons' offers further implications. Moving from pastiche of the Nights to hommage, Yeats places himself in the position formerly held by Kusta ben Luka, wise man and geomancer. Robartes, mage and prophet, now occupies the position formerly held by Giraldus. Both Giraldus and Kusta ben Luka move into a penumbra of folklore, always at hand, always recoverable. They too assume a 'chief place in the story'. The dancers are replaced by Robartes' pupils, all named from literature as legend, all moving to his tune, carrying out his 'whim, or fancy, or creative vision'.[67] To reject readings of 'The Dance of the Four Royal Persons' as parable involves setting the characters in all of these fictions into a more multitudinous patterning than is accountable to biographical allegory.[68] Thus 'The Gift of Harun Al-Rashid' was surely not dropped from A Vision [B] solely for biographical reasons, nor even necessarily for aesthetic ones. It is simply that the poem, along with the rest of the Kusta ben Luka material, is always recoverable as folklore, through the acroamatic reading Yeats forces us to give to A Vision, that is, within the context of the rest of his work.

I now turn briefly to the abandoned Robartes story, before looking at the closing pages of A Vision [B]. 'Michael Robartes Foretells' has occasioned a disagreement between W. K. and C. K. Hood, two textual scholars of A Vision, who dispute[69] its dating. They agree that it cannot, from internal evidence, predate the death of Lady Gregory (May 1932). They disagree about whether 'Michael Robartes Foretells' or Denise de L'Isle Adam's interpolated story is the extra Robartes story referred to in a 1936 letter. Neither, however, asks whether it might have been written subsequently to the publication of *A Vision [B]* for inclusion in *Discoveries* in the delayed 'Edition de Luxe'.[70]

'Michael Robartes Foretells', as W. K. Hood argues, was probably intended (whenever it was written) as a closing frame to the doctrinal sections of *A Vision [B]*. In it, Hudden, Dudden and Denice (*sic*) foregather at Thoor Ballylee seven years after the disappearance of Robartes and the others to the East to hatch Leda's egg. The connection of the group with Yeats is thus tightened by the choice of locale. O'Leary consults some notes of Robartes' conversations, made before the retreat to Arabia. The notes indicate what Robartes and his pupils 'might safely prophesy' (*YO*, p. 220) concerning the next cycle. The prophecies follow. Robartes has been non-commital: 'he made them up while talking and didn't know whether they were true or not: he knew nothing of the next cycle except that it would be the reverse of ours'. Such a disappointment is an extraordinarily rich fictive device, allowing as it does for Winters' 'formula of alternate possibilities'[71] and what I have called the formula of reunification by disavowal. W. K. Hood's thesis is that 'Michael Robartes Foretells'

> would, therefore, have framed *A Vision* within the fiction, and the intervention of the text of *A Vision* would have suggested the passage of seven years after Robartes' departure. Most important, . . . [it] would have suited the prophetic tone and content of the historical section, 'Dove or Swan'. . . . Possibly, then, [it] . . . was one of Yeats's attempts to deal with the future; it would have had the advantage (which Yeats specified in a letter) of allowing the rather harsh prophecy to come from the persona of Robartes rather than from Yeats himself.
>
> (*YO*, pp. 216–17)

This is a reasonable point, but there are also good reasons for seeing 'Michael Robartes Foretells' as a conventional, rather than a self-swallowing, framing device. As such, it would have been an inferior conclusion to that provided by 'The End of the Cycle'. The *Stories of Michael Robartes and his Friends* provide an open inner frame for the five books of doctrine, and 'The End of the Cycle' and 'All Souls' Night' provide a return to the outermost frame of Yeats's reverie. 'The End of the Cycle' is Yeats's meditation on the system, his system. In *A Vision [A]* it had been Robartes' system, though mediated by Yeats. Now 'The End of the Cycle' is as much self-critique (a mode in which Yeats is usually very convincing) as reverie. It briefly considers not prophecies, but the impossibility of prophesying, and it ends in frustration.

> Then I draw myself up into the symbol and it seems as if I should know all if I could but . . . find everything in the symbol. . . . But nothing comes – though perhaps this moment was to reward me for all my toil. Perhaps I am too old. Surely something would have come when I meditated under the direction of the Cabalists. . . . How work out upon the phases the gradual coming and increase of the counter-movement, the *antithetical* multiform influx.   (*AV[B]*, pp. 301–2)

Here too, of course, is a dependent text. The 'Arabian host' of 'The Gift of Harun Al-Rashid' has been replaced by something European and everyday.

> What discords will drive Europe to that artificial unity – only dry or drying sticks can be tied into a bundle – which is the decadence of every civilisation? . . .
> Then I understand. I have already said all that can be said. The particulars are the work of the *Thirteenth Cone* or cycle, which is in every man and called by every man his freedom. Doubtless for it can do all things and knows all things, it knows what it will do with its own freedom but it has kept the secret.   (Ibid.)

A brief coda leads in to the closing riddling questions, the method becoming more inscrutable still. Then the final enclosure, into 'All Souls' Night', which we read in a new way, as Yeats surely intended. His apocalypse laid at our feet, as it were, history brought down to the present[72] and the future previewed, Yeats himself retreats into this extraordinary poem of solipsism. No conventional fictional framing device would have sufficed: any such would have foreclosed an open future in which Chance and Choice would interact. Here the self is closed, its limits recognised. Chance and Choice remain free.

Just as at the end of 'The Phases of the Moon' the light is snuffed out, all is now swaddled in mind's wandering'. Even Robartes now returns to his origins and re-emerges as plain MacGregor.[73]

Such thought – such thought have I that hold it tight
Till meditation master all its parts,
. . .
Such thought, that in it bound
I need no other thing,
Wound in mind's wandering
As mummies in the mummy-cloth are wound.

(*AV[B]*, p. 305)

Ultimately then, I propose that there is no disjunction between the 'constructed ruin' (*YO*, p. 226) of the 'Robartes set', *A Vision [A]* and *A Vision [B]*. A study of the growth of these fictions demonstrates not only new erections on old foundations, but also the paradoxical progressive distancing of new fictions from old, which the more closely reunites old and new in a larger fictional structure. Such a perspective is only available to the student who will see that *A Vision* demands to be read acroamatically, and not as a tractate or an instruction manual. Such a view of it as a continually evolving book,[74] a 'moving image' of its author's developing thought, helps us understand the riddles of that conclusion, partly quoted above.

'Man can embody[75] truth but he cannot know it' (*L*, p. 922) is the ultimate apprehension of the unconscious mummer. Yeats accepts that a limited cosmo-conception is all that is his due as a character in a congeries of texts. Ellmann and Hough[76] reply to the charge that Yeats's system is deterministic, seeing that the 'doctrine of the Thirteenth Cone was to make the will even more free'. We may add to this that it does so by positing the infinitude of the scenario in which any particular will operates, and the limitation of its own perspective upon that scenario. 'The End of the Cycle', then, symbolises in that 'Thirteenth Cone' that the drama that men write and in which they are written is not wholly knowable. It is Yeats's way of saying, 'But Allah knows All'.

NOTES

Books published in London unless otherwise stated. Wherever possible, page references to various standard works identified in notes 1, 3, 4 below are given in the text, identified by the abbreviations specified there.

1. *The Book of the Thousand Nights and One Night*, rendered into English from the literal and complete French translation of Dr J. C. Mardrus by Powys Mathers (Casanova Society, 1923) III, 75. Yeats owned this edition, which is henceforth cited as *M&M*. Yeats adopts the motif of writing 'upon the corner of an eye' in 'His Confidence', *The Variorum Edition of the Poems of W. B. Yeats*, ed. Peter Allt and Russell K. Alspach (New York: Macmillan, 4th imprint 1968) pp. 517–18. This edition is henceforth cited as *VP*. References to the standard first editions of the *Arabian Nights* as translated by Burton (Benares: Kamashastra Society, 1885 *et seq.*) and Payne (Villon Society, 1882 *et seq.*) are identified by the abbreviations *B* and *P*, respectively.
2. Suheil Bushrui, 'Yeats's Arabic Interests', in *In Excited Reverie: A Centenary Tribute to William Butler Yeats*, ed. A. Norman Jeffares and K. G. W. Cross (Macmillan, 1965) pp. 280–314. See also Ahmed El-Ghamrawi, *W. B. Yeats and the Culture of the Middle East* (Cairo: Anglo-Egyptian Bookshop, n.d.).
3. Michael J. Sidnell, 'Mr Yeats, Michael Robartes and their Circle', in *Yeats and the Occult*, ed. George Mills Harper (Toronto: Macmillan, 1975) pp. 225–54. See p. 226. This volume is henceforth cited as *YO*.
4. References to other standard works by Yeats will be cited in the text using the following abbreviations: *AV[A]* for *A Critical Edition of Yeats's 'A Vision' (1925)*, ed. George Mills Harper and Walter Kelly Hood (Macmillan, 1978); *AV[B]* for *A Vision* (Macmillan, 1937, repr. 1962); *Au* for *Autobiographies* (Macmillan, 1955); *E&I* for *Essays and Introductions* (Macmillan, 1961); *Ex* for *Explorations*, selected by Mrs Yeats (Macmillan, 1962); *Myth* for *Mythologies* (Macmillan, 1959); *L* for *The Letters of W. B. Yeats*, ed. Allan Wade (Rupert Hart-Davis, 1954); *UP2* for *Uncollected Prose by W. B. Yeats*, collected and edited by John P. Frayne and Colton Johnson, vol. 2: *Review Articles and other Miscellaneous Prose 1897–1939* (Macmillan, 1975); *VSR* for *The Secret Rose, Stories by Yeats: A Variorum Edition*, ed. Phillip L. Marcus, Warwick Gould and Michael J. Sidnell (Ithaca, NY: Cornell University Press, 1981); *LMR* for *Ah, Sweet Dancer: W. B. Yeats – Margot Ruddock, a Correspondence*, ed. Roger McHugh (Macmillan, 1970); *VPl* for *The Variorum Edition of the Plays of W. B. Yeats*, ed. Russell H. Alspach and Catharine C. Alspach (New York: Macmillan, 1966); *LDW* for *Letters on Poetry from W. B. Yeats to Dorothy Wellesley*, intro. Kathleen Raine (Oxford University Press, 1964); *Y&T* for *Yeats and the Theatre*, ed. Robert O'Driscoll and Lorna Reynolds (Macmillan, 1975).
5. A copy of *Five Favourite Tales from the Arabian Nights in Words of One Syllable*, ed. A. and A. E. Warner (H. K. Lewis, 1871), still in Yeats's library, was inscribed for him by his father. See also El-Ghamrawi, *W. B. Yeats and the Culture of the Middle East*, p. 42.

6. Burton's footnote states that the passage is not in the Macnaghten edition (and is therefore not in *P*, viii). I am grateful to Peter Caracciolo for tracing this fugitive reference.
7. Jorge Luis Borges, *Labyrinths: Selected Stories and Other Writings* (Harmondsworth: Penguin, 1970) p. 34.
8. Yeats's most recent editor treats al-Rashid, Jaffer and others *merely* as historical figures. See W. B. Yeats, *The Poems: A New Edition*, ed. Richard J. Finneran (New York: Macmillan, 1983) p. 689. Sidnell (*YO*, p. 249) finds Stallworthy's reading in part 'ridiculous and unsupportable', but offers an 'allegorical' reading himself. See Jon Stallworthy, *Between the Lines: Yeats's Poetry in the Making* (Oxford: Clarendon Press, 1963) p. 63.
9. Mia Gerhardt, *The Art of Story-Telling: A Literary Study of the Thousand and One Nights* (Leiden: Brill, 1963) p. 93.
10. Frank Kermode, *The Genesis of Secrecy* (Cambridge, Mass.: Harvard University Press, 1979) pp. 81ff, upon 'midrash' which 'entail[s] narrative alterations or interpolations, sometimes very free'. Kusta ben Luka, of course, knowing that he only *has* existence in a text, can foresee such a process as inevitable: the passage is extraordinary in providing evidence of Yeats's intuitive grasp of the implications of his own fictional method. Robert Hampson alerted me to the parallel.
11. Stallworthy, *Between the Lines*, pp. 79–80. The reading does not depend upon Stallworthy's 'allegorical' interpretation of the poem as concealed biography.
12. The shape-changing 'dusky demon' of book ii of 'The Wanderings' (*VP*, 39–40) may well have been drawn from the afrit of the battle in the Second Calender's tale (*B*, i, 134–5).
13. Borges, *Labyrinths*, pp. 84–5, 231. The citation is from Carlyle's essay 'Count Cagliostro', first published in *Fraser's Magazine*, nos 43 and 44 (July, Aug 1833), repr. in *Critical and Miscellaneous Essays*, iii (1857) 250–1. I am grateful to Rosemary Ashton for tracing it for me. Carlyle refers to the 'grand sacred Epos, or Bible of World History, infinite in meaning as the *Divine Mind* it emblems; wherein he that is wise can read a line, and there a line, this same Bible . . . that all men, in all times, with or without clear consciousness, have been unwearied to read, what we may call *read*; and again to write, or rather to be written'.
14. See 'The Tale of the Porter and the Three Young Girls' (*M&M*, i, 68–168) as an example of such self-chronicle.
15. Daniel A. Harris, in 'The "Figured Page": Dramatic Epistle in Browning and Yeats' in *Yeats Annual No. 1*, ed. Richard J. Finneran (Macmillan, 1982) pp. 133–95, finds no reason to mention the *Nights*.
16. J. C. Mardrus courts the 'monstrous' possibility of the 602nd night with this conclusion. See Borges, *Labyrinths*, p. 230 on the problem of that 'night'.
17. See for example 'Zumurrud and Ali Shar' and 'Delilah the Wily' (*M&M*, ii, 362–3, 736). Other sources for Yeats's bride of the poem can be found in 'Sympathy the Learned' (*M&M*, ii, 197–236; also in *B*, v, 189–245, esp. 228–9, where the learned girl recites the twenty-

eight mansions of the moon – the incident is not in M&M). The bride-gift motif can be found in 'Heart's Miracle, Lieutenant of the Birds' (M&M, IV, 430–73), referred to in AV[A], p. 197, and AV[B], p. 286; 'The Arab Girl at the Fountain' (M&M, IV, 698); 'The Tale of Ghanim ibn Ayyub and his Sister Fitnah' (M&M, I, 428–67); and many others.

18. For example, Sidnell (in YO) and Walter Kelly Hood, 'Michael Robartes: Two Occult Manuscripts' (YO, pp. 204–24). Also see William H. O'Donnell, A Guide to the Prose Fiction of W. B. Yeats (Ann Arbor: UMI Research Press, 1983) pp. 139–46; and Connie K. Hood, 'The Remaking of A Vision', in Yeats: An Annual of Critical and Textual Studies, Vol. I, 1983, ed. Richard J. Finneran (Ithaca, NY: Cornell University Press, 1983) 33–67. Steven Helmling, 'Yeats's Esoteric Comedy', Hudson Review, xxx, no. 2 (Summer 1977) 230–46, notes the retention of the 'original, farcical account' and its 'counterposing . . . with the "new" genuine account' (p. 239). Since Hazard Adams' Blake and Yeats: The Contrary Vision (Ithaca, NY: Cornell University Press, 1955), the most suggestive account of the shape of A Vision is that of Eugene Korkowski in 'YEATS' Vision as Philosophic Satura', Eire – Ireland, XII, no. 3 (Fomhar/Autumn 1977) 62–70. Commenting upon A Vision as Menippean satire, Korkowski does not, however, cite the Nights among his many sources, but he concludes,

> Had Yeats even been oblivious of the generic conventions of the Menippean satura, however, he would still have had the same needs, in terms of literary logistics, that the Menippean didascalicists had had. Like them, he must sweeten bitter and difficult learning . . . lend fable to exposition . . . mix prose and verse . . . lull away disbelief through such means as creating imaginary dialogues, and . . . move in very cautiously toward the making of emphatic metaphysical statements. If A Vision is not consciously a Menippean satura, it is nonetheless in what turns out to be the Menippean shape. (p. 70)

19. See infra, p. 271; and cf. YO, pp. 215ff., and C. K. Hood, in Yeats: An Annual . . . 1983, p. 47.

20. The cante-fable structure is consciously imitated, from the Nights especially. Cante-fable structure in the Nights is discussed in Joseph Jacobs, 'Childe Rowland', Folk Lore, II, no. 11 (1891) 182–97 (p. 196). Yeats also sought a design at once abstract yet symbolical; the 'Persian carpet' was one of his own images for such design (VPl, p. 805), ultimately dependent upon both an exterior system and a concrete dramatis personae. Cf. Sidnell, in YO, p. 248. Cante-fable is also the standard form of old Irish poetry.

21. The term is that of Douglas R. Hofstadter, in Gödel, Escher, Bach: An Eternal Golden Braid: A Metaphorical Fugue on Minds and Machines in the Spirit of Lewis Carroll (Brighton: Harvester, 1979) ch. 20. Peter Caracciolo alerted me to the applicability of Hofstadter's terms to this study.

22. Suheil Bushrui (in In Excited Reverie, ed. Jeffares and Cross, pp. 298ff.), explains why Yeats chose Qusṭā ibn-Lūqā (died c. 912–13), doctor and

translator, for his wise man. However, in addition, Qusṭā, who is best known for his *Liber de Differentia Spiritus et Animae* (references to which Yeats may have found in his reading of the Cambridge Neo-Platonists), was alive during the reign of al-Muktadir, wrote a treatise on sand divination, one on 'The Great Astronomical Cones', an introduction to astrology and a work entitled 'The Paradise of History'. Much of this information upon him was not easily available in English until after Yeats had chosen to insert Kusta into his fictions, but may have been conveyed to him by Sir Edward Denison Ross.

23. There are 'surprisingly few clues' to assist the dating of this section of *A Vision* (*AV[A]*, Introduction, p. xxxvi). I am grateful to Professor George Mills Harper for supplying me with relevant copies of manuscripts for inspection.

24. See *YO*, p. 210; *AV[A]*, pp. xxxi–xlix. No stories or supporting fictions with titles such as 'The Holy Women with the Two Kalendars' or 'The Dance of the Eunuch with the Favourite Wife' seem to have survived.

25. Yeats owned a copy of Wyndham Lewis's *The Caliph's Design: Architects! Where is your Vortex?* (The Egoist, 1919), which casually employs an *Arabian Night*-ish frame tale to introduce its theme.

26. The quoted words are a catchphrase of Yeats's: see *LDW*, p. 26; *E&I*, p. 340. The source is *Troilus and Criseyde*, II.18 ('For as myn auctour seyde, so sey I', but there is a striking resonance with the reply of the youth in the story of Wird Khan quoted above, pp. 245–6: 'My father taught it me'.

27. Disclaiming has been commented upon by Helmling (in *Hudson Review*, xxx, no. 2, 239) and Korkowski (in *Eire – Ireland*, xII, no. 3, 64), yet neither sees it as the principle of fictional growth, whereby stories becomes both self-sufficient yet interdependent. For a reading of the story as a 'parable of artistic and intellectual sincerity' see Sidnell, in *YO*, p. 248.

28. See Korkowski, in *Eire – Ireland*, xII, no. 3, 69.

29. Yeats used this as the title of a poem (*VP*, p. 486) and calls 'The Seven Wise Masters' 'that most ancient book of fables' (*UP2*, pp. 334–6).

30. Katharine Slater Gittes, 'The Canterbury Tales and the Arabic Frame Tradition', *PMLA*, xcvIII, no. 2 (Mar 1983) 237–51 (p. 249).

31. See Sidnell, in *YO*, p. 225. The studied dating of the various books of *A Vision [A]* serves the purpose of demonstrating the compilation of a dossier of testimonies. It does not (as Harper and Hood state) tell us very much about the actual dates of composition (*AV[A]*, pp. xxxvi–xxxviii).

32. A variant of this idea is 'man can embody truth but he cannot know it' (*L*, p. 922). Other formulations include 'Man does not perceive the truth in God but God perceives the truth in man', and the Goethean 'Man knows himself by action only, by thought never' (*AV[A]*, p. 80 and n.; *Y&T*, pp. 31, 77).

33. The subdivisions of *AV[A]* are Urizenic, and occasionally awry. The title *A Vision* appears after the fly-title 'Book I' with its epigraph, and the third subsection of this book is headed 'Part I' without being

succeeded by any 'Part II'. I am grateful to Professor Harper for confirming for me that such inconsistencies are probably accidental.

34. Graham Hough, *The Mystery Religion of W. B. Yeats* (Brighton: Harvester, 1983) p. 103. Hough's last chapter is the clearest available commentary upon *A Vision*.

35. Hofstadter, *Gödel, Escher, Bach*, ch. 20, *passim*.

36. Hough, *Mystery Religion*, p. 103.

37. *VP*, 469–70. The last lines recall the terrible vision in 'The Two Lives of Sultan Mahmud' (*M&M*, iv, 21).

38. This metaphor is more fully explored in *AV[B]*, esp. pp. 83–4. See also Ruth Nevo, 'Yeats and Schopenhauer', in *Yeats Annual No. 3*, ed. Warwick Gould (Macmillan, 1985) pp. 15–32).

39. See also 'Under the Round Tower' (*VP*, p. 331).

40. As in Hough, *Mystery Religion*, p. 109 ('an orrery'); Nevo, in *Yeats Annual No. 3* ('theatrum mundi'); Colin McDowell, 'To "Beat upon the Wall": Reading *A Vision*', *Yeats Annual No. 4*, ed. Warwick Gould (Macmillan, 1986) pp. 219–20. Richard Ellmann, *Yeats: The Man and the Masks* (Oxford University Press, 1979) p. xxxvii, discusses Yeats's 'private philosophy'.

41. *L*, p. 917. Needing philosophy, but keeping it out of his work was a maxim for the poet Yeats took from Goethe: see also *E&I*, p. 154; *L*, p. 832 (quoted *infra*, p. 265).

42. In its current annotated edition, *A Vision [A]* has grown by the accretion of scholarly introduction and notes written by two editors, and seems to contain within it a principle of growth.

43. Most critics note it casually. W. K. Hood (in *YO*, p. 215) is a good example of the credence given to Yeats's biographical justifications of the fictions of *AV[A]*.

44. For a representative discussion see however Hough, *Mystery Religion*, pp. 97ff.; C. K. Hood, in *Yeats: An Annual...1983*, pp. 33–67.

45. Entitled in the 1929 volume 'Introduction to the Great Wheel' and preceded by 'Meditations upon Death', which introduces Yeats's multitudinous conception of incarnate and discarnate life.

46. C. K. Hood is unnecessarily detained by this question (in *Yeats: An Annual . . . 1983*, p. 46).

47. Gerhardt, *The Art of Story-Telling*, p. 420 discusses the compositeness of the *Nights* and observes that such a work of art is a 'rather exceptional phenomenon'.

48. In the 1929 version the passage reads, '. . . he has best imagined reality who has best imagined justice'.

49. William Blake, *Complete Writings with Variant Readings*, ed. Geoffrey Keynes (Oxford University Press, 1966 etc.) p. 516. See also *E&I*, p. 172; *VSR*, p. 117.

50. British Library Add. MS 55727 ff. 271–3. The edition was first proposed on 27 December 1930. The other plural volume-titles were *Autobiographies, Mythologies, Essays, Poems* and *Plays*.

51. C. K. Hood, in *Yeats: An Annual . . . 1983*, pp. 47, 60; *L*, p. 859.

52. See *supra*, n. 41.

53. *M&M*, iii, 37–8, 'Moral Anecdotes from the Perfumed Garden'.

54. Owen Aherne had desired to travel 'into many lands, that I may know all accidents and destinies, and when I return, I will write my secret law'. Avatar of the Age of the Holy Spirit, Aherne exactly descries the connection between encyclopaedic compilation and individual self-knowledge, in this story of 1896 (*VSR*, p. 158).
55. Balzac's letter to Eve Hanska, quoted in Norman Denny's translation of André Maurois, *Prometheus: The Life of Balzac* (Harmondsworth: Penguin, 1965) p. 286.
56. See *E&I*, pp. 438–47; *Ex*, pp. 269–72. Yeats would have endorsed Wilde's view that the 'nineteenth century . . . is largely the invention of Balzac. . . . We are merely carrying out, with footnotes and unnecessary additions, the whim or fancy or creative vision of a great novelist' – *The Artist as Critic, Critical Writings of Oscar Wilde*, ed. Richard Ellmann (Allen, 1970) p. 309).
57. *The Unconscious Mummers and other Stories*, tr. Ellen Marriage with a Preface by George Saintsbury (New York: Temple; London: Dent, 1897) p. xii. Yeats's own copy has annotations which reveal something of an obsession with ordering the *Comédie*.
58. Robartes does this by means of visions: the doctrine behind it may be explored in *VSR*, p. 142, and *E&I*, p. 28.
59. Sidnell (in *YO*, pp. 228–30) finds the 'fictive paraphernalia' of *AV[A]* significant, but not 'pervasive' (ibid., p. 247). Noting that these fictions 'gobble up' the earlier versions, he does not see the same principle at work in *AV[B]*. What he sees there as 'rather contrived' (ibid.), I see as wholly contrived. Without the perspective the *Nights* provides he sees the set as abandoned (ibid., p. 249) and unsuccessfully allegorical. O'Donnell sees the fictions as 'nonsequitous, hopelessly disjointed', with 'little merit' beyond 'extravagance' (*Guide to the Prose Fiction*, pp. 138–9).
60. 'Donald and his Neighbours' in *Fairy and Folk Tales of the Irish Peasantry*, which Yeats edited in 1888 (pp. 299–303). His source was *The Royal Hibernian Tales*, via Thackeray's *Irish Sketchbook*. Another recension of the story, in Joseph Jacobs' *Celtic Fairy Tales* (Nutt, 1892) pp. 47–56, employs a motif deriving from the tale of Ali Baba.
61. 'Long John Brown & Little Mary Bell' and 'William Bond', in Blake, *Complete Writings*, pp. 434–6.
62. *VP*, pp. 821, 852, 853; *YO*, p. 254.
63. *YO*, p. 230.
64. See *infra*, p. 271.
65. *Frank Pearce Sturm: His Life, Letters and Collected Work*, ed. Richard Taylor (Urbana: University of Illinois Press, 1969). See also Warwick Gould, 'The Poet at the Breakfast Table', *English*, xxvii, nos 128–9 (Summer–Autumn 1978) 222–39, esp. pp. 232–4.
66. It also recalls the central symbol of the interpenetrating gyres which die 'each other's life' and live 'each other's death' (*AV[B]*, p. 68).
67. See *supra*, n. 56.
68. Sidnell and Stallworthy see fiction merging into autobiography, yet when the *Nights* are perceived as a text upon which the poem depends it is not disturbing to note that Kusta's bride (unlike Mrs Yeats) is 'a

merry girl with no more interest in [occult] matters than other girls of her age' (*VP*, p. 829).

69. *L*, p. 859; W. K. Hood in *YO*, pp. 215–24; C. K. Hood, pp. 47, 60, 61.

70. In 1936–7 Yeats, annotating a draft list of contents for *Discoveries* in his Macmillan Edition de Luxe, suggested that the volume might contain, in addition to *A Vision* in its 1937 format, something entitled 'Michael R' but cancelled in his hand. This possibly suggests that he had thought of adding 'Michael Robartes Foretells' as a sort of 1002nd Night. But he did not so add it.

71. Yvor Winters, *In Defence of Reason* (Routledge and Kegan Paul, 1960) p. 170. The remark is made of the style of *The Scarlet Letter*.

72. Yeats, like Milton, stands at a critical distance from belief in his encyclopaedic compilation. As Frye remarks, 'In a period of romance the poet . . . has become a human being . . . his function now is primarily to remember' – *Anatomy of Criticism: Four Essays* (New York: Atheneum, 1969) pp. 56–7. 'Unwilling belief' (*Ex*, p. 277) best characterises Yeats's own relation to his *Vision*. Joseph A. Wittreich Jr provides an apposite comment: 'Epic poets and prophets alike impose historical pattern upon historical pattern: but, whereas the epic poet translates pattern into model, the prophet searches beyond pattern for a new model, his search causing him to turn closed patterns into open ones . . .' – *Visionary Poetics: Milton's Tradition and its Legacy* (San Marino, Calif.: Henry E. Huntington Library and Art Gallery, 1979) p. 52.

73. Cf. Sidnell, in *YO*, pp. 232, 252.

74. See C. K. Hood, in *Yeats: An Annual . . . 1973*, p. 67.

75. Yeats as an art student 'embodied' the *Nights* for one comrade at least: 'At 19 or 20 when he posed for his father's King Goll the outside of his head was a beautiful as the inside. . . . I used to think him like a young prince out of the *Arabian Nights* he was so dusky and handsome' – quoted in Alan Denson, *John Hughes* (Kendal: Alan Denson, 1969) p. 163. I am grateful to Deirdre Toomey for alerting me to this passage and for much else. J. B. Yeats's portrait of W. B. Yeats as King Goll, which accompanied 'The Madness of King Goll' in *The Leisure Hour*, Sep 1887, can also be found in *Yeats Annual No. 4*, plate 16.

76. Both men's views can be found in Hough, *Mystery Religion*, pp. 116–18. George Mills Harper's *The Making of Yeats's 'A Vision'* (Macmillan, 1987) appeared after this essay had been completed. As a study of the automatic script, it does not change my views on the overall shape of either of Yeats's published versions of *A Vision*.

11

The King of the Black Islands and the Myth of the Waste Land

JOHN HEATH-STUBBS

Without going into all the details of a very complicated set of narratives, we will remind the reader that the continuation of the Fisherman and the Genie is the tale of the Young King of the Black Islands. This story deals with a sultan who, in the course of his quest, first passes by a lake full of white, red, yellow or blue fishes, next finds in a deserted palace this enchanted king. The victim of his wife, a wicked and depraved sorceress, he has been turned to black marble from the waist downwards. Having detected her in an amour with a hideous black, the king had attacked this negro, rendering him apparently dead, though in fact speechless and unable to move. The wicked queen then went into mourning and erected a magnificent monument in which after a year she installed her lover, whom she tended and nursed. Finally outraged by this behaviour, the king threatened her with his drawn sword. The queen now recognised her lover's assailant, and revenged herself by reducing him to this semi-petrified state. Furthermore, she changed his kingdom of four islands into as many mountains, withdrawing the water that surrounded them into the lake already mentioned. His subjects she transformed into fishes – the white ones being the Muslims, the red Zoroastrians, the yellow Jews and the blue Christians (these are said to have been the colours of the turbans assigned to the four religions under the Abbasid caliphate).[1] The sultan espouses the cause of the wronged king, slays the negro, and forces the wicked queen to disenchant her husband and to restore the kingdom and his subjects to their former state. She releases the king by sprinkling him with water from a little bowl. The body of the negro is cast into a well and that of the queen dismembered.

There seem to me to be some interesting parallels between this story and the medieval European romances of the Holy Grail. In the latter, the hero comes to the Waste Land, the realm of the Fisher King. This king has been the guardian of two sacred relics – the Holy Grail (the cup or platter used by Christ at the Last Supper, and in which His Blood was collected at the Crucifixion) and the Lance or Spear with which the centurion pierced Christ's side. Through some fault of his, disaster has fallen on the Fisher King. He has been pierced through the thighs by the sacred Spear and is thus crippled. At the same time his country has been stricken with barrenness and become waste. The hero of the quest is able by use of the right ritual formula to restore the king to health and fertility to his land.

Jessie M. Weston in her book *From Ritual to Romance* (a book now celebrated for having suggested the structure of T. S. Eliot's *The Waste Land*) first proposed that behind these Christian legends could be traced the pre-Christian pattern of a fertility ritual of the kind postulated in Frazer's *The Golden Bough*. We must suppose a primitive stage of culture in which this symbolism is centred in the person of the divine king. The latter reigns by virtue of his relationship to the goddess who also personifies his land. His continuing virility ensures the fertility of the latter, and when this wanes he must be slain to be replaced by a successor. This successor may be considered as himself reborn or resurrected. Thus we find in the ancient Near East the concept of the dying god, Attis, Adonis or Osiris. He is the lover, husband or son of the goddess, who mourns when he is slain with the dying year and rejoices when he returns with the new vegetation of spring. Robert Graves in *The White Goddess*, basing his analysis on the myths of a number of differing cultures, suggested a pattern whereby the goddess divides her favours between two consorts, the god of the Waning Year and the god of the Waxing Year, who alternately win and are defeated in a ritual combat.

Looked at from this point of view, we can see in the crippling of the Fisher King, and the turning to stone of the King of the Black Islands, fairly obvious symbols of sexual impotence whereby their respective lands are also stricken. In the Arabian story, the goddess has become the wicked queen, who transfers her favours to a new consort who is wounded and mourned as Adonis and Osiris were mourned. In the Holy Grail stories the goddess seems to be represented by the Loathly Maiden, who appears in many of them as the messenger or bearer of the Grail, and whose ugliness is really one with the barrenness of the Waste Land. The water-sprinkling by the queen in the Arabian story doubtless reflects a rain-making ritual. Her bowl is of minor significance compared to the Holy Grail. Christian commentators have been rather reluctant to see in the Grail and the Spear feminine and masculine fertility symbols respectively; to me there is nothing very disturbing in the idea that the positive life-giving symbols of a primitive state of culture could be transvalued and spiritualised in a higher religious context.

The questing sultan or knight in both stories represents the new or reborn king who restores fertility to the stricken land. In neither story does he replace the former king, as we may suppose he did in the original myth; in the Arab story there is indeed a reversal of roles, since the questing king finally adopts the King of the Black Islands as his son.

Both the Holy Grail stories and the Arabian story must, I think, be considered as deriving from a common source. Each contains features wanting in the other, but which taken together illuminate the hypothetical myth ritual pattern. Jessie Weston's belief that the ritual pattern which she detected behind the Holy Grail stories was brought to the West in early times by Phoenician traders must now be considered as rather simplistic. In particular, there is no real evidence that the Phoenician tin traders ever reached Britain. Nevertheless ancient Phoenicia, where the cult of the fish goddess Atergatis or Derceto was important, might well be the starting point.

It has, of course, often been suggested that the stories of medieval Western romance incorporate material of Arabian origin. This is certainly frequently the case, but the main elements in the Holy Grail legends seem to go a long way back to Celtic tradition. The fact that the kingdom over which the king in the story we have been dealing with ruled is called the Black Islands opens up an interesting possibility. Have we here a case of a Western story migrating eastwards?[2] Could the Black Islands by any chance in fact be Ingeltera, Skotlandya and Arlandya – whose existence, however, remote, was certainly known to early Arab geographers?

NOTES *(compiled by the editor)*

Books published in London unless otherwise stated.

1. Lane (*Nights*, i, 135 n. 55) finds in the sumptuary laws of Mohammad Ibn Kala-oon, Sultan of Egypt, a date for the composition of the *Nights*: 'the eighth century of the Flight, or fourteenth of our era'; however, Burton (*Nights*, i, 71) points out that 'the custom was much older'.
2. On the difficulty of determining the origins of a story such as Ali Baba, see Max Lüthi, *The Fairy Tale as Art-form and Portrait of Man*, tr. J. Erickson (Bloomington, Ind.: Indiana University Press, 1984) p. 187 n. 256. Of these 'orphan stories', as Mia Gerhardt has called those tales in the Galland collection for which no certain Arabic source text has been found, at least one, 'The Envious Sisters' is 'a European fairy tale to all appearances'. See Gerhardt, *The Art of Story-Telling: A Literary Study of the Thousand and One Nights* (Leiden: Brill, 1963) pp. 14–15; also D. B. Macdonald 'The Earlier History of the Arabian Nights', *Journal of the Royal Asiatic Society*, 1924, pp. 353–97. Although it has been suggested that Celtic legends of the Grail were influenced by Solomonic tradition, Wolfram von Eschenbach's own claim as to the Arabian origin of his material is discounted by both R. S. Loomis, in *Arthurian Literature in the Middle Ages* (Oxford: Clarendon Press, 1959) pp. 293–4, and A. C. L. Brown, in *The Origin of the Grail Legend* (New York: Russell and Russell, 1966). The trouble with some diffusionists, such as Flavia Anderson in her *The Ancient Secret: In Search of the Holy Grail* (Gollancz, 1953), is that they are unable to credit the people of 'the Western World', with enough imagination to invent compelling tales of their own. While, to a certain extent, such a restricted approach to inter-cultural transactions flaws E. L. Ranelagh's otherwise persuasive study, *The Past We Share: The Near Eastern Ancestry of Western Folk Literature* (Quartet, 1979), Bob Quinn in his *Atlantean: Ireland's North African and Maritime Heritage* (Quartet, 1986) concedes that 'Ireland was not always a kind of sponge passively absorbing . . . there was a two-way traffic' (p. 99). The connections between the Arabian and Celtic cycles are further examined by Michael Barry in 'Arthur's Round Table and the Arabian Nights', forthcoming in *Temenos*, ed. Kathleen Raine *et al.*

The False Caliph

ROBERT G. HAMPSON

1

heat or no heat,
the windows have to be shut.
nights like this,
the wind winds down
through the mountain passes
and itches the skin
on the backs of necks:

anything can happen.

2

voices on the radio
drop
soundless as spring rain
into the
murmur of
general conversation.

his gloved hands
tap lightly
on the table-top
as he whistles
tunelessly
to himself.

his partner
picks through
a pack of cards,
plucks out the jokers
and lays down a mat
face down in front of him.

the third
hones his knife
on the sole of his boot:

tests its edge with his thumb.

3

Harry can't sleep.

Mezz and the boys,
night after night,
have sought
means to amuse him –
to cheat the time
till dawn brings the tiredness
that finally takes him.

but tonight
everything has failed.

neither card-tricks nor knife-tricks –
not even the prospect
of nocturnal adventures
down in the old town
has lifted his gloom.

they're completely
at a loss.

then the stranger
enters:
the same build
the same face
the same dress

right down to
the identical
black leather gloves
on the hands

which now tap
contemptuously
on the table
while he whistles
tunelessly
as if to himself.

Appendix

W. F. Kirby's 'Comparative Table of the Tales in the Principal Editions of the Thousand and One Nights' from the Burton Edition (1885).

[List of editions]

1. Galland, 1704–7
2. Caussin de Perceval, 1806
3. Gauttier, 1822
4. Scott's MS (Wortley Montague), 1797–8
5. Ditto (Anderson; marked A), 1798
6. Scott's *Arabian Nights*, 1811
7. Scott's *Tales and Anecdotes* (marked A), 1800
8. Von Hammer's MS, *c.* 1800
9. Zinserling, 1823
10. Lamb, 1825–6
11. Trébutien, 1828
12. Bulac text, 1835
13. Lane, 1839–41
14. Breslau text, 1835–43
15. Habicht, 1825
16. Weil, 1837–41
17. Macnaghten text, 1839–42
18. Torrens, 1838
19. Payne, 1882–4
20. Payne's *Tales from the Arabic* (marked I, II, III), 1884
21. Calcutta text, 1884–8
22. Burton, 1885–8
23. Lady Burton, 'Prepared for household reading', 1886

As nearly all editions of the *Nights* are in several volumes, the volumes are indicated throughout, except in the case of some of the texts. Only those tales in No. 5, not included in No. 4, are here indicated in the same column. All tales which there is good reason to believe do not belong to the genuine *Nights* are marked with an asterisk.

	Burton (Sir R. F.)	Burton (Lady)	Calcutta	Payne	Torrens	Mac. Text	Weil	Habicht	Breslau Text	Lane	Bul. Text	Trébutien	Lamb	Zinserling	Von Hammer's MS	Scott	Scott's MS	Gautier	Caussin de Perceval	Galland
Introduction	1	1	+	1	1	+	1	1	+	1	+					−	1		1	−
Story of King Shahryar and his Brother	1	1	+	1	1	+	1	1	+	1	+					1	1	1	1	1
1. Tale of the Bull and the Ass	1	1	+	1	1	+	1	1	+	1	+					1	A	1	1	1
Tale of the Trader and the Jinni	1	1	+	1	1	+	1	1	+	1	+					1	1	1	1	1
a. The First Shaykh's Story	1	1	+	1	1	+	1	1	+	1	+					1	1	1	1	1
b. The Second Shaykh's Story	1	1	+	1	1	+	1	1	+	1	+					1	1	1	1	1
c. The Third Shaykh's Story	1	1	+	1	1	+	1	1	+	1	+					1	1		−	−
2. The Fisherman and the Jinni	1	1	+	1	1	+	1	1	+	1	+					−	1	1	1	1
a. Tale of the Wazir and the Sage Duban	1	1	+	1	1	+	1	1	+	1	+					1	1	1	1	1
ab. Story of King Sindibad and his Falcon	1	1	−	1	1	+	1	−	−	1	+					−	?		−	−
ac. Tale of the Husband and the Parrot	1	1	+	−	−	−	1	1	+	1	+					1	?	1	1	1
ad. Tale of the Prince and the Ogress	1	1	+	1	1	+	1	1	+	1	+					1	?	1	1	1
b. Tale of the Ensorcelled Prince	1	1	+	1	1	+	1	1	+	1	+					1	?	1	1	1
3. The Porter and the Three Ladies of Baghdad	1	1	+	1	1	+	1	1	+	1	+					1	1	1	1	1
a. The First Kalandar's Tale	1	1	+	1	1	+	1	2	+	1	+					1	1	1	1	2
b. The Second Kalandar's Tale	1	1	+	1	1	+	1	2	+	1	+					1	1	1	1	2
ba. Tale of the Envier and the Envied	1	1	+	1	1	+	1	2	+	1	−					1	?	1	1	2
c. The Third Kalandar's Tale	1	1	+	1	1	+	1	2	+	1	+					1	1	1	1	2

(Full contents from Introd. to No. 4 not given: 3c and 4 are apparently wanting.)

Tale	Lv														
d. The Eldest Lady's Tale	2	2	1	1	+	+	1	2	+	1	1	+	1	1	1	1
e. Tale of the Portress	2	2	1	1	+	+	1	2	+	1	1	−	1	1	1	1
Conclusion of the Story of the Porter and Three Ladies			1	2			1			1	1		1	1	1	1
4. Tale of the Three Apples	2	2	1	2	+	+	1	3	+	1	1	+	1	1	1	1
5. Tale of Nur Al-Din and his Son Badr Al-Din Hasan	3,4	2	2	1	+	+	1	3	+	1	1	+	1	1	1	1
6. The Hunchback's Tale	4	2	2	2	+	+	1	3	+	1	1	+	1	1	1	1
a. The Nazarene Broker's Story	4	2	2	1	+	+	1	3	+	1	1	+	1	1	1	1
b. The Reeve's Tale	4	2	2	1	+	+	1	3	+	1	1	+	1	1	1	1
c. Tale of the Jewish Doctor	4	2	2	?	+	+	1	3	+	1	1	+	1	1	1	1
d. Tale of the Tailor	4,5	3	2	1	+	+	1	3	+	1	1	+	1	1	1	1
e. The Barber's Tale of Himself	5	3	2	2	+	+	1	4	+	1	1	+	1	1	1	1
ea. The Barber's Tale of his First Brother	5	3	2	1	+	+	1	4	+	1	1	+	1	1	1	1
eb. The Barber's Tale of his Second Brother	5	3	2	2	+	+	1	4	+	1	1	+	1	1	1	1
ec. The Barbar's Tale of his Third Brother	5	3	2	?	+	+	1	4	+	1	1	+	1	1	1	1
ed. The Barber's Tale of his Fourth Brother	5	3	2	1	+	+	1	4	+	1	1	+	1	1	1	1
ee. The Barber's Tale of his Fifth Brother	5	3	2	1	+	+	1	4	+	1	1	+	1	1	1	1
ef. The Barber's Tale of his Sixth Brother	5	3	2	1	+	+	1	4	+	1	1	+	1	1	1	1
The End of the Tailor's Tale	5	3	2	1	+	+	1	4	+	1	1	+	1	1	1	1
	5	3	2	2	+	+	1	4	+	1	1	+	1	1	1	1
7. Nur Al-Din Ali and the Damsel Anis Al-Jalis	7	4	3	1	+	+	1	5,6	+	1	1	+	1	1	1	2
8. Tale of Ghanim Bin Ayyub, the Distraught, the Thrall o' Love	8	4,5	4	1	+	+	1	8	+	2	2	+	1	1	1	2
a. Tale of the First Eunuch, Bukhayt			4	?	+	+	−		+	2	2	+		1	1	2
b. Tale of the Second Eunuch, Kafur			4	?	+	+	1		+	2	2	+	1	1	1	2

Story	Galland	Caussin de Perceval	Gauttier	Scott's MS	Scott	Von Hammer's MS	Zinserling	Lamb	Trébutien	Bul. Text	Lane	Breslau Text	Habicht	Weil	Mac. Text	Torrens	Payne	Calcutta	Burton (Lady)	Burton (Sir R. F.)
9. Tale of King Omar Bin Al-Nu'uman, and his sons Sharkan and Zau Al-Makan						1				+	−			3	+	+ 1(p)	2		1,2	2,3
a. Tale of Taj Al-Muluk and the Princess Dunya						1				+	1			3	+		2		2	2,3
aa. Tale of Aziz and Azizah						1				+	1			3	+		2		2	2,3
b. Tale of the Hashish-Eater						?				+	−			−	+		2		2	3
c. Tale of Hammad the Badawi						1				+	−			−	+		2		2	3
10. The Birds and Beasts and the Carpenter						(Nos. 10–19 represented by 7 Fables.)				+	2			2	+		3		2	3
11. The Hermits										+	−			2	+		3		2	3
12. The Water-fowl and the Tortoise										+	−				+		3		2	3
13. The Wolf and the Fox										+	2				+		3		2	3
a. Tale of the Falcon and the Partridge										+	2			2	+		3		2	3
14. The Mouse and the Ichneumon										+	−				+		3		2	3
15. The Cat and the Crow										+	−				+		3		2	3
16. The Fox and the Crow										+	−				+		3		2	3
a. The Flea and the Mouse										+	−				+		3		2	3
b. The Saker and the Birds										+	−				+		3		2	3
c. The Sparrow and the Eagle										+	−				+		3		2	3
17. The Hedgehog and the Wood Pigeons										+	−				+		3		2	3
a. The Merchant and the Two Sharpers										+	−				+		3		2	3
18. The Thief and his Monkey										+	−				+		3		2	3

No.	Title													
	a. The Foolish Weaver													
19.	The Sparrow and the Peacock	5,6	3			1	3		+	+	3		2	3
20.	Ali Bin Bakkar and Shams Al-Nahar	6	3,4	3		1	3	4	+	+	3	+	2	3
21.	Tale of Kamar Al-Zaman		3	2,3		1	3	5	2	+	3		2	3
	a. Ni'amah bin Al-Rabia and Naomi his Slave-girl		3		1,2	1	3		2	+	3		2	3,4
22.	Ala Al-Din Abu Al-Shamat	9				1	3	13	2	+	3		2	4
23.	Hatim of the Tribe of Tayy	9				1	3	13	2	+	3		2	4
24.	Ma'an the son of Zaidah and the three Girls					1	3		2	+	3		2	4
25.	Ma'an son of Zaidah and the Badawi				2	1	3		2	+	3		2	4
26.	The City of Labtayt				2	1	3		2	+	3		2	4
27.	The Caliph Hisham and the Arab Youth				2	1	3		2	+	3		2	4
28.	Ibrahim bin Al-Mahdi and the Barber-Surgeon				2	1	3		2	+	3		2	4
29.	The City of Many-columned Iram and Abdullah son of Abi Kalabah				2	1	3	13	2	+	3	+	2	4
30.	Isaac of Mosul	7			2	1	3		2	+	3		2	4
31.	The Sweep and the Noble Lady	2			2	1	3		2	+	3		3	4
32.	The Mock Caliph	9			2	1	3	4	4	+	3		3	4
33.	Ali the Persian				2	–	–		2	+	3		3	4
34.	Harun Al-Rashid and the Slave-Girl and the Imam Abu Yusuf				2	1	3		4	+	3		3	4
35.	The Lover who feigned himself a Thief				–	–	–		2	+	4		3	4
36.	Ja'afar the Barmecide and the Bean-Seller				2	1	3		2	+	4		3	4
37.	Abu Mohammed hight Lazybones	9			–	–	–	13	4	+	4		3	4
38.	Generous dealing of Yahya bin Khalid the Barmecide with Mansur				–	–	–		2	+	4		3	4
39.	Generous dealing of Vahya son of Khalid with a man who forged a letter in his name				–	–	–		2	+	4		3	4

	Galland	Caussin de Perceval	Gautier	Scott's MS	Scott	Von Hammer's MS	Zinserling	Lamb	Trébutien	Bul. Text	Lane	Breslau Text	Habicht	Weil	Mac. Text	Torrens	Payne	Calcutta	Burton (Lady)	Burton (Sir R. F.)
40. Caliph Al-Maamun and the Strange Scholar						2	1		3	+	2				+		4		3	4
41. Ali Shar and Zumurrud						2	1		1	+	2	+		2	+		4		3	4
42. The Loves of Jubayr Bin Umayr and the Lady Budur						2	1		1	+	2	+		2	+		4		3	4
43. The Man of Al-Yaman and his six Slave-Girls						2	1		3	+	–	+		2	+		4		3	4
44. Harun Al-Rashid and the Damsel and Abu Nowas						2	1		3	+	–	+		2	+		4			4
45. The Man who stole the dish of gold whereon the dog ate						2	1		3	+	2	+		4	+		4		3	4
46. The Sharper of Alexandria and the Chief of Police						2	1		3	+	2	+		4	+		4		3	4
47. Al-Malik Al-Nasir and the three Chiefs of Police						2	1		3	+	2	+		4	+		4		3	4
a. Story of the Chief of the new Cairo Police						2	1		3	+	2	+		4	+		4		3	4
b. Story of the Chief of the Bulak Police						2	1		3	+	2				+		4		3	4
c. Story of the Chief of the Old Cairo Police										+							4		3	4
48. The Thief and the Shroff						–	–		–	+	2	+		4	+		4		3	4
49. The Chief of the Kus Police and the Sharper						–	–		–	+	–	+		4	+		4		3	4
50. Ibrahim bin al-Mahdi and the Merchant's Sister						2	1		3	+	2	+			+		4		3	4

No.	Title													
51.	The Woman whose hands were cut off for almsgiving	2	1		3	+	2	+		4	+	4	3	4
52.	The devout Israelite	2	1		3	+	2	+		4	+	4	3	4
53.	Abu Hassan Al-Ziyadi and the Khorasan Man	2	1		3	+	2	+		4	+	4	3	4
54.	The Poor Man and his Friend in Need	–	–		–	+	2	+		4	+	4	3	4
55.	The Ruined Man who became rich again through a dream	2	1		3	+	2	+		4	+	4	3	4
56.	Caliph Al-Mutawakkil and his Concubine Mahbubah	2	1		3	+	2	+		4	+	4	3	4
57.	Wardan the Butcher's Adventure with the Lady and the Bear	2	1		3	+	–			4	+	4	4	4
58.	The King's Daughter and the Ape	2	1		3	+	–			4	+	4	4	4
59.	The Ebony Horse	11 7 5 5	2	–	–	+	2	+	9	1	+	4	3	5
60.	Uns Al-Wujud and the Wazir's Daughter Rose-in-Hood	6 4 5 6	2	1	1	+	2	+	11	2	+	4	3	5
61.	Abu Nowas with the Three Boys and the Caliph Harun Al-Rashid	2	1	–	+	–	+		2	+	4		5
62.	Abdullah bin Ma'amar with the Man of Bassorah and his Slave-Girl	2	1	–	+	–	+		4	+	4	3	5
63.	The Lovers of the Banu Ozrah	2	1	3	+	2	+		4	+	4	3	5
64.	The Wazir of Al-Yaman and his young Brother	–	–	–	+	2	+	11	4	+	4	3	5
65.	The Loves of the Boy and Girl at School	2	1	3	+	–			4	+	4		5
66.	Al-Mutalammis and his Wife Umaymah	2	1	3	+	2	+		4	+	4	3	5
67.	Harun Al-Rashid and Zubaydah in the Bath	–	–	–	+	–	+		4	+	4	3	5
68.	Harun Al-Rashid and the Three Poets	2	1	3	+	2	+		2	+	4	3	5 5
69.	Mus'ab bin Al-Zubayr and Ayishah his Wife	2	1	3	+	–	+			+	4	3	5 5
70.	Abu Al-Aswad and his Slave-Girl	–	–	–	+	–	+			+	4	3	5 5

Appendix

No.	Title	Galland	Caussin de Perceval	Gauttier	Scott's MS	Scott	Von Hammer's MS	Zinserling	Lamb	Trébutien	Bul. Text	Lane	Breslau Text	Habicht	Weil	Mac. Text	Torrens	Payne	Calcutta	Burton (Lady)	Burton (Sir R. F.)
71.	Harun Al-Rashid and the two Slave-Girls						2	1		3	+	–	+			+		4			5
72.	Harun Al-Rashid and the Three Slave-Girls						–	–		3	+	–				+		4		3	5
73.	The Miller and his Wife						2	1		3	+	2	+			+		4		3	5
74.	The Simpleton and the Sharper						–	–		–	+	2	+			+		4		3	5
75.	The Kazi Abu Yusuf with Harun Al-Rashid and Queen Zubaydah					A	–	–		–	+	–	+		4	+		4		3	5
76.	The Caliph Al-Hakim and the Merchant				A		2	1		3	+	2	+			+		4		3	5
77.	King Kisra Anushirwan and the Village Damsel						2	1		3	+	2	+		4	+		4		3	5
78.	The Water-carrier and the Goldsmith's Wife						2	1		3	+	–	+		4	+		4		3	5
79.	Khusrau and Shirin and the Fisherman						2	1		3	+	2	+			+		4		3	5
80.	Yahya bin Khalid and the Poor Man						–	–		–	+	2	+			+		4		3	5
81.	Mohammed al-Amin and the Slave-Girl						–	–		–		2				+		4		3	5
82.	The Sons of Yahya bin Khalid and Said bin Salim						–	–		–		2				+		4		3	5
83.	The Woman's Trick against her Husband						2	1		3	+	2	+			+		4		3	5
84.	The Devout Woman and the Two Wicked Elders						2	1		3	+	–	+		4	+		4		3	5

85.	Ja'afar the Barmecide and the old Badawi	2	1	3	+	2	+	4	+	4	3	5
86.	Omar bin Al-Khattab and the Young Badawi	2	1	3	+	–			+	4	3	5
87.	Al-Maamun and the Pyramids of Egypt	2	1		+	2	+		+	4	3	5
88.	The Thief and the Merchant	2	1	3	+	–	+	4	+	4	3	5
89.	Masrur the Eunuch and Ibn Al-Karibi	2	1	3	+	2	+	4	+	4	3	5
90.	The Devotee Prince	2	1	3	+	2	+	4	+	4	3	5
91.	The Schoolmaster who fell in Love by Report	2	1	3	+	–	+	4	+	4	3	5
92.	The Foolish Dominie	–	–		+	–	+		+	4	3	5
93.	The Illiterate who set up for a Schoolmaster	2	1	3	+	2	+	4	+	4	3	5
94.	The King and the Virtuous Wife	2	1	3	+	–	+		+	4		5
95.	Abd Al-Rahman the Maghribi's story of the Rukh	2	1	3	+	2	+		+	4	3	5
96.	Adi Bin Zayd and the Princess Hind	2	1	3	+	–	+		+	4	3	5
97.	Di'ibil Al-Khuza'i with the Lady and Muslim bin Al-Walid	2	1	3	+	–	+	4	+	4	3	5
98.	Isaac of Mosul and the Merchant	2	1	3	+	–	+	4	+	4	3	5
99.	The Three Unfortunate Lovers	2	1	3	+	–	+	4	+	4	3	5
101.	The Lovers of the Banu Tayy	2	1	3	+	2	+	4	+	4	3	5
102.	The Mad Lover	2	1	3	+	2	+	4	+	4	3	5
103.	The Prior who became a Moslem	2	1	3	+	2	+	4	+	4	3	5
104.	The Loves of Abu Isa and Kurrat Al-Ayn	2	1	3	+	2	+	4	+	4	3	5
105.	Al-Amin and his Uncle Ibrahim bin Al-Mahdi	2	1	3	+	–	+		+	4		5
106.	Al-Fath bin Khakan and Al-Mutawakkil	2	1	3	+	–	+		+	4		5
107.	The Man's dispute with the Learned Woman concerning the relative excellence of male and female	2	1	3	+	–	+		+	4		5

	Galland	Caussin de Perceval	Gautier	Scott's MS	Scott	Von Hammer's MS	Zinserling	Lamb	Trébutien	Bul. Text	Lane	Breslau Text	Habicht	Weil	Mac. Text	Torrens	Payne	Calcutta	Burton (Lady)	Burton (Sir R. F.)
108. Abu Suwayd and the pretty Old Woman						2	1		3	+	–	+			+		4			5
109. Ali bin Tahir and the girl Muunis						2	1		3	+	–	+			+		4			5
110. The Woman who had a Boy, and the other who had a Man to lover						2	1		3	+	–	+			+		4			5
111. Ali the Cairene and the Haunted House in Baghdad						2	1		1	+	2	+			+		4			5
112. The Pilgrim Man and the Old Woman						2	1		3	+	2			4	+		4		3	5
113. Abu Al-Husn and his Slave-girl Tawaddud						2	1		1	+	–				+		4		3	5
114. The Angel of Death with the Proud King and the Devout Man						2	1		3	+	–			4	+		5		3	5
115. The Angel of Death and the Rich King						2	1		3	+	–			4	+		5		3	5
116. The Angel of Death and the King of the Children of Israel						2	1	3	3	+	2				+		5		3	5
117. Iskandar zu Al-Karnayn and a certain Tribe of Poor Folk						2	1		3	+	–			4	+		5		3	5
118. The Righteousness of King Anushirwan						2	1		3	+	–			4	+		5		3	5
119. The Jewish Kazi and his Pious Wife						2	1		3	+	–			4	+		5		3	5
120. The Shipwrecked Woman and her Child						2	1		3	+	–			4	+		5		3	5
121. The Pious Black Slave						2	1		3	+	–			4	+		5		3	5
122. The Devout Tray-maker and his Wife						2	1		3	+	2			4	+		5		3	5

No.	Title															
123.	Al-Hajjaj bin Yusuf and the Pious Man					2	1	3	+				+	5	3	5
124.	The Blacksmith who could Handle Fire Without Hurt					2	1	3	+	-		4	+	5	3	5
125.	The Devotee to whom Allah gave a Cloud for Service and the Devout King											4	+	5	3	5
126.	The Moslem Champion and the Christian Damsel					2	1	3	+	-		4	+	5	3	5
127.	The Christian King's Daughter and the Moslem					2	1	3	+	2		4	+	5	3	5
128.	The Prophet and the Justice of Providence					2	1	3	+	-			+	5	3	5
129.	The Ferryman of the Nile and the Hermit					2	1	3	+	2		4	+	5	3	5
130.	The Island King and the Pious Israelite					2	1	-	+	-			+	5	3	5
131.	Abu Al-Hasan and Abu Ja'afar the Leper			6		2	1	3	+	-	10	4	+	5	3	5
132.	The Queen of the Serpents					2	1	3	+	-		4	+	5	3	5
a.	The Adventure of Bulukiya					2	1	3	+	-		4	+	5	3	5
b.	The Story of Janshah					2	1	3	+	-		4	+	5	3	5
133.	Sindbad the Seaman and Sindbad the Landsman	3	2	2	3	-	+	3	+	1		2	+	5	3	6
a.	The First Voyage of Sindbad the Seaman	3	2	2	3	-	+	3	+	1		2	+	5	3	6
b.	The Second Voyage of Sindbad the Seaman	3	2	2	3	-	+	3	+	1		2	+	5	3	6
c.	The Third Voyage of Sindbad the Seaman	3	2	2	3	-	+	3	+	1		2	+	5	3	6
d.	The Fourth Voyage of Sindbad the Seaman	3	2	2	3	-	+	3	+	1		2	+	5	3	6
e.	The Fifth Voyage of Sindbad the Seaman	3	2	2	3	-	+	3	+	1		2	+	5	3	6

Tale	Galland	Caussin de Perceval	Gautier	Scott's MS	Scott	Von Hammer's MS	Zinseling	Lamb	Trébutien	Bul. Text	Lane	Breslau Text	Habicht	Weil	Mac. Text	Torrens	Payne	Calcutta	Burton (Lady)	Burton (Sir R. F.)
f. The Sixth Voyage of Sindbad the Seaman	3	2	2		2	3	–		–	+	3	+	3	1	+		5	–	4	6
ff. The Sixth Voyage of Sindbad the Seaman										–	3	–			–		III	+		–
g. The Seventh Voyage of Sindbad the Seaman	3	2	2		2	3	–		–	+	3	+	3	1	+		5	–	4	6
gg. The Seventh Voyage of Sindbad the Seaman	–						–		–	–	3	–		1	–		III	+	4	6
134. The City of Brass					–	–	–		–	–	3	–		–	–		5	+	4	6
135. The Craft and Malice of Women						3	2	1	1	+	3	+		2	+		5	+	4	6
a. The King and his Wazir's Wife				A	A	3	–	1	1	+	3	+	15		+		5		4	6
b. The Confectioner, his Wife and the Parrot				A	A				–	+	3	+	15		+		5		4	6
c. The Fuller and his Son				A	A	(Would include subordinate tales.)				+	–	+			+		5		4	6
d. The Rake's Trick against the Chaste Wife				A	A					+	–	+			+		5		4	6
e. The Miser and the Loaves of Bread				A	A					+	–	+	15		+		5		4	6
f. The Lady and her two Lovers				A	A					+	3	+	15		+		5		4	6
g. The King's Son and the Ogress				A	A					+	–	+	15		+		5		4	6
h. The Drop of Honey				A	A					+	3	+	15		+		5		4	6
i. The Woman who made her husband sift dust				A	A					+	3	+	15		+		5		4	6
j. The Enchanted Spring				A	A					+	3	+	15		+		5		4	6
k. The Wazir's Son and the Hammam-keeper's Wife				A							+		15		+		5		4	6

Ref	Title											
l.	The Wife's Device to cheat her Husband		A	+	3	+	15	+	5		6
m.	The Goldsmith and the Cashmere Singing-girl	1	A	+	3	+	1	+	5	4	6
n.	The Man who never laughed during the rest of his days		A A	+	3	+	15	+	5	4	6
o.	The King's Son and the Merchant's Wife		A A	+	−	+	15	+	5	4	6
p.	The Page who feigned to know the Speech of Birds			+	−	+		+	5	4	6
q.	The Lady and her five Suitors		A A	+	−	+		+	5	4	6
r.	The Three Wishes or the Man who longed to see the Night of Power			+	−	+	15	+	5	4	6
s.	The Stolen Necklace		A A	+	3	+	15	+	5	4	6
t.	The Two Pigeons		A A	+	3	+	15	+	5	4	6
u.	Prince Behram and the Princess Al-Datma		A A	+	3	+	15	+	5	4	6
v.	The House with the Belvedere		A A	+	3	+	15	+	5	4	6
w.	The King's Son and the Ifrit's Mistress			+	−	+		+	5	4	6
x.	The Sandal-wood Merchant and the Sharpers			+	3	+	15	+	5	4	6
y.	The Debauchee and the Three-year-old Child			+	−	+	15	+	5	4	6
z.	The Stolen Purse			−	3	+	15	−	5	4	6
aa.	The Fox and the Folk			+	3	+		+	6	4	6
136.	Judar and his Brethren	3 2 1 1		+	−	+		+	6	4	6
137.	The History of Gharib and his Brother Ajib	3 2 1 3		+	3	+	15	+	6	4	6,7
138.	Otbah and Rayya	3 2		+	3	+	15	+	6	4	7
139.	Hind, daughter of Al-Nu'man and Al-Hajjaj	3 2 3		+	−	+		+	6	4	7

Story	Galland	Caussin de Perceval	Gauttier	Scott's MS	Scott	Von Hammer's MS	Zinserling	Lamb	Trébutien	Bul. Text	Lane	Breslau Text	Habicht	Weil	Mac. Text	Torrens	Payne	Calcutta	Burton (Lady)	Burton (Sir R. F.)
140. Khuzaymah bin Bishr and Ekrimah al-Fayyaz						3	2		3	+	3			4	+		6		4	7
141. Yunus the Scribe and the Caliph Walid bin Sahl						3	2		3	+	3			4	+		6		4	7
142. Harun Al-Rashid and the Arab Girl						3	2		3	+	–				+		6		4	7
143. Al-Asma'i and the three girls of Bassorah						3	–		–	+	–				+		6		4	7
144. Ibrahim of Mosul and the Devil						3	–		3	+	–				+		6		4	7
145. The Lovers of the Banu Uzrah			6	4	6	3	–		3	+	3		11		+		6		4	7
146. The Badawi and his Wife						3	2		3	+	–				+		6		4	7
147. The Lovers of Bassorah						3	2		3	+	–				+		6		4	7
148. Ishak of Mosul and his Mistress and the Devil						3	2		3	+	3				+		6		4	7
149. The Lovers of Al-Medinah						3	2		3	+	–	+		4	+		6		4	7
150. Al-Malik Al-Nasir and his Wazir						3	2		3	+	–	+			+		6		4	7
151. The Rogueries of Dalilah the Crafty and her Daughter Zaynab the Coney-Catcher						3	2		3	+	–	+			+		6		4	7
a. The Adventures of Mercury Ali of Cairo							2		–		–			4					4	7
152. Ardashir and Haya Al-Nufus				7		3	2	1	2	+	3			2	+		6		4	7
153. Julnar the Sea-born and her son King Badr Basim of Persia	7	4	3		3,4		–		2	+	3	+	6	3	+		7		4	7
154. King Mohammed bin Sabaik and the Merchant Hasan				1		3	2		2	+	3	+		–	+		7		4	7
a. Story of Prince Sayf Al-Muluk and the Princess Badi'a Al-Jamal				1		3,4	2		2	+	–	+		2	+		7		4,5	7,8

155. Hasan of Bassorah	3	4	3	2	2	+	3	+	2	+	7	5	8
156. Khalifah the Fisherman of Baghdad		4	3	2	2	+	3	+	2	+	7	5	8
a. The same from the Breslau Edition		4	3	2	2	+	−	−	+		7	5	8
157. Masrur and Zayn al-Mawassif		4	3	2	2	+	−	−	+		8	5	8
158. Ali Nur al-Din and Miriam the Girdle-Girl		4	3	2	2	+	−	+	+		8	5	8,9
159. The Man of Upper Egypt and his Frankish Wife		4	3	−	3	+	−	+	+		8	5	9
160. The Ruined Man of Baghad and his Slave-Girl		4	3	−	3	+	3	+	4	+	8	5	9
161. King Jali'ad of Hind and his Wazir Shimas, followed by the history of King Wird Khan, son of King Jali'ad, with his Women and Wazirs													
a. The Mouse and the Cat		4	3	3	3	+	−	+	4	+	8	5	9
b. The Fakir and his Jar of Butter		4	3	3	3	+	−	+	4	+	8	5	9
c. The Fishes and the Crab		4	3	3	3	+	−	+	4	+	8	5	9
d. The Crow and the Serpent		4	3	3	3	+	−	+	4	+	8	5	9
e. The Wild Ass and the Jackal		4	3	3	3	+	−	+	4	+	8	5	9
f. The Unjust King and the Pilgrim Prince		4	3	3	3	+	−	+	4	+	8	5	9
g. The Crows and the Hawk		4	3	3	3	+	−	+	4	+	8	5	9
h. The Serpent-Charmer and his Wife		4	3	3	3	+	−	+	4	+	8	5	9
i. The Spider and the Wind		4	3	3	3	+	−	+	4	+	8	5	9
j. The Two Kings		4	3	3	3	+	−	+	4	+	8	5	9
k. The Blind Man and the Cripple		4	3	3	3	+	−	+	4	+	8	5	9
l. The Foolish Fisherman		4	3	3	3	+	−	+	4	+	8	5	9
m. The Boy and the Thieves		4	3	3	3	+	−	+	4	+	8	5	9
n. The Man and his Wife		4	3	3	3	+	−	+	4	+	8	5	9
o. The Merchant and the Robbers		4	3	3	3	+	−	+	4	+	8	5	9
p. The Jackals and the Wolf		4	3	3	3	+	−	+	4	+	8	5	9
q. The Shepherd and the Rogue		4	3	3	3	+	−	+	4	+	8	5	9
r. The Francolin and the Tortoises		4	3	3	3	+	−	+	4	+	8	5	9

Story	Burton (Sir R. F.)	Burton (Lady)	Calcutta	Payne	Torrens	Mac. Text	Weil	Habicht	Breslau Text	Lane	Bul. Text	Trébutien	Lamb	Zinserling	Von Hammer's MS	Scott	Scott's MS	Gauttier	Caussin de Perceval	Galland
162. Abu Kir the Dyer and Abu Sir the Barber	9	5		8		+	4		+	3	+	3	1	3	4					
163. Abdullah the Fisherman and Abdullah the Merman	9	5		8		+			+	3	+	3	1	3	4					
164. Harun Al-Rashid and Abu Hasan the Merchant of Oman	9	6		9		+	2		+	–	+	3	3	3	4					
165. Ibrahim and Jamilah	9	6		9		+				3	+	3	1	3	4					
166. Abu Al-Hasan of Khorasan	9	6		9		+				–	+	3	1	3	4					
167. Kamar Al-Zaman and the Jeweller's Wife	9	6		9		+	4			–	+	3	1	3	4					
168. Abdullah bin Fazil and his Brothers	9	6		9		+				–	+	3	3	3	4					
169. Ma'aruf the Cobbler and his wife Fatimah	9	6		9		+	4			3	+	3	3	3	4					
170. Asleep and Awake	10	6		9		+				2	+	3	3	3	4					
a. Story of the Lackpenny and the Cook	1			1			1	7	+	–						4		4	5	9
171. The Caliph Omar ben Abdulaziz and the Poets	1			1					+											
172. El Hejjaj and the Three Young Men	1			1			2		+	–										
173. Harun Er Reshid and the Woman of the Barmecides	1			1					+	–										
174. The Ten Viziers, or the History of King Azadbekht and his Son	1			1			2	10	+	–								6	8	
a. Of the uselessness of endeavour against persistent ill-fortune																				
aa. Story of the Unlucky Merchant	1			1			2	10	+	–								6	8	

	Galland	Caussin de Perceval	Gautier	Scott's MS	Scott	Von Hammer's MS	Zinserling	Lamb	Trébutien	Bul. Text	Lane	Breslau Text	Habicht	Weil	Mac. Text	Torrens	Payne	Calcutta	Burton (Lady)	Burton (Sir R. F.)
177. Ibn Es-Semmak and Er-Reshid												+					I			I
178. El Mamoun and Zubeideh												+					I			I
179. En Numan and the Arab of the Benou Tai												+					I			I
180. Firouz and his Wife												+					I			I
181. King Shah Bekht and his Vizier Er Rehwan												+	14				I			I
a. Story of the Man of Khorassan, his son and his governor												+	14				I			I
b. Story of the Singer and the Druggist												+	14				I			I
c. Story of the King who knew the quintessence of things												+	14				I			I
d. Story of the Rich Man who gave his fair Daughter in Marriage to the Poor Old Man												+	14				I			I
e. Story of the Rich Man and his Wasteful Son												+	14				I			I
f. The King's Son who fell in love with the Picture												+	14				I			I
g. Story of the Fuller and his Wife												+	14				I			I
h. Story of the Old Woman, the Merchant, and the King												+	14					I			I
i. Story of the credulous Husband												+	14			I	I			I
j. Story of the Unjust King and the Tither												+	14				I			I
jj. Story of David and Solomon												+	14				I			I

	Galland	Caussin de Perceval	Gautier	Scott's MS	Scott	Von Hammer's MS	Zinserling	Lamb	Trébutien	Bul. Text	Lane	Breslau Text	Habicht	Weil	Mac. Text	Torrens	Payne	Calcutta	Burton (Lady)	Burton (Sir R. F.)
y. Story of the Foul-favoured Man and his Fair Wife												+	14				II			I
z. Story of the King who lost Kingdom and Wife and Wealth, and God Restored them to him																				
aa. Story of Selim and Selma												+	14				II			I
bb. Story of the King of Hind and his Vizier												+	14				II			I
182. El Melik Ez Zahir Rukneddin Bibers El Bunducdari and the Sixteen Officers of Police												+	14				II			II
a. The First Officer's Story												+	14				II			II
b. The Second Officer's Story												+	14				II			II
c. The Third Officer's Story												+	14				II			II
d. The Fourth Officer's Story												+	14				II			II
e. The Fifth Officer's Story												+	14				II			II
f. The Sixth Officer's Story												+	14				II			II
g. The Seventh Officer's Story												+	14				II			II
h. The Eighth Officer's Story												+	14				II			II
ha. The Thief's Story												+					II			II
i. The Ninth Officer's Story												+	14				II			II
j. The Tenth Officer's Story												+	14				II			II
k. The Eleventh Officer's Story												+	14				II			II
l. The Twelfth Officer's Story												+	14				II			II
m. The Thirteenth Officer's Story												+	14				II			II

n. The Fourteenth Officer's Story					+	14	II	II
na. A Merry Jest of a Thief					+	14	II	II
nb. Story of the Old Sharper					+	14	II	II
o. The Fifteenth Officer's Story					+	14	II	II
p. The Sixteenth Officer's Story					+	14	II	II
183. Abdallah Ben Nafi, and the King's Son of Cashgar					+	14	II	II
a. Story of the Damsel Tuhfet El Culoub and Khalif Haroun Er Reshid					+	14	II +	II
184. Women's Craft	2	3	6		+	14	II	II
185. Noureddin Ali of Damascus and the Damsel Sitt El Milah					+	15	III	II
186. El Abbas and the King's Daughter of Baghdad					+	15	III	II
187. The Two Kings and the Vizier's Daughters					+	15	III	II
188. The Favourite and her Lover					+	15	III	II
189. The Merchant of Cairo and the Favourite of the Khalif El Mamoun El Hakim bi Amrillah					+	15	III	II
190. Conclusion	4	3	3 + 3	+	+	15	III 9 &	III 6 10
191. History of Prince Zeyn Alasnam	8	5	4	4	6	3		III
192. History of Codadad and his Brothers	8	5	4	4	6	3		III
a. History of the Prince of Deryabar	8	5	4	4	6	3		III
193. Story of Aladdin, or the Wonderful Lamp	9,10	5,6	4	4,5	7,8	3		III
194. Adventures of the Caliph Harun Al-Rashid	10	6	5	5	8	3		III
a. Story of the Blind Man, Baba Abdallah	10	6	5	5	8	3		III
b. Story of Sidi Numan	10	6	5	5	8	3		III
c. Story of Cogia Hassan Alhabbal	10,11	6	5	5	8	3		III

	Galland	Caussin de Perceval	Gautier	Scott's MS	Scott	Von Hammer's MS	Zinserling	Lamb	Trébutien	Bul. Text	Lane	Breslau Text	Habicht	Weil	Mac. Text	Torrens	Payne	Calcutta	Burton (Lady)	Burton (Sir R. F.)
*195. Story of Ali Baba and The Forty Thieves	11	6	5		5								9	3						III
*196. Story of Ali Cogia, a Merchant of Baghdad	11	7	5		5								9	3						III
*197. Story of Prince Ahmed and the Fairy Peri Banou	12	7	5		5								9	3						III
*198. Story of the Sisters who envied their younger sister	12	7	5		5								10	3						III
199. (Anecdote of Jaafar The Barmecide, = No. 39)														2						
200. The Adventures of Ali and Zaher of Damascus														4						
201. The Adventures of the Fisherman, Judar of Cairo, and his meeting with the Moor Mahmood and the Sultan Beibars														4						
202. The Physician and the young man of Mosul				1																
203. The Story of the Sultan of Yemen and his three sons			6	3	6								11							
204. Story of the Three Sharpers and the Sultan			6	3	6								11							
a. Adventures of the Abdicated Sultan			6	3	6								11							
b. History of Mahummud, Sultan of Cairo			6	3	6								11							

c. Story of the First Lunatic	8	6	3	6	11
d. (Story of the Second Lunatic = No. 184)	2	6	3	6	11
e. Story of the Sage and his Pupil		6	3	6	11
f. Night Adventure of the Sultan		6	3	6	11
g. Story of the first foolish man			3		
h. Story of the broken-backed Schoolmaster		6	3	6	11
i. Story of the wry-mouthed Schoolmaster		6	3	6	11
j. The Sultan's second visit to the Sisters		6	3	6	11
k. Story of the Sisters and the Sultana, their mother		6	3	6	11
205. Story of the Avaricious Cauzee and his wife		6	3	6	11
206. Story of the Bang-Eater and the Cauzee		6	3	6	11
a. Story of the Bang-Eater and his wife		6	3	6	11
b. Continuation of the Fisherman, or Bang-Eater's Adventures		6	3	6	11
207. The Sultan and the Traveller Mhamood Al Hyjemmee		6	3	6	11
a. The Koord Robber (= No. 33)			3	6	
b. Story of the Husbandman			3	6	
c. Story of the Three Princes and Enchanting Bird		6	3	6	11
d. Story of a Sultan of Yemen and his three Sons		6	4	6	
e. Story of the first Sharper in the Cave		6	4	6	11
f. Story of the second Sharper		6	4	–	
g. Story of the third Sharper			4	–	
h. History of the Sultan of Hind	5	4	6		
208. Story of the Fisherman's Son		6	4	6	10

Story	Galland	Caussin de Perceval	Gauttier	Scott's MS	Scott	Von Hammer's MS	Zinserling	Lamb	Trébutien	Bul. Text	Lane	Breslau Text	Habicht	Weil	Mac. Text	Torrens	Payne	Calcutta	Burton (Lady)	Burton (Sir R. F.)
209. Story of Abou Neeut and Abou Neeuteen			6	4	6								11							
210. Story of the Prince of Sind, and Fatima, daughter of Amir bin Naomaun			6	4	6								11							
211. Story of the Lovers of Syria, or the Heroine			6	4	6								11							
212. Story of Hyjauje, the tyrannical Governor of Confeh, and the young Syed				4	6															
213. Story of the Sultan Haieshe				4	–															
214. Story told by a Fisherman				4	–															
215. The Adventures of Mazin of Khorassaun			6	4,5	6									10						
216. Adventure of Haroon Al Rusheed			6	5	6									11						
a. Story of the Sultan of Bussorah				5	–															
b. Nocturnal adventures of Haroon Al Rusheed				5	6															
c. Story related by Munjaub				5	6															
d. Story of the Sultan, the Dirveshe and the Barber's Son				5	6															
e. Story of the Bedouin's Wife				5	6															
f. Story of the Wife and her two Gallants				5	–															
217. Adventures of Aleefa, daughter of Mherejaun, Sultan of Hind, and Eusuff, son of Sohul, Sultan of Sind			6	5	6									11						

	Galland	Caussin de Perceval	Gauttier	Scott's MS	Scott	Von Hammer's MS	Zinserling	Lamb	Trébutien	Bul. Text	Lane	Breslau Text	Habicht	Weil	Mac. Text	Torrens	Payne	Calcutta	Burton (Lady)	Burton (Sir R. F.)
241. Adventures of the Cauzee, his Wife, &c.			6	7	6									11						
a. The Sultan's Story of Himself			6	7	6															
242. Story of Shaykh Nukheet the Fisherman, who became favourite to a Sultan														11						
a. Story of the King of Andulusia				7	–															
243. Story of Teilone, Sultan of Egypt				7	–															
244. Story of the Retired Man and his Servant				7	–															
245. The Merchant's Daughter who married the Emperor of China				7	–															
*246. New Adventures of the Caliph Harun Al-Rashid		8	7		–								12							
*247. The Physician and the young Purveyor of Baghdad		8	7										13							
*248. The Wise Heycar		8	7										13							
*249. Attaf the Generous		9	7										13							
*250. Prince Habib and Dorrat-al-Gawas		9	1										12							
*251. The Forty Wazirs													1							
a. Story of Shaykh Shahabeddin			1										1							
b. Story of the Gardener, his Son, and the Ass			1										1							
c. The Sultan Mahmoud and his Wazir			1										1							
d. Story of the Brahman Padmanaba and the young Fyquai			1										1							

Tale		
*e. Story of Sultan Akshid	1	1
*f. Story of the Husband, the Lover and the Thief	1	1
*g. Story of the Prince of Carisme and the Princess of Georgia	1	1
*h. The Cobbler and the King's Daughter	1	1
*i. The Woodcutter and the Genius	1	1
*j. The Royal Parrot	1	1
*252. Story of the King and Queen of Abyssinia	6	10
*253. Story of Prince Amina	7	12
*a. Story of the Princess of Tartary	7	12
*b. Story told by the Old Man's Wife	7	12
254. Story of Ali Johari	7	12
*255. Story of the two Princes of Cochin China	7	12
*256. Story of the two Husbands	7	12
*a. Story of Abdallah	7	12
*b. Story of the Favourite	7	12
*257. Story of Yusuf and the Indian Merchant	7	12
*258. Story of Prince Benazir	7	12
259. Story of Selim, Sultan of Egypt	7	13
*a. Story of the Cobbler's Wife	7	13
*b. Story of Adileh	7	13
*c. Story of the scarred Kalender	7	13
*d. Continuation of the story of Selim	7	13
*260. Story of Seif Sul Yesn	7	14
261. Story of the Labourer and the Chair	A	A
262. Story of Ahmed the Orphan	A	A

NB. In using this table, some allowance must be made for differences in the titles of many of the tales in different editions. For the contents of the printed text, I have followed the lists in Mr Payne's *Tales from the Arabic*, vol. III. [W. F. K.]

Index

Abdullah of the Land and Abdullah of the Sea, 50
Aberdeen, George Hamilton Gordon, 4th Earl of, 139
'Aboulhassan, Ali Ebn Becar and Shemselnihar, History of', 201
Abu Hassan (character), 163, 166, 224; *see also* 'Sleeper Awakened, The'
Abu Kir, 153, 192
Abu Nawās, 169n19
Abu Sir, 153, 192
Adams, Robert M., 233
Addison, Joseph: reads Galland version of *Nights*, 1; on Barmecide banquet, 184; and Thackeray, 186; and barber's fifth brother, 197; retells 'History of Chec Chahabeddin', 241; *Vision of Mirza*, 8
Aden, 106
Administrative Reform Association, 139
Afghan campaign, 160–1
Aherne, John (Yeats figure), 266–9
Aherne, Owen (Yeats figure), 247, 252–7, 260, 266
Ahmed, Prince, and the Peri Banou, 13, 35, 52, 60, 179, 195, 204, 210–11
Aladdin (character), 19, 24, 28; in pantomime, 1, 54, 91, 236; Byron on, 20; and children, 22; parallels, 30; De la Mare on, 49; C. S. Lewis and, 52; Stevenson and, 193–4; Meredith and, 209–10, 213
Aladdin: story published separately, 91–2
Alcestis myth, 56
Alderson, Brian, 39–40
Alfred, Mike, 79n137
Alhambra (Spain), 58, 146
Ali Baba (character), 31, 131; in

pantomime, 1, 22, 236; Byron on, 20; parallel with Mercury, 57; Thackeray and, 186; Wells and, 225
Ali Baba: story published separately, 91
'Ali Cogia', 131, 170n22
All the Year Round (journal), 133, 158, 161
Allen and Unwin (publishers), 55
Allott, Miriam, 20
Alnaschar (character), 14–15, 185–7, 197, 208
Alphonsus, Petrus, 5
Ambrus, Victor, 92
Amgiad, Prince (character), 35
'Amina the Ghoul Wife', 132, 184–5, 199, 250
Amina (character in 'The Porter and the Ladies of Baghdad'), 87, 99
Andersen, Hans Christian, 89
angels, orders of: Coleridge on, 119–20
Anstey, F. (Thomas Anstey Guthrie), 46
anti-feminism, 41
anti-Modernism, 54
Arabian Nights: publishing history, xiv, xv, 2, 6, 21; tables, 289–315; serialised, 2–3; origin of tales, 4–6; nexus of conditions favouring its use, 19; orthography, xxviii, 21–2; adapted for children, 39–40, 82–93; propagandist editions, 41; individual stories excerpted, 90–1; narrative structure, xvii, 155–7; and British knowledge of orient, 159–60; eating and drinking in, 184; *see also* individual tales under titles; *also* illustrations; translations

General Magazine, 3
Gentleman's Magazine, 6, 96
Gerhardt, Mia I., 52, 115, 194, 218–19
Germany: *Nights* in, 44
ghouls, 26–7, 32, 132, 228–9
Gibbon, Edward, 2
Gildon, Charles: *Golden Spy*, 2
Gillman, James, 128n29
Giraldus: Dulac portrait of, 256, 267, 268, 270
Gittes, Katharine Slater, 256
Godwin, Mary Jane, 91
Goethe, J. W. von, 66n42, 71n84, 265
Gollancz (publishers), 46
gourds, 65n30
Grabar, Oleg: *The Alhambra*, 58
Graham, Robert Cunninghame, 226
Grail, Holy, 282–3
Grant, Allan, 7
Graves, Robert, 56; *The White Goddess*, 282
Greek myth, 125n13, 126n14
Green, Roger Lancelyn, 51
Greene, Graham, 49, 54–6
Gregory, Pope, 56
Gregory, Augusta, Lady, 270
Grimm Brothers, 22, 89
Grisewood, Harman, 52
Guardian (newspaper), 57
Gurdjieff, George (Yuri), 56

'Habib and Dorathil-goase, or The Arabian Knight', 9
Habicht, Maximilian, 21
Hajji Baba, see Morier, James Justinian
Hammer-Purgstall, Joseph, Freiherr von, 15, 21, 148
Harar (Somaliland), 106
Harris, Augustus, 44
Harris, John, 91
Hart, Clive, 234
Harun al-Rashid, Caliph: historical figure, 43, 105, 126n16; name, 141n11; Dickens and Collins as, 147; Stevenson as, 191;

Meredith's view of, 213; and Wells' stories, 224–5; parallel with Proteus, 230; Joyce and, 230–1, 236; Yeats' allusions to, 246–9, 252–3, 257–9, 268
Harvey, William, 33–4, 46, 89
Hasan of Basra (character), 59
'Hasan of El-Basra', 32, 151
Hauff, W.: 'The Caliph Turned Stork', 191
Hawker, R. S., 31
Hawkesworth, John, 2
Hayes, Michael, 79n137
Hazlitt, William, 67n46
'Heart's Miracle, Lieutenant of the Birds', 259–60, 276n17
Heath-Stubbs, John, 42–3
Henley, W. H., xiv, xv, 36–7, 223
Heron, Robert: *The Arabian Tales* (translation of *Continuation of the Arabian Nights*), 6, 9–10
Hindbad (character), 91, 192, 214
History of Sinbad the Sailor, 90–1
Hitopadesa, 58
Hodder and Stoughton (publishers), 42, 46
Hofmannsthal, Hugo von, 71n84
Hofstadter, Douglas R., 53, 61
Hole, Richard: *Arthur, or, The Northern Enchantment*, 7; *Remarks on the Arabian Nights Entertainments*, 3–5, 7, 10, 17–18, 57, 82, 122n1
Holman Hunt, William, 33, 170n23
Holmes, Sherlock (fictitious figure), 37
Homer, 2, 12, 218, 220
Hood, W. K. and Connie K., 270–1
Hope, Thomas: *Anastasius*, 98
horse, enchanted, 5, 34, 46, 132, 135, 169n15; *see also* 'Enchanted Horse, The Story of the'
Hough, Graham, 258, 273
Houghton, Arthur Boyd, 33–4, 89, 170n23
Household Words (journal), 130, 136, 139, 198
Housman, Laurence, 41–2, 46, 60